D1093228

# Atheism and Secularity

# Atheism and Secularity

Volume 1
Issues, Concepts, and Definitions

**Edited by**
PHIL ZUCKERMAN

*Praeger Perspectives*

PRAEGER
*An Imprint of ABC-CLIO, LLC*

A B C 🐦 C L I O

Santa Barbara, California • Denver, Colorado • Oxford, England

Copyright 2010 by Phil Zuckerman

All rights reserved. No part of this publication may be reproduced, stored in a retrieval system, or transmitted, in any form or by any means, electronic, mechanical, photocopying, recording, or otherwise, except for the inclusion of brief quotations in a review, without prior permission in writing from the publisher.

**Library of Congress Cataloging-in-Publication Data**

Atheism and secularity / Phil Zuckerman, editor.
    p. cm.
    Includes bibliographical references and index.
    ISBN 978-0-313-35181-5 (hard copy : alk. paper) — ISBN 978-0-313-35182-2 (ebook) — ISBN 978-0-313-35183-9 (hard copy vol. 1 : alk. paper) — ISBN 978-0-313-35184-6 (ebook vol. 1) — ISBN 978-0-313-35185-3 (hard copy vol. 2 : alk. paper) — ISBN 978-0-313-35186-0 (ebook vol. 2) 1. Irreligion and sociology. 2. Atheism. 3. Secularism. I. Zuckerman, Phil.
    BL2747.A85 2010
    211'.6—dc22      2009036682

ISBN: 978-0-313-35181-5
EISBN: 978-0-313-35182-2

14  13  12  11  10    1  2  3  4  5

This book is also available on the World Wide Web as an eBook.
Visit www.abc-clio.com for details.

Praeger
An Imprint of ABC-CLIO, LLC

ABC-CLIO, LLC
130 Cremona Drive, P.O. Box 1911
Santa Barbara, California 93116-1911

This book is printed on acid-free paper ∞

Manufactured in the United States of America

# Contents

# Introduction:
# The Social Scientific Study
# of Atheism and Secularity

## Phil Zuckerman

In 1972, almost forty years ago, Colin Campbell, then a lecturer at the University of York, published a book titled *Toward a Sociology of Irreligion*.[1] The inside jacket cover dubbed it "the first serious study of the social phenomenon of the rejection of religion." In this groundbreaking treatise, Campbell observed that sociologists have "entirely ignored irreligion."[2] He sought to vigorously address this major lacuna by calling for a new focus of study within sociology, that is, the study of people who live their lives indifferent to, without, or in opposition to religion. Campbell began his work by pondering why it is that sociologists have ignored secularity over the years, and he then went on to broach a variety of significant topics ripe for inquiry and attention: the role antireligious and/or humanist movements play in spreading secularization within society; the various forms and definitions of irreligion; irreligion and morality; irreligion and politics; the social functions of irreligion, and so on. Campbell's work remains significant for its insights, its thoughtfulness, and its incontrovertible prescience. But what is perhaps most striking about the work is this: it fell on deaf ears. Campbell's call for a widespread sociological analysis of irreligion went largely unheeded.

The publication of this two-volume set seeks to redress that regrettable outcome, to hear and to heed Campbell's call, and to finally take seriously the social scientific task of exploring, investigating, documenting, and analyzing various aspects of atheism and secularity. The authors of the chapters contained in this collection have attempted to do just that and thereby offer studies of irreligiosity with the same level of interest and rigor that social scientists have devoted to studying the topic of religiosity for well over a century.

While bemoaning the dearth of scholarship on atheism, irreligion, and secularity that has typified the social sciences,[3] it must also be acknowledged that a significant amount of academic writing and scholarship has in fact been devoted to the topic of *secularization*—the historical process whereby religion weakens, fades, or loses its hegemonic dominance or public significance. A plethora of scholars have been aggressively debating secularization for years.[4] Despite the impressive amount that has been published on secularization, nearly all of it—at least that I am aware of—is generally theoretical, typological, or broadly historical in nature, and doesn't actually deal with secular life or atheism as they are actually lived, expressed, or experienced by irreligious men and women in the here and now. Nor does the cottage industry of scholarship on or about secularization entail a direct focus on the social, anthropological, and/or psychological particulars of how secularity actually manifests itself or "plays itself out" in the contemporary world.

As with work on secularization, when it comes to the advocacy of atheism—or the debunking of religion—there's also a lot out there, to be sure. Thousands of books, essays, and articles have been published since the days of David Hume (1711–1776) and Baron D'Holbach (1723–1789), which argue against theism, critique the Bible, deride religion, harangue clergy, and/or promote naturalism, materialism, agnosticism, humanism, freethought, and so on. Most recently, a spate of best sellers have been published in this formidable vein, including *The End of Faith: Religion, Terror, and the Future of Reason* (2004) by Sam Harris,[5] *God Is Not Great: How Religion Poisons Everything* (2007) by Christopher Hitchens,[6] and *The God Delusion* (2006) by Richard Dawkins[7]—the last of which has sold over 1.5 million copies as of this writing. These books, however, are not studies of atheists and/or secular people, per se. They are distinctly polemical works with the expressed goal of convincing people that theism is false and/or that religion is a bad or harmful thing. Such endeavors, however thought provoking, are not social science. Nor are they meant to be. Lest the reader be confused, this point bears stressing: the advocacy of atheism and/or the urging of secularity are not to be mistaken for the social-scientific study of atheism and secularity—just as one wouldn't confuse works that advocate faith and religion with those that seek to study, explain, or analyze faith and religion. And as stated above, when it comes to the advocacy of atheism and secularity, one finds a rich, diverse, and undeniably copious corpus of work. But when it comes to the study and analysis of atheism and secularity, one doesn't find much. As William Sims Bainbridge recently lamented, "we know surprisingly little about Atheism from a social-scientific perspective."[8]

That said, for one to suggest that absolutely *no* social science has been undertaken devoted to the study of atheism or secularity since Campbell's call would be untrue. In fact, several years just prior to the publication of Campbell's book, N. J. Demerath wrote what may very well be the first sociological investigations of irreligion ever published in academic journals; one, coauthored with Victor Thiessen and published in 1966, was an article on the Freie Gemeinde, a small free-thought movement in Wisconsin and the other, published in 1969, was an article on the Society for Ethical Culture and the American Rationalist Federation.[9] Also in 1969, Armand Mauss published an article on religious defection among Mormons.[10] And one year prior to the publication of Campbell's book, Rocco Caporale and Antonio Gumelli edited a volume titled *The Culture of Unbelief*, which was an assemblage of papers delivered at a symposium held in Rome on the very topic of the lack of religious belief in the contemporary world. Most of the papers in this publication, however, tended to be highly tentative and/or speculative, for as one contributor noted, there is an "appalling lack of empirical data on unbelief" and "we do not know enough about the phenomenon of unbelief to formulate even a minimum inventory of validated propositions that may constitute the basis of further analysis."[11] While a slew of studies emerged in the 1970s and 1980s with a focus on apostasy,[12] aside from these and a few additional disparate books and articles,[13] in the words of Talal Asad, "social scientists ... have paid scarcely any attention to the idea of the secular."[14]

That sociologists, anthropologists, and psychologists have largely neglected the study of secularity is truly remarkable, especially given the fact that secular, irreligious, nonreligious, and antireligious men and women have always existed.[15] Even Rodney Stark and Roger Finke can admit that atheism is "probably as old as religion."[16] Today, we know that atheists and secular folk represent a large slice of humanity; one recent (and conservative) estimate of nonbelievers in God places the number somewhere between 500 million and 750 million people worldwide.[17] And if the category were to be widened to include those who self-identify as simply "nonreligious" or "unreligious," these numbers would no doubt increase dramatically. The fact is, the portion of humans who reject, have no interest in, or are indifferent to belief in God and/or religion is not limited to some miniscule batch of angry deviants or disgruntled "village atheists." On the contrary, for if our estimates are correct, nonbelievers in God as a worldwide group come in fourth place after Christianity, Islam, and Hinduism in terms of the global ranking of commonly held belief systems. Put another way, there are 58 times as many nonbelievers in God as there are Mormons, 35 times as many nonbelievers in God as there are Sikhs, and twice as many nonbelievers in God as there are Buddhists.

Granted, in most nations, the irreligious may represent but a small minority.[18] However, in many other nations—such as Sweden, the Czech Republic, and Japan—the nonreligious or irreligious most likely constitute a majority of the population.[19] In the United States, over 15 percent of Americans (approximately 35 million people) claim "None" as their religion when asked by pollsters; of those 35 million, one study reports that 4 percent self-identify as atheists and another 6 percent as agnostics, with most of the remaining people simply saying that they have "no religion."[20] Some estimates of irreligious Americans are even slightly higher; according to the 2008 U.S Religious Landscape Survey carried out by the Pew Forum on Religion and Public Life, more than 16 percent of Americans identify as "unaffiliated."[21] This is quite an increase in irreligiosity, for back in the 1950s only 3 percent of Americans claimed "none" as their religion.[22] Thus, the percentage today (15 or 16 percent) represents a quadrupling of "none's" in one generation. And just to give readers some perspective, these percentages mean that there are more unaffiliated or "none's" in the United States than there are African Americans. When it comes to God-belief specifically, a recent Harris poll from 2008 found that 10 percent of Americans do not believe in God, with an additional 9 percent who said "not sure."[23] That means that nearly one American in five is either an atheist or possible agnostic. We're talking about 60 million Americans who are nontheists. These numbers and percentages render any suggestion that secular folk are atypically unhappy, alienated, elitist, or otherwise unwell or unnatural manifestly untenable, if not downright quaint.

Whether atheists and secular folk represent a very small minority of a nation's population (as in the case of, say, Ghana or Zimbabwe), or a very large percentage (as in the case of, say, the Netherlands or France), the bottom line is that, in the succinct and understated words of Darren Sherkat, "not everyone desires religious goods."[24] Such irreligious women and men—their identities, worldviews, associations, and experiences—deserve to be studied. Of particular interest for social scientists is how atheism, and/or secularity, intersects with, is influenced by, and in turn influences other aspects of the social world.

Fortunately, it appears as though a new day is dawning for the social-scientific study of atheism and secularity. In addition to the founding in 2005 of the Institute for the Study of Secularism in Society and Culture—the first of its kind to be established in North America—a growing body of research and scholarship has begun to emerge that focuses specifically on the irreligious. Some of the more noteworthy, pioneering efforts include *Atheists: A Groundbreaking Study of America's Nonbelievers* by Hunsberger and Altemeyer,[25] *Secularism and Secularity: Contemporary International Perspectives* edited by Kosmin and Keysar,[26] *The Cambridge Companion to Atheism* edited by Michael Martin,[27] my own *Society Without God: What the Least Religious Nations Can Tell Us about*

*Contentment,*[28] and finally, this publication. The essays in this two-volume set have been assembled and published in a concerted effort to not only begin filling a major lacuna within the social sciences, but more hopefully, to inspire further social-scientific research on irreligiosity in all its numerous dimensions and varied manifestations.

## NOTES

1. Colin Campbell, *Toward a Sociology of Irreligion* (New York: Heider and Heider, 1972).

2. Ibid., 8.

3. In the words of Benjamin Beit-Hallhami: "Those who shaped the modern human sciences have been preoccupied with explaining the phenomena of religion and religiosity. Accounting for the absence of religious faith has never been of much concern to them." Benjamin Beit-Hallahmi, "Atheists: A Psychological Profile," in *The Cambridge Companion to Atheism*, ed. Michael Martin (Cambridge: Cambridge University Press, 2007), 300.

4. For some major works on secularization, see Karel Dobbelaere, *Secularization: An Analysis at Three Levels* (Bruxelles: P.I.E.-Peter Lang, 2002); William Swatos and Daniel Olson, *The Secularization Debate* (Lanham, MD: Rowman and Littlefield, 2000); Steve Bruce, *God is Dead: Secularization in the West* (Oxford, UK: Blackwell Publishing, 2002); Peter Berger, ed., *The Desecularization of the World: Resurgent Religion and World Politics* (Grand Rapids, MI: William B. Eerdmans, 1999); David Martin, *A General Theory of Secularization* (New York: Harper and Row, 1978); Peter Glasner, *The Sociology of Secularization: A Critique of a Concept.* (London: Routledge of Kegan Paul, 1977); Peter Berger, *The Sacred Canopy* (New York: Anchor, 1967).

5. Sam Harris, *The End of Faith: Religion, Terror, and the Future of Reason* (New York; W.W. Norton, 2004).

6. Christopher Hitchens, *God is Not Great: How Religion Poisons Everything* (New York: Twelve, 2007).

7. Richard Dawkins, *The God Delusion* (Boston: Houghton Mifflin, 2006).

8. William Sims Bainbridge, "Atheism," *Interdisciplinary Journal of Research on Religion* 1 (2005): 3.

9. N. J. Demerath and Victor Theissen, "On Spitting against the Wind: Organizational Precariousness and American Irreligion," *The American Journal of Sociology* 7, no. 6 (1966): 674–87; N. J. Demerath, "A-Religion, and the Rise of the Religion-less Church: Two Case Studies in Organizational Convergence," *Sociological Analysis* 30, no. 4 (Winter 1969): 191–203.

10. Armand Mauss, "Dimensions of Religious Defection," *Review of Religious Research* 10, no. 3 (1969): 128–35.

11. Rocco Carorale and Antonio Grumelli, eds., *The Culture of Un-Belief* (Berkeley, CA: University of California Press, 1971), 3–4.

12. Including David G. Bromley, ed., *Falling From the Faith: The Causes and Consequences of Religious Apostasy* (Newbury Park, CA: Sage Publications, 1988); David Caplovitz and Fred Sherrow, *The Religious Drop-Outs: Apostasy among College Graduates* (Beverly Hills, CA: Sage Publications, 1977); Roger Louis

Dudley, "Alienation from Religion in Adolescents from Fundamentalist Religious Homes," *Journal for the Scientific Study of Religion* 17, no. 4 (Dec. 1978): 389–98; Bruce Hunsberger, "Apostasy: A Social-Learning Perspective," *Review of Religious Research* 25 (1983): 21–38; Bruce Hunsberger, "A Re-examination of the Antecedents of Apostasy," *Review of Religious Research* 21 (1980): 158–70.

13. J. Russell Hale, *The Unchurched* (San Francisco, CA: Harper and Row, 1980); W. Feigelman, B. S. Gorman, and J. A. Varacalli, "Americans Who Give up Religion," *Sociology and Social Research* 76 (1992): 138–44; Bon Altemeyer and Bruce Hunsberger, *Amazing Conversions: Why Some Turn to Faith and Others Abandon Religion* (Amherst, NY: Prometheus Books, 1997); Michael Hout and Claude S. Fischer, "Why More Americans Have No Religious Preference: Politics and Generations," *American Sociological Review* 67 (2002): 165–90.

14. Talal Asad, *Formations of the Secular: Christianity, Islam, and Modernity* (Palo Alto, CA: Stanford University Press, 2003), 17.

15. Jennifer Michael Hecht, *Doubt: A History* (New York: Harper Collins, 2003); James Thrower, *Western Atheism: A Short History* (Amherst, NY: Prometheus Books, 2000).

16. Rodney Stark and Roger Finke, *Acts of Faith* (Berkeley, CA: University of California Press, 2000), 13.

17. Phil Zuckerman, "Atheism: Contemporary Numbers and Patterns," in *The Cambridge Companion to Atheism*, ed. Michael Martin (Cambridge: Cambridge University Press, 2007).

18. Pippa Norris and Ronald Inglehart, *Sacred and Secular: Religion and Politics Worldwide* (New York: Cambrdige University Press, 2004).

19. Phil Zuckerman, "Atheism: Contemporary Numbers and Patterns," in *The Cambridge Companion to Atheism*, ed. Michael Martin (Cambridge: Cambridge University Press, 2007).

20. http://www.trincoll.edu/secularisminstitute/.

21. http://religions.pewforum.org/affiliations/.

22. C. Kirk Hadaway and Wade Clark Roof, "Apostasy in American Churches: Evidence from National Survey Data," in *Falling From the Faith: The Causes and Consequences of Religious Apostasy*, ed. David G. Bromley (Newbury Park, CA: Sage Publications, 1988).

23. http://www.harrisinteractive.com/harris_poll/index.asp?PID=982/.

24. Darren E. Sherkat, "Beyond Belief: Atheism, Agnosticism, and Theistic Certainty in the United States," *Sociological Spectrum* 28 (2008), 438.

25. Bruce E. Hunsberger and Bob Altemeyer, *Atheists: A Groundbreaking Study of America's Nonbelievers* (Amherst, NY: Prometheus Books, 2006).

26. Barry A. Kosmin and Ariela Keysar, eds., *Secularism and Secularity: Contemporary International Perspectives* (Hartford, CT: Institute for the Study of Secularism in Society and Culture, 2007).

27. Michael Martin, ed., *The Cambridge Companion to Atheism* (New York: Cambridge University Press, 2007).

28. Phil Zuckerman, *Society without God: What the Least Religious Nations Can Tell Us about Contentment* (New York: New York University Press, 2008).

# Chapter 1

# What Is Atheism?

## Jack David Eller

More than a century after Nietzsche announced the death of God, and more than twenty-four centuries after Socrates was sentenced to death for impiety toward the gods, there is still confusion and controversy over precisely what "atheism" is. Some of this confusion and controversy is real, some of it manufactured by those who prefer to dominate rather than describe, to undermine rather than to understand—and this on both "sides" of the "controversy." The fact that both religion and atheism have emerged, or reemerged, in the twenty-first century as vocal social forces has raised the profile, and the stakes, for both.

At its core, atheism is a profoundly simple idea: derived from the Greek *a-* for "no/without" and *theos* for "god," it merely designates a position (not a "belief"; see below) that includes or asserts no god(s). In practice—which for most of recorded history has meant in *theist* practice—the term has been less a descriptive term and more a judgmental one, and a negative and relative judgment at that. For instance, Christians, against whom modern Western atheism particularly strives, were originally condemned as atheists in ancient Rome. The Romans surely did not accuse the Christians of lacking a god-belief but rather of lacking or flatly denying belief in the Roman gods, which were the real and/or relevant gods. Muslims call nonbelievers "infidels" not because non-Muslims are without god-beliefs (Hindus, for instance, are clearly theists) but because non-Muslims are without belief in the Muslim god, who is, according to them, the only true god. Indeed, such is the common approach of the theist: if you do not believe in *my* god(s), even if you believe in some other god(s), which are almost necessarily false god(s), then you believe in no god(s) and are an a-theist.

An atheist who avows the term for himself or herself, on the other hand, is not merely an atheist "from some theist's point of view," that is, a person who disbelieves in some god(s) while believing in some other god(s). An atheist is one who possesses no belief in any god(s), a person for whom "god" is a foreign and inert concept—and nothing more than a concept, literally a word without a referent. By this understanding—the understanding of the atheist him/herself and not one imposed by theists—atheism is actually quite a common position, even within religion.

## ATHEISM, THEISM, AND A-THEISTIC RELIGIONS

Before we can proceed, it is critically important to realize that the entire "debate" in Western civilization about atheism and religion has been conducted in religious, and more specifically theistic, terms. Two gross, and false, assumptions have driven this debate. The first is that religion, and more specifically theism, is the default position: most people are religious/theists, and atheism is the exception: something not only to be explained but to be opposed. The second is that religion *is* theism, and therefore atheism is "a-religion" and "anti-religion."

The second assumption is explicable, although not defensible, from the utter hegemony that Christianity has had over the Western world for two millennia. Through most of Western history people have only known one religion (Christianity) or even only one variety of that religion (Catholicism), and of course the religious institution has aimed to keep it that way. "The Church" sought, and for the majority of the Christian era achieved, a monopoly of religion. People knew about Judaism (also theistic) and occasionally about Islam (also theistic), so it seemed to them—and was urged on them—that religion was theism and that theism was religion. Even worse, religion was *mono* theism, and *mono* theism was religion.

The intellectual and political value of equating the local religion with religion itself is apparent enough. However, as European Christians began to encounter other societies with their own religions, the claim simply became unsupportable. For one thing, not all theisms are monotheisms. In fact, the vast majority of theisms in human history have been polytheisms, pantheons, or systems of multiple gods, often each with a particular power or portfolio (e.g., a god of thunder, a god of war, and a god of the sea). Furthermore, not all of these gods had the alleged qualities of the Christian god: immortality, omnipotence, omniscience, ultimate creativity, and absolute moral goodness. Thus, "theism" is not a single religious position but a congeries of incompatible and often contradictory god-claims.

Anthropology has discovered something yet more discomforting to theism: *not all religions have gods at all*. Classical Christianity and the philosophies and social sciences based on it have presupposed that god(s) are necessary and universal components of religion, the very essence of religion. This presupposition is false. Theism is one "kind" or component of religion but not a universal and not even the most common one. Other religions, especially the numerous small "tribal" or "traditional" religions, often lacked god-concepts in favor of other, equally religious, concepts. For instance, a recurrent idea across religions is that there exist "nature spirits," such as those residing in and animating plants and animals or physical locations like hills and streams or natural phenomena like the sun and moon and wind and rain. Nature spirits (in a system commonly referred to as "animism") cannot justifiably be called gods, since they share few if any of the qualities ordinarily attributed to gods. Other religions focus on dead human ancestors, who continue to interact with and affect society; whereas some ancestors may become gods (indicating an open boundary between humans and gods), most are not gods, and ancestor-spirit belief (not properly called "ancestor worship," since many societies did not worship their ancestors and sometimes actually dreaded them) is not theism. Finally, still other religions posit supernatural forces that run through the world, like "mana" and "chi," typically not "persons" and lacking attributes like mind or will or intention, such forces cannot be regarded as gods; this notion is designated animatism. Worst of all for theists, these various religious conceptions can and do coexist: any one religion can include god(s) along with nature spirits, dead ancestors, and impersonal forces.

These discoveries prove two things. First, theism is not only not the essence of religion, it is not even a distinct "type" of religion; it is merely one building block in religious systems. In other words, a theism can or usually does include other, nontheistic elements too. Second, many, perhaps most, religions *are a-theisms* in that they do not include a god-concept at all. Surprisingly, atheism is not the opposite or lack, let alone the enemy, of religion *but is the most common form of religion*. Religions based on nature spirits, dead ancestors, and supernatural forces do not "doubt" gods, nor "disbelieve in" gods, nor "argue against" gods. They simply and unproblematically *lack* gods. They function fine without gods.

## DEFAULT THEISM AND NATURAL ATHEISM

The cross-cultural comparison of religions therefore answers the first assumption that we identified above, that theism is the natural and default position. Theism—in the familiar sense of a religion that focuses primarily or exclusively on one or a few gods—is in reality a rare and recent development in religion and neither natural nor default, although it is easy to see why theists might want to maintain otherwise. If one accepts the "default theism" claim, then atheism has a severe handicap, logically and socially. Logically, it appears to bear the entire burden of proof, since theism is "true until proven false." Socially, atheism can only exist, and thrive, by extricating itself from the overwhelmingly "popular" (and highly institutionalized) theistic system. As a minority position, it must necessarily be oppositional, critical, defensive, and argumentative—trying to "disprove" what is generally held to be true.

However, across religions it is simply not the case that theism is the default position. Most religions do not advance theistic claims at all, or it might be more accurate to say that most religions to not "talk about god(s)" at all. There is no such word, no such concept, no such "belief." It would be incorrect to say that these religions "disbelieve" in god(s) and still more incorrect to say that they "oppose" or "criticize" or "argue against" god(s). Most of the time, they have never even heard of such things as god(s).

In fact, where would one hear of such things as god(s)? God(s) is (are) not obvious to the naked eye, as, say, sun and water are; the idea of a spirit or mind or "person" in or of the sun or water is a small step. Further, no child, from all we can tell, is born with a god-concept; if they were, we would expect to find the god-concept everywhere, which we do not. Rather, as the theist John Wesley, founder of Methodism, realized:

> After all that has been so plausibly written concerning "the innate idea of God"; after all that has been said of its being common to all men, in all ages and nations; it does not appear, that man has naturally any more idea of God than any beasts of the field; he has no knowledge of God at all; no fear of God at all; neither is God in all his thoughts. Whatever change may afterwards be wrought . . . he is, by nature, a mere Atheist.[1]

In other words, Wesley admitted that atheism, not theism, is the default, the "natural," stance. Of course, he considered this a thoroughly bad thing, but then he surely would. The point is that an honest theist grasps that humans are not "natural theists"; that is why it takes so many years of teaching and indoctrination, so much institutional weight, so much colonization of experience, to instill the concept of theism. Humans are natural atheists—not in the sense of attacking god(s) but in the sense of lacking god(s).

No newborn human has any ideas about, let alone any "beliefs in," god(s)—or for that matter, any other religious entities. It is not that humans lack god-beliefs at birth but possess nature-spirit or dead-ancestor beliefs; they lack all such notions. There is a new and persuasive school of thought that humans may have innate tendencies to attribute mind or intention or "agency" to the nonhuman world (as when children think their toys have thoughts and feelings), but this is not religion or any specific religious concept. It is rather the raw material out of which a religion may be constructed. This native and intuitive "animism" must not only be coached and encouraged but given concrete expression: humans may tend to ascribe mind to nonhuman phenomena, but they must be taught to identify that mind as *nats* (nature spirits in Burmese village Buddhism), *atua* (spirits/gods in Pacific islands), *kwoth* (divinity/spirits/god in African Nuer religion), *wakan* (holy beings in Lakota religion), *razana* (ancestor spirits of Madagascar Imerina), or God, Allah, Vishnu, Odin, Zeus, and so on.

What would happen if a child were never told a word about any of these religious concepts? It is unlikely that he or she would spontaneously invent his or her own religious concepts, and astronomically unlikely that he or she would reinvent Burmese village Buddhism or Lakota religion or Christianity. No human is born a Burmese Buddhist or a Lakota religionist or a Christian. No human is born a theist. Humans are born without any god-concepts. Humans are natural atheists.

There are two fates that a natural atheist can follow. If she is never exposed to the idea of god(s), never urged to "believe" in any god(s), she will retain her natural atheism—even if it is tainted with other religious but nontheistic notions. But under the pressures of a theistic milieu, the great majority of natural atheists will have their natural atheism replaced with an acquired theism, that is, they will be turned into or converted into theists. Some of these learned-theists will, for various reasons, come to question, "doubt," and ultimately reject the theism thrust on them and will "deconvert" into "recovered atheists." Whether a recovered atheist is quite the same species as a natural atheist is open to discussion: an analogy might be a person who has recovered from a viral infection as opposed to a person who never contracted it in the first place or a person who quite smoking as opposed to one who never started.

## ATHEISM AND ITS VICISSITUDES

The most fundamental distinction within atheism, then, is between what we might call "anthropological atheism" or the lack of any god-concept in a culture or religion and "argumentative atheism" or the rejection of the god-concept proffered by the theistic religion in one's culture. Because all of us live in a society informed by theism, argumentative atheism is immediately relevant for us, in which we find other real or putative diversity. One of the frequent assertions is that two types of atheism, positive and negative or strong and weak, exist and even compete. The distinction has been characterized as the difference between "not believing" and "believing not." Negative/weak atheism, on the one hand, is generally taken to designate the claim that one does not believe in god(s), that one lacks such a belief that such an entity exists; it does not, ostensibly, imply that no such entity actually exists. As the term connotes, positive/strong atheism makes a stronger assertion, that the belief in god(s) is unjustified and false. Thus, the putative positive/strong atheist states, "I not only lack the belief in god(s), I assert the non-existence of god(s)."

On the surface this may seem like a valid distinction, but upon closer inspection it is not. There are three sources of confusion on the subject. The first is the false dichotomy between "not believing" and "believing not," that is, not believing in god(s) and believing that there is no such thing as god(s). Indisputably, someone who maintains that there is no such thing as god(s) does not believe in them; to maintain otherwise is to be incoherent. Indisputably, someone who believes in god(s) maintains that there is such a thing; to maintain otherwise is equally incoherent. But what other possibilities are there? Can one maintain that there is no such thing as god(s) yet believe in them? Not without contradicting oneself. Can one maintain that there is such a thing as god(s) yet not believe in them? Not in any sensible way. So, it emerges that there are only two consistent positions: either one claims that there is such a thing as god(s) and believes in them, or one claims that there is no such thing as god(s) and does not believe in them. The dichotomy, then, is not between positive and negative atheism but between theism and atheism.

The second and more pernicious source of error is the attribution of "belief" to atheists, sometimes literally the insistence that atheism *is* a belief. Theists certainly, and atheists occasionally too, will say that atheism is a belief—the belief that god(s) does (do) not exist. This is a familiar and seductive way of thinking, since "belief" is such a ubiquitous and powerful concept. Surely, Christians argue, belief is universal and essential to religion; still more, religion is only one kind of belief. Theists often go so far as to call science a belief-system, to equate all knowledge with belief. On this count they have an ally in philosophy, which has frequently defined knowledge as "justified true belief." But such a definition cannot suffice, if only because the adjectives "justified" and "true" suggest that belief, unmodified with adjectives, is not justified or true—a conclusion I suspect most believers would want to avoid. In other words, if the existence of the Christian god is a belief and not (yet) knowledge, then it is (so far) either unjustified or untrue or both.

I have argued the case for the radical distinction between knowledge and belief elsewhere. The relevant point for current purposes is that absence of a belief, even active rejection of a belief, is not itself a belief. The animist who lacks any notion of god(s) whatsoever does not *disbelieve* in god(s) and certainly cannot be said to have a *belief* in the non-existence of gods. As a case in point, the Warlpiri of aboriginal Australia have a religious term *jukurrpa*, sometimes translated as "dreaming" or "dreamtime." It would be false and meaningless to say that most Christians disbelieve in *jukurrpa* or believe in the nonexistence of *jukurrpa*, if only and precisely because *most Christians have never even heard of* jukurrpa. Christians are, if you will, natural a-*jukurrpa*-ists. They lack the very concept, having never been exposed to and pressured into believing in it.

Natural atheists, including all members of religions that lack a god-concept as well as people like myself who have never found any validity in the available god-concept, do not "believe" in the nonexistence of god(s). They and we simply do not have the concept; it is a foreign language to them and us. However, it might be presumed that recovered atheists, those who have had to fight and argue their way out of theism, have a belief, just a belief-not. Unhappily for theists, this analysis is false. Imagine, for example, that a person is led to believe in childhood that Santa Claus exists. Through personal effort or counter-teaching, she learns or concludes that there is no Santa. Would you reasonably now say that she "believes that there is no Santa Claus"? Of course not. The rejection of the Santa-belief is not the belief in no-Santa. It is not a belief at all. It is the absence of a belief, the overthrow of a belief, the freedom from a belief. To argue otherwise is equivalent to saying that a person who kicks the habit of smoking now has the habit of not-smoking, or that a person gives up the hobby of collecting stamps now has the hobby of not-collecting stamps. In a word, the absence of a belief is not another belief; if it were, then believers would have more not-beliefs (i.e., in all the other religious entities across the world) than beliefs.

The third and more subtle source of confusion is the failure to distinguish between the point and the tactics of atheism. Atheism says one thing and one thing only: that there is no such thing as god(s). However, there are two quite different strategies for arguing that point in a world where the majority believe in god(s). Consider the analogy of a courtroom, where the "case" concerns the existence of god(s). Thus, the prosecution argues the case for god(s). The atheist represents the defense, which has two non-mutually exclusive tactics at its disposal. It can argue a "negative" case, demonstrating the inadequacy of the prosecution's evidence and logic, on the basis of the "burden of proof." Given the presumption of innocence, which amounts to the presumption that the charge or claim is false, the atheist/defense can simply punch holes in the prosecution's case and prevail; in fact, the atheist/defense has no obligation to make its own case at all, since if the prosecution's case is insufficient, the defense wins by default. As we stated above, if we consider atheism, not theism, the default position—if we, that is, start from the "presumption of atheism"[2]—then a negative atheist case, or no atheist case at all, carries the day.

The negative case, highlighting the flaws of theism or the reasons *not* to accept a belief in god(s), is so-called "negative atheism." However, if atheism as defense can mount its own case, offer its own evidence and logic for why such a thing as god(s) cannot and do not exist, then this constitutes "positive atheism." In a word, positive atheism not only demonstrates what is wrong with theism but what is right with atheism. But the position of atheism is the same in both approaches. It is only the argumentative strategy that differs.

## ATHEISM AND AGNOSTICISM

There might be another way to conceive of variations in or alternatives to atheism. One common tendency is to distinguish between atheism and agnosticism. Quite literally, many people who do not avow an active belief in god(s) eschew the term "atheist" and dub themselves "agnostics" instead. This is partly a tactical decision too: "atheist" still has serious pejorative connotations in the Western theist world. But for a large number of people, the choice to don the cloak of agnosticism is more intentional—presumably to avoid the two "extremes" of theism and atheism and to stake out a middle ground, to postpone or circumvent a stand on the question of god(s).

In a way, this attempt is understandable, but it is based on bogus notions of atheism, of agnosticism, and of the nature of the god-question. First, atheism is not an "extreme" position, any more than theism is (most theists do not see themselves as extremists). Atheism is actually a very humble claim, that there is no reason to conclude that there is any such thing as god(s) and therefore that it is inadvisable and impermissible to jump to such a conclusion. Atheism, as we have established, is not a "belief" that there is no such thing as god(s) but a default or a reasoned lack of any such belief.

While atheism is not a belief in any form, some people suggest that it might be possible or necessary to place atheism and theism at opposite ends of a belief spectrum—theism on the "have god-belief" pole and atheism on the "do not have god-belief" pole. The standard notion of agnosticism, then, that it is somewhere in between. But this is the wrong understanding of agnosticism. The very word, a- for "not/without" and gnosis for "knowledge," indicates that agnosticism is referring to something quite different. If we examine the original formulation of the meaning of agnosticism, given by Thomas Huxley over a century ago, the point becomes clearer:

> Agnosticism is not a creed but a method, the essence of which lies in the vigorous application of a single principle. . . . Positively the principle may be expressed as, in matters of the intellect, follow your reason as far as it can carry you without other considerations. And negatively, in matters of the intellect, do not pretend the conclusions are certain that are not demonstrated or demonstrable. It is wrong for a man to say he is certain of the objective truth of a proposition unless he can produce evidence which logically justifies that certainty.[3]

Notice—and this is of critical importance—that agnosticism is explicitly not a "belief" at all but a method, a process, and one for evaluating knowledge-claims and thus of avoiding "belief."

Thus, it is plain to see that agnosticism is not a "middle position" between theism and atheism because *it is not a position at all*. It is, rather, a means of arriving at a position. We might be better served to use the term in an adverbial sense, in the sense of thinking or judging "agnostically." But when we make this shift, we see that "agnostic" means nothing more than "rational," for to use reason is to follow the facts and only the facts, to base conclusions only on what can be demonstrated or detected in some way, and to refrain from "jumping to conclusions" on the basis of personal preference, emotion, or "faith."

So agnosticism is not a third position on the theism/atheism spectrum, because it is not a position at all and therefore not a position about belief, certainly not about religious belief in particular. One can—and should—advance agnostically on all subjects. But if agnosticism is neither a position nor a belief-related concept, then it cannot be an alternative to theism and atheism. In fact, if we accept agnosticism as a *method or process* rather than as a position, then the only question is: What is the outcome of applying that method to questions of god(s)? The answer can only be, since we have no clear demonstrations of god(s), no certain evidence of god(s), and no trustworthy way to detect god(s), that we should reject any talk of god(s), affirm the presumption of atheism, and conclude that there is no such thing as god(s).

For, despite the insincere attempt at humility inherent in conventional agnosticism, the god-question only has two possible answers: yes there is such a thing as god(s) or no there is no such thing as god(s). Agnosticism notwithstanding, there is no third position; there is no spectrum. Even if one were to come down on the affirmative side, there would still be other vexing questions to answer, like how many gods and with what specific qualities—questions that might still cause theism to crash on the rocks of evidence and logic, not to mention other theisms. But to the fundamental question, the answer is either yes or no. There might, indeed, be occasions, in religion as elsewhere, on which one postpones calling the question—for want of evidence, for instance. But, in religion as in law and science, if one does not explicitly conclude yes, then one tentatively concludes no. No sensible jurist or researcher would say, "We have no evidence that this defendant is guilty or that this drug is safe and effective, but let's put him in jail/prescribe it until we do." There is no third position between being in jail and not being in jail, or between prescribing a medicine and not prescribing it. Hesitating—often a wise course—is tentatively *not doing*. The conventional agnostic may think that she is hesitating to decide between god(s) and not-god(s), but in the meantime she is *not believing in god(s)*. In other words, agnosticism in the everyday sense is implicit or tacit or tentative atheism. From the conventional descriptions of the Christian god, he would not make the distinction.

## ATHEISM, SECULARISM, AND OTHER ISMS

Atheism is also associated with another constellation of terms, such as rationalism, materialism, skepticism, humanism, irreligion, and of course secularism, a central topic in modern politics and society and in the present volumes. In the small space available here it is impossible to explore thoroughly these related but distinct concepts. Let it be said that not all humanists are atheists (there are those who call themselves "religious" or "spiritual" humanists, although the sense of that identity escapes me), but presumably all atheists are humanists, since what else could they be? Skepticism (of the nonepistemological variety, epistemological skepticism positing that all knowledge is impossible) is merely another name for agnosticism: being wary of claims on one's credulity unless evidence can be demonstrated. One could (and should) be a skeptic about any and all subjects, and the "skeptic community" expends at least as much energy on pseudoscience as on religion. Ideally, most if not all, atheists are rationalists and materialists, although indisputably not all can give nuanced philosophical accounts of either. However, some atheists call themselves "spiritual," and as we have shown above, atheism in its broadest sense does not preclude other religious concepts like nature spirits, dead ancestors, and supernatural forces. Therefore, it would be inappropriate, except in the theist-dominated Western context, to equate atheism with irreligion, since as we now know, most religions have been a-theistic. However, I would propose that a rationalist atheist would also dismiss claims about nature spirits, ancestor spirits, and the entire line of "spiritual" thinking, as nothing more than a metaphor run amok.

With little doubt, the most common and important idea in the social and political struggle over religion/theism and atheism is "secular" and its permutations (e.g., secularism, secularization, and secularity). To many observers, secular is tantamount to atheism: the eminent scholar of religion Martin Marty actually regards secularism as a form of "unbelief," which he defines as "any kind of serious or permanent departure from belief in God (as symbolized by the term 'Trinity') and from the belief that God not only is but acts (as symbolized by the historic reference 'Incarnation')."[4] The nonsensical and prejudicial nature of this statement is self-evident: it is so Christian-centered, and even more specifically Christian-trinitarian–centered, that not only Islam and Hinduism and Buddhism would have to classified as secularism and unbelief but so would Unitarianism and many if not most forms of Protestant Christianity. The persistent and pernicious bias in favor of Christianity in the theism/atheism and the secularism debates is apparent even in the work of David Martin, who confesses in his *A General Theory of Secularization* that "by the term 'religion' in this context I mean Christianity."[5] But this can never under any circumstances be acceptable.

Since secularism is the theme of the chapters to follow and is often construed to be the equivalent of atheism if not a stealth version of atheism, it is worth dwelling on the subject for a moment. In short, "secular" or its permutations is one of those concepts that needs to be unpacked and relativized in its cross-cultural context. Let us begin with the observation that, at least since the time of Durkheim and echoed in other scholars like Eliade, it has been commonplace in social science to propose a dichotomy between the spiritual/religious and the secular, often in the form of "sacred" versus "profane." Naturally, this habit is once again an importation from conventional Christianity, which, from its earliest days, has drawn a line between two irresolvable worlds ("My kingdom is not of this world," Jesus is reported to have said). Augustine gave the classic formulation, separating the "city of the world" from the "city of God." The division is not unique to Christianity: Islam also distinguishes between the *dar al-harb* or the domain of strife and nonbelief and the *dar al-islam* or the domain of peace and true belief (that is, Islamic belief).

While it may be common to separate, or try to separate, the sacred from the secular, it is by no means universal nor is it ultimately successful. Even within Christianity, "secular" was not always the opposite or absence of "sacred": a "secular priest" was still a religious figure, simply one who participated in the ordinary world versus one who took monastic vows and secluded himself from the world (but still unavoidably lived in it). Secular could even refer to the laity, who might be and hopefully were quite religious. Worse for Christian thinking, not all religions entail the same dualistic and mutually exclusive, even hostile, division of worlds. In many religions, the concerns of religion are not (at least entirely) "otherworldly" at all, nor is "spirit" or "the sacred" cloistered in some remote inaccessible dimension. Buddhism and Confucianism locate their primary interests and practices very much in this world. Shinto is as social and political as a religion can be. In Hua (Papua New Guinea) religion, the main concern is ingesting the correct "substance" (*nu*), which is regarded as both supernatural and natural and "distinctly nonspiritual," which ultimately takes the form of eating the right foods prepared by the right persons.[6] Finally, Driberg has argued convincingly that ancestor spirit belief in Africa is essentially secular, since "The idea behind the whole [ancestor spirit] business is nothing sacred, but a social recognition of the fact that the dead man has acquired a new status and that . . . he is still one with [the community]."[7]

In fact, with a little thought it is obvious that a religion cannot be perfectly "spiritual" or "otherworldly," no matter how hard it tries.

Humans, even the most stubborn fundamentalists, live in the real world (although they may gripe that they are "not of the world"). The objects and symbols of religion—crosses, churches, bells, candles, statues, "holy" water, or what have you—are natural, physical things. The concerns of religion are always closely tied to the mundane world—health, long life, fertility, wealth, luck, and so on. And religion enters into everyday life in myriad and almost unnoticed ways—the foods we eat, the clothes we wear, the ways we groom our bodies, our social institutions, our calendar systems, and the very space that we occupy (e.g., with "sacred grounds" and religious buildings).

The point is that the sacred/secular dichotomy is, like most dichotomies, false. "Secular" certainly does not mean "atheistic" or without religion, definitely not anti-religion; in fact, as I illustrate in a chapter in the second volume of this collection, there is a proud tradition of "Islamic secularism." Despite the predictions of the "secularization theorists" like Marx and Weber, "modern" or secular processes have not meant the demise of religion and have actually proved to be quite compatible with religion—have even led, at least in the short term, to a surprising revival of religion. The problem with earlier secularization theories is that they presumed that secularization was a single, all-encompassing, and unidirectional phenomenon. However, as Peter Glasner has more recently shown, "secular" and "secularization" embrace a variety of diverse processes and responses, not all of which—indeed, few of which—are inherently antithetical to religion.[8]

Glasner identifies ten different versions of secularization, organized in terms of whether their thrust is primarily institutional, normative, or cognitive. They include

- Decline—the reduction in quantitative measures of religious identification and participation, such as lower church attendance/membership or decreased profession of belief
- Routinization—"settling" or institutionalizing through integration into the society and often compromise with the society, which tends to occur when the religion becomes large and is therefore one mark of *success* as a religion, although it is less intense and distinct than in its early formative "cultish" or new-religious-movement stage
- Differentiation—a redefined place or relation to society, perhaps accepting its status as one religion in a plural religious field or morphing into a more "generic" and therefore mass-appeal religion
- Disengagement—the detachment of certain facets of social life from religion
- Transformation—change over time (Glasner cites Weber's analysis of Protestantism as a transformation of Christianity for a new social milieu)
- Generalization—a particular kind of change in which it becomes less specific, more abstract, and therefore more inclusive, like the supposed "civil

religion" in the United States; it moderates its more controversial and potentially divisive claims and practices

- Desacralization—the evacuation of "supernatural" beings and forces from the material world, leaving culture and rationality to guide humans instead
- Segmentation—the development of specialized religious institutions, which take their place beside other specialized social institutions
- Secularization—the processes of urbanization, industrialization, rationalization, bureaucratization, and cultural/religious pluralism through which society moves away from the "sacred" and toward the "profane"
- Secularism—the only form that leads to outright rejection of religion, amounting to atheism

The upshot of this analysis is that secularism most assuredly does not translate simply and directly into atheism. Many good theists support the secularization of the American government in the form of the "separation of church and state," and all of them go about at least part of their day without doing religion. "Secular" in this sense does not mean "antireligious" but rather "religiously neutral." Despite the objections of some critics, religious neutrality, even the absence of religion from certain human phenomena, is not atheism. When people do their banking, or play baseball, or go on vacation without references to their god(s), this is hardly a rejection of their god(s). Religious people most assuredly may and do bring their religion into nonspiritual activities and occasions, but that merely proves the point that secularization can work in two entirely opposite directions. It can mean, and more conventionally means, the evacuation of religion from social territories it formerly occupied (like disestablishing a state religion). But it can also mean the penetration of religion into social territories it did not formerly occupy and which serve no essential religious function, like forming a church basketball league. In fact, religion is all too keen, and all too effective, at "secularizing" in this latter sense: notice that the "mega-churches" in the United States offer not only "spiritual" services but everything from child day care to sports to movie nights to book clubs to foreign language classes. Wasn't it the Catholic church that discovered long ago the religious value of "secular" activities like bingo and potluck dinners?

## THE "NEW ATHEISM" AND THE FUTURE OF ATHEISM

Atheism has been very much in the public eye in recent years, partly due to the anti-religion backlash in response to the faith-based violence and terrorism that has swept the world (not least in the September 11, 2001, attacks by fanatical Muslims) and partly due to the series of surprisingly blunt and commercially successful books published since 2004. Actually, the current "push" of atheism can perhaps be dated to two earlier books: George Smith's 1989 *Atheism: The Case against God*[9] and Dan Barker's 1992 *Losing Faith in Faith: From Preacher to Atheist*.[10]

But atheism entered an unprecedented period of confidence and enthusiasm with the publication of Sam Harris' best-selling 2004 offering, *The End of Faith*.[11] It was quickly followed by Daniel Dennett's *Breaking the Spell: Religion as a Natural Phenomenon* and Richard Dawkins' *The God Delusion*, and Harris' follow-up *Letter to a Christian Nation*, all published in 2006, not to mention Christopher Hitchens' 2007 contribution, *God Is Not Great: How Religion Poisons Everything*.[12] More quietly, a small industry of atheist publishing has produced a wave of activity, including two of my own books, *Natural Atheism* in 2004 and *Atheism Advanced* in 2008.[13]

It is especially noteworthy that the "big four" of Harris, Dennett, Dawkins, and Hitchens have not only enjoyed significant market and media success but that they obtained major publishers for their work; one can imagine a time not so long ago when a prominent popular press would not have touched such titles. Collectively, these writers are regarded as the founders of the so-called "new atheism," which is, if nothing else, profitable and vociferous. However, precisely how new is it, what does it add to the discussion of atheism/theism/religion, and where does atheism go from here?

There is no doubt that the new atheism is unabashed, even aggressive, and more than a little in-your-face. There is some debate within the atheist community as to whether this is a good thing. Some go so far as to disown the very moniker "atheist" in favor of other identities like "humanist," "freethinker," "secularist," "agnostic," or such original names as "bright" or "universist." Others, on the contrary, consider these concessions a kind of appeasement, a way of "passing" in a society that is controlled by theists and in which "our kind" are as unwelcome as blacks or gays used to be (and sometimes still are).

The political/identity issues inherent in the new atheism are one thing. A greater concern, from my perspective, is the content. For the most part, there is nothing particularly new offered at all; what is new is mostly that their atheism is, as we might say, "loud and proud." But much of the new atheism is aimed in two well-worn and not entirely wise directions. The first is the never-ending effort to "disprove god(s)" or worse, "disprove God." Many of these works, and their less famous counterparts, tirelessly rehearse arguments against god(s), a project to which no new ideas have been added in decades, if not generations or millennia. Quite frankly, everyone (including an honest theist) recognizes that arguments in favor of god(s) fail, and if they did succeed, they would not establish the existence of any particular god(s) over all the others; that is to say, the tired old cosmological or ontological or teleological arguments would defend Zeus or Odin or Vishnu as effectively as Yahweh or Allah.

There are two other problems with the new atheism. One is that much of its rhetoric is targeted not at the falsity of theism but at the *danger* of theism. Harris' major book pounds away at religious terrorism, giving Islam in particular a sound thrashing. Hitchens insists that religion ruins everything. Both essentially argue that religion is not so much wrong as bad. And of course much of the criticism of religion is directed, explicitly or implicitly, at religious fundamentalism (although Harris uniquely and equally condemns "moderate religion" as an excuse for and virtually a gateway drug to fundamentalism). No one, it turns out, likes fundamentalism, except for the fundamentalists themselves, and so the analysis of and attack on fundamentalism not only fails to move us very far but mischaracterizes religion.

The objection to the religion-is-bad, or more pointedly the religion-is-violent, argument is that not all religion is violent and, quite frankly, it is irrelevant whether or not religion is bad or violent for determining if religion is true or false. It is not inconceivable that theism might be correct—there really is such a thing as god(s)—and violent too: if a violent god, or a god of war, or a mortal threat to the religious community exists, then religious violence would be a natural and justifiable part of the picture. Further, the supposed case against religion/theism is just an instance of the famous but refuted "argument from benefit" in reverse: atheism has insisted over the years that religion's alleged benefits are not germane to questions of truth, so it cannot now insist that religion's alleged costs are germane to those questions. In fact, in the end, this new strategy provides an out for religion: if atheism is only against bad/violent theism, then it might have to be for, or at least tolerate, good/peaceful theism. That is a possible position, but it is not the position of atheism.

At the deepest level, the new atheism suffers from the same syndrome that virtually all atheism has suffered since the beginning of theism—namely, taking the local theism as the essence of religion itself. The new atheism, and all past argumentative atheism, is as much in the theist universe as theism is; in fact, so far all atheism that argues against Christianity has been as much in the Christian universe as Christianity is: notice that the titles, and the contents, of the new atheism offerings tilt with "God" over and over again (e.g., *The God Delusion, God is Not Great,* and *God: The Failed Hypothesis*) and never with Zeus or Odin or Vishnu, let alone nature spirits, dead ancestors, or supernatural forces. The new atheism is trapped in the gravitational pull of theism generally and Christianity specifically as surely and securely as any Christian congregation. If recent psycholinguistics is right, then arguing *against* god(s) is just as effective at perpetuating god-concepts as arguing *for* god(s). No doubt, this is why theists love to debate atheists: they can get atheists publicly talking about their god(s)!

If the purported new atheism is a worthwhile first step—it certainly has atheists energized and self-congratulatory, it is only a first step.

What is the future for atheism, in a god-saturated world? There are those who claim that it has no future; Alister McGrath already detects the "twilight of atheism," the "fall of disbelief in the modern world."[14] That is as may be: just as secularization theorists prematurely predicted the death of religion, so the likes of McGrath may be prematurely predicting the death of atheism.

A different point appears in John Haught's recent criticism of the new atheism, which he calls "amateur," lacking profundity and pathos.[15] The *real* atheists—Marx and Nietzsche and Camus—knew and felt the full weight of their rejection of god(s), or, as Nietzsche saw it, their *murder* of god(s). Not for nothing was it a madman who announced Nietzsche's death of God:

> What did we do when we unchained this earth from its sun? Whither is it moving now? Whither are we moving now? Away from all suns? Are we not plunging continually? Backward, sideward, forward, in all directions? Is there any up or down left? Are we not straying as through an infinite nothing? Do we not feel the breath of empty space? Has it not become colder? Is not night and more night coming on all the while?[16]

What Nietzsche described is the classic condition of nihilism, and Haught demands that atheists confront and perhaps dwell in their nihilism as the "hard-core atheists" of the nineteenth century did. The new, "soft-core atheists," these trivializers of humanity's greatest achievement or crime (depending on your perspective), delusionally imagine "that life will go on as usual once religion disappears."

Yet one wonders in the twenty-first century whether the (melo)drama of nineteenth-century atheism is not more than a little overwrought. Perhaps in Marx's and Nietzsche's time, when atheism was still comparatively strange and scary, it seemed that losing the Christian god actually was like losing the sun, like losing all light and sense and direction. Presumably the Greeks and the Norse and the Egyptians felt the same: without Zeus or Odin or Osiris there was nothing, only nothingness. But when Zeus and Odin and Osiris, and countless other gods and non-god supernatural beings passed into historical obscurity, the sun kept shining. Even better, new light, new sense, and new direction appeared. Two things are true: humans cannot live without sense, and humans create their sense. For was it not also Nietzsche who wrote, in his grand atheistic mythology *Thus Spoke Zarathustra*, that humans are camels who bear the burden of someone else's truths, someone else's religion, someone else's god(s)? When the burden becomes too great, humans throw off and destroy these ancient tablets of good and evil, becoming lions, nay-sayers, perhaps even nihilists, certainly egoists. This is the stage at which atheism has lingered for centuries, at which the new atheism still pauses or expires. But a really new atheism, an atheism of the future, an atheism that humans can live in, will come from Nietzsche's third meta-morphosis, the child, the yes-sayer and creator:

> To create new values—that even the lion cannot do; but the creation of freedom for oneself for new creation—that is within the power of the lion. The creation of freedom—for that, my brothers, the lion is needed. To assume the right to new values—that is the most terrifying assumption for a reverent spirit that would bear much. . . . For the game of creation, my brothers, a sacred "Yes" is needed: the spirit now wills his own will, and he who had been lost to the world now conquers his own world.[17]

What may be most interesting of all about twenty-first-century atheism is that this challenge, this project, now sounds familiar, even welcome, even easy.

The poorly named new atheism may actually prove to be the last shots of the old atheism—the last arguments, the last struggles against someone else's god(s), the last nay-saying. The future of atheism is not in disproving god(s) but, as with the nontheistic and pretheistic religions, in not talking about god(s) at all. It is in creating new institutions, new practices, new habits, new celebrations, and new ways of life that have nothing whatsoever to do with god(s). It is in reclaiming from theism what theism usurped from humans in the first place—time, space, nature, even our very bodies. Religion, theism or otherwise, creates little or nothing: without religion, there would still be birth and death, love and marriage, growth and the passage of time, norms and morals, and occasions for joy and sorrow. Religion, theism or otherwise, barges into these situations and demands a place among them; worse yet, it asserts that it invented them, that these and all other natural and social things depend on it. When Nietzsche's madman killed the local god, birth and death and love and time and morals and joy all survived—to many people's, including Professor Haught's, surprise. Once, atheism meant the opposition to, the resistance against, god(s). Now, it only means freedom, to establish new norms and new institutions, and to tear them down and establish new ones again. Like the day when smoking ends once and for all and anti-smoking campaigns become extinct, so when believing in god(s) ends atheism—as an anti-god(s) campaign—will become extinct. But on that day, everyone will be a nonsmoker, just as everyone will be a non-god-er, and both will have their health and their freedom to do with what they will.

## NOTES

1. John Wesley, Sermon 95: On the Education of Children, http://www.godrules.net/library/wsermons/wsermons95.htm (accessed July 16, 2008).

2. Antony Flew, *God, Freedom, and Immorality: A Critical Analysis* (Buffalo, NY: Prometheus Books, 1984).

3. Thomas Huxley, Agnosticism, http://www.infidels.org/library/historical/thomas_huxley/huxley_wace/part_02.html (accessed July 16, 2008).

4. Martin E. Marty, *Varieties of Unbelief* (New York: Anchor Books, 1966 [1964]), 30.

5. David Martin, *A General Theory of Secularization* (New York, Evanston, IL, and San Francisco: Harper & Row Publishers, 1978), 2.

6. Anna S. Meigs, *Food, Sex, and Pollution: A New Guinea Religion* (New Brunswick, NJ: Rutgers University Press, 1984).

7. J. H. Driberg, "Supplement: The Secular Aspect of Ancestor-Worship in Africa," *Journal of the Royal African Society* 35 (1936): 7.

8. Peter E. Glasner, *The Sociology of Secularisation: A Critique of a Concept* (London: Routledge & Kegan Paul, 1977).

9. George Smith, *Atheism: The Case Against God* (Amherst, NY: Prometheus Books, 1989).

10. Dan Barker, *Losing Faith in Faith: From Preacher to Atheist* (Madison, WI: Freedom from Religion Foundation, 1992).

11. Sam Harris, *The End of Faith: Religion, Terror, and the Future of Reason* (New York: W. W. Norton & Company, 2004).

12. Daniel C. Dennett, *Breaking the Spell: Religion as a Natural Phenomenon* (New York: Viking, 2006); Richard Dawkins, *The God Delusion* (Boston and New York: Houghton Mifflin, 2006); Sam Harris, *Letter to a Christian Nation* (New York: Knopf, 2006).

13. David Eller, *Natural Atheism* (Cranford, NJ: American Atheist Press, 2004); David Eller, *Atheism Advanced: Further Thoughts of a Freethinker* (Cranford, NJ: American Atheist Press, 2008).

14. Alister McGrath, *The Twilight of Atheism: The Rise and Fall of Disbelief in the Modern World* (New York: Doubleday, 2004).

15. John F. Haught, "Amateur Atheists: Why the New Atheism Isn't Serious," *Christian Century* February 26, 2008.

16. Walter Kaufmann, *The Portable Nietzsche* (Harmondsworth, U.K. and New York: Penguin Books, 1977 [1954]), 95.

17. Ibid., 139.

# Chapter 2

# Atheism, Secularity, the Family, and Children

## *Christel Manning*

What is the impact of atheism and secularity on the family and children? Specifically, how are atheist and/or secular families different from religious ones, and how does a nonreligious upbringing affect children? This is a difficult question to answer, not only because of definitional problems addressed elsewhere in this volume, but because the topic carries such ideological baggage. The fact that we even ask this question says a lot about the cultural significance of religion in America. Although the number of people with no religious affiliation is growing, there is a common perception that religion is good for family and children and that atheism and secularism therefore weaken families and put children at risk. That perception is supported not just by conservative religious pundits but by the supposedly liberal academic establishment, resulting in guilt and worry among many secular parents.

I should say, at the onset, that I am one of those parents. I am secular in the sense of not identifying or affiliating with religion in my adult life, but I was raised in a family in which religion was a powerful presence. Religion provided moral structure. My sisters and I could not watch television or listen to rock music (considered a corrupting influence) and we were made to kneel and pray in front of our beds before we went to sleep. But religion also provided magic and mystery. I remember Christmas at my German grandmother's house, how she closed the door to the living room while she decorated the tree, forbidding entry until Christmas Eve when we would all file in while she played *Silent Night* on the piano. There were real candles on the tree, the room smelled of wax and pine needles, incense and cinnamon, and everything glittered with light reflecting off the glass ornaments and tinsel and the brightly wrapped boxes below. The entire family would sing, children would recite poems, and adults would lead religious readings and prayers. Eventually, the children were sent off to bed, dreaming of the presents that awaited them in the morning, while the adults sat drinking and talking until late into the night. My daughter, now seven, has none of that. Although I cannot, with integrity, raise her with religion, I often wish I could give her what I had. It is this quandary that led to my research on unchurched parents, some of the results of which are presented here.

This chapter will argue that the impact of atheism and secularity on family and children is complex and not necessarily negative. The literature suggests that secularism may impact families in at least two ways: its effect on family structure and its effect on children. However, a critical review of that literature reveals that the exact nature of that impact remains disputed. The impact of secularism on family structure is unclear because it is impossible to determine the exact causal role of religion. The impact of secularism on children's behavior and well-being is unclear because existing studies do not adequately define secularism or distinguish between different types of secularism. Preliminary research that corrects for these problems suggests that children affiliated with secular organizations can get benefits similar to those provided by religious affiliation.

## THE PERCEIVED CONNECTION BETWEEN RELIGION AND FAMILY

Paradoxically, even as secularism increases among American families, the perception remains widespread that religion and family go together. One reason is that many of those counted as secular really aren't. Recent surveys find the number of Americans indicating no religious preference has almost doubled.[1] But most of that increase comes from increases in unchurched believers.[2] Previous research[3] has consistently shown the majority of the unaffiliated to be religious, with most holding traditional beliefs about God, Jesus, and the Bible and many engaging in regular religious practice such as prayer or scripture reading. Even those who reject traditional religion will often identify as spiritual and adhere to beliefs and practices originating outside denominational religious institutions.[4] The highest levels of secularism are found among the young, but this may be a temporary phenomenon. Smith's recent survey of American teenagers found that many young people who are disengaged from religion are not rejecting it, but see it as something they plan to return to at a later stage in life when they marry and start a family.[5] Secularism is perceived as an individual pursuit tied to the freedom and exploration associated with youth—something we all must leave behind when we settle down to adult commitments.

The identification of religion with family is also rooted in bias and ignorance about atheism. Secularism may be rising, but atheism remains a minority position, one that is perceived as deviant by many Americans.[6] According to a recent Pew survey, 63 percent of Americans would be less likely to vote for a presidential candidate if she or he were atheist—more than might be influenced by the candidate being Muslim (46 percent) or homosexual (46 percent).[7] It should come as no surprise, then, that divorced parents have had custody rights denied or limited because of atheism[8] and that seven in ten Americans would be troubled if a member of their immediate family married an atheist.[9] Most of what the public knows about atheist families comes from media coverage about atheist parents fighting to protect their kids from religious influence in public schools: prayer, pledge of allegiance, and study of creationism. Such accounts are unrepresentative of most atheist parents who are not political activists. Worse, we are left with the impression of atheist parents as ideologues, using their children as pawns to promote their own political agenda.

Religion is also tied to family because of political rhetoric. In the culture war over gender and sexual orientation that has divided this nation for more than 30 years, religious conservatives have skillfully appropriated the word "family" for political ends. Legislation discouraging abortion or women's employment were labeled "profamily," and "family values" became a code word for conservative Christian morality. The Family Channel is actually a major Christian television broadcaster, and Focus on the Family is a conservative Christian lobby group. The liberal use of individual-choice language (e.g., prochoice, sexual preference) has reinforced the perceived link of religion and family, and the media's repeated use of family as codeword for religion has further cemented that meaning.[10]

However, it is not just religious conservatives who identify religion with family—even many secularists do. Most contemporary secularists are individuals who were themselves raised with religion, and whatever their misgivings or disinterest in religion as adults, they often cherish the memories of childhood associated with religion: the excitement and mystery of a first communion, the smells and sounds of family gatherings at Christmas or Passover, the struggle to remain still while kneeling in a hard wooden pew. Fay cites nostalgia and fantasy to be an important reason why secular parents want religion for their children, giving numerous examples of parents who insist on having their children baptized or conducting a traditional religious circumcision ceremony even though they themselves no longer believe in god. She writes, "However relaxed parents might be about going it alone metaphysically or morally, few I spoke to were sanguine about what they perceived as the emotional and cultural loss to their children of being raised without religion's shaping and celebratory power, without its stories and its poetry, without its web of symbols, and its magic."[11]

Parent's don't want to deprive their kids of something that is widely perceived as good—and religion is. Even liberal academics such as psychologist Robert Coles assert that children are "naturally spiritual"[12] and for the last 50 years, numerous studies report that children who grow up with religion do better on most measures of behavior and well-being than those who don't (this literature is further discussed below). While most parents do not read scholarly journals, the conclusions are picked up by the popular press. The result is that many secularists and atheists worry about how their children will fare without religion and often appear defensive in explaining their secular parenting choices.

Popular magazines and newspapers regularly run editorials (usually around Christmas time) about the impact of atheism on children, both in terms of the prejudice they face as a minority group, and in terms of what they might lose (joy, comfort, and moral values) by lacking religion.[13] In the early 1990s *New York Times* reporter Martha Fay, a lapsed Catholic, published a book entitled, *Do Children Need Religion?*, in which she reported on the growing number of secular parents and the ways they raised their children. The parents Fay interviewed were themselves disconnected from church, but saw religion as a source of moral guidance and community, and worried about whether or not their children could "become good and loving people" and "find a place in the culture" without it. Secular parents receive little guidance on answering these questions, compared to the vast literature of advice books on Christian parenting. Fay's was among the first in a small but growing literature directed at secular parents that has more recently included books about pagan, Buddhist, and atheist parenting.[14] The authors of these essays usually conclude that secular children will be fine, but the very existence of these writings is testament to their need to persuade themselves and the rest of the culture.

With all the hand-wringing, it is surprising that there has been no systematic study of secular families and childrearing in the United States. The literature suggests that secularization impacts family and children in at least two ways: family structure and children's well-being, but there is little consensus about either subject.

## Secularization and Family Structure

Secularization's influence on family structure is closely tied to issues of gender and sexuality that are discussed in detail elsewhere in this volume, so I will present only a brief overview here. The issue has been widely debated and carries considerable political baggage. Conservatives argue that secularization weakens family ties by legitimating divorce, contraception, abortion, and sex outside of marriage, including homosexual relationships. Liberals dispute those claims, emphasizing the ways in which secularization has liberated oppressed groups from patriarchal authority. While both arguments have merit, it is all but impossible to sort out who is right.

The structure of the American family has changed significantly over the last century. What is often termed the traditional family (male breadwinner married to female homemaker with several children) is no longer demographically typical. For the last 25 years, the majority of women with children have worked outside the home, and National Public Radio recently reported that for the first time in history the majority of mothers under 30 were unmarried. The contemporary family includes a diversity of models, including single-parent families, blended families, and gay and lesbian families.

Secularization does seem to have played a role in that change. Historically, secularization has gone hand in hand with the decline in family size and a weakening of parental authority. As modern societies become more secular, people have fewer children, women go off to work, the divorce rate rises, childrearing becomes more permissive, and young people are less deferent to their elders. Demographic statistics for the contemporary United States bear this out. Secularization is associated with lower fertility rates and weaker marriage ties. Single adults, especially males, are most likely to indicate no religious preference; individuals with no religious preference have lower fertility rates. Secularism is more common among people who are single, divorced, or childless than among those who are married with children, and single and unwed mothers are more likely to be secular.[15]

But it is not at all clear that religion or lack thereof plays a causal role in determining family structure. There is an obvious logical connection as secular ideas challenge traditional theologies which legitimate large families, heterosexuality, and patriarchal authority. If prohibitions of contraception or divorce or homosexual relationships are no longer perceived as a mandated by god, it is easier to break them. But religious arguments can be made for small families and/or for women's liberation. Among Victorian Protestants, small families were encouraged as a sign of sexual restraint, and by some accounts the feminist movement had religious rather than secular origins.[16]

There are other causal factors that contributed to family change independent of secularization, such as economics, education, reproductive technology, and the sexual and gender liberation movements.[17] The rising cost of having children, for example, has a significant impact on fertility. In the farm based economy of colonial America, and the emergent industrial economy of the nineteenth century, children contributed to family income by working alongside their parents. But legislation mandating education and outlawing child labor meant that children became a drain on the family pocketbook. The recent shift to a service and technology based economy and the associated expectation that every child must go to college has only aggravated that pattern, creating strong incentives for all parents to reduce family size, regardless of religion. The causal relationship between secularization and family structure may also be reversed. The education and employment of women, for example, made them more independent and thus more likely to challenge male authority, which may contribute to the weakening of religious authority. Self selection also plays a role. Divorced and never-married mothers, for example, are more likely to be secular, but that doesn't mean that secularism made them get a divorce or prevented them from getting married. Rather, such individuals probably became secular because so many religions groups condemn unwed motherhood.

Some historians dispute the significance of the changes in family structure, asserting that the so-called traditional family was never typical of America. As Stephanie Coontz's influential study points out, "today's diversity of family forms, rates of premarital pregnancy, productive labor of wives, and prevalence of blended families, for example, would all look much more familiar to colonial Americans than would 1950s patterns."[18] Other researchers such as Finke and Stark have questioned whether America really is more secular than it was a century ago.[19] Changes in family structure have occurred in both the religious and secular population, and although many religious institutions resisted that change, others have supported them.[20] In short, all we can say for sure is that secularization legitimates and may therefore accelerate changes in family structure that have a variety of causes.

## Secularization and Children

A clearer picture seems to emerge from the literature on secularism and children. For more than half a century, research reports have statistically linked childhood religious affiliation to positive outcomes.[21] While many of these studies were small, they are confirmed by Christian Smith's groundbreaking study of teens and religion. Smith's research, drawing on nationwide surveys and follow-up interviews with hundreds of teens found that religious involvement is significantly associated with positive life outcomes. Religious teens were significantly less likely than secular teens to engage in high-risk behavior such as smoking, drinking, or drug use, and they were less likely to drop out of school or be sexually active. They expressed higher levels of emotional well-being and more meaningful relational ties to parents and other adults. They placed higher values on honesty, expressed more compassion for the less fortunate, and were more actively engaged in their community. These findings held even when Smith controlled for gender, age, race, region, parental marital status, parental education, and family income.

The association of secularism and childhood risk factors is far more disturbing that the link, if any, between secularism and changes in family structure. The public is deeply divided over the desirability of changes in family structure, but nobody wants their kids to drop out of school, use drugs, or be depressed. It is essential therefore to evaluate whether secularity, and atheism in particular, pose a risk for children. A critical analysis of the available evidence suggests that it does not.

## THE CAUSAL LINK BETWEEN RELIGION AND POSITIVE CHILDHOOD OUTCOME REMAINS DISPUTED

It is difficult to establish the causal process in studies linking religious involvement with positive childhood outcomes. As Smith himself acknowledges, the "association is most likely the result of a combination of complex social processes" including both religious and nonreligious factors such as personality selection (risk averse or joiner personalities are more likely to be religious), reverse causation (some teenagers who get in trouble drop out of religious involvement), and indirect religious effects (e.g., religion supports strong families, which reduces the risk of teen delinquency).[22] It is hard to dispute his conclusion, however, that such factors cannot explain away the religious influence entirely.

Religious affiliation provides many social benefits that children need. Smith describes these benefits as falling into three broad categories. The first is the provision of a moral order. Religion provides not only moral directives grounded in the authority of tradition, but an organizational context for spiritual experiences that help solidify moral commitments, and adult and peer group role models for moral behavior. A second benefit of religious affiliation is that youth can acquire learned competencies including life and leadership skills, coping skills, and cultural capital such as biblical literacy. A third benefit is the social and organizational ties that go with religious affiliation: religion provides one of few institutional contexts that are not age-stratified, providing youth with access to caring adults outside their family as well as networking opportunities to other organizations.[23] A close look at all of these benefits, however, shows they are tied to the organizational aspects of religion, the fact that church or synagogue is a community of caring adults that guides children and provides support for a shared moral order. This suggests that those benefits could also be had from affiliation with a secular organization.

## WE LACK GOOD DATA ABOUT ATHEIST AND SECULAR FAMILIES

Unfortunately, the information available about such families is limited, and what is available is often biased and/or marred by conflicting and inaccurate definitions of secularism. While there is a large body of research about the impact of religion on raising children, there has been no systematic study of atheist or secular parenting in the United States. Large-scale national studies of youth and religion often ignore atheist and other secular denominations altogether because the numbers are so small. And, as noted in Pasquale's chapter in this volume, we have no studies that account for the variations in the secular population, which has significant implications for the impact on children.

What we do know about the subject comes from studies on religion that treat atheism and secularism as the absence of religion, rather than an alternative worldview that has many diverse variations with possibly distinct outcomes. Such an approach tends to presume the a priori value of religion, simply assuming that children who lack religion have "nothing," without investigating the differences that may exist between different types of secular families. The American Religious Identification Survey, for example, asked only couples in mixed marriages about their children's religious education.[24] The study authors seem to simply assume that parents with no religious affiliation would not provide any worldview education for their children, thus ignoring many atheists and humanists who raise their children as Humanists or Unitarians. It is significant that the risks associated with secularism in Smith's and other studies focus on individuals who are weak or lacking in religious commitment. What these studies do not address is what happens when individuals are committed to something else.

A major source of these biases is the lack of clear definitions. Atheism and secularity are defined in opposition to religion, with atheism (the rejection of theism) often perceived as an extreme form of secularism (the decline of religious influence over society). But atheism is a narrow term referring to a specific belief (that there is no god), whereas secularism has various meanings, including a range of attitudes (such as religious indifference, doubt, agnosticism, and atheism) as well as behaviors (such as lack of regular church attendance or disregard for traditional religious morality). Yet the literature on family and children often does not clearly articulate which of those many meanings is in use and usually does not differentiate between atheism and secularism. In many studies, atheist families are subsumed under the category of "none" or "no religious preference," which includes agnostics, pagans, and others who are in fact religious. By the same token, those who do claim religious affiliation include many who are functionally secular.[25]

## SECULAR FAMILIES VARY CONSIDERABLY

Secularism, like religion, comes in many flavors. Nobody would ever assume that being raised in a fundamentalist Mormon household would have the same impact on kids as a liberal Protestant upbringing, but that is, in essence, how many people look at secularism. As more recent studies are beginning to demonstrate, secularism is every bit as diverse as religion and should therefore be expected to have diverse impact on children.

My own research on secularism confirms the variations discussed elsewhere in this volume. Over the last three years I interviewed 46 family members who claimed "no religious preference" and "no religious affiliation" about the upbringing of their children. Previous research[26] has shown significant regional differences in religious disaffiliation: the lowest rates are in the South or states where Evangelical Christianity dominates the culture; the highest rates are in the West and the urban Northeast (depending on whether affiliation is measured by attendance or identification). So my respondents were selected to reflect these differences: from Connecticut, Massachusetts, and California where "nones" are more numerous and from Colorado Springs and Jacksonville, Florida, where they are less common. Previous research has shown higher rates of secularism in single-parent households,[27] so an effort was made to include both married and unmarried respondents. Respondents ranged in age from 23 to 55. There were 16 men and 30 women: all were white and had completed at least some college, and all were employed or supported by someone who was employed (I did not ask questions about income). Almost all respondents had themselves been raised with religion; their religious background included Catholic, mainline Protestant, conservative Protestant, Jewish, Mormon, Unitarian, and Bahai. Interviews were conducted in person, using a semi-structured format, and usually lasted about an hour. This was a qualitative study which included many respondents who were in fact religious, so the numbers of actual secularists were small. Nonetheless, the findings provide concrete illustrations of the diversity among secular families, providing valuable pointers for future research.

The analysis of my interview data, which is still ongoing, suggests that there is considerable variation among secular families that is likely to impact the ways in which they raise their children. One source of variation is their worldview, that is, the set of beliefs and values that gives meaning and order to their lives. Another is whether or not they affiliate with a community that shares and supports that worldview.

## VARIETY IN WORLDVIEW

The respondents to my study were selected because they had no religious affiliation and did not identify as religious. Many of them, however, turned out to be not secular in the sense of rejecting theism or supernatural beliefs or basic Judeo-Christian values, and those who did varied considerably in what kinds of worldviews they adopted instead.

## Pure Secularism

I will define as pure secularists those respondents who were committed to a nontheistic, materialist worldview, one that is characterized by questioning rather than accepting particular assertions about the world. Such individuals identified themselves by a variety of labels such as atheist, humanist, or skeptic, but were united by their "faith" in rational empiricism. The meaning of our existence, to these respondents, lies not in god but in the pursuit of truth. That pursuit requires the opposite of religious faith, a default position of skepticism, which subjects every assertion about the world to rational, empirical testing. Thus pure secularists saw the scientific method as the only honest path to truth.

Pure secularists often dismissed religion as irrational and misleading. David, a married father of three young children, identifies as an ethical humanist. He does not believe in god or a higher power. "As a way or truth to this existence, it [theism] doesn't hold much truth. I am very grounded in trying to find out what is real . . . we are what we are today and then you're done, and so I try to live life as if this is all I have, because I think that's probably true." Raised Presbyterian, David's father was a minister, but he became "alienated from traditional church teachings from a scientific perspective . . . my undergraduate degree is in theoretical mathematics, and so the whole notion of any real understanding of something beyond the concrete is doubtful." Bob, divorced father of two teenagers, identifies as an atheist. He too rejects religion on logical grounds. Like David, he was raised Protestant and actually intended to become a minister. It was in seminary that he became alienated from religion. "The first problem was actually the problem of any one religion's claim to being true, it seemed like the competing claims of the religions just negated them." If Christianity, Islam, and Hinduism all claim divine revelation, and "those religions have conflicting views of the world, then all you can do is stand in a room and shout at one another, I've got revelation, no, I've got a revelation . . . obviously that's ridiculous. And the basis for these claims cannot be established otherwise, empirically. . . . The second big problem was the age old problem of evil, how do I maintain traditional Christian theism in the face of all the evil and suffering in the world, there's a tsunami, 160,000 people killed, it doesn't make any sense." If Bob's ultimate purpose is finding truth, then the logical conclusion is that religion must be rejected.

Others see religions not only as false but dangerous, legitimating oppression, intolerance, and violence. Rosemary, married with two children in college and one still at home, jokingly calls herself a "Pastafarian. You know, the flying spaghetti monster." She says she is "neither spiritual nor religious, does not believe in god or higher power or spirit or energy. Nothing." Rosemary has done her share of seeking, studying the ancient scriptures, the Bhagavad-Gita, the Gnostics. But she ultimately rejected religion "because I find that, and no matter how pure the intentions, religion is used to justify what we do, and I reject that entirely." Religion to Rosemary is too often a tool of self-deception, allowing us to deny the true motives or our actions.

If pure secularism's source of meaning is the pursuit of truth, morality is grounded in the human responsibility to be rational rather than indulge our often selfish and childlike emotions. Pure secularist respondents often resonated with best-selling atheist author Sam Harris, who describes evil as rooted in irrationality and blames religion for rejecting reason in favor of faith, thus contributing to much cruelty and violence. To pure secularist respondents, right action is not "some rule you blindly follow" but the result of critical reflection to determine "what is best for humanity." That isn't easy, human nature being prone to self-deception, but it is something we can learn and practice, and pure secularist parents actively encouraged such practice in their children. The importance of teaching children to "question everything" was a recurrent theme in my interviews. According to Rosemary, "one of the things that I have stressed with the kids for a long time is to understand that a word does not mean the same thing for everybody, and that being called to service does not mean for instance joining the Marines, you need to question how the word is used and for what purpose, and what it supports." However, pure secularist ethics is more than just skepticism of other people's morals; it is also a substantive ethical system. Children learn that "there is only our natural world. There are no gods, no devils, no heavens or hell. By careful thinking and by using science we can try to understand our world, and we can try to solve our problems. We are all citizens of the same world, and all people should work together to make a better world where all people can live together peacefully. And we want to protect the Earth both for ourselves and for all people in the future."[28] Contrary to the popular notion that science is value free, pure secularist respondents argued that rational, scientific thinking *can* provide a basis for morality that transcends individual subjectivity. As Rosemary put it: "we are all particles in the universe when we are alive, our actions speak, and we can never know where on the wave we are on a massive wave of history, and we could be the person that turns the way, and so it will force us to be ethical and even kind because kind is good." Pure secularism, then, is not just the rejection of religion, but a positive embrace of a meaningful moral order that parents actively convey to their children.

### Naturalism

I define as naturalist those respondents who expressed an earth-centered worldview, characterized by the belief that nature is sacred, deserving respect as much as humans do. Like pure secularist respondents, naturalists rejected theism, but unlike pure secularists they drew on Buddhist or Pagan ideas. They often described a force or energy that animates the universe but were quite adamant that this is not god and should not be worshipped. Tansy, married mother of three, was raised a Southern Baptist, but rejected the religion of her childhood because it made no sense to her intellectually. Instead, she came to ". . . believe in a force, very Jedi-ish," and laughs, "I'm not kidding, people may laugh at me, but I believe that there's probably a force that connects us together, it's a not a sentient being, I wouldn't call it a god so I wouldn't worship him, it's an energy out there that that keeps people together, probably a natural thing." Similarly, Ella, a young woman in her twenties, who was raised Unitarian, says: "I believe in an energy or force, would probably be the best way to describe it, we have a spiritual connection to the rest of the planet, I believe that there is a force that connects everyone and that when we die we become a part of that, and the energy becomes reincarnated, not the person."

To these respondents, the meaning of our existence lies in our connection to the natural world. As Barbara, a middle-aged, formerly Methodist woman, put it, "I think God is a construct that we humans have created to explain things that we don't understand, so that word doesn't resonate with me, I don't like to meditate, I don't like quiet. However, I do love going to the mountains, and walking in nature, and if ever there was a time that I felt spiritual that would be the time that I felt that way." Naturalists seem less enchanted than pure secularists with the power of rationality, which the former often blame for environmental degradation and the mechanization of human life. Nature is where we reconnect with what makes us essentially human, our bodies and our senses, and reflect on our purpose, which is to enjoy this planet and make it a better place to live.

To naturalists, morality is grounded in our responsibility to the planet. Evil is rooted not so much in irrationality as in human arrogance and greed, our habit of seeking to control this planet for our own selfish purposes. They point out that most of the major problems in this world—war, crime, poverty—are not just human but ecological problems. Fred, for example, is a married man with two grown children who is an active environmentalist. "Look at how the wars in Iraq and Afghanistan have caused environmental degradation, they bombed the oil fields, burned down forests, wipe out people's crops, there is no water, and that breeds poverty and crime and terrorism, and then we get new rounds of warfare." To be a good person means to live sustainably on this earth, but that isn't easy, especially if you live in the United States and have become accustomed to a lifestyle that carries a huge environmental footprint. Many naturalists will assign some of the blame for that footprint to the influence of Judeo-Christian religion that has "encouraged man to dominate and exploit this planet." Instead naturalists often look to Native American culture as an ethical model. Vicky, for example, was raised Baptist in Arkansas, but left in her teens. Now a young mother of a preschool age child, she says we must learn to live in balance, to "take only what we need, and fix what we have broken, and to pay respect to nature, like the Native Americans did, I really resonate with that." She and other naturalists talk about the ethical challenge of making daily small decisions that support sustainability. "It's like every time I go to the supermarket, the organic veggies are more expensive, sometimes two dollars more per pound, same with fair trade coffee, or toys made in the United States rather than in China, actually they are almost impossible to find . . . but then I remind myself, this is what will help the earth, the small farmers, the workers in poor countries, this is the right thing to do." Vicky and other naturalist parents engage their children in these moral challenges. "I've explained to her about how hot water uses energy, and how making energy pollutes the air and how that hurts people and the planet. She understands pretty well." Perhaps too well, as Vicky's daughter now nags her about taking long showers. A sustainability ethic, then, provides a coherent moral order for naturalists to live by and raise their children in.

## Pluralism

The majority of my respondents did not reject religion, but were unaffiliated because they refused to commit themselves to one of them. These pluralists, as I call them, see the world's religions as different paths to the same place, though they often find one or two they are most at home in. Their conceptions of the divine varied: many were agnostic, some believed in a personal god and others in pantheism, but they are united in their conviction that "ultimately, it doesn't matter."

Anne, married mother of a 9-year-old boy, was raised Greek Orthodox, and began studying other religions in college. "I saw how similar people who were called masters or saints are, like there are masters in the Buddhist tradition and there are Christian monks . . . the Sufi masters, their divine encounters or mystical experiences were so similar, I started thinking about it." Anne eventually became a devotee of a Hindu guru, but she rejects all labels. "I do not feel that any of these traditions is mine, I feel like they all are, but I don't feel like I have to belong to one of them." Now living in California, Anne may seem like the stereotypical hippie seeker, but there are many pluralists who are not. Susan, raised as a conservative Jew and living in Connecticut, says: "I'm a pluralist, I believe all religions are valid and true, so the question for me is which ritual system speaks most to my heart, and makes most sense to me intellectually and personally, I guess I would choose Judaism, but it's hard to be Jewish, there are a lot of rituals you're supposed to keep . . . that at this point I'm thinking I'm not going to do, and is it ok for me to simply go to synagogue but not be kosher and not hold Passover one year . . . but I also really love Buddhism, it absolutely makes sense to me, it's about human nature and meditation practice keeps me grounded and peaceful. So I enjoy Judaism and Buddhism for very different reasons, I like the practice of Buddhism but Judaism has a tradition based on my past and my family and also has god at its center, which I do want in a religious tradition, so I don't think I'll choose one or the other, I'm figuring out how to make the two work for me." Susan, married to a Jewish man, has considered joining a synagogue, for her son's sake, but she can't find one that "fits my needs."

To pluralists, meaning is rooted in their own personal experience. What matters is not an over-arching principle such as truth or sustainability, but as Anne puts it, what "I feel." As Susan phrases it, a worldview must "speak to the heart" and it must "work for you." The pluralist moral order is similarly subjective, often in reaction to respondents' own experience of religion as associated with dogmatic and rigid morality. Thus Ken, a young married man who does not yet have children, says: "my biggest fear about religion, and this is probably from having grown up in Colorado Springs, is the attitude that this is right and this is wrong, this is good and this is bad, it's so black and white for a lot of people who don't think." He says he "would be nervous if I ended up indoctrinating my child with any sort of dogma about this is right and this is wrong. Of course there are certain things like murder or—but even then there are certain situations where killing may be right." If the pluralist morality is rooted in anything, it would be the primacy of personal choice. Traditional Hindu morality, for example, is rooted in the concept of karma, which Anne interprets in terms of personal choice. "It does not mean you do something bad and then you have to pay for it. Karma means self-awareness of choosing the right thing rather than the easy thing. And a lot of times the question is what is the right thing. . . the right thing in general is to do the least amount of damage, not because its sinful, but if you have a choice, and you live in a society where there are so many choices." Thus she has explained to her son why they are vegetarians, "because that does the least amount of damage," but ultimately, it is up to him, "he must make his own choices, and whatever he decides that's ok too." Anne's expression of discomfort with making moral judgments about others is typical of pluralists who seem to view intolerance as the root of all evil. Moral relativism, so often blamed on secularism, turned out to be far more common among pluralists, the most religious among my respondents.

## Religious Indifference

A small group of my respondents were those who were religiously indifferent. Unlike atheists, they do not so much reject religion as ignore it. Some, like Peter, hold vaguely Christian beliefs. "The idea that Jesus was a spiritual being who came to earth and died, I suppose I believe that, but I do not consciously following any Christian dogma or ethics and we don't go to church." Yet his disaffiliation is not rooted in any kind of resentment against organized religion. "I mean I don't know why I don't [attend church], I don't have that in my life, it's more like why would I? Rather than why don't I?" He and his wife had their three children baptized, but when asked if he had considered sending them to Sunday school, he responded: "Fleetingly." And what happened? "I let the thoughts pass out of my head." Peter might be called an indifferent Christian. Others, like Tom, are atheist. He does not believe in god or a higher power and does not identify as spiritual or religious. "Spiritual to me is more of an inner thing, when someone is interested in and thinking about spiritual matters," whereas religious means commitment to organized religion. "I'm neither." Yet Tom has no animus against religion; he remembers the church he grew up in with fondness and claims that he and his wife talked about joining a church, but "we're out of town at the ski condo two to three Sundays per month, and Sundays we're here we still don't go." He does not see any inconsistency in joining without belief because religion just isn't important to him.

Both Peter and Tom were raised Protestant. Like most Indifferents, they left the religion of their childhood not because they disagree with it, but because they are too busy with other things to be bothered. When asked if there was some other philosophy or worldview that gave meaning to their life, the Indifferent's answer was usually a long silence, followed by, "I really haven't thought much about that." Yet Christianity was often named as a source of morality: respect your parents, don't kill, don't lie, don't steal, treat others the way you want to be treated. As Peter puts it, "I think that my behavior . . . fits into, like, basic Christian values." Given that the religiously indifferent have never actually rejected religion, this should not be surprising. Religion to them is a social resource that is sometimes useful, but mostly not.

Pure Secularists, Naturalists, Pluralists, and the religiously indifferent are just four of many types of secularists that are out there. They illustrate the difficulties in defining secularism discussed earlier in this chapter. All of these respondents are secular in the sense that they do not identify or affiliate with any religion, but most are committed to alternative worldviews that could be considered equivalent to religion in the sense of providing a coherent system of meaning and values.

Moreover, the differences between these worldviews have significant implications for how respondents raise their children. One such difference was in the way that parents use their worldview to provide moral guidance. Religion has historically functioned as a powerful provider of moral order. All major religions warn against the inherent human inclination to seek "more, more, more for me, me, me" and to ignore the harm we inflict on others and the world. Thus perhaps the most damaging critique of secularism is its perceived materialism, selfishness, and moral relativism. Smith's study confirms this critique, showing that secular teens were more likely than religious teens to view right and wrong purely in terms of pleasure and personal benefit. But Smith's study does not differentiate between different kinds of secularism, some of which reject the consumerism and hedonism of contemporary society as much as religions do. It is noteworthy that many religiously "disengaged" teens were no more materialistic or relativistic than religiously "devoted" teens: 39 percent of the former rejected relativism, 60 percent would not "choose to do whatever made them happy," 84 percent would not "choose to do whatever helped them get ahead," 33 percent care very much about the needs of the poor, and 39 percent care about racial equality.[29] One must wonder whether the difference in value orientation comes not from a family's religious affiliation but from their commitment to a meaningful moral order that grounds the individual in something greater than themselves.

Among my respondents it was pluralists, the most religious group, who most embraced a subjectivist and relativist moral order, and pure secularists who most rejected it. As described above, pluralists sought to teach their children tolerance, a term they interpreted to mean acceptance of all religions as equally valid. Pure secularists, by contrast, saw all religions as equally false. Although pure secularists asserted intellectual support for religious tolerance, they tended to judge one worldview—skepticism—as superior to all others. Both pure secularist and pluralist parents had enrolled their kids in religious education programs so that they might better understand other people. Pluralists hoped that providing such choices would help their child "choose the religion that's right for them." For pure secularists the purpose of understanding others is not to accept all religions as valid, but to question any worldview you encounter. As Rosemary puts it, "the most important thing that I hope I've taught my kids is that there is nothing else that you can be sure of other than what you have now, you live your life, you live it in the best, the fullest, and the most complete way that you can in any moment, you develop your skills, whether they be thinking skills or ice-skating, and you don't live in isolation, but you were here. *If anybody tries to sell you anything beyond what you have here, you need to question their motives.*" For Rosemary, Bob, and David, a this-worldly worldview is true in an absolute sense because it can be empirically supported. All other worldviews are suspect.

In their passionate commitment to objective truth and suspicion of "false" worldviews, pure secularist parents resemble Evangelical Christians and other religious conservatives. Just as Evangelicals resist the secularism of mainstream America, pure secularist parents often see themselves as embattled, seeking to protect their kids from the religious majority. David and his wife, for example, joined a Humanist community because "it is really hard being unchurched when you live on the edge of the Bible Belt. We feel different enough anyway, to be ethical humanists in this society that dumps on people trying to exercise their right to be free from religion, it's very hard to be atheist in America." And it is even harder in Jacksonville "because everybody is affiliated with the church, and the first thing people ask when you move here is, what church do you belong to? Or, have you found a congregation yet? They all want to recruit you." Such recruitment begins in school. "Kids here, they will ask, have you been saved? And, why don't you go to church? So if my son can say he belongs to a church, they are more likely to leave him alone." David and other pure secularists such as Rosemary educate their children about the principles of Humanism as well as about traditional religions "so that they can have ammunition" to fight a wider culture that they see as saturated with religion. Pure secularist parents also resemble Evangelicals in taking their worldview public, fighting lawsuits over school curriculum or prayer at children's camps and ballgames. That willingness to fight publicly for what they believe is true sends a powerful moral message to the children of pure secularist parents: that truth is not just what feels good to each individual and that we can objectively determine what is right and what is wrong.

## VARIETY IN AFFILIATION

A second source of variation among people who claim no religious identification or affiliation is whether or not they affiliate with an alternative organization that supports and enacts their secular worldview. Affiliation matters because most of the benefits that children supposedly get from religion are tied to organizational membership. It is therefore significant that the majority of my respondents were organizationally affiliated. Although Indifferents showed little interest in joining a community, Pure Secularists, Naturalists, and Pluralists often do belong to an organization of like-minded individuals. Some of these organizations were intentionally created to provide an alternative to religion: what I call free-thinking denominations. Others have political purposes such as environmental or peace activism.

### Freethinker Denominations

A growing number of secularists are affiliating with free-thinker denominations that closely resemble churches in structure and activities. There are national secularist organizations such as the American Humanist Association that have chapters in many states. There are also independent secular churches such as the North Texas Church of Free

Thought or the First Humanist Society of New York. Just as some people who claim to belong to a church but never attend, some secular individuals affiliate in name only. Many others, however, gather weekly and on special occasions for sermons, readings, and rituals. Depending on size, some secular associations meet independently in people's homes; others are large enough to have their own facility. Some organizations serve a particular secularist population such as atheists or humanists, and others provide a home to a variety of both secular and religious families.

The Humanist Community of Silicon Valley (HCSV), California, is an example of a community serving a particular secular population, those who identify as humanist. Serving San Jose, Silicon Valley, Stanford, and the Peninsula since 1962, HCSV offers regular Sunday Forums and children's programs and celebrates weddings and funerals, as well as holidays significant to the atheist community such as Darwin Day or Martin Luther King Day. In other locations where they are less numerous or not as well funded, secularists may pool their resources with other free-thinkers. In many states, Unitarian Universalist societies provide a home not only for liberal religious folk but for various types of secularists, including atheists. A recent survey of the Unitarian Universalist Society in New Haven (UUNH), Connecticut, for example, found that 28 percent identify as atheist or humanist. Unitarian Universalism is a nondoctrinal community, sharing commitment to a set of ethical principles rather than a supernatural belief and celebrating a variety of religious holidays to mark the diversity of their community. UUNH has served the greater New Haven area since 1951. They offer two services each Sunday, life cycle rituals, a religious education program, and small groups and are deeply involved in social activism particularly on issues such as opposing the Iraq war and supporting gay rights.

It is not surprising to find secular organizations in urban areas on the east and west coasts, given the liberal reputation of these locations. But I found vibrant secular communities in more conservative regions such as Colorado Springs or Jacksonville as well. Colorado Springs, for example, is a medium-sized city where you can find an Evangelical church on almost every corner, as well as the headquarters of Focus on the Family, but it also boasts two Unitarian Universalist churches that provide a home for many secularists for whom belonging to a community of like-minded individuals is a significant source of support in raising their children.

Secularists seem aware of children's need for affiliation with a moral community. Thus some free-thinker organizations offer worldview education and youth programming that replicates much of what churches provide in terms of moral values, learning opportunities, and social networking. The "dogma free Sunday school" of HCSV was established in 2004 in response to an expressed need by community members for "children who are used to hearing their classmates talk about god to have a safe refuge to explore all the alternatives." Held parallel to the adult Sunday meetings, the children's program focuses on thinking and asking questions (rather than learning a particular doctrine) and emphasizes human (rather than supernatural) answers for how to live in a human world. Unitarian Universalist children's programs have been in existence longer and are therefore more comprehensive. They are actually called "religious education," but they too are nondogmatic, teaching children about Unitarian Universalist principles and presenting the teachings of world religions as well as humanism as equally valid alternatives. The curriculum has several levels geared to different age groups, as well as providing opportunities for youth to engage in the wider community. The Highland Park Unitarian Universalist Congregation in Colorado Springs, for example, sends teenagers on a trip to a Indian reservation where they engage in cultural exchange and social outreach activities. In all Unitarian Universalist congregations, children are encouraged to interact with adults, for example, by conducting annual membership surveys and by participating in the first 15 minutes of the religious service.

In addition to alternative Sunday school programs, secularists have also established children's summer camps. The first atheist summer camp, Camp Quest, was established in 1996 in northern Kentucky to provide children in the greater Cincinnati area with a secular alternative to religiously based summer camps such as Boy Scouts and summer Bible camps. The camp, which first met in a Baptist facility, provided much of what religious camps offer: roasting marshmallows and telling stories at campfires, sleeping in cabins with other kids, swimming, hiking, and arts and crafts, as well as educational activities such as learning about lake ecology or astronomy. But other activities reflect the camp's secular identity: morning tai chi, a field trip to endangered wetlands, and—instead of Bible school—instruction in secular humanism. The success of Camp Quest, which continues going strong, soon spawned branches in Ohio and other states such as Quest West in Sacramento, California.[30]

Clearly, the organizational resources are available to provide children secular equivalents of the "benefits" associated with religious affiliation. As described above, free-thinking organizations can provide a moral order grounded in a larger intellectual tradition—the Humanist and the Unitarian Universalist traditions, for example, are both more than a century old and are associated with a vast body of learned literature. In their Sunday schools, camps, trips, and volunteer activities, secular organizations provide children and youth with opportunities to learn life, leadership, and coping skills as well as acquire cultural capital such as religious literacy and ethics. Perhaps most importantly, free-thinker organizations engage kids with other caring adults as well as with the wider community.

**Socio-political Organizations**

Not all secularists belong to organizations that are religion equivalents. It could be argued, however, that some unaffiliated secularists
may have some other community involvement that provides similar
benefits. Parents who are deeply involved in social activism, perhaps for
peace or the environment, illustrate this pattern. The membership of the
Environmental Justice Network (EJN) in New Haven where I live is an
example. There are several parents who regularly bring their children to
monthly EJN meetings; when working on a particular crisis issue, the
meetings may be more frequent. The children play while the adults talk,
but the children are also involved in both the values and actions of the
organization. Parents explain to children what is at stake (the proposed
reopening of a diesel fueled power plant or the construction of a trash
incinerator in a poor urban neighborhood), and children learn about
right and wrong, truth and justice. Children and youth participate in
activism with their parents, attending public hearings, picketing, and
riding a bus on a "toxic tour" of polluted areas in the inner city. Some
children have literally grown up in this organization, as their parents
have been members for five or ten years. Like children who grow up in
a church, EJN kids are provided with a moral order and an organizational context that supports that order; they learn life and leadership
skills that are particularly valuable in becoming active citizens, and they
have access to caring adults beyond their own family as well as networking opportunities to other organizations. It seems reasonable to
expect that children growing up in this environment would experience
similarly positive outcomes as those raised in religious communities.

**CONCLUSION**

It is clear that we need more and better research investigating the
impact of atheism and secularity on the family and children. Although
the literature suggesting a positive association between religious affiliation and childhood well-being is compelling, it does not follow that
children raised in secular environments are at risk, especially if families
are committed to positive alternative worldviews and communities that
may offer the same benefits as religion. It is not my intention to suggest that such benefits can be derived from just any organization; that
would be reductionist. The religious environment surely does matter in
the sense that it provides a meaningful moral order that transcends the
individual's subjective experience and a community that shares and
supports that order. I am simply arguing that such an order and community need not be theist or supernatural in character. Until research
on religious affiliation and identification recognizes that secularism can
be more than just the absence of religion and takes into account the

variety of secular worldviews, our findings will only confirm existing prejudices.

We are beginning to see some hopeful signs that secular worldviews are being recognized as religious equivalents. In Great Britain, for example, the National Framework for Religious Education now suggests that the teaching of secular philosophies such as atheism and humanism be included in the curriculum of state schools. Such a policy reflects a recognition that children "can learn from atheism as well as about it; in other words, that atheism could offer opportunity for spiritual development."[31] The weakness of secular worldviews, if any, lies in their resistance to organization. There is an inherent strain of individualism in many secular worldviews, perhaps because secularists are resisting what they perceive as the rigid and intrusive character of organized religion. As one of my respondents put it, "church is a place where you are forced to believe a certain way and they are always asking you for money." But, as this chapter has illustrated, some secular parents are beginning see the value of a moral community and to build their own alternatives.

Although studies such as Smith's are often cited to prove that secularism is bad for children, what it really shows is that a moral order is meaningful only if it actually is lived out in a community. It is telling that many of today's secularists are people who were themselves raised with religion but turned away because of the perceived hypocrisy of its practitioners. Thus, what matters is not whether children learn religious or secular values, but whether or not those values are put into practice. As Fay put it, "what parents do, how they themselves behave, what they expect of their children remain the critical factors in the formation of moral perspective, whether the parents conviction is expressed in weekly church attendance or in dragging one's child to a peace march when she would rather go to a friend's birthday party."[32] In short, it may be the integrity of a family's commitment to something greater than themselves that is most important to moral development and emotional well-being in children.

## NOTES

1. Barry Kosmin and Ariela Keysar, *Religion in a Free Market: Religious and Non-religious Americans* (New York: Paramount Publishing, 2006).

2. Michael Hout and Claude Fisher, "Why More Americans Have No Religious Preference: Politics and Generations." *American Sociological Review* 67 (2002): 165–190.

3. Gallup conducted two national surveys, *The Unchurched American* (1978) and *The Unchurched American—10 Years Later* (1988), both available from Princeton Religion Research Center. For unchurched Protestants, see Dean Hoge, Benton Johnson, and Donald A. Luidens, *Vanishing Boundaries: The Religion of Mainline Protestant Baby Boomers* (Louisville, KY: Westminster/John Knox Press, 1994).

4. Robert Fuller, *Spiritual, But Not Religious: Understanding Unchurched America* (New York: Oxford University Press, 2001).

5. Christian Smith, *Soul Searching: The Religious and Spiritual Lives of American Teenagers* (New York: Oxford University Press, 2005).

6. Richard Jenks, "Perception of Two Deviant and Two Non-deviant Groups," *Journal of Social Psychology* 126 (1986): 783.

7. Michael Luo, "God '08: Whose, and How Much, Will Voters Accept?" *New York Times Week in Review*, July 22, 2007.

8. Eugene Volokh, "Parent-Child Speech and Child Custody Speed Restrictions," *New York University Law Review* 81 (2006): 631–733.

9. Council for Democratic and Secular Humanism, "Atheists Still Remain Black Sheep of Families," *Free Inquiry* 21, no. 4 (2001): 29.

10. James D. Hunter, *Culture Wars: The Struggle to Control the Family, Art, Education, Law, and Politics in America* (New York: Basic Books, 1992); George Lakoff, *Don't Think of an Elephant* (White River Junction, VT: Chelsea Green Publications, 2004).

11. Martha Fay, *Do Children Need Religion? How Parents Today Are Talking about the Big Questions* (New York: Pantheon Books, 1993): 124.

12. Robert Coles, *The Spiritual Life of Children* (Boston: Houghton Mifflin, 1990).

13. See, for example, Lawrence Kutner, "Parent & Child," *New York Times*, Dec. 20, 1990, 7; Patricia Pearson, "Mommy, Is Santa Jesus's Uncle?" *Maclean's* (Dec. 22, 2003): 20–25; Dana Tierney, "Coveting Luke's Faith," *New York Times Magazine*, Jan. 11, 2004, 66; Tayari Jones, "Among the Believers," *New York Times*, July 10, 2005: OP 13; Paul Asay, "Who Is God? Even Kids Raised without Religion Need Spiritual Questions Answered," *Colorado Springs Gazette*, Aug. 26, 2006, LS 1; Nica Lalli, "Am I Raising Atheist Children?" *USA Today*, March 17, 2008.

14. For example, Kristin Madden, *Pagan Parenting: Spiritual, Magical, and Emotional Development of the Child* (Woodbury, MN: Llewellyn Publications, 2000); Greg Holden, *Karma Kids: Answering Everyday Questions with Buddhist Wisdom* (Berkley, CA: Ulysses Press, 2004); Dale McGowan, ed., *Parenting Beyond Belief: On Raising Ethical, Caring Kids without Religion* (New York: Amacom, 2007).

15. Kosmin and Keysar, 94–97.

16. Nancy Hardesty, *Women Called to Witness: Evangelical Feminism in the 19th Century* (Nashville, TN: Abingdon Press, 1984).

17. J. A. Banks, *Victorian Values: Secularism and the Size of Families* (Boston: Routledge, Kegan & Paul, 1981); Stephanie Coontz, *The Way We Never Were: American Families and the Nostalgia Trap* (New York: Basic Books, 1992); Susan M. Ross, ed., *American Families Past and Present: Social Perspectives on Transformations* (Princeton, NJ: Rutgers University Press, 2006).

18. Coontz, 183.

19. Roger Finke and Rodney Stark, *The Churching of America, 1776–2005: Winners and Losers in Our Religious Economy* (Princeton, NJ: Rutgers University Press, 2005).

20. Christel Manning, *God Gave Us the Right: Conservative Catholic, Evangelical Protestant, and Orthodox Jewish Women Grapple with Feminism* (Princeton, NJ: Rutgers University Press, 1999).

21. For an excellent survey of this literature, see Smith, 330–31; see also Kenneth Hyde, *Religion in Childhood and Adolescence: A Comprehensive Review of the Research* (Birmingham, AL: Religious Education Press, 1990).

22. Smith, 234.

23. Smith, 240–51.

24. For extended discussion of ARIS results, see Kosmin and Keysar.

25. Martin Ashley, "The Spiritual, the Cultural, and the Religious: What Can We Learn from a Study of Boy Choristers?" *International Journal of Children's Spirituality* 7 (2002): 257–272; Penny Long Marler and Kirk Hadaway, "Being Religious or Being Spiritual in America: A Zero Sum Proposition?" *Journal for the Scientific Study of Religion* 41 (2002): 289–300.

26. Christian Smith, David Sikkink, and Jason Bailey, "Devotion in Dixie and Beyond: A Test of the 'Shibley Thesis' on the Effects of Regional Origin and Migration on Individual Religiosity," *Journal for the Scientific Study of Religion* 37 (1998): 494–506; Roger Stump, "Regional Variations in the Determinants of Religious Participation." *Review of Religious Research* 27 (1986): 208–225.

27. Kosmin and Keysar, 94–97.

28. Vern Uchtman, "Camp Quest 96," *Free Inquiry* 17 (Winter 1996/97): 27.

29. Smith, 227–228.

30. Cathy Lynn Grossman, "Camps Sign Up Freethinkers," *USA Today*, July 17, 2006.

31. Jaqueline Watson, "Can Children and Young People Learn from Atheism for Spiritual Development? A Response to the National Framework for Religious Education," *British Journal of Religious Education* 30 (2008): 49–58.

32. Fay, 99.

# Chapter 3

# A Portrait of Secular Group Affiliates

## Frank L. Pasquale

"Atheism" and "secularity" are windows into a complex domain in human ideas and affairs. The former is comparatively narrow (at least semantically, if not always as used); the latter is somewhat broader. There are other windows into this domain, each with a distinctive slant, such as irreligion, religious doubt, unbelief or nonbelief, freethought, agnosticism, (secular) humanism, rationalism, materialism, philosophical naturalism, and (religious) skepticism, among others. What these terms have in common—from a negative vantage and to varying degrees—is nonaffirmation, rejection, or doubt concerning theistic, supernatural, or (ontologically) transcendental ideas and phenomena *or* something called "religion." From a positive vantage, and to varying degrees, they reflect what intellectual historian James Thrower has called an "alternative tradition"[1] in human thought about the nature of what exists (and probably or definitely does not exist)—call this "naturalistic" or "this-worldly."

There have been countless historical, philosophical, polemic, and apologetic treatments of these subjects, but social scientific research that focuses directly on them has been limited and sporadic.[2] There are recent signs of increasing interest in secularism, atheism, irreligion, and related subjects.[3] But as observed nearly forty years ago, there remains "an appalling lack of empirical data on unbelief."[4] Although there have been notable exceptions along the way,[5] secular group affiliates and their organizations have been largely neglected.

Whether attributable to the lack of detailed knowledge or attention, or a culturally reflexive tendency to narrowly frame these phenomena within a dichotomy between something-called-religion and its absence, "seculars" or the "nonreligious" or "atheists" are habitually treated as though "they were one homogeneous category."[6] More than thirty years ago, Paul Pruyser confronted this habit, noting "the complexity of unbelief" and suggesting that "unbelief is at least as diversified as religious belief."[7] As he observed,

> Irreligion is not merely the absence of something, and certainly not simply the missing of something good, desirable, or pleasant. It is much closer to adopting an active stance or posture, involving the act of excluding another posture which, despite its popularity or naturalness, is deemed to be a poor fit in an acquired life style. Irreligion, like religion, can be zealous, militant, declarative, dogmatic, or [persuasive]. Like religion, it can be the product of training, existential decision-making, or drifting. And all too often it can be the product of religious instruction![8]

Pruyser suggested that the "study of belief and unbelief must come down from the height of global generalities to the untidy details of concrete experience in order to produce that as yet unwritten tome: *The Varieties of Experiencing Irreligion.*"[9] His challenge prompted the research to be described here. The aim has been to cast a net wide enough in scope, but fine enough in weave, to identify both shared and distinctive characteristics among those who describe themselves as substantially or affirmatively nonreligious, philosophically naturalistic, or secular.

## SAMPLE AND METHODS

Secular individuals are an elusive research target. The vast majority tends not to associate, at least formally or institutionally, on the basis of their secularity.[10] In order to produce a detailed portrait, several methods were used to gather data over an extended period:

1. Participant observation (2001–2006) in local and regional secularist groups in the Pacific Northwest (primarily secular humanist, Jewish Humanist, and atheist), together with attendance at national organizational meetings (humanist, secular humanist, skeptic, and atheist), and monitoring of websites, e-mail exchanges, and printed material (for local, regional, and national "atheist," "freethought," "humanist," "secular humanist," "Jewish Humanist," "rationalist," "secular," "skeptic," and similar groups).

2. Semi-structured interviews (fall, 2006) lasting 1.5 to 3 hours with 50 individuals, of whom 25 were male and 25, female; 25 were members of secularist groups and 25 were not; ranging in age from 18 to 87, with a mean of 62.4 years. All described themselves as "nonreligious" or "secular" and reported no religious identification or affiliation. The interview protocol focused on individuals' ways of describing and speaking about their existential or metaphysical worldviews, family background and

upbringing, the development of their ways of thinking over time, attitudes toward or about "religion," moral and ethical point of view, politics, and everyday life (family and social life, work, hobbies and
avocations, community activity, and voluntarism or philanthropic support of preferred social causes).

3. A survey of affiliates of groups that explicitly embrace secular worldviews in the Pacific Northwest (winter, 2006–2007). Hard-copy-by-mail
was used rather than on-line survey methods because the latter would
likely have underrepresented less Internet-savvy members of a population known to have an older age skew. The process itself was instructive.

An effort was made to identify all free-standing secularist groups in
Oregon, Washington, and southern British Columbia.[11] This included
groups that describe themselves as "secular," "humanist" (secular,
Jewish, or Unitarian), "atheist," "freethought," "rationalist," and/or
"skeptic." Questionnaires were distributed by postal mail or by hand
to 1,638 individuals on the mailing lists of 22 such groups from
September of 2006 through January of 2007. These were distributed in
manila envelopes containing a cover letter, the questionnaire, and a
self-addressed, post-paid return envelope addressed to a post office
box in Portland, Oregon. The cover letter requested group members'
participation in a study of people in the Pacific Northwest whose ways
of thinking are substantially secular, nonreligious, skeptical, nonsupernatural, or naturalistic. Anonymity was assured and it was indicated
that "survey findings will not be reported for any particular group or
organization by name." The letter was signed by the investigator as a
research associate with the Institute for the Study of Secularism, Trinity
College, Hartford, Connecticut.

Forty-one questionnaires were returned by the postal service as
undeliverable. Questionnaires were returned by 951 individuals, but
because of membership in multiple groups some individuals received
more than one copy. To avoid data duplication (i.e., more than one
completed survey from anyone), recipients were asked to complete a
cover sheet for each duplicate questionnaire received, indicating the
group for which they had already completed and returned the survey,
and the group(s) from which they received the duplicate(s). Twenty-
eight respondents did so, yielding 922 completed surveys for analysis,
or an effective response rate of 58.76 percent (of a nonduplicative distribution of 1,569). Ten questionnaires were partially completed, but
because they provided usable data in some sections, they were not
excluded from the sample for analysis.

Anecdotal reports (as well as written notes on completed forms) indicated that some of those receiving more than one survey did not return
duplicate surveys with completed cover sheets, as requested. Another
indication of multiple group membership (and so, likely receipt of more

than one questionnaire) was provided by a survey item on respondent membership in local religious, philosophical, or nonreligious groups. Sixty-six respondents indicated affiliation with two or more of the targeted groups. The resulting response rate is thus a conservative estimate, since the actual (net) number of individuals in the distribution sample was likely closer to 1,500 than 1,600. It is reasonable to conclude that a response rate of roughly 60 percent was achieved.[12]

A commitment was made to all participating groups that data would not be reported for any individual group by name, but rather, for distinguishable group or philosophical types based on self-descriptions (in group names, in materials or Web sites, and by group members and representatives). Assignment of groups to categories was straightforward in most cases, based on self-descriptive distinctions made by the groups themselves. Groups were assigned to the Unitarian Humanist category on the basis of an indicated relationship with a Unitarian church or fellowship, substantial numbers of Unitarian church/fellowship members among respondents, and/or explicit self-description as Unitarian Humanists.[13] Seven respondents each who were affiliated with Ethical Culture and "Brights"[14] groups, who described themselves as "atheist(ic)" and/or indicated dual membership in a regional atheist group, were included in the Atheist group category. Comparatively low response variability for the Atheist group category on many items reinforced confidence in the appropriateness of this allocation.

One small group (n = 11) that labeled itself "freethought" was excluded from the analyses presented here. Analysis of responses suggested that its members were markedly and consistently different from all other groups in the distribution sample. Most indicated profoundly "religious," "spiritual," supernatural, and/or "mystical" views. Aggregation with affiliates of other freethought groups yielded results with high response variability that did not fairly represent either of two apparently very different "takes" on "freethought." This points up an apparent distinction in popular use and meaning of "freethought" and "freethinker."

One widely cited dictionary definition of freethought/freethinker refers to "one who forms opinions on the basis of reason independently of authority; especially one who doubts or denies religious dogma." Two of three groups in the distribution sample use these terms in what may be called the (majority or standard) "rationalist" sense.[15] Here, emphasis is on reason (or rigorous application of logic and empirical evidence to the evaluation of truth claims) and denial of religious doctrine or supernatural ideas. The response patterns of the outlier group, however, suggested a very different interpretation. Here, thinking may be set free from the perceived constraints of "traditional" or institutional religious adherence, belief, or doctrine, but also from those of rationalism, skepticism, naturalism, or nontranscendentalism. (This might best be called an "unfettered" sense of "freethought"/ "freethinker.") Such variation in usage is not restricted to the groups sampled here. A check of the World Wide Web indicates that although the rationalist usage seems most common, there are those (such as a "Freethought Church") for whom these terms mean freedom from *either* religious or rationalist/empiricist discipline (with consequent inclusion of pagan, gnostic, mystical, magical, "neo-pagan polytheistic," and "bohemian" references).

Following these adjustments, the final sample for analysis included 911 respondents in six categories:

| Group/type | Oregon/Washington* | British Columbia* | Total respondents[†] |
|---|---|---|---|
| Humanist/Secular[16] | 4 (256) | 3 (129) | 385 (42.3) |
| Humanist/Jewish | 2 (110) | | 110 (12.1) |
| Humanist/Unitarian | 3 (129) | | 129 (14.2) |
| Atheist | 2 (104) | | 104 (11.4) |
| Skeptic, rationalist | 3 (153) | | 153 (16.8) |
| Freethought[17] | 2 (30) | | 30 (3.3) |
| Totals | 16 (782) | 3 (129) | 911 (100.1) |

*Values are number of groups, with number of individuals in parentheses.
[†]Values are number of respondents, with percentage of total in parentheses (total percentage is greater than 100% due to rounding error).

The focus on one region enabled the use of both intensive and extensive methods on a limited budget.[18] This said, given the mobility of North Americans, the sample reflects a wide range of geographical backgrounds. Among the U.S. affiliates, 26 percent were Northwest born and bred. Roughly 15 percent each were raised in the West, Midwest, or Northeast; 8 percent were from central or southern states, 12 percent were raised in multiple locations, and 8 percent were raised internationally. This, in fact, broadly reflects the regional distribution of seculars throughout the United States.[19]

## WHO ARE THEY?

The secularist group affiliates tend to be older, middle-class "white" Euro-Americans, generally more often male than female, and overwhelmingly the product of religious upbringings. Most are well educated, long-term seculars who are socially and politically liberal, but notably modest with regard to their lifestyles.

## Age

The average age of the group affiliates was 62.68 and median age was 64, with a range of 15 to 92 years of age. This is consistent with available evidence on age distribution in secular humanist organizations, for example. McTaggart[20] reported mean age of 57 and median age of 60 among Canadian secular humanists. At the Council for Secular Humanism there is a similar skew among the readership of their flagship publication, *Free Inquiry*, which provides a fair indication of membership (with 50.8 percent over 60, 73.4 percent over 50, and only 1.9 percent between 18 and 30 years of age).[21] Hunsberger and Altemeyer[22] found that the median age of atheist and humanist group affiliates in the San Francisco Bay area was 60.

This said, there were notable differences among the Pacific Northwest groups (Table 3.1). The younger age profile of Atheist affiliates in this sample is attributable to one of the constituent groups that grew out of a local "atheist meet-up" (n = 45; mean age = 43.6). Meet-up. com is "an online social networking portal that facilitates offline group meetings in various localities around the world. Meet-up allows members to find and join groups unified by a common interest. . . ."[23] As such, participation skews toward a younger, Internet-savvy audience. More recently, I observed the coalescence of another atheist meet-up (also with a younger membership profile) that chose to become a chapter of the Center for Inquiry (the parent organization of the Council for Secular Humanism and Committee for Skeptical Inquiry). The Internet has clearly become a medium for the formation of new secularist groups and recruitment into existing organizations, particularly because there is an overrepresentation of young "nones" (no religious preference) among Internet users.[24]

By contrast, the Unitarian Humanists consist largely of long-time Unitarian affiliates who have reacted critically to a decades-long swing in Unitarian Universalism away from a nonsupernatural or nontranscendental ("humanist") orientation toward "God-talk," "New Age" beliefs, and spiritualism.[25] Some continue to participate in UU

## Table 3.1
**Age distribution among secularist groups**

| Group type/ affiliation | Mean (years) | N | Standard deviation | Median |
|---|---|---|---|---|
| Secular Humanist | 65.61 | 377 | 13.582 | 67.00 |
| Jewish Humanist | 59.38 | 107 | 13.105 | 56.00 |
| Unitarian Humanist | 70.96 | 129 | 9.842 | 72.00 |
| Atheist | 50.83 | 103 | 16.863 | 50.00 |
| Skeptic, rationalist | 58.76 | 153 | 13.618 | 59.00 |
| Freethought | 62.60 | 30 | 11.944 | 62.50 |
| Total | 62.68 | 899 | 14.597 | 64.00 |

N = number of respondents.

fellowships; some, who have tired of trying to hold a secular line within their fellowships, have migrated to explicitly secular (humanist) organizations, which have also struggled with aging World War II and Baby Boom memberships and ways of attracting younger members.[26] The comparatively younger skew among Jewish Humanist affiliates is attributable, at least in part, to a strong focus on the transmission of Jewish culture (sans supernaturalism) to the next generation. As such, more members are family-establishment age. Consonant with this family focus, membership is typically recorded in families/households rather than individuals.

## Gender

Overall, roughly 56 percent of respondents were male and 44 percent were female (Table 3.2). Again, this is consistent with substantial prior indications that females tend, in general, to be more (or males less) religious with regard to belief, identification, affiliation, or behavior. Differences in gender distribution among group types or philosophies are also consistent with this general tendency. Men are more strongly represented in groups with a more analytical or critical focus (e.g., Skeptic, Atheist) and women in groups that tend to be more focused on cultural values and transmission (Jewish and Unitarian Humanist).[27]

**Table 3.2**
**Gender distribution by group type**

| Group type/affiliation | Gender | | Totals |
|---|---|---|---|
| | Male | Female | |
| Secular Humanist | 210 (55.4) [58.5%] | 169 (44.6) [41.5%] | 379 (100.0) |
| Jewish Humanist | 33 (30.6) [40.5%] | 75 (69.4) [59.5%] | 108 (100.0) |
| Unitarian Humanist | 63 (48.8) [48.0%] | 66 (51.2) [52.0%] | 129 (100.0) |
| Atheist | 69 (67.0) [69.3%] | 34 (33.0) [30.7%] | 103 (100.0) |
| Skeptic, rationalist | 113 (74.3) [70.0%] | 39 (25.7) [30.0%] | 152 (100.0) |
| Freethought | 18 (60.0) [N/A] | 12 (40.0) [N/A] | 30 (100.0) |
| Total respondents | 506 (56.2) | 399 (43.8) | 901 (100.0) |

Values are number of respondents, with percentage of total respondents in parentheses and estimated actual percentage of male and female group affiliates (based on membership and mailing lists) in brackets. N/A, not available.

## Education, Vocation, and Socioeconomic Status

Again, consistent with prior data on secular affiliates, "nones," or the nonreligious,[28] this is a well-educated group, with more than three-quarters holding college degrees and nearly half holding advanced degrees, far higher than among all U.S. citizens 25 years of age or older (Table 3.3).

Work and careers run the gamut, from accountant to zoologist, with a white-collar skew. Secularist affiliates have done their neighbors' taxes, prepared their wills, built their houses, taught their children, groomed their pets, shipped their goods, and diagnosed their ailments. One intriguing vocational fact was a strong concentration of educators—something that has been observed before among secularist affiliates. Colin Campbell, for example, found that among members of the British Humanist Association in the 1960s "by far the most significant individual occupation engaged in by the respondents [was] that of teaching. Approximately 1 in 5 of all respondents indicated that they were (or had been, if retired) teachers other than university teachers."[29] Among the Northwest group affiliates 31.4 percent indicated that they had been educators at some point in their lives at the elementary level (7.9 percent), junior high or high school (7.2), community college or university (11.2), or at multiple levels (4.8). One hundred eighty respondents (19.5 percent) indicated teaching as their primary or current profession. A number of factors may be involved.

There is some evidence of a relationship between education and nonreligiosity.[30] Educators are themselves better educated than the general population. Some have suggested that higher (liberal arts)

## Table 3.3
## Group affiliates' educational attainment

|  | Total sample (%) | U.S. sample (%)[a] | U.S. population (%)[b] |
|---|---|---|---|
| High school only | 4.4 | 3.4 | 31.7 |
| Some college, no degree | 16.0 | 15.5 | 17.0 |
| Specialist/associate degree | 5.1 | 4.2 | 8.7 |
| Baccalaureate | 28.8 | 30.3 | 18.3 |
| Master's degree | 28.2 | 28.7 | 6.8 |
| Doctoral degree/professional (J.D., M.D., Ph.D.) | 17.4 | 17.7 | 2.9 |

Values are percentage of respondents (or census data for U. S. population).
[a]Excluding British Columbia groups.
[b]Among individuals 25 years of age and older (=191,884,000).
*Source*: U.S. Census, 2006 at http://www.census.gov/population/socdemo/education/cps2006/tab01-01.xls/.

education fosters increased critical thinking, and so, religious skepticism. Others have suggested a selection factor involved in the pursuit of higher education: those with a drive to question may be motivated or encouraged to pursue advanced education, particularly in the sciences. Those who are drawn to teaching may tend to be driven to explain the nature of things, prompting them to question religious tenets, as well. It may also be that those who have had teaching careers miss the intellectual discourse in retirement that secularist groups tend to provide. Fully 54 percent of the group affiliates are retired (or "semi-retired"), and the most frequently cited reason for affiliating was intellectual stimulation and information exchange. The most prominent activity among such groups consists of lectures, book groups, and discussion groups on a wide range of topics (such as science and world affairs, as well as religion and secularity).

In keeping with education levels and careers, the majority of affiliates are middle class. Sixty percent of the U.S. affiliates report annual incomes of $40,000 or more and 50 percent reported $60,000 or more. This said, by no means all are "well-heeled": 8.7 percent reported incomes of $20,000 or less. Most of these (61 percent) are retirees. Annual incomes thus tend to underrepresent economic condition. Eighty percent (of the U.S. group affiliates) reported net household assets of $100,000 or more; 43.8 percent, $500,000 or more; and 21 percent, $1 million or more.

## Cultural Background

The group affiliates are overwhelmingly white and of European descent. Among 899 individuals supplying this information, 79.8 percent described themselves as "Euro-Caucasian," with another 16.4 percent "Jewish" or "Jewish"+"Euro-Caucasian" and 3.8 percent as other (including [East] Asian descent, Indian [South Asian], Middle Eastern [Persian, Iraqi], African American, and Native American).

Those of Jewish descent are overrepresented among group affiliates. Among the U.S.-based groups (n = 782), 17.5 percent indicated Jewish backgrounds. Excluding the two Jewish Humanist groups, 7.1 percent of respondents indicated Jewish backgrounds among the remaining groups. This compares with an estimated 2.2 percent in the U.S. population and 0.7 percent in Oregon and Washington.[31]

By contrast, Asian, African, and Latin Americans are noticeably underrepresented. Only ten group affiliates (or 1.1 percent) indicated East Asian or Asian + Euro descent, and two indicated South Asian/ Indian descent (or 0.2 percent). Based on 2006 census data (East and South), Asian Americans make up 4.4 percent of the U.S. population and 5.5 percent of the population of Oregon and Washington. Only seven affiliates indicated African American or African + Euro descent (or 0.78 percent). This compares with 12.8 percent in the United States and 3.0 percent in Oregon and Washington. Only one individual (0.1 percent) indicated Hispanic/Latino descent, whereas there are an estimated 14.8 percent in the United States and 9.4 percent in Oregon and Washington.[32] These data are reinforced by observation and discussion at annual and regional meetings of several national secularist organizations (atheist, secular humanist, skeptic, and freedom from religion). Organized secularity tends to be an activity of (non-Latino) Euro-Americans, most of whom have had Christian or Jewish upbringings. This is not new: in their 1932 survey of Atheist affiliates, Vetter and Green reported that only two of 350 respondents were not "white."[33]

The underrepresentation of African Americans and Latin Americans is consistent with more recent data on religious (non)affiliation in the general population, but the underrepresentation of those of Asian descent is not. In prior survey data on religious nonaffiliates or "nones" (no named religious preference), Asian Americans have been disproportionately represented. In the Pew Forum's "U.S. Religious Landscape Survey 2008,"[34] for example, the percentage of religious nonaffiliates (atheist, agnostic, or secular) was highest among Asian Americans compared with other major cultural/ethnic groups (Table 3.4).

Why does organized secularity seem to be a substantially (non-Latino) Euro-American activity? One explanation for this enduring fact may be cultural—specifically the character and role of religious identity and affiliation in these subcultures. Religion has been, and continues to be, significant in the African American experience, and despite recent signs of religious disaffiliation among Hispanics, religion (specifically Catholic) remains a significant force.[35] The Pew data affirm this continuing role, because African Americans and Latin Americans were least likely to describe themselves as atheist, agnostic, or secular.

Other Pew data indicate that religious Asian Americans predictably identify more often with various Asian religio-philosophical traditions compared with other cultural and ethnic groups. Monotheistic traditions (Judaic, Christian, and Islamic) tend to be more exclusive (with

**Table 3.4**
**Religiosity of cultural/ethnic groups in the United States**

|                        | White | Black | Asian | Other | Latino | Total |
|------------------------|-------|-------|-------|-------|--------|-------|
| Atheist                | 2     | <0.5  | 3     | 1     | 1      | 2     |
| Agnostic               | 3     | 1     | 4     | 3     | 1      | 2     |
| Secular unaffiliated   | 7     | 3     | 11    | 7     | 4      | 6     |
| Religious unaffiliated | 5     | 8     | 5     | 9     | 8      | 6     |
| Total                  | 17    | 12    | 23    | 20    | 14     | 16    |

Values are percentage of Pew survey respondents.
Source: Pew Forum. "U.S. Religious Landscape Survey 2008." http://religions.pewforum.org/.

expectations for devotion to a single doctrine or "identity," metaphysically comprehensive and definitive, and more highly institutionalized) than Asian traditions (such as Buddhist, Confucian, Daoist, Hindu, and native or ancestral traditions). The comparatively "tighter" or more stringent and all-encompassing demands for adherence among the former may elicit more vehement critical reactions than the latter. (To this point, aggressively nontranscendental or anti-"religious" schools of thought have been comparatively rare in Asian intellectual history.) Although data gathered in the research reported here do not afford a direct test of this observation, data on the strictness of religious/philosophical upbringing among the secularist group affiliates offer relevant insights.

## UPBRINGING AND WORLDVIEW DEVELOPMENT

When asked when they "realized they were nonreligious," as has been typically been found in prior research[36] the majority indicated that this was early in life (most notably during adolescence or very early adulthood; Figure 3.1). To some extent this may be a personal construction developed later in life. More detailed questions about shifts in religious or philosophical views through life, together with prior research with adolescents whose worldviews had recently changed, suggest that the adoption of "nonreligious" worldviews is a process of questioning over time rather than an instantaneous

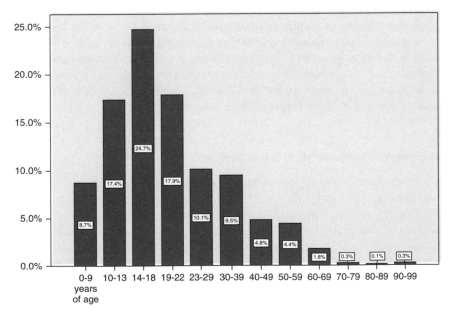

**Figure 3.1.** Age respondent realized s/he was nonreligious

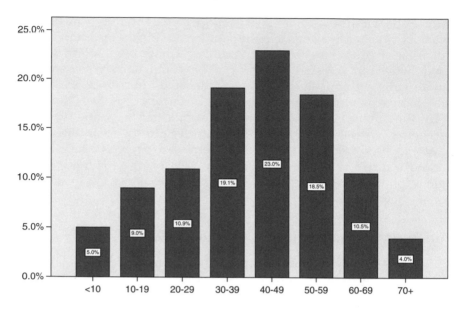

**Figure 3.2.** Number of years nonreligious (Current age minus age at realization)

decision.[37] Nonetheless, these responses reflect a point in life when individuals recall that religious uncertainty, doubt, or rejection became conscious or explicit in their lives. Few reported "religious relapses" once the process of religious questioning began. (Those who reclaimed a religious identity following earlier abandonment do not, of course, appear in this sample.) Both affiliates and interviewees tended to describe their secularity as unidirectional and stable over time rather than transient or "developmental," with a majority having been nonreligious for many years (Figure 3.2).

### Religious/Philosophical Upbringing

Differences in the reported nature of respondents' religious or philosophical backgrounds offer some insight into the stances they adopted. McTaggart referred to members of Canadian humanist groups as "re-affiliates," because the majority affiliated on the basis of their world-views after having abandoned religious upbringing, but this time on the basis of irreligiosity.[38] The same is true of the Pacific Northwest affiliates (Table 3.5). About 79 percent indicated religious backgrounds (both parents religious and some family religious participation), 12 percent indicated secular or nonreligious backgrounds, and 9 percent indicated mixed religious and/or nonreligious backgrounds.

**Table 3.5**
**Secularist group affiliates' religious/philosophical backgrounds**

| Religious/philosophical background | Total |
|---|---|
| Protestant/Christian parents, education | 461 (51.5) |
| Roman Catholic parents, education | 129 (14.4) |
| Religiously Jewish/Judaic parents, education | 115 (12.8) |
| None/nonreligious, secular humanist, agnostic, atheist parents | 104 (11.6) |
| Nonreligious + religious parents | 50 (5.6) |
| Spiritual(ist), Deist, Unitarian Universalist, religious humanist parents | 20 (2.2) |
| Other/mixed religious parents, education | 16 (1.8) |
| Total respondents | 895 (100.0) |

Values are number of respondents, with percentage in parentheses.

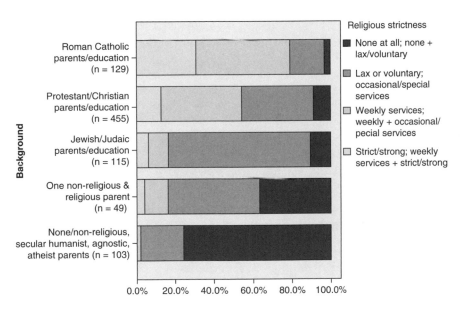

**Figure 3.3.**   Reported strictness of religious/philosophical backgrounds

Reported (or recalled) strictness varied considerably among religious/philosophical family backgrounds (Figure 3.3). Those raised Roman Catholic were most likely to describe their religious upbringings as strict/strong or disciplined (attending weekly services and/or multiyear parochial schooling). As one respondent (a former Catholic priest) wrote in a survey response, "I still have lots of anger about what Catholic school training did to me during the 1930s and 1940s." Another attributed his irreligiosity to "negative reactions to oppressive Catholic upbringing." Those raised in Protestant/Christian family contexts generally characterized their upbringings as less strict, on average, than Catholics.[39] By contrast, those with Jewish/Judaic backgrounds viewed their religious upbringings as lax or voluntary—more similar to those with Secular or mixed (religious and nonreligious parental) backgrounds than to those raised Catholic or Protestant.

The attitudes of Catholic-raised respondents about "religion" tended to be comparatively more severe, those raised Jewish/Judaic were less severe, and those with Secular, Protestant, or mixed backgrounds, middling. For example, those raised Catholic were most likely to describe themselves as "antireligious" (Table 3.6). Fewer with Jewish/Judaic backgrounds did so. Those raised Catholic indicated greater anger, on average, compared with respondents raised Protestant, Jewish/Judaic, and Secular (Table 3.7). Those raised Jewish/Judaic were less likely, on average, to indicate that a reason for group affiliation was to "counteract religion" (Table 3.8; 1-5 response scale used for this item). Lastly, those raised Catholic were somewhat more likely to indicate conflict about religion (with parents, with siblings, and at work).[40] Those raised Jewish/Judaic generally indicated less conflict, as did those with Secular backgrounds (except with friends; Table 3.9).

The strongest critical reaction to something-called-religion, then, was evident among those raised Catholic, who also rated their religious upbringings most strict, on average. By comparison, those with Jewish or secular backgrounds reported both less strictness in their religious/ philosophical upbringings and less severity in their attitudes about "religion."

## Intolerance for Inconsistencies; Tolerance for Uncertainty

Many factors have been proposed to explain the adoption of personal secularity or irreligion (particularly for those who abandon religious backgrounds) including education, personal or social maladjustment, familial problems, rebellion against parents or authority, and childhood trauma or parental loss, among others. Each may conceivably play a part in various individuals' development, but evidence for them is highly variable.[41]

One theme that was pervasive throughout my observations, interviews, and survey results was sensitivity to inconsistencies or contradictions. These may be internal logical inconsistencies among ideas (such as religious tenets or texts), external contradictions with "common sense" or empirical evidence, inconsistencies between espoused principles and exhibited behavior, or inconsistency over time (contrary to asserted universal or eternal truths). Personal explanations for the

**Table 3.6**
**Choice of "anti-religious" as a self-description**

| | Protestant/ Christian parents/ upbringing | Roman Catholic parents/ upbringing | Jewish/ Judaic parents/ upbringing | None, secular, nonreligious, humanist, agnostic/ athiest parents | One religious + one nonreligious parent; varied upbringing | Other/mixed religious parents/ upbringing | Total |
|---|---|---|---|---|---|---|---|
| Chose "antireligious" as self-description | 130 (28.3) | 53 (41.4) | 25 (21.9) | 29 (27.9) | 17 (34.0) | 7 (19.4) | 261 (29.3) |
| Total respondents | 460 | 128 | 114 | 104 | 50 | 36 | 892 |

Values are number of respondents, with percentage of category in parentheses.

**Table 3.7**
**Religious background and anger about religion**

| | Protestant/ Christian parents/ upbringing | Roman Catholic parents/ upbringing | Jewish/ Judaic parents/ upbringing | None, secular, nonreligious, humanist, agnostic/athe- ist parents | One religious + one nonreli- gious parent; varied upbringing | Other/mixed religious parents/ upbringing | Total |
|---|---|---|---|---|---|---|---|
| Anger about religion (Scale: 1 = not at all; 7 = very) | 5.46 | 5.89 | 5.42 | 5.26 | 5.63 | 5.75 | 5.51 |
| Standard deviation | 1.68 | 1.54 | 1.60 | 1.87 | 1.78 | 1.46 | 1.68 |
| Number of respondents | 450 | 123 | 112 | 101 | 46 | 36 | 868 |

# Table 3.8
## Religious background and motivation to affiliate with group (to counteract religion)

| Reason for affiliating | Protestant/ Christian parents/ upbringing | Roman Catholic parents/ upbringing | Jewish/ Judaic parents/ upbringing | None, secular, nonreligious, humanist, agnostic/athe- ist parents | One religious + one nonreli- gious parent; varied upbringing | Other/mixed religious parents/ upbringing | Total |
|---|---|---|---|---|---|---|---|
| To counteract religion[a] | 3.81 | 3.85 | 3.26 | 3.68 | 3.94 | 3.81 | 3.74 |
| Standard deviation | 1.28 | 1.30 | 1.44 | 1.44 | 1.24 | 1.22 | 1.33 |
| Number of respondents | 401 | 115 | 100 | 88 | 47 | 31 | 782 |

[a]Values are means. Scale: 1 = not at all, 5 = very.

59

**Table 3.9**
**Reported conflict involving religion**

| Background | Conflict reported with | | | | | |
|---|---|---|---|---|---|---|
| | Parents | Siblings | Children | Spouse | Friends | Coworkers |
| Roman Catholic (n = 128) | 37.5 | 20.3 | 6.3 | 8.6 | 25.8 | 23.4 |
| Protestant (n = 469) | 24.3 | 14.3 | 6.0 | 10.0 | 24.9 | 10.9 |
| Jewish/Judaic (n = 115) | 18.3 | 5.2 | 3.5 | 9.6 | 10.4 | 10.4 |
| Secular (n = 105) | 2.9 | 3.8 | 1.9 | 10.5 | 20.0 | 13.3 |

Values are percentage of respondents reporting conflict. n = total number of respondents.

emergence of religious doubt or rejection offered by survey respondents make this clear:

- "Absurdity of religious teachings. (Never believed in Santa, either.) Too silly. My own independent thoughts brought me there. I didn't know anyone else who thought that way. Don't know why I did. Never discussed it with others until confirmation class, age 15–16. Very gradual."

- "The Bible—even as a kid it didn't seem logical; existence of God, Jesus; concept of heaven and hell; the idea that one religion is the "right" religion and everyone else who believes just as strongly, but in a different set of beliefs are wrong; lack of tolerance for those that are different"

- "Internal inconsistencies . . . willingness to suspend reason to defend beliefs"

- "Realized as a child a great contradiction in a vengeful/loving God"

- "Contradictory claims, supernatural explanations for physical events"

- "Experiences at church that were illogical or caused cognitive dissonance"

- "Claim of being the only truth; faith over reason; logical contradictions; ethnocentricity; conflicts with science"

- "Even as a child I found Biblical stories to be impossible and far-fetched. It was obvious to me. I couldn't believe people fell for it."

- "Careful scrutiny of religious claims—if God is all-knowing, what is the point of prayer? (epiphany)"

- "Belief without evidence, belief in the face of massive counter-evidence"

- "Lack of questioning, faith instead of facts"

- "The idea of a superman in the sky; contradictions in the Bible"

- "Hypocrisy of those who profess to believe"

When asked to explain the emergence of their secularity, one of the most frequently occurring phrases was that "things didn't make sense." Whether attributable to modeling or education by a parent, teacher, or other significant adult, oft-mentioned voracious reading and reflection, strong observational skills, memories for detail, and/or inherited characteristics (that give rise to a strong analytical bent or "intellectualism," autonomy, boldness, curiosity, confidence, stubbornness, or rebelliousness), secularists repeatedly report and exhibit strong resistance to (or drive to resolve) logical or empirical inconsistency. When this cannot be resolved, there is voiced willingness to suspend judgment and accept uncertainty pending further data or to actively challenge such contradictions if logic or available evidence warrant. Taken together with the findings on religious upbringing, it is not unreasonable to suggest that more aggressive or stringent doctrinal or behavioral expectations will tend, on average, to produce greater numbers of individuals who experience confusion, conflict, or critical reaction.

## WORLDVIEW COMPLEXITY AND DIVERSITY

On the surface there is substantial unanimity among these individuals—nontheistic and "nonreligious." But the more deeply worldviews are probed, the more diversity becomes apparent. Consider, for example, the following interviewees (both group affiliates and independents; names are fictitious; ages are in parentheses):

Ruth (72) is intensely and a-religiously absorbed in life, particularly in art (as a print-maker, lecturer, museum docent, and avid student). She was raised in a "nonpracticing" Jewish home. Her father, whom she admired greatly, was openly critical of supernatural religion. She has had a passing "sociological" interest in the "curious phenomenon" of religion, but this is one of many aspects of the species about which she is naturally curious. This said, she has little inclination to focus substantial time or energy on the subject. Unlike her husband (or her father) she is not vocally or uniformly critical of religion. She can see how it helps some, but also how it can be and has been harmful. Unless asked, she is too busy to give the matter much thought.

Ellen (76) is a life-long skeptic and atheist who was reared in a loosely Protestant household in a small midwestern town. She read voraciously from an early age and concluded that supernatural phenomena were mythological rather than real. But this said, she always loved ritual and social celebration, particularly as developed in religions. Following intermittent exploration of a number of religious and philosophical traditions, she found a comfortable balance of ideas, inspiration, and ritual—that allowed her to quietly retain her atheism—in a liberal Jewish temple. She then became aware of Sherwin Wine, dubbed the "atheist rabbi" who founded a Jewish (secular) humanist movement, and Ellen became an active participant. This offers a satisfying balance of community, cultural richness, and ritual without supernaturalism.

**Warren** (87) was raised on a remote farm in eastern California. For reasons he cannot explain, he began doubting religious beliefs early in life. Exposure to Darwin's theory of evolution in his adolescence sealed his doubt. As a young man he served in the Pacific alongside Aussies in WWII. He brought an Australian bride back to the United States after the war, and together they built a life, a family, and a farm. His atheism never wavered, but neither did his live-and-let-live attitude about religion. Others can believe whatever they wish so long as they don't try to change his views. He doesn't get "riled" about such things.

**Josh** (50) is a professional artist who was carefully educated in a virtual Protestant cocoon through college. He married in the faith and planned to raise his children in it, as well. But in early adulthood doubts arose, exacerbated by marital difficulties. After years of increasing discomfort, one day in his late thirties he resolved to probe as deeply inward as possible to "find God." He could not, however, find "Him." Nor could he reconcile much of what he had been told about God with what he knew of nature. This triggered an intense anger at having been fooled by false "truths." After brief involvement in secularist groups that tended to intensify his anger, further alienating family and friends, he realized he needed to find ways to rein this in. He began a regimen of Yoga and Buddhist group meditation as therapeutic means to tame his anger and find greater perspective and peace. At the same time, he maintains a stance that is affirmatively atheistic, empirical, and critical of supernatural religion. He actively pursues a strong interest in the sciences.

**Rajinder** (48) is a student of science and a skeptic reared in India, but was educated in American universities and is now a citizen. Although he does not accept the reality of religious supernaturalism, after careful reading of many religious and philosophical texts, he has adopted a "metaphorical" posture. For example, he embraces notions of *samsara* and *karma* as useful ethical reminders that what one does (or does not do) is not self-contained, but has larger ("ripple") effects for good or ill, even though he does not accept their ontological reality.

**Bruce and Jill** (48, 50). Bruce is Jewish by descent (only) and the product of three generations of atheists. He reports only passing interest in religion and spends little time asking ultimate questions, preferring to focus on his work, his friends, his wife, recreation, and a practical absorption with business, economics, and politics. With regard to metaphysical questions, such as an afterlife, his attitude is, "Who knows. We'll see. Nobody, to my knowledge, has ever returned from the grave with a reliable report." His wife is a product of a Catholic upbringing that left her critical of the social, historical, and psychological effects of established and institutional religion, but open to "spiritual" possibilities. It is not clear to her what is real or imagined but this makes little difference, because there is something valuable in human experience that may be meaningfully called "spiritual."

**Monica** (22) was raised by a nominally religious single mother following an early divorce. Reflecting the influence of selected teachers, she developed an intense idealism regarding human, civil, and women's rights and human well-being. In late elementary and early high school, she concluded that religion (particularly Christian—the only one with which she said she is familiar) has too often been a force in opposition to these ideals. In college, she became a vocal antireligious (specifically anti-Christian) activist. Her writings, in fact, came to the attention of a cable television personality, who cited her as an example of what has gone wrong in American society and education. She considers the episode a badge of honor. Having just graduated, she does not know what she will do, but hopes to continue advocating for, and writing about, human rights and environmentalism. She cannot imagine abandoning her atheist stance.

The closer people's worldviews are probed—even among self-described secular or nonreligious individuals—the more difficult it is to neatly place many into the major categories that frame Western discourse on "theism" and "atheism" or "religion" or "irreligion." Survey data among group affiliates provided evidence of worldview diversity and complexity, as well.

If attention is restricted to customary (that is, "personal" and monotheistic) notions of "God," this is a strongly nontheistic and apparently naturalistic sample. Respondents were asked, for example: Do you think that the degree of order or patterning we perceive in nature is most likely attributable to

1. Properties that are intrinsic to the nature of the physical universe or all that exists, and nothing more

2. A coherent organizing principle that we cannot, or do not yet, fully comprehend that is pervasive throughout the physical universe or all that exists

3. An organizing principle or force that in some way transcends the physical universe or all that exists

4. An impersonal, but in some sense intelligent, creative force that has brought all that exists into being

5. A personal, and in some sense intelligence creative force, or "God," with which human beings can make contact or have a communicative relationship

6. An omniscient, omnipotent, intelligent God that designed and created all that exists

Based on responses to this item alone (n = 875), this is a substantially naturalistic group, with 78.6 percent choosing response 1, 17 percent choosing response 2, and 1.1 percent choosing both 1 and 2. Only 2.7 percent chose responses 3 or 4 (which could be considered alternative expressions of "deism"), one individual chose response 5, and none chose

6. In related texts, fourteen individuals made reference to the human tendency to perceive or impose pattern whether or not it is "really there." (One stated definitively that "there is no order or patterning in nature!") Had there been a response option attributing "order" to human perception (or human perceptual bias, alone) rather than to nature, more individuals might well have indicated this view.

Diversity became more apparent as worldviews were probed more deeply about concepts such as the following:

- A *transcendent entity*: "a being, entity, or higher power beyond, apart from, or transcending nature (call this "God" if you wish)
- A *"personal essence*, spirit, or soul apart from our physical bodies or continuing beyond our physical lives (or through multiple lifetimes)"
- An *"impersonal force* or energy that courses through and connects all living things or all that exists" (call this "spiritual" if you wish)
- An *"ultimate purpose* or direction in human life or all of existence"

Response options for each of these items were as follows:

- *Meaningless/nonexistent*: "This makes no sense to me; I don't think there is any such thing."
- *Unknowable*: "I don't know, and don't think this is something human beings can know."
- *Maybe/unsure*: "This may be; I'm just not sure."
- *Sometimes*: "Sometimes I think this is so and sometimes I do not."
- *Metaphorical*: "Even though I doubt or reject the reality of this, or view this as a human construction, I like to think *as though* there is."
- *Probably*: "There is probably something like this, but I have no idea about its actual nature."
- *Definitely*: "This is something I definitely think exists or is the case."

Strong majorities rejected the notions of a transcendent entity and continuing personal essence ("spirit" or "soul") as meaningless/nonexistent or unknowable (Table 3.10).[42] But when it came to the question of an ultimate purpose or direction in human life or all of existence, rejection weakened. Somewhat surprisingly it was the notion of an impersonal force that courses through and connects all (living) things that elicited the most diverse response. A substantial number of respondents (roughly 30 percent) accepted this maybe/sometimes, probably, or definitely, with an additional 6 percent embracing this metaphorically.

Again, there were notable differences among group types. Atheist affiliates were predictably most likely to reject the concept of a transcendent entity, followed by Secular humanists, Skeptics, and

**Table 3.10**
**Response patterns for several worldview items**

| Transcendent entity | | | | |
|---|---|---|---|---|
| **Meaningless/ nonexistent** | **Maybe or sometimes** | **Metaphorical (as though)** | **Probably or definitely** | **Total** |
| 775 (86.6) | 50 (5.6) | 28 (3.1) | 42 (4.7) | 895 (100.0) |

| Personal essence | | | | |
|---|---|---|---|---|
| **Meaningless/ nonexistent** | **Maybe or sometimes** | **Metaphorical (as though)** | **Probably or definitely** | **Total** |
| 749 (84.0) | 61 (6.8) | 35 (3.9) | 47 (5.3) | 892 (100.0) |

| Ultimate purpose | | | | |
|---|---|---|---|---|
| **Meaningless/ nonexistent** | **Maybe or sometimes** | **Metaphorical (as though)** | **Probably or definitely** | **Total** |
| 632 (72.4) | 58 (6.6) | 107 (12.3) | 76 (8.7) | 873 (100.0) |

| Impersonal force | | | | |
|---|---|---|---|---|
| **Meaningless/ nonexistent** | **Maybe or sometimes** | **Metaphorical (as though)** | **Probably or definitely** | **Total** |
| 566 (63.9) | 127 (14.3) | 57 (6.4) | 136 (15.3) | 886 (100.0) |

Values are number of respondents, with percentage of total in parentheses. Response options compressed to simplify presentation.

Freethinkers. More Jewish and Unitarian Humanists viewed this as unknowable, with slightly greater numbers allowing its possibility to varying degrees. Responses concerning a personal essence (soul) were similar, except that fewer Jewish Humanists flatly rejected the concept and more considered this unknowable or were unsure.

Response patterns shifted markedly with regard to ultimate purpose and an impersonal force. A substantial number of respondents (12.3 percent overall) viewed ultimate purpose metaphorically. A slightly greater percentage of males (13.3 percent) than females (10.7 percent) indicated this view. The concept of an impersonal connecting force or energy elicited the greatest response variation among groups. Jewish Humanists were most likely to allow the possibility or reality of such a phenomenon, followed by Unitarian Humanists. Females more often accepted an impersonal force maybe/sometimes (17.5 percent of women; 11.8 percent of men), or probably/definitely (22.2 percent of women; 11.4 percent of men). But both male and female Jewish Humanists accepted the concept more often than those in other groups.

Although substantially non*theistic*, group affiliates were by no means equally *naturalistic*. This was further evidenced by data on something called "spiritual/ity."

### "Spirituality"—Supernatural, Immanent, and Psychological

The degree to which group affiliates allowed or accepted the existence of an "impersonal force or energy that courses through and connects all living things or all that exists" (and not in a metaphorical sense) suggests the salience of something-called-spirituality, however defined, among some secular affiliates. As one female affiliate of a secular humanist group once confided, her greatest challenge and complaint as a member was that she felt compelled to "check her spirituality at the door." The following survey item was devised to assess the meanings and relevance of "spiritual/ity" among group affiliates:

With regard to "spiritual" and "spirituality" . . . (check any that apply to you)

__ I (tend to) avoid these terms; they do not apply to me or my experience.
__ I (may) use these terms, but only in psychological or experiential terms,
  __ as a special state of being at peace or equilibrium or harmony.
  __ as a process or experience of greater awareness or higher consciousness.
  __ as a general feeling or experience of connection with others or nature.
__ I use these terms to refer to something that exists beyond physical nature and its properties (a force, energy, or entity, or multiple forces or entities), with which I/we can make contact.

Among 896 respondents to this item, 58 percent indicated "avoid/ do not apply" and 38 percent indicated that they may use the terms in a psychological/experiential sense. Only 3.5 percent indicated transcendental usage. Among the respondents who specified psychological usage (Table 3.11), most indicated a feeling or experience of connection with others or nature. Fewest indicated a process or experience of higher awareness or consciousness. Fittingly, being at peace, harmony, or equilibrium was in between.

Written texts were provided by 250 respondents (in response to an "Other" prompt after the scaled item). The great majority of these conveyed naturalistic or nontranscendental uses and meaning of "spiritual/ity." The following were the most frequent meanings:

- Experience of/in nature
- Awe, wonder, gratitude, or appreciation (about existence, nature, the universe)

**Table 3.11**
**Use of "spiritual/ity" in specifically psychological/experiential senses**

| | |
|---|---|
| 1. As being at peace, harmony, equilibrium | 46 (14.5) |
| 2. As process/experience of higher awareness, consciousness | 18 (5.7) |
| 3. As feeling/experience of connection with others/nature | 146 (46.1) |
| Responses 1 and 3 | 35 (11.0) |
| Responses 2 and 3 | 14 (4.4) |
| Responses 1, 2, and 3 | 58 (18.3) |
| **Total** | **317 (100.0)** |

Values are number of respondents, with percentage in parentheses.

- A sense of social connection or generalized connectedness
- Intense emotional experience
- Reaction to art, literature, music, aesthetic beauty
- Psychological process
- Sense of something greater than oneself (but not ontologically transcendental).

As indicated in Table 3.12, there were notable differences in the propensity to apply "spiritual" terms or concepts based on worldview type, self-descriptions,[43] and group types. Just as notably, however, use of these terms or concepts was not restricted to the "softer" secularists, alone. Even among those with thoroughgoing naturalistic worldviews (Level 1 secularists who flatly rejected a transcendental entity, personal essence, impersonal force, and ultimate purpose—about one-third of the entire sample), 15.7 percent indicated willingness to use these terms nontranscendentally (to describe a kind of personal or human experience), even though they resolutely resist using "spiritual" to describe themselves in general.

Unsurprisingly, those who described themselves as "atheist(ic)" or "anti-religious"[44] were most averse to "spiritual/ity." Those who described themselves as "agnostic" or "naturalistic" were most likely to make nontranscendental or transcendental references to it. For some, "agnostic" denotes the affirmative unknowability of matters transcendental, and for others, open-ended indecision about them. Written comments also suggested that "naturalistic" is often construed as an affinity for nature rather than philosophical rejection of transcendental phenomena. As one respondent wrote, "I'm naturalistic—after all, I'm a veterinarian."

Among group types, Atheist and Skeptic affiliates were most averse to the concept, and Jewish and Unitarian Humanists, least. The Jewish Humanists were most likely to make reference to "spiritual/ity" in both

**Table 3.12**
**Uses and meanings of "spirituality" among secular affiliates**

| | N | Uses of "spiritual/ity"[a]* | | | Describe self as "spiritual"[b]† |
| | | Avoid term | Psychological | Transcendental | |
|---|---|---|---|---|---|
| **Worldviews**[c]‡ | | | | | |
| Level 1 | 299 | 83.3 | 15.7 | 0.0 | 1.06 |
| Level 2 | 453 | 77.7 | 21.2 | 0.0 | 1.13 |
| Level 3 | 534 | 74.7 | 23.4 | 0.0 | 1.14 |
| Level 4 | 700 | 65.9 | 32.6 | .1 | 1.34 |
| **Self-descriptions** | | | | | |
| Atheist(ic) | 555 | 67.0 | 30.8 | .5 | 1.34 |
| Anti-religious | 264 | 62.9 | 34.8 | .8 | 1.55 |
| Skeptical | 449 | 60.6 | 35.6 | 2.0 | 1.57 |
| Freethinker | 415 | 58.3 | 37.3 | 2.4 | 1.62 |
| Secular | 497 | 53.7 | 41.8 | 3.0 | 1.54 |
| Agnostic | 323 | 48.3 | 47.1 | 2.5 | 1.90 |
| Naturalistic | 292 | 47.6 | 45.5 | 4.8 | 1.87 |
| **Group affiliations** | | | | | |
| Atheist | 101 | 75.2 | 23.8 | 0.0 | 1.15 |
| Skeptic, rationalist | 151 | 65.7 | 29.8 | 2.0 | 1.48 |
| Secular Humanist | 381 | 62.5 | 33.3 | 2.4 | 1.55 |
| Freethought | 30 | 50.0 | 50.0 | 0.0 | 1.90 |
| Unitarian Humanist | 126 | 47.6 | 47.6 | 3.2 | 2.04 |
| Jewish Humanist | 107 | 30.8 | 59.8 | 8.4 | 2.82 |

[a]Values are percentage of respondents.
[b]Values are means (Scale: 1 = not at all; 7 = very much).
[c]Level 1 = God/soul/force/purpose meaningless/non-existent ("straight-ticket rejecters")
Level 2 = God/soul/force/purpose meaningless/ non-existent OR don't know/unknowable
Level 3 = God/soul/force meaningless/non-existent OR don't know/unknowable
Level 4 = God/soul meaningless/non-existent OR don't know/unknowable

nontranscendental and transcendental terms (most of the latter were female). Written comments, discussions, and interviews indicated that a distinction between definitively nontranscendental (social, psychological, or metaphorical) and transcendental senses of the "spiritual" (such as an immanent force *in* nature) was important and clearly drawn among some, but fuzzy or indecisive among others—whereas an overtly "supernatural" notion of the "spiritual" (as in an entity existing *apart from* nature) was overwhelmingly rejected.

## Attitudes About "Religion" and the "Religious"

Concern about the perennial role of "religion" in human affairs, and its public resurgence in the United States and elsewhere, was pervasive among those observed, interviewed, and surveyed. Roughly two-thirds of the affiliates indicated that they had become more nonreligious, vocal, or actively involved with secularist groups because of the "resurgence of religion in recent times."

When asked to what extent they would say they are "angry about the role, dominance, and/or effects of religion in the world," nearly 80 percent indicated anger affirmatively (Table 3.13; scaled responses from 5 to 7; 1 = not at all angry; 7 = very angry). Written comments provided by 79 individuals indicated a range of reactions other than anger, such as "concerned," "distressed," "disappointed," "distraught," "frustrated," "puzzled," "sad," "troubled," "upset," "worried," and "aghast." Although some writers made it clear that "anger" was apt and warranted, others said that there are more reasonable or productive sentiments.

Respondents were also asked to what extent they considered religion a harmful or positive force in human affairs (1 = harmful; 7 = positive). Roughly three-quarters of respondents considered religion more harmful than positive, but again there were considerable differences among

**Table 3.13**
**Reported anger about the role and effects of religion in the world**

|  | Secular Humanist | Jewish Humanist | Unitarian Humanist | Atheist | Skeptic, rationalist | Free-thought | Total |
|---|---|---|---|---|---|---|---|
| Angry (5–7)[a] | 298 (80.1) | 83 (76.9) | 98 (79.0) | 86 (86.0) | 106 (71.6) | 24 (82.8) | 695 |
| Total number of respondents | 372 | 108 | 124 | 100 | 148 | 29 | 881 |

[a]Values are number of respondents, with percentage in parentheses. Scale: 1 = not at all angry; 7 = very angry.

groups (Table 3.14). Jewish Humanists were least likely to consider religion a harmful force followed by Unitarian Humanists; Freethought, and Atheist affiliates were most likely to be of this opinion.

Respondents were offered the opportunity to indicate that "religion is too complex a phenomenon to generalize about in this way" in addition to, or instead of, a scaled response.

In Table 3.14, those who chose this option *instead of* a scaled response are reported. In Table 3.15, those who chose this option *whether or not* they provided a scaled response are reported. In both cases, Jewish Humanists were most likely to feel that "religion" is too complex to generalize about in such a manner, followed by Unitarian Humanists; Freethought, and Atheist affiliates were least likely to do so.

Overall, more than a third of respondents felt that "religion" was too complex to characterize or evaluate simply (whether or not they provided scaled responses).

Additional items provided further insight into respondents' attitudes about "religion" and related issues. In general, Jewish Humanists were less critical of "religion" and more (self-critical) of "skeptical and nonreligious people" than others, with the Unitarian Humanists close by. Close inspection of the data indicated that this was true of both males and females in comparison with other groups. Atheist and Freethought affiliates tended to be most critical of "religion." Skeptic and Secular humanist affiliates generally held the middle ground, with Secular humanists more severe, on average, and Skeptics somewhat less so.

## Purpose and Meaning in Life

There was strong unanimity about the value or personal meaningfulness of life among group affiliates and interviewees, as long as this is carefully qualified. When asked to what extent they considered their own lives worthwhile (1 = not at all; 7 = very), an overwhelming majority of affiliates affirmed that they did (91.8 percent responded between 5 and 7; 5.9 percent at the scale midpoint; n = 891).

When it came to generalized meaning attributable to human life, however ("Do you feel that human life or existence is, in general, not at all [or] very meaningful?"), matters changed. Response to this item dropped to 670 individuals. Of these, the majority responded affirmatively (71.8 percent, 5–7), but a substantial minority did not (17.2 percent, 1–3; 11 percent, midpoint). Moreover, 272 individuals chose an optional item indicating that "this is not a meaningful question to me" whether or not they responded to the question on meaningfulness. Written comments clearly indicated that whatever meaning there is in human life is assigned *by* human beings to their own lives. Many expressed discomfort speaking about general "meaningfulness" of life at all (in order to avoid even a hint of any transcendental or ultimate meaning).

**Table 3.14**
**Religion as a harmful or positive force in human affairs**

| Secular | Secular Humanist | Jewish Humanist | Unitarian Humanist | Atheist | Skeptic, rationalist | Freethought | Total |
|---|---|---|---|---|---|---|---|
| Religion a harmful force[a] | 302 (78.6) | 61 (56.0) | 81 (63.8) | 90 (87.4) | 110 (72.4) | 29 (96.7) | 673 (74.4) |
| Religion too complex to generalize about[b] | 50 (13.0) | 29 (26.6) | 19 (15.0) | 5 (4.9) | 14 (9.2) | 0 (0) | 117 (112.9) |
| Total respondents | 384 | 109 | 127 | 103 | 152 | 30 | 905 |

[a]Values are number of respondents rating religion a harmful force (1 to 3 on a scale with 1 = harmful force, 7 = positive force); percentage in parentheses.

[b]Values are number of respondents who gave no scaled response and indicated that religion is much too complex a phenomenon to generalize about in this way; percentage in parentheses.

**Table 3.15**
**Religion too complex to evaluate generally as a harmful or positive force in human affairs**

| | Group type/affiliation | | | | | | |
|---|---|---|---|---|---|---|---|
| | Secular Humanist | Jewish Humanist | Unitarian Humanist | Atheist | Skeptic, rationalist | Freethought | Total |
| Religion too complex to generalize about | 126 (32.8) | 53 (48.6) | 55 (43.3) | 30 (29.1) | 48 (31.6) | 7 (23.3) | 319 (35.2) |
| Total respondents | 384 | 109 | 127 | 103 | 152 | 30 | 905 |

Values are number of respondents, with percentage in parentheses.

Yet, in response to an open-ended query about "what gives *you* the greatest sense of meaning in life," respondents readily listed a range of experiences and activities—particularly family and social relations, productive work and personal achievement, contributing positively to the quality of human life, the acquisition of knowledge, and the experience of nature:

Family (235 mentions)
Helping, caring for others (177)
Nature (experience of, connection with, being part of; 167)
Learning, knowledge, understanding (165)
People, social relations in general (160)
Friends, friendship (157)
Contributing, improving things, ethical action (146)
Children, child-rearing, parenting (144)
Enjoyment, happiness, satisfaction in living (96)
Love, loving (92)
Beauty (experience of; 78)
Work, accomplishment (63)
Meaningful personal activity in general (58)
Art (28)
Experience in general (27)
Music (24)
Creativity (23)
Political action, involvement (22)
Engagement, involvement in general (15)
Hope (13)

They overwhelmingly consider their lives worthwhile, but meaning is assigned to life by those who live it. The sources of meaning in their lives are remarkable for their unremarkableness: familial, social, educational, creative, contributive, and experiential.

## Attitudes About Death

The value of living is generally not diminished or threatened by the inevitability of death. Indeed, some indicated that the value of living is enhanced by the fact of our mortality. Group affiliates were asked: "To what extent would you say that you fear death?" (1 = not at all; 7 = quite a lot) and "What is your attitude about death?" (open-ended item). The distribution of responses concerning fear of death was broad, but with a clear skew toward little or no fear (Table 3.16). In a secular humanist meeting, one young affiliate admitted that he has long harbored an inexplicable fear of death. On the other hand, an 83-year-old secular humanist affiliate, with whom I spent a good deal of time in his last weeks in hospice, maintained his acerbic wit and skeptical assumption that the end was the end—to the very end.

**Table 3.16**
**Reported fear of death**

| | | | Scale | | | | |
|---|---|---|---|---|---|---|---|
| **1** | **2** | **3** | **4** | **5** | **6** | **7** | **Total respondents** |
| 284 | 182 | 109 | 102 | 65 | 36 | 21 | 799 |
| (35.5) | (22.8) | (13.6) | (12.8) | (8.2) | (4.5) | (2.6) | (100.0) |

Values are number of respondents, with percentage in parentheses. Scale: 1 = not at all; 7 = quite a lot.

Attitudes about death most often mentioned in written texts made mention of

- finality—the end, it happens, inevitable, unavoidable, no afterlife
- acceptance—part of life, the natural process of living organisms
- neglect—no attitude, ignore it, not worth thinking about (can't do anything about it, anyway)
- resistance or fear—(of death or, more often, the process of dying)
- desire for control over dying process—(including suicide if warranted)
- mystery—unknown, uncertainty, wonder.

Notably, the older the respondents, the *less* the reported fear of death. Although this relationship was modest, it was statistically significant ($r = -0.272$; $p < 0.01$, two-tailed). A pervasive theme was, in a word, "acceptance." The sense among many was that this is an attitude worth cultivating no matter how difficult this may be. Death is a part of life/nature, it happens, it's unavoidable, it's final, and there is little to be done about it other than to do what one can to live a healthy and positive, productive life. In text responses, many respondents distinguish between fear of death "in principle" and fear of the process of physical decline or dying. It was repeatedly made clear that scaled responses pertained to the former rather than the latter. The importance of personal control over the dying process was also mentioned by many.

It may be that because secularists tend to reject the notion of an afterlife or the suggestion that belief is necessary for acceptance of death, the reported lack of fear may reflect a degree of dismissive bravado that conceals deeper or neglected fear. Relevant texts and interview discussions suggest that this is likely true among some, but not all. Many respondents wrote on the general theme of inevitability, acceptance, and getting on with the business of living to the best of one's ability.

This is not to deny, entirely, that the fact of death is an unsettling one (because of the natural tendency for consciousness to want to persist). It is, rather, to say that the mature individual is one who accepts reality—however undesirable—without whining or throwing a tantrum. It is even, some suggested, possible to embrace death as a beneficial conclusion to human life, in both natural and personal terms. It is possible for human beings to cultivate a mindset concerning mortality that nullifies death's "sting." This is a model of mature human living to which many secularists say they openly aspire. This said, some noted in interviews and survey comments that it is the quality of *life* that is important, leading them to support "death with dignity" and "physician-assisted suicide" measures like those in Oregon or the Netherlands.

## WHAT DO THEY VALUE AND HOW DO THEY LIVE?

As just indicated, a majority of group affiliates cited social relationships as a significant source of meaning in life. Indeed, 63.8 percent mentioned social life (family, friends, people in general); 39.2 percent mentioned personal experience or pursuits (work, creativity, experience of nature or art); and 33.8 percent mentioned social or political engagement (making a contribution, volunteering, political action, helping and caring for others). These commitments are not in word, alone.

Most affiliates were married or partnered at the time of the survey (68 percent; n = 907). Most (76.6 percent) had children (whether "biological," adopted, or by marriage). Among those providing this information (n = 860), 11 percent had never been married, 50.9 percent had been married but never divorced, and 38.1 percent had been divorced at least once.

To understand their value systems, a distinction must be made between what may be called ethical "essentials" and moral "preferentials." The former are principles and behavior patterns considered essential for acceptable (or desirable) social life. The latter are personal or cultural preferences that are not felt to be critical for achieving a desirable quality of life—individual or societal. Matters such as honesty/truthfulness/trustworthiness, treating others fairly or considerately, and justice are considered essential for personal and societal well-being, and so the importance of these values is strong and virtually unanimous (Table 3.17; 1 = not at all, 7 = extremely important). This said, many questioned the specific *meaning* of justice and the degree to which it is applied equally and fairly.

Responsibility for improving the world and helping others in need received strong endorsement, if not quite as strong or unanimous as honesty, fairness, or justice. This said, the most frequently mentioned ethical principle in interviews with both affiliated and independent secularists was the "golden rule." This is considered a fundamental

**Table 3.17**
**Respondents' rated importance of selected values**

| | | Importance | |
|---|---|---|---|
| Values | Total respondents | Mean[a] | Standard deviation |
| Honesty, truthfulness, trustworthiness | 917 | 6.74 | 0.565 |
| Treating others fairly | 912 | 6.61 | 0.671 |
| Justice | 911 | 6.59 | 0.786 |
| Treating others considerately | 912 | 6.45 | 0.815 |
| Compassion | 911 | 6.43 | 0.905 |
| Responsibility for improving world | 913 | 6.02 | 1.159 |
| Helping others in need | 905 | 5.90 | 1.105 |
| Moderation of own appetites, emotions | 908 | 5.15 | 1.455 |

[a]Scale: 1 = not at all important; 7 = extremely important.

insight into the nature of human social life that, many noted, predated Christianity.

With regard to "moderation of one's own appetites and emotions," endorsement was notably weaker and more variable. The question arises: how much moderation, and of what appetites or emotions? In a study of the ethical values of religious "skeptics" and "believers" by Middleton and Putney,[45] a pertinent distinction was made between "ascetic" and "social" ethical standards. They found that social standards (that devalue actions intrinsically harmful to social life, such as lying, stealing, or physical injury) were held strongly and equally among religious "skeptics" and "believers." By contrast, "ascetic" standards (concerning personal behavior such as smoking, gambling, alcohol consumption, or sexual activity) were stronger among religious believers than skeptics.

Moderation of one's appetites and emotions, at least in general principle, would seem to fall into the "ascetic" category. Even so, when asked whether it is "important to focus our own and our children's attention on values and aims beyond material consumption or consumerism," 95 percent of the group affiliates agreed (5 to 7 on a 1–7 scale; mean = 6.42). Moreover, the manners and lifestyles of the secularists whom I have come to know well over the past several years, both independent and affiliated, can only be described as modest (to the point, some would say, of being downright "square"). These are, in the main, responsible and generally serious-minded parents, employees, and citizens whose attitudes and actions—apart from their worldviews—would attract little attention from their neighbors. Indeed, because many report that they tend to be strategically circumspect about their views in public or in unfamiliar contexts, little *does* attract attention and most blend quietly into middle-class North American life. This

**Table 3.18**
**Affiliates' attitudes about controversial "moral" issues**

|  | N[a] | Completely acceptable | Accept with reservations | Should be limited or discouraged | Completely unacceptable |
|---|---|---|---|---|---|
| Same-sex marriage | 749 | 79.6 | 10.7 | 4.9 | 4.8 |
| Divorce | 752 | 69.9 | 21.8 | 6.6 | 1.6 |
| Sex before marriage | 753 | 60.0 | 31.4 | 6.1 | 2.4 |
| Sex between a legal adult and a minor | 740 | 2.4 | 7.9 | 27.6 | 62.0 |
| Embryonic stem cell research | 757 | 87.6 | 9.1 | 5.0 | 2.8 |
| Genetic research in general | 744 | 44.1 | 48.6 | 5.0 | 2.3 |
| Physician-assisted suicide | 760 | 68.8 | 26.1 | 2.8 | 2.4 |
| Death penalty | 740 | 16.2 | 18.5 | 29.4 | 35.9 |

[a]These items were added to the end of the survey following distribution to the first three groups (n = 141; one Atheist, Secular Humanist, and Humanist Unitarian group, each); total sample size for these items was therefore 770.
Values are percentage of respondents. N = total number of respondents.

said, with regard to matters considered preferential rather than essential for individual and societal well-being, both interviewed and surveyed secularists live up to their self-descriptions as politically (or socially) "liberal" (83.6 percent) or "moderate" (11.4 percent).

Most consider same-sex relations or marriage matters of personal choice that do not threaten the common good, and therefore acceptable (Table 3.18). Similarly, divorce and physician-assisted suicide, though regrettable, are sometimes preferable to an intolerable quality of personal or family life. They are acceptable, in principle, as long as they are decided upon responsibly on a case by case basis. (The same can be said of abortion.)

Ethical lines are drawn more carefully or sharply on some issues. For example, sexual relations between an adult and a minor, in principle, are completely unacceptable (62 percent) or should be limited or discouraged (27.6 percent). It is, after all, the law, and the law is reasonably designed to protect the young from sexual predation and victimization. Again, the prime directive is ensuring individuals' well-being—in this case, children. Even so, reasonable judgment must be applied, as in the case, say, of a 17- and 21-year-old "in love." As a result, general-principle responses were frequently qualified with "it depends on the circumstances."

Although there is strong support for the use of embryonic stem cells in research on, for example, chronic illnesses (over and against religious objections), many have reservations about genetic research in general. The latter covers a broad range of phenomena with both potentially desirable and undesirable outcomes. Some express concern about potentially harmful environmental and human impact of genetically modified plants, and although knowledgeable, voluntary, and carefully monitored termination of one's own life is deemed an intrinsic human right, the state's right to punitively take individuals' lives (and the deterrent value or justness of the death penalty) is viewed more critically.

The common thread in such matters is the application of prudent judgment and critical reason with the aim of discerning what is, or is not, likely to advance or threaten individuals' well-being and the common good. Not surprisingly, among the most highly regarded values was that of critical reasoning. Nearly 98 percent endorsed the importance of "critical, logical thinking" and nearly 96 percent endorsed the value of "guiding children to think critically and logically" (5 to 7 on a 1–7 scale with 7 = extremely important).

Many of the affiliated secularists were noticeably less confident about what, exactly, the *content* of children's philosophical guidance should be or how this should be provided. Because the majority experienced, and then rejected, religious upbringing, moral "inculcation" and religious (*or* philosophical) "proselytizing" are anathema. The line between "education" and "proselytizing" is difficult to draw, and there are frequent discussions of this issue in secularist meetings. So it is that when asked on two occasions, a year apart, one secular humanist group was split down the middle about the advisability of a children's program.[46] A few members have struggled for more than a decade with limited success to institute a children's educational program. They are not alone. Among the groups observed and surveyed here, only the Jewish Humanist groups have maintained multiyear children's educational programs (that focus on Jewish cultural heritage and general ethical principles embodied in that heritage—such as *tikkun olam*, one's responsibility to "repair the world" and contribute to the welfare of the community).

There are signs that ambivalence about children's instruction in organized secularity is beginning to abate. Widely publicized atheist and skeptic summer camps have emboldened some locals to renew calls for children's educational programs in critical thinking, logic, ethics, values, and philosophy, as has the appearance of a volume on *Parenting beyond Belief—On Raising Ethical, Caring Kids without Religion.*[47] The secular humanist group just mentioned now has an active children's program committee and a fledgling program. And the secular humanist chapter that emerged from an atheist meet-up includes several young parents or parents-to-be who are motivated to participate in the creation of an environment in which their children can be educated—"not proselytized"—to judge truth claims critically and intelligently and find their own philosophical way (hopefully, promoters admit, along skeptical and secular lines). The degree to which these endeavors can overcome a strong and abiding emphasis on philosophical individualism or autonomous discovery—and so, endure—remains to be seen.

## SUMMARY

These findings are consistent with Beit-Hallahmi's conclusion that "the modal atheist in Western society today . . . is much more likely to be a man, married, with higher education"[48] and Hunsberger and Altemeyer's conclusion that "[d]emographically, active [or affiliated] atheism appears to be mostly an educated, 'left-winger,' old, guy, thing."[49] To these characterizations might be added "a substantially white, Euro-American" thing. This said, there are signs that affiliated secularism continues to replenish itself with younger participants, in part through the mechanism of the Internet as a marketing, sorting, and assembling mechanism.

There has been an observable tendency over the past 200—and 2,000—years for particular skeptical or secularist movements and collectives to emerge and fade away, continually replenished by new ones under new leadership and labels with distinctive slants, from the *kakodaimoniotai* to "brights."[50] Substantial or affirmative secularity has been a minority position throughout Western history, and organized secularity has perennially attracted an infinitesimal portion of the secular or skeptical population. But this persists, even as it waxes and wanes over time and across societies.

No research takes place in a historical vacuum, and it is important to acknowledge the environment in which the data just presented were gathered. Secularists of various stripes have been wrested in recent years from a comforting mid-twentieth-century presumption of inexorable, straight-line secularization (heading toward the positions they themselves hold). Both independent and affiliated secularists have been upset by a resurgence of religion in governance, public life, and world affairs in recent decades. Many have become more vocal, assertive, and/or engaged *as* secularists. They have been emboldened, to some extent, by a series of published tracts that give voice—sometimes quite strident—to their perspectives and concerns.[51] Reference is often made to the "gay revolution" as a model to be emulated: proudly asserting one's identity and equal political, human, and civil rights.

But it is equally important to recognize that this is not a uniform response, nor are secularists a homogeneous mass—even among the small minority of secularists who affiliate on this basis. Peter Steinfels and Barry Kosmin[52] have suggested that much as religiosity may be viewed along a continuum from orthodox or fundamentalist to liberal, so forms of secularity must be distinguished, from "hard" to "soft," with respect to worldviews, values, attitudes about something-called-religion, the place of religious expression in government or public discourse, and much else. Psychologist Frank Barron[53] once suggested distinctions between "fundamentalist" and "enlightened" forms of "belief" *and* "unbelief." Although his nomenclature may have a "politically incorrect" ring today, the import of his observation is valuable. Regardless of the content of existential/metaphysical worldviews—naturalistic or supernaturalistic—these (or the personalities of their holders) range from authoritarian, dogmatic, or prejudicial to tolerant, nuanced, and accepting or live-and-let-live.

It is sometimes asked whether secularists are more or less dogmatic or prejudicial than the "religious."[54] The question may be framed too broadly because there is considerable diversity on both "sides," including those who describe themselves as "atheist(ic)." The answer depends on degrees and types of secularity (and the personalities of those who hold varying positions), much as it depends on degrees and types of religiosity. Gordon Allport, and a legion of researchers following him, distinguished between "mature" or "intrinsic" and "immature" or "extrinsic religion," with the latter tending to be more dogmatic or broadly prejudicial than the former.[55] Similar consideration has not yet been extended to "atheists" (or "secularists") in the social sciences.

The answer also depends on the target(s), breadth, and intensity of judgmental generalization. Affiliated Atheists hold comparatively critical views of something-called-religion, much as many Americans generalize broadly (and negatively) about something-called-atheism. But this is hardly uniform among self-described atheists or across a broader spectrum of distinguishable secular types. Recall that roughly a third of the secular affiliates felt that it is not possible to make blanket judgments about something-called-religion, from 30 percent of the Atheists to 50 percent of the Jewish Humanists. Moreover, this is not uniform concerning targets, since the affiliated Atheists and fellow secularists are comparatively nonjudgmental about homosexuality, for example.

Are the secularists interviewed and surveyed here critical of "traditional" monotheistic notions of "God" or an "afterlife," or perceived excesses in human behavior attributed to these? Overwhelmingly. However, when probed more deeply, only about one-third categorically rejects "God," "soul," "ultimate purpose," *and* an impersonal force. Another third is receptive to the "spiritual" notion of an immanent connecting force ("within nature") sometimes, probably, definitely, or metaphorically. And another quarter is similarly receptive to some kind of ultimate purpose or directionality in human life or existence in general.

The more closely we probe peoples' worldviews and lifeways, as evidenced by the data presented here, the more difficult it becomes to neatly place many (and quite possibly a growing number) into some of the central categories that frame much "Western" discourse, such as "theist" or "atheist," "religious" or "nonreligious." Even if secularization is not a straight-line trajectory culminating in "hard secularity," there is evidence of increasing individuality and eclecticism in people's constructions of their existential and metaphysical worldviews.[56]

The more closely we look at affiliated secularists, the more cultural diversity becomes apparent among the institutions they create. The central preoccupations, and institutional ethos, in Atheist, Skeptic, and Secular, Jewish, or Unitarian Humanist groups are not the same, even if they share a degree of doubt or disapproval concerning certain culturally prevalent "religious" ideas or institutions. This shared characteristic has earned them a marginal and culturally symbolic position, particularly in the United States. As such, secularists (often encapsulated as "atheists") have long been viewed as homogenous figures set against a "religious" ground.

As Penny Edgell and her colleagues have observed, the notion of "atheist," even among those who do not think they know (or have ever known) one, serves as a symbolic cultural and moral boundary marker that defines (for some) what it is (and is not) to be "an American":

> Some people view atheists as problematic because they associate them with illegality, such as drug use and prostitution—that is, with immoral people who threaten respectable community from the lower end of the status hierarchy. Others saw atheists as rampant materialists and cultural elitists that threaten common values from above—the ostentatiously wealthy who make a lifestyle out of consumption or the cultural elites who thing they know better than everyone else. Both of these themes rest on a view of atheists as self-interested individualists who are not concerned with the common good.[57]

In contrast to this, both affiliated and independent secularists describe themselves as rational, reasonable, and thoughtful, as well as ethical, law-abiding, and responsible. They express concern about improving the quality of life "here and now" and in the future (principally but not exclusively for human beings). Well aware of survey data on mainstream attitudes about "atheists," "nonbelievers," or "secular humanists," they view themselves as widely misunderstood, misrepresented, and unreasonably maligned, particularly in the United States.[58] Many find it incredible that they and their forebears and fellows are castigated for holding essentially "conservative" positions—or as comic Bill Maher once put it, for saying "I don't know"—about ultimate existential or metaphysical questions. They overwhelmingly consider their lives worthwhile and find meaning, most of all, in family, friends, personally enriching experience, productive work, and positive contributions. Ironically, but for their secularist stances or naturalistic worldviews, their values and lifestyles tend to be substantially similar to those of many (moderate or liberal) "religious" neighbors in their communities.

The secularists studied here, taken together, resemble another population that has perhaps been better served by research—scientists and academics, particularly social scientists.[59] Both affirmative secularists and scientists tend to be well educated and serious minded, with a decidedly intellectual bent. They tend to be male somewhat more often than female. There is shared dedication to the empirical investigation and understanding of nature, even among those who accommodate transcendental or variously "spiritual" or "religious" ideas and commitments within their worldviews. Substantial numbers of both are educators. They extol and exhibit the values of individualism and autonomous thought, but are nonetheless collaborative and sociable. And they tend to be politically liberal citizens whose lifestyles typically blend quietly into the North American cultural standards of their neighborhoods.

## NOTES

1. Thrower, 1980.

2. This has been observed repeatedly by, for example, Vernon, 1968; Caporale and Grumelli, 1971; Hale, 1977; Pruyser, 1992; Bainbridge, 2005; Hunsberger and Altemeyer, 2006; see also, Pasquale, 2007b.

3. For example, Bainbridge, 2005; Beit-Hallahmi, 2007; Cimino and Smith, 2007; Hunsberger and Altemeyer, 2006; Kosmin and Keysar, 2007; Pasquale, 2007b; Zuckerman, 2007 and 2008.

4. Caporale, 1971, 3.

5. Such as Budd, 1967; Campbell, 1965, 1969, and 1972; Cimino and Smith, 2007; Demerath, 1969; Demerath and Thiessen, 1966; Black, 1983; McTaggart, 1967; Hunsberger and Altemeyer, 2006.

6. Hale, 1977, 97.

7. Pruyser, 1974, 195.

8. Ibid., 174.

9. Ibid., 196.

10. Pasquale, 2007a.

11. Atheist, skeptic, or rationalist student groups at some universities in the region were not sought out for inclusion in the study. Membership is typically small and shifts annually as students matriculate and graduate.

12. It should also be noted that the nature and quality of mailing lists varied noticeably among the groups. This reflects, in part, differences in the purposes, activities, and nature of affiliation in these groups. Some exhibit formal organizational structure with governing boards, committees, regular meetings, and clearly defined levels of membership. Others are less structured networks of interested individuals and supporters who meet irregularly, distribute newsletters or other bulletins, maintain continuing contact largely via e-mail, and have less well-defined affiliation levels or requirements, As a result, some were clearly regularly updated lists of active or dues-paying members, whereas others were less frequently updated and/or more inclusive lists covering both active participants (in meetings, e-mail correspondence, or other activities) as well as people who had inquired about the group or asked to receive electronic or printed newsletters.

13. Nearly 60 percent of Unitarian humanist affiliates indicated affiliation with a Unitarian church or fellowship; in other groups 10.5 percent or less did so.

14. A secularist movement dedicated to "illuminating and elevating the naturalist worldview." See http://www.the-brights.net/.

15. As in, for example, Robertson, 1936, or Jacoby, 2004.

16. From here on, when referring specifically to the surveyed groups, the group category names will be capitalized.

17. Because of small sample size, limited reference will be made to results for the Freethought group affiliates.

18. I am grateful for a Shand Award from the Society for the Scientific Study of Religion (2006), which helped defray survey distribution costs.

19. Preliminary analysis of response patterns among the United States and British Columbia humanists disclosed no strong or systematic differences for many of the variables reported here. Data are therefore reported for the full sample.

20. McTaggart, 1997.

21. Personal communication, Tom Flynn, ed., *Free Inquiry*, September 13, 2007.

22. Hunsberger and Altemeyer, 2006.

23. http://en.wikipedia.org/wiki/Meetup (accessed June 24, 2008).

24. Bainbridge, 2005.

25. Lee, 1995.

26. Members, organizers, and young visitors at established secularist groups have repeatedly mentioned that the old-age skew is a recruitment problem, because young secularists do not feel at home among a majority of "elders."

27. Gender distribution of survey respondents was a fair reflection of the actual gender distributions in the groups (based on mailing list counts or group reports; indicated in brackets).

28. For example, Beit-Hallahmi and Argyle, 1997; Roozen, 1980; Stark, 1963; Vetter and Green, 1932.

29. Campbell, 1965, 333.

30. See, for example, Argyle, 1958; Beit-Hallahmi and Argyle, 1997; Spilka, Hood, Hunsberger, and Gorsuch, 2003; Thalheimer, 1965; Vetter and Green, 1932.

31. http://www.jewishvirtuallibrary.org/jsource/US-Israel/usjewpop.html. Source: Ira M. Sheskin and Arnold Dashefsky, "Jewish Population of the United States, 2006," in *American Jewish Year Book 2006*, Vol. 106, ed. David Singer and Lawrence Grossman (New York: American Jewish Committee, 2006).

32. http://quickfacts.census.gov/qfd/states/41000.html, U.S. Census Bureau; State & County Quickfacts.

33. Vetter and Green, 1932, 185.

34. http://religions.pewforum.org/.

35. Kosmin and Keysar, 2006.

36. For example, Altemeyer and Hunsberger, 1997; Roozen, 1980; Vetter and Green, 1932.

37. Altemeyer and Hunsberger, 1997.

38. McTaggart, 1997.

39. Distinctions were not made among fundamentalist or liberal Protestant denominations or sects. Differences in perceived strictness might well vary among these.

40. Respondents were asked to indicate (yes/no) if they had experienced conflict over religion with (a list of) others.

41. For example, research suggesting significant involvement of early family maladjustment or rebelliousness (e.g., Caplovitz and Sherrow, 1977) has not been borne out by later work (e.g., Altemeyer and Hunsberger, 1997).

42. Response categories have been compressed to simplify presentation.

43. Repondents were asked to indicate which (if any) of several listed descriptors applied to them.

44. Note that despite the widespread criticism of something-called-religion, less than one-third of the sample (264) was willing to apply the term "anti-religious" to themselves.

45. Middleton and Putney, 1962.

46. December, 2005, mean = 3.3 on a 5-point scale (1 = not at all; 5 = very) concerning the importance of a children's educational program, n = 98; November, 2006, mean = 3.32, n = 111. Part of the reason for this ambivalence is likely attributable, as well, to limited personal investment, since most members were well past child-rearing age.

47. McGowan, 2007.

48. Beit-Hallahmi, 2007, 313.

49. Hunsberger and Altemeyer, 2006, 106.

50. See, for example, Budd, 1977; Campbell 1972; Marty, 1961; Robertson, 1936; Thrower, 1980; Warren, 1943. Will Durant writes (1966, 361) that in ancient Greece "Lysias tells of an atheistic society that called itself the *kakodaimoniotai*, or Devils' Club, and deliberately met and dined on holy-days set apart for fasting."

51. For example, Dawkins, 2006; Harris, 2004; Hitchens, 2006.

52. Steinfels, 2006; Kosmin, 2007.

53. Barron, 1963.

54. For example, Hunsberger and Altemeyer, 2006.

55. Allport, 1950; Batson, Shoenrade, and Ventis, 1993.

56. Consider the increase in religious "nones" (no specific religious affiliation) or "spiritual but not religious" in recent decades (Kosmin and Keysar, 2007; Roof, 1999).

57. Edgell, Gerteis, and Hartmann, 2006, 225 and 227.

58. A majority of group affiliates agreed that "people with my way of thinking are discriminated against in society."

59. See, for example, Beit-Hallahmi, 1977 and 2007; Brown, 2003; Ecklund and Scheitle, 2007; Roe, 1953.

## REFERENCES

Allport, Gordon. 1950. *The individual and his religion*. New York: Macmillan.

Altemeyer, Bob, and Bruce Hunsberger. 1997. *Amazing conversions: Why some turn to faith & others abandon religion*. Amherst, NY: Prometheus Books.

Argyle, Michael. 1958. *Religious behaviour*. London: Routledge & Kegan Paul.

Bainbridge, William Sims. 2005. Atheism. *Interdisciplinary Journal of Research on Religion* 1:(Article 2). http://www.religjournal.com.

Barron, Frank. 1963. *Creativity and psychological health: Origins of personal vitality and creative freedom*. New York: D. Van Norstrand.

Batson, C. Daniel, Patricia Schoenrade, and W. Larry Ventis. 1993. *Religion and the individual: A social-psychological perspective*. Oxford: Oxford University Press.

Beit-Hallahmi, Benjamin. 1977. Curiosity, doubt, and devotion: The beliefs of psychologists and the psychology of religion. In *Perspectives in the psychology of religion*, ed. H. Newton Malone, 381–391. Grand Rapids, MI: Wm. B. Eerdmans.

———. 2007. Atheists: A psychological profile. In *The Cambridge companion to atheism*, ed. Michael Martin, 300-313. New York: Cambridge University Press.

Beit-Hallahmi, Benjamin, and Michael Argyle. 1997. Apostasy, atheism, and disbelief. In *The psychology of religious behaviour*. London: Routledge.

Black, Alan W. 1983. Organised irreligion: The New South Wales Humanist Society. In *Practice and belief: Studies in the sociology of Australian religion*, ed. Alan W. Black, 154–166. Sydney: George Allen & Unwin.

Brown, C. Mackenzie. 2003. The conflict between religion and science in light of the patterns of religious belief among scientists. *Zygon* 38:603–632.

Budd, Susan. 1967. The humanist societies: The consequences of a diffuse belief system. In *Patterns of sectarianism: Organization and ideology in social and religious movements*, ed. Bryan R. Wilson, 377. London: Heineman.

Campbell, Colin. 1965. Research note: Membership composition of the British Humanist Association. *The Sociological Review* 13 (3): 327–337.

———. 1969. Humanism in Britain: The formation of a secular value-oriented movement. In *A sociological yearbook of religion in Britain*, Vol. 2, ed. David Martin, 157–172. London: SCM Press.

———. 1972. *Toward a sociology of irreligion*. New York: Herder and Herder.

Caplovitz, David, and Fred Sherrow. 1977. *The religious dropouts: Apostasy among college graduates*. Beverly Hills: Sage Publications.

Caporale, Rocco, and Antonio Grumelli. 1971. *The culture of unbelief*. Berkeley, CA: University of California Press.

Cimino, Richard, and Christopher Smith. 2007. Secular humanism and atheism beyond progressive secularism. *Sociology of Religion* 68 (4): 407–424.

Dawkins, Richard. 2006. *The God delusion*. New York: Houghton Mifflin.

Demerath, Nicholas J., III. 1969. Religion, a-religion, and the rise of the religion-less church: Two case studies in organizational convergence. *Sociological Analysis* 30 (4): 191–203.

Demerath, Nicholas J., III, and Victor Thiessen. 1966. On spitting against the wind: Organizational precariousness and American irreligion. *American Journal of Sociology* 71:674–687.

Durant, Will. 1966. *The story of civilization, II: The life of Greece*. New York: Simon and Schuster.

Ecklund, Elaine Howard, and Christopher P. Scheitle. 2007. Religion among academic scientists: Distinctions, disciplines, and demographics. *Social Problems* 54 (2): 289–2307.

Edgell, Penny, Joseph Gerteis, and Douglas Hartmann. 2006. Atheists as "Other": Moral boundaries and cultural membership in American society. *American Sociological Review* 71:211–234.

Hale, J. Russell. 1977. *Who are the unchurched? An exploratory study.* Washington, D. C.: Glenmary Research Center.

Harris, Sam. 2004. *The end of faith: Religion, terror, and the future of reason.* New York: W. W. Norton & Co.

Hitchens, Christopher. 2007. *God is not great: How religion poisons everything.* New York: Twelve, Hachette Book Group.

Hunsberger, Bruce, and Bob Altemeyer. 2006. *Atheists: A groundbreaking study of America's nonbelievers.* Amherst, NY: Prometheus Press.

Jacoby, Susan. 2004. *Freethinkers: A history of American secularism.* New York: Metropolitan Books.

Kosmin, Barry A., and Ariela Keysar. 2007. *Secularism & secularity: Contemporary International Perspectives.* Hartford, CT: Institute for the Study of Secularism in Society and Culture, Trinity College.

———. 2006. *Religion in a free market: Religious and non-religious Americans.* Ithaca, NY: Paramount Market Publishing.

Lee, Richard Wayne. 1995. Strained bedfellows: Pagans, New Agers, and "starchy Humanists" in Unitarian Universalism. *Sociology of Religion* 56 (4): 379–396.

Marty, Martin E. 1961. *The infidel.* Cleveland, OH: World Publishing.

McGowan, Dale, ed. 2007. *Parenting beyond belief.* New York: Amacon.

McTaggart, John Mitchell. 1997. Organized humanism in Canada: An expression of secular reaffirmation. In *Leaving religion and religious life. Religion and the social order*, Vol. 7, ed. Mordecai Bar-lev and William Shaffir (David Bromley, Series Editor), 61–75. Greenwich, CT: JAI Press.

Middleton, Russell, and Snell Putney. 1962. Religion, normative standards, and behavior, *Sociometry*, 25 (2): 141–152.

Pasquale, Frank L. 2007a. The "nonreligious" in the American Northwest. In *Secularism & Secularity: Contemporary International Perspectives*, ed. Barry A. Kosmin and Ariela Keysar, 41–58. Hartford, CT: Institute for the Study of Secularism in Society and Culture, Trinity College.

———. 2007b. Unbelief and irreligion, empirical study and neglect of. Entry in *The New Encyclopedia of Unbelief*, 760–66. Amherst, NY: Prometheus Press.

Pruyser, Paul W. 1992. Problems of definition and conception in the psychological study of religious unbelief. In *Changing perspectives in the scientific study of religion*, ed. Allan W. Eister 185–200. New York: John Wiley & Sons.

Robertson, J. M. 1936. *A history of freethought.* London: Watts & Co.

Roe, Anne. 1953. A psychological study of eminent psychologists and anthropologists, and a comparison with biological and physical scientists. *Psychological Monographs: General and Applied* 67 (2): 1–55.

Roof, Wade Clark. 1999. *Spiritual marketplace.* Princeton, NJ: Princeton University Press.

Roozen, D. A. 1980. Church drop-outs: Changing patterns of disengagement and re-entry. *Review of Religious Research* 21:427–450.

Spilka, Bernard, Ralph W. Hood, Jr., Bruce Hunsberger, and Richard Gorsuch. 2003. *The psychology of religion: An empirical approach.* 3rd ed. New York: Guilford.

Steinfels, Peter. 2006. Hard and soft secularism. *Religion in the News* (Winter supplement), 8 (3): 8, 11.

Stark, Rodney. 1963. On the incompatibility of religion and science: A survey of American graduate students. *Journal for the Scientific Study of Religion* 3:3–20.

Thalheimer, Fred. 1965. Continuity and change in religiosity: A study of academicians. *Pacific Sociological Review* 8:101–108.

Thrower, James. 1980. *The alternative tradition: Religion and the rejection of religion in the ancient world.* The Hague: Mouton.

Vernon, Glenn. 1968. The religious "nones": A neglected category. *Journal for the Scientific Study of Religion* 7:219–229.

Vetter, George V., and Martin Green. 1932. Personality and group factors in the making of atheists. *Journal of Abnormal and Social Psychology* 27:179–194.

Warren, Sidney. 1943. *American freethought, 1860–1914.* New York: Gordian Press.

Zuckerman, Philip. 2007. Atheism: contemporary numbers and patterns. In *The Cambridge companion to atheism,* ed. Michael Martin, 47–65. New York: Cambridge University Press.

———. 2008. *Society without God.* New York: New York University Press.

# Chapter 4

# Sexuality and the Secular

*Thomas J. Linneman*
*Margaret A. Clendenen*

We begin with a quick exercise in word association. What images does the phrase "religion and homosexuality" most readily bring to mind? Pastor Fred Phelps brandishing a sign reading "God Hates Fags"? Jerry Falwell warning of the gay ways of Teletubby Tinky Winky? Mega-church pastor Ted Haggard drummed out of his church due to his trysts with a gay masseur? The controversy over gay Episcopal bishop Gene Robinson? Such high-profile examples dominate the ways we connect homosexuality and religion, both within popular culture and academe.

The literature surrounding the intersection of religion and homosexuality has concentrated primarily on two themes: how Christians understand and react to homosexuality and how gay men and lesbians attempt to reconcile their sexuality with their faith. Recent examples of the former[1] demonstrate how and why Christian conservatives feel threatened by the lesbian and gay rights movement and the ways in which they have responded to the many successes this movement has achieved. Examples of the latter demonstrate that religion can be both an inhibitive[2] and a liberating[3] force within the everyday lives of gay men and lesbians. Both themes, however, focus on the role of religion and practices of religious faith. Indeed, a prevalent assumption in both sociological literature and the culture at large is that discrimination against gay men and lesbians is rooted in conservative religious beliefs.[4] Though the lively battle between these groups seduces our attention, it distracts us from considering how those living apart from religion view homosexuality and the movement for lesbian and gay rights. Without considering atheists' and agnostics' views of homosexuality, we cannot develop a comprehensive understanding of beliefs about homosexuality: what happens to these attitudes when God is not in the picture? If you remove the "God" from Phelps' "God Hates Fags," does the hate necessarily disappear as well?

Studies consistently have shown that atheists are more liberal and more likely to be politically radical than their religious peers.[5] Yet, does this mean that atheists are also more likely to be accepting of homosexuality? Thomas Clark, the founder and director of The Center for Naturalism, contends in a 1994 article in *The Humanist* that all arguments about the immorality of homosexuality and the threat of the gay rights movement are based in religious ideology.[6] Similarly, in a 2006 article in the secular humanist magazine *Free Inquiry*, sociologist Phil Zuckerman demonstrates that the eighteen countries that are most accepting of homosexuality also have high levels of atheism among their populations.[7] The only mention of homosexuality in Beit-Hallahami's chapter is a 1949 study that showed that people with high degrees of "religionism" were more intolerant of criminals, homosexuals, unwed mothers, and "conscientious objectors" than people with low degrees of "religionism."[8] Yet, in the sixty years since this study was published, we have witnessed the 1969 Stonewall riots and the subsequent rise of the lesbian and gay rights movement. Surely it is time to reconsider what people with low degrees of "religionism" think about homosexuality.

Some researchers have analyzed connections between sexuality and religion, but these studies do not adequately allow for the study of atheists' attitudes because of their lack of specificity in measuring atheism. For example, Hoffman and Miller's research on the effects of religion on social attitudes, while careful about measuring various types of Protestantism, simply has an "Unaffiliated" category.[9] Laumann and his coinvestigators' survey of American sexual behavior, widely considered the most definitive study of sexuality in recent decades, offers only a category of "No Religion at All."[10] However, Hout and Fischer show that those who express "no religion" in surveys are in reality often unchurched people who hold religious beliefs.[11] These studies, therefore, do not allow us specifically to study atheists and sexuality.

A body of research that addresses both atheism and homosexuality focuses on quantitative measures of discrimination against atheists and gays and lesbians. Most of this research[12] has used General Social Survey (GSS) data to compare people's willingness to grant civil liberties to "atheists" with their willingness to grant civil liberties to homosexuals, militarists, and racists. GSS questions regarding atheists are prefaced by the following statement: "There are always some people whose ideas are considered bad or dangerous by other people. For instance, somebody who is against all churches and religion." The use of the word "against" ascribes a certain degree of militancy to atheists that they may or may not have, and the use of "churches" and "religion" suggests a definition of atheism far beyond a lack of belief in God. Thus, instead of reflecting people's willingness to grant civil liberties to atheists in general, these questions more likely elicit opinions regarding people who are actively opposed to organized religion. In addition, this research gives us no insight into the minds of atheists themselves.

More recent research from Penny Edgell, Joseph Gerteis, and Douglas Hartmann[13] provides a better measure of levels of discrimination against atheists and gays and lesbians. As part of the larger Minnesota Mosaic Project, researchers asked a random sample of American adults whether certain groups shared their vision of America. Of all groups listed (atheists, Muslims, homosexuals, conservative Christians, recent immigrants, Hispanics, Jews, Asian Americans, African Americans, and white Americans), atheists were the least likely to be seen as sharing people's visions of America. Edgell, Gerteis, and Hartmann view the greater level of reported discrimination against atheists as opposed to homosexuals as particularly notable: "The possibility of same-sex marriage has widely been seen as a threat to a biblical definition of marriage . . . and the debate over the ordination of gay clergy has become a central point of controversy within many churches. In our study, however, concerns about atheists were stronger than concerns about homosexuals."[14] But again, here we have the atheist as object: people are concerned about atheists, but we have no idea what concerns atheists themselves.

We do have some evidence regarding how atheists feel about the prejudice they experience. The differing levels of stigma identified by Edgell and her coauthors are reflected in everyday comparisons made by atheists between themselves on the one hand and lesbians and gay men on the other. Through content analysis of the secular humanist magazine *Free Inquiry*, interviews with participants and leaders of atheist/secular humanist organizations, and participant observation at atheist/secular humanist meetings and events, Cimino and Smith found that atheists and secular humanists frequently employ language appropriated from the gay rights and women's rights movements.[15] They particularly note the prevalence of "coming out" rhetoric among atheists. Individual atheists with whom they spoke discussed the process of revealing their atheist identity to others in terms analogous to those used to describe the process of "coming out," among gay men and lesbians. They also found coming-out rhetoric to be prevalent in atheist publications, such as in a *Free Inquiry* editorial written by philosopher Paul Kurtz, the founder/leader of the Council for Secular Humanism. In this editorial, titled "Letting Atheists Come out of the Closet," Kurtz called for action: "Let us declare: 'We are secular humanists, atheists, and agnostics and proud of it! We demand equal access and equal rights'."[16] After "coming out," individual atheists also discussed discovering "pride" in their identity, analogous to lesbian and gay pride.[17]

Cimino and Smith further argue that secular humanists and atheists have begun to construct themselves as a minority movement, termed the freethought movement. As examples of the progression of the movement and its claiming of minority status for atheists and secular humanists, they point to the founding of the Center for Atheism in Washington, D.C., a political lobbying group, and the Anti-Discrimination Support Network, a group based out of the Freethought Society of Greater Philadelphia to which one can report incidents of discrimination against nontheists. Similarly, there has been some discussion among atheists regarding the use of a more positive-sounding word than "atheist" to describe those who do not believe in God. One prominent organization, The Brights Network, promotes the use of the word "Bright" instead of e.g., atheist or agnostic, claiming that transitioning to using this more positive-sounding word is analogous to the gay rights movement encouraging the use of "gay" instead of "homosexual."[18] Thus, as gay men and lesbians had to make conscious decisions to organize and to construct themselves as a minority movement[19] so have some atheists begun to organize as an emerging social movement and identity politics is a key tactic within this movement. Like other contemporary movements, different groups and organizations within the freethought movement make use of the Internet and other forms of media to promote their message and to allow individuals active in the movement to connect, organize, and "try on" atheist/activist identities.[20]

In this chapter, using both analysis of national survey data and analysis of Internet discussions from a major atheist organization, we explore the ways in which atheists and agnostics think about homosexuality and the movement for lesbian and gay rights. We move beyond the assumption that, given their common freedom from religion, atheists and agnostics will similarly and overwhelmingly support the movement for gay and lesbian rights. Using both sources of data, we show that atheists think about homosexuality in multifaceted ways.

## SECONDARY ANALYSIS

### Methods

To analyze the attitudinal connections between secularism and homosexuality, we use data from the GSS between the years 1988 and 2006. The GSS is an almost annual face-to-face interview survey conducted by the National Opinion Research Center. The population from which the GSS samples are drawn is all noninstitutionalized Americans aged 18 and above. The multistage probability sampling procedures used for the survey have consistently produced response rates between 73 and 82 percent.

We begin in 1988 because this was the first year in which the GSS asked a question they call simply GOD:

Please look at this card and tell me which statement comes closest to expressing what you believe about God:

1. I don't believe in God.
2. I don't know whether there is a God, and I don't believe there is any way to find out.
3. I don't believe in a personal God, but I do believe in a Higher Power of some kind.
4. I find myself believing in God some of the time, but not at others.
5. While I have doubts, I feel that I do believe in God.
6. I know God really exists, and I have no doubts about it.

For the analyses below, we excluded respondents who chose responses 3, 4, or 5 because we wanted to analyze only those who had the more clear-cut religious attitudes. Those who claimed they don't believe in God we labeled atheists, those who claimed they don't know whether there is a God we labeled agnostics, and those who have no doubts about the existence of God we labeled believers. We also used the GSS measures for religious preference (RELIG), attendance at religious services (ATTEND), and prayer habits (PRAY).

The GSS also regularly asks questions about respondents' attitudes regarding homosexuality. One of these questions, labeled HOMOSEX, deals directly with sexual behavior: "What about sexual relations between two adults of the same sex—do you think it is always wrong, almost always wrong, wrong only sometimes, or not wrong at all?" Three other questions deal with civil rights issues. Beginning with "And what about a man who admits that he is a homosexual?"; the three questions are as follows:

Suppose this admitted homosexual wanted to make a speech in your community. Should he be allowed to speak, or not?

Should such a person be allowed to teach in a college or university, or not?

If someone in your community suggested that a book he wrote in favor of homosexuality should be taken out of your public library, would you favor removing this book, or not?

The wording of these questions is not ideal. For example, in the HOMOSEX question, it is hard to determine what a respondent means if she chose that such behavior is "wrong only sometimes" (fortunately, respondents tended to choose one of the extreme responses to this question). In addition, the word "admits" at the beginning of the civil rights questions adds bias. But one must keep in mind that the GSS began asking these questions in 1973, the same year the American Psychiatric Association removed homosexuality from its list of disorders.[21] To maintain the ability to measure opinion trends over time, the GSS has kept the wording of these questions the same.

For the dependent variable in our regression equations, we combined these homosexuality questions into a single additive index. We gave equal weight to the attitudes regarding sexual behavior and attitudes regarding civil rights. That is, we took the HOMOSEX variable, with values ranging from zero to three, and combined it with the dichotomous civil rights variables (0/1, 0/1, 0/1) to create an index that ranged from zero to six. Respondents scored a zero on the index if they believed gay sex was always wrong and they denied civil rights on all three questions. Respondents scored a six on the index if they believed that gay sex was not wrong at all and supported all three civil rights.

In addition to these attitudinal questions, since 1991 the GSS has asked a subset of its respondents about their sexual behaviors. We use the variable SEXSEX5, which asks: "Have your sex partners in the last five years been exclusively male, both male and female, or exclusively female?" By combining this question with the respondent's own sex, we are able to identify those respondents who, for example, identify as male and claim that their sex partners have been male. Using these variables, we classified people into two categories: those whose sexual behavior has been exclusively heterosexual and those whose sex life in the past five years has involved same-sex behavior. We realize that this technique is less than ideal: those engaging in same-sex behavior may not identify as gay, lesbian, or bisexual. In addition, people who have not had a sex partner in the last five years bear the additional misfortune of being left out of these analyses.

## Findings

### Atheists and Agnostics: An Overview of Demographics and Religious Behaviors

The GSS has included the GOD question in seven different years of its administration. Of the 11,335 people who have responded to this question, 7,042 of them (64.1 percent) are believers, 269 of them (2.4 percent) are atheists, and 454 of them (or 4.1 percent) are agnostics. Because of these small frequencies for the atheists and agnostics, we did not conduct trend analyses, as the frequencies of these groups for each year of data would simply be too small. Table 4.1 illustrates some differences among the three groups. Although some of the differences between believers and the other groups are to be expected (and reflect previous research[22]), there are also some interesting differences between atheists and agnostics. For example, the average agnostic has

**Table 4.1**
**Demographic differences among the groups**

|                                  | Believers | Atheists | Agnostics |
| -------------------------------- | --------- | -------- | --------- |
| Mean years of education          | 12.74     | 13.79    | 14.54     |
| Percent male                     | 37        | 64       | 65        |
| Mean age (years)                 | 47.19     | 43.92    | 41.16     |
| Percent middle/upper class       | 47        | 55       | 66        |
| Mean political views[a]          | 4.31      | 3.45     | 3.61      |

[a]Based on the GSS variable POLVIEWS, where 1 = very liberal and 7 = very conservative.

0.75 more years of education and is 2.75 years younger than the average atheist. Also notice that, with regard to overall political views, atheists tend to be slightly more liberal than agnostics. These differences will come up again in our regression analyses.

Another aspect that will arise in later analyses concerns the effects of religious behaviors on the attitudes of atheists and agnostics. One might assume that those who state they do not believe in God would not exhibit religious behaviors. This is not always the case. Where Hout and Fischer identified "unchurched believers" in their research,[23] we identify "churched nonbelievers." Just over half of the atheists (55 percent) and agnostics (51 percent) express no religious denominational preference. Therefore, there are GSS respondents who identify as Protestants or Catholics but who do not believe in God. One explanation for this is some of the respondents may have been raised in particular religious traditions and still identify with these on a cultural level. Perhaps more interesting is the finding that only a third of atheists (32 percent) and agnostics (34 percent) claim they never pray, and only half of the atheists (55 percent) and agnostics (52 percent) claim they never attend religious services. Of course there are the stories of the atheist who is dragged to church during the holidays, but the GSS contains a number of respondents who, although they claim they don't believe in God, attend religious services on a regular basis (even once a week or more). This allows us to examine the effect of connection with religious communities on the attitudes of atheists and agnostics, and we do so below.

### Atheists' and Agnostics' Attitudes toward Sexuality

Table 4.2 offers the first examples of an unexpected finding. Although atheists' overall political views are slightly more liberal than the views of agnostics, when it comes to issues regarding homosexuality, atheists are significantly more antigay in their attitudes than agnostics. As one would expect, atheists, compared to believers, hold more progay attitudes, but agnostics are even less likely than atheists to be

**Table 4.2**
**Attitudes toward homosexuality**

|                                              | Believers | Atheists | Agnostics |
| -------------------------------------------- | :-------: | :------: | :-------: |
| Percent who believe same-sex behavior is wrong | 75        | 42       | 29        |
| Percent against gay college teacher          | 33        | 21       | 10        |
| Percent against gay book in library          | 35        | 21       | 11        |
| Percent against gay public speaker           | 24        | 13       | 6         |

against same-sex sex or against civil rights. Even though the sample sizes of atheists and agnostics are small, all of the differences between these two groups reach statistical significance at the $p < 0.05$ level (based on simple cross-tabulations). To what can we attribute these differences? One reason may be the more dichotomous and dogmatic worldview held by some atheists. Agnostics, in contrast, might be less willing to make definitive stands, and thus may be less likely, for example, to say that homosexuality is "always wrong."

Another set of possibilities involves the demographic differences we described above. Perhaps these differences between atheists and agnostics can explain away their differences in opinion around homosexuality. To address this, we turn to Table 4.3, which presents a set of regression models that use the index of attitudes toward homosexuality as the dependent variable. Model 1 shows a 0.59 point difference between atheists and agnostics on the six-point index: a significant difference ($p < 0.01$, as judged by a simple difference-of-means test). Recall that agnostics had on average 0.75 more years of education than atheists. It is a well-known finding that education increases support for gay and lesbian issues.[24] Including education in Model 2 does decrease the difference between atheists and agnostics, from 0.59 to 0.42, and it increases the explained variation from 7 to 16 percent. However, almost a half-point difference remains, so education is not the entire explanation. Adding in the other variables also does not decrease the effect. In fact, adding Political Views in Model 5 actually increases the size of the effect. The difference between atheists and agnostics is quite robust.

This difference is limited to attitudes toward homosexuality and does not apply to other sexuality-related issues. We constructed a nine-point attitudinal index using three GSS variables with similar response choices to the HOMOSEX variable: variables concerning premarital sex, extramarital sex, and sex between teenagers 14 to 16 years old. Atheists and agnostics, while differing significantly from believers on this index, do not differ from each other in any statistically significant way. With regard to sex-related behaviors measured by the GSS (watching X-rated

**Table 4.3**
**Explaining attitudes toward homosexuality**

| Independent variables | Model 1 | Model 2 | Model 3 | Model 4 | Model 5 |
|---|---|---|---|---|---|
| Atheist[a] | 1.41 | 1.23 | 1.32 | 1.31 | 1.01 |
| Agnostic[a] | 2.00 | 1.65 | 1.73 | 1.68 | 1.46 |
| Education | — | 0.19 | 0.19 | 0.17 | 0.18 |
| Female | — | — | 0.33 | 0.36 | 0.33 |
| Age | — | — | — | −0.02 | −0.02 |
| Political Views | — | — | — | — | −0.30 |
| Constant | 2.69 | 0.22 | 0.00 | 1.22 | 2.34 |
| $R^2$ | 0.07 | 0.16 | 0.16 | 0.19 | 0.23 |
| n | 4627 | 4622 | 4622 | 4617 | 4460 |

[a]The coefficients for atheist and agnostic are in reference to the omitted category of Believers.
The dependent variable used was index of attitudes toward homosexuality; score: 0 = no support; 6 = full support. — = not applicable. All coefficients are significant at the $p < 0.01$ level. $R^2$ = Pearson correlation coefficient; n = number of respondents.

movies, frequency of sexual intercourse, and number of sexual partners over the past five years), atheists and agnostics are more sexually occupied than believers, but they do not differ from each other on any of these measures.

The differences between atheists and agnostics with regard to attitudes toward homosexuality become even more intriguing when we take into account attendance at religious services (a rough measure of connection to religious community). Above we described the unusual fact that a number of atheists and agnostics attend religious services on a regular basis. Does this regular exposure to religious community affect their attitudes towards homosexuality? To address this question, we used regression analysis to examine the interaction effect between the religious attendance variable and the categories in the GOD variable, again using the index as the dependent variable. Among the believers, attendance has the expected effect: believers who often attend religious services (more than once a week) score 1.44 points lower on the attitude index than believers who do not attend religious services (1.71 versus 3.15). Among the agnostics, attendance has little effect. In fact, it has the opposite effect (though this effect is small): agnostics who often attend religious services score 0.16 points *higher* on the attitude index than agnostics who do not attend religious services (4.85 versus 4.69). In stark contrast to this, atheists who often attend religious services are far more likely to be homophobic than their atheist counterparts who do not attend religious services. The difference between these two groups on the attitude index is a striking 2.64 points (1.80 vs. 4.44). Notice that atheists who often attend differ very little from believers who often attend: 1.80 versus 1.71. It seems that involvement in religious community trumps the effect of atheistic beliefs. Yet somehow agnostics are unaffected by such religious participation.

### God Hates Fagnostics? And Gaytheists?

Given their often unpleasant experiences with organized religion, are gay men, lesbians, and bisexuals more likely to be atheist or agnostic? Since the GSS began asking respondents about their sexual behavior, 10,533 people have responded to these questions. Of these, 10,108 (96 percent) claim exclusively heterosexual behavior and 425 (4 percent) claim lesbian, gay, or bisexual sexual behavior (hereafter, for the sake of concision, referred to as LGB). This did not leave us with a huge sample size, especially once we took into account the fact that only 284 of these 425 LGB respondents answered the GOD question. It is for this reason that we do not break these respondents out into separate categories of gay men, lesbians, bisexual men, and bisexual women. The number of cases simply gets too small. However, even with a sample size of only 284, significant (well below p < 0.01) differences exist between heterosexual and LGB respondents. Whereas 62 percent of heterosexual respondents are believers, only 42 percent of LGB respondents are believers. The LGB respondents are more likely to be atheists than were heterosexuals: only 2.5 percent of the heterosexual respondents claim they do not believe in God, compared to 5.6 percent of the LGB respondents. Whereas 4 percent of the heterosexual respondents are agnostics, 12 percent of LGB respondents are. Thus, according to the GSS data, GLB people are nearly three times more likely than heterosexuals to respond to the GOD question in an atheistic or agnostic way. Although there are millions of LGB people who do have active faith lives and their integration into various religion communities remains an unfortunately troublesome issue for many denominations and congregations,[25] it does seem that some LGB people completely forsake God altogether. Another possibility for these results involves reversing this causality: GLB atheists and agnostics, free from religious strictures, are more able than believers to acknowledge their sexuality to the GSS interviewer.

Given that GLB respondents make up 10 percent of the atheists/agnostics in the GSS samples, one might wonder what effect their inclusion has on the regression results presented in Table 4.3. We ran these regression models excluding the GLB respondents and the results remained essentially the same. Using Model 5, the difference between atheists and agnostics on the homosexuality index moved from 0.45 to

0.52 (keeping in mind that taking into account the SEXSEX5 variable decreased the number of cases by nearly 1,700). Running the results with only the LGB respondents erases the difference between atheists and agnostics completely, but it also reduces the number of valid cases to 106, making comparability to the previous results questionable.

We also ran simple cross tabulations using a GSS variable regarding gay marriage. Unfortunately, this variable appeared in only the 1988 and 2006 GSS, leaving us with a small number of cases. Atheists and agnostics hardly differ in their attitudes toward gay marriage: 35 percent of atheists and 31 percent of agnostics either disagree or strongly disagree with gay marriage. Removing the GLB respondents from this crosstab produces altered results: these percentages change to 42 percent for atheists and 25 percent for agnostics. Given the very small number of cases left for such an analysis, this difference does not reach statistical significance. However, it is at least in the direction that the other results had shown: atheists seem less supportive of GLB people.

The results from the GSS analyses shed some light on the heretofore unexamined relationships between homosexuality and secularism. As with findings from most exploratory research, these results raise more questions than they answer. We were also troubled by our reliance on a single survey question to measure atheism and agnosticism, especially when we realized that those who claim they don't believe in God sometimes engage in religious behaviors. We decided it was important to study how avowed atheists, people for whom atheism is a significant component of their lives, discuss the issue of homosexuality. To hear these voices, we turned to the Brights, one of the largest groups in the freethought movement today.

## DISCUSSION FORUM ANALYSIS

### Methods

We collected the data for this research component from the Brights' Movement Forum, the official Web forum of the Brights' movement. Although we recognize that people who post on an atheist Web forum are likely to view "atheist" as a more important part of their identity than most atheists, we felt that this was the best way to begin to understand the complexity of atheists' opinions about homosexuality. Using the Web forum also allows us to gain insight into the everyday organizing and socializing among people active in the freethought movement.

The Brights' movement was founded in 2003 by Mynga Futrell and Paul Geisert, two teachers in Sacramento, California. The movement is currently supported by Daniel Dennett, a leading atheist philosopher at Tufts University, and Richard Dawkins, an evolutionary biologist and the author of the best-selling *The God Delusion*.[26] A bright is defined as a person with a naturalistic worldview, and a naturalistic worldview is defined as being free of mystical and supernatural elements (a Bright with a capital *B* is someone who has registered as a bright on the Brights' Web site). Thus, while most Brights are atheists, not all atheists are Brights; an atheist who checks her horoscope every day, for example, cannot be considered a Bright because she still places some stake in a mystical force. There are registered Brights in over 140 countries, and as of March 2008, the Brights movement had 40,000 registered members.[27]

The discussion forum includes a search engine. Terms entered into the search engine pull up every thread that contains the specified word. The terms we used for our searches were: lgbt, glbt, lgbtq, glbtq, lgbtqqa, glbtqqa, gay, lesbian, bisexual, queer, homosexuality, homosexual, same-sex marriage, civil union(s), dyke, faggot, fag, coming out, sexual orientation, and sexual preference. We found and compiled every discussion or mention of homosexuality on the forum from the year 2007. This amounted to approximately 1,100 single-spaced pages of text. We then coded each discussion entry for the themes that emerged. We also compiled the age, sex, and current location of everyone who participated in a discussion related to homosexuality. However, we are relying on their self-reports of this information, and many chose not to do so. Of the 39 percent of the participants who specified their sex (67 of 172), 79 percent were male and 21 percent were female. Of the 55 percent of the participants who identified their age, 3 percent were under 18 years of age, 25 percent of people were between 18 and 25, 25 percent were between 26 and 35, 21 percent between 36 and 45, 17 percent between 46 and 55, and 10 percent were 56 years or older. Sixty-eight percent of the participants identified their location. Participants in discussions about homosexuality were from 19 different countries, with the top three being the United States (45 percent), the United Kingdom (16 percent), and Canada (11 percent).

## Results

The Brights' Movement Web forum covered a vast array of topics relating to the lives of the participants. Some of the posts to the forum were mundane, but often the participants engaged each other in extensive discussions on a wide variety of political and social issues. Discussions of homosexuality were quite prevalent within the forum. Of the total number of threads on the forum, 7.2 percent mentioned homosexuality. In compiling and analyzing the discussions and mentions of homosexuality from the Brights' movement Web forum, three dominant themes emerged. Below, we critically examine each of these themes by analyzing the parts of the discussions in which the themes were most clearly demonstrated. We attempt to offer representative examples. We note when there was dissenting commentary and also note the reactions to such dissent. Words or phrases in bold were emphasized in the original posts.

## The Morality of Homosexuality

Atheists are frequently cast as immoral. According to one argument in this vein, atheists are unable to be moral because they lack belief in the religious faiths that define morality for many in society.[28] In contrast to this assertion, however, we found discussions of morality to be quite prevalent on the Brights' forum. Clearly, we were particularly interested in conversations about the morality of homosexuality. With regard to all issues, though, the consensus definition of morality was that moral actions are those that do not infringe on the rights or privacy of others. This was described succinctly by a 21-year-old female from Australia, in response to a question about how to define morality: "Simple . . . , 'if I do this, will it cause suffering of any kind for any length of time towards any living thing of reasonable consciousness?'"

When this definition of morality is applied specifically to gay men and lesbians, forum participants argue that because homosexual sex between consenting adults does not hurt anyone, there is no reason to define it as immoral. Although there were a few exceptions to this attitude, the discussions on the forum were overwhelmingly affirming of the morality of gay and lesbian relationships, and these exceptions were all quickly challenged by others on the forum. The overall consensus can be characterized by these comments from forum participants:

> In the case of homosexuality, and this is key: **there is absolutely nothing by nature harmful about a homosexual relationship**. If gay people are in gay relationships and they're having sex and finding intimacy and they're loving all of it, **good. Very good.** If they're having bad sex or find themselves in bad relationships, I mean, it's bad, but it's bad when it happens to heterosexuals, as it regularly does, and it happens irrespective of the sex of the partners, everything aside. So the homosexuality question is so easily and simply and strongly answered that it's really sick that as a species we even have to discuss it. (16-year-old male from Canada)
>
> There is no rational reason to condemn homosexuality. That's the issue. There are plenty of rational reasons to condemn pederasty, bestiality, yadda, yadda, yadda, but what consenting adults do at night, in private, is of no concern to me, until it leaves the house. That's a general statement; if they're in there plotting a murder, I don't care, until they come outside to commit the act. (28-year-old male stationed in Iraq)

Sometimes, Brights discussed homosexuality as simply one example among a litany of social/political issues that have been wrongly cast as immoral by our culture and/or government:

Intermixing drug prohibition (alcohol prohibition), polygamy, obscenity, gay marriage, even suicide, etc., with immoral acts is a religious tactic to confuse the issue [to] justify passing legislation against them. Some call these victimless crimes. I call them issues of virtue and personal freedom. In either case, they should be left as individual choices, and not made illegal. (from the United States, sex and age unspecified)

Thus, in conversations relating to the morality of homosexuality, Brights affirmed the morality of homosexuality and, likewise, tended to criticize actions by the government that infringe on what they perceive as the rights of lesbians and gay men. However, this type of support is less than ideal when one considers many of the goals of the lesbian and gay rights movement. These discussions of morality concentrate a great deal of attention on the sexual acts themselves and give little consideration to issues of identity and civil rights so important to lesbians and gay men. Granted, there were discussions on the forum about civil rights, especially gay marriage. However, by focusing their morality discussions on individual acts and by comparing homosexuality with act-based issues (such as obscenity or bestiality), some participants in the discussion forum construct homosexuality in a particular way that often fails to recognize lesbian and gay identities and denies the complexity of lesbian and gay lives.

### The Discriminatory Nature of Religion

If, as Brights argue, homosexuality and homosexual sex are not inherently immoral, from where do discriminatory beliefs and attitudes regarding gays and lesbians originate? Consistent with sociological research and cultural assumptions concerning the origin of discriminatory attitudes towards gays and lesbians, Brights frequently describe prejudice and discrimination against gays and lesbians as being rooted in organized religion:

Situations like this are where religion and "commonsense morality" part ways—like homosexuality, stem cells, drugs, pornography, blasphemy. Since [religious people] believe in an ultimate morality that isn't based on suffering and rights, you have suffering, on many levels and massive scales, *caused* by the supposed guiding light of mankind. (45 years old, from the United States, sex unknown)

I say it is generally irrational attempts to oppress others in areas like sex, pornography, homosexuality, censorship, attempts to denounce love, and general persecution of those they deem "immoral" out of no explanation but their religion that not only made me give up the idea of religion altogether, but in fact I have a very negative view on it. Curiously, I have a negative view on Christianity, Islam . . . and Judaism . . . but none against Buddhism, Wicca, and several other religions. This is because I have never heard of Buddhists or Wiccans going around to oppress others irrationally in the name of their belief. (no personal information given)

For many Brights, then, organized religion is seen as problematic not only because Brights lack the belief in God necessitated by most religions, but also because they claim that believing in God inspires a host of other damaging social and political ramifications. The way some religions treat homosexuality provides these Brights with a clear example of one of their primary problems with religion. In making their case, some Brights (such as in the first quote above) paint religion with a single, wide brush. They do not acknowledge the wide diversity of religious thought on homosexuality, much of which has developed only in recent years, both among and within various religious traditions.[29] The second quote above takes a step toward making distinctions among religions, but still puts all Christian traditions into a single, discriminatory category.

Brights also discussed the ways in which damaging beliefs have affected individual gays and lesbians, criticizing these beliefs both for their content and their effects.

When you base your morality on an ancient book that "says" it's the ultimate authority, instead of what alleviates human suffering, you are willing to forsake your [gay] children. Throw in some silly antiquated view of what is manly, and you have the potential for a whole lifetime of human suffering. (30 years old, from the United States)

There are issues that we, Brights, would never even imagine they have to deal with . . . Knowing about religious gays who struggle with their homosexuality always evokes deep emotions in me; I'm convinced that non-believer gays actually suffer much less than believer gays— because at least they don't have to battle with their own selves. (20-year-old female from England)

One thirty-three-year-old Bright from the United States discussed the example of Fred Phelps and the Westboro Baptist Church. As noted at the very beginning of this chapter, Phelps is notorious for protesting using the phrase "God Hates Fags":

I would almost have to give Phelps & Co. props, if they weren't causing pain to so many already suffering people. I'm sure many fundamentalists dislike the WBC [Westboro Baptist Church] because it strips away the "love the sinner, hate the sin" line that said fundamentalists like to dish out for PR purposes, and exposes the basic message of religion-based homophobia for what it is. (33 years old, from the United States)

One word arises again and again in these postings: suffering. These Brights construct gay men and lesbians as victims whose lives have been tormented by conservatives in the name of religion. Given the prominence of the battle between Christian conservatives and gays and lesbians in recent decades and the potent imagery this brings to mind, it is no surprise that Brights would use this battle to offer stirring examples of the harm religion can cause. Yet Dawne Moon, in her insightful study of how Methodist congregations deal with the issue of homosexuality, cautions us regarding the use of suffering as a political tool:

> When people use the language of pain in politics, they risk perpetuating hierarchy and further isolating people, and there can also be broader unintended political effects as well. The politics of emotion has contributed, of late, to a political climate where being a victim, being wronged or pained, is what gives people a right to challenge the way things are; victimhood has become *the* righteous position from which to make political interventions, the only political position from which to make political interventions, the only political position that is not immediately suspect.[30]

These Bright discussion participants put lesbians and gay men in the position of "sufferers," and, according to Moon, this limits the political possibilities for achieving change. In addition, Brights are in the odd position of pitying the suffering of gay men and lesbians while at the same time envying the progress the lesbian and gay rights movement has made, as the next section makes clear.

### The Lesbian and Gay Rights Movement as a Model

By far the most prevalent theme related to homosexuality on the Brights' forum concerned comparisons between the Brights and the lesbian and gay rights movement. Like the atheists and secular humanists interviewed by Cimino and Smith,[31] Brights frequently drew comparisons between their struggles for equality and the struggles that the lesbian and gay rights movement has had to endure. This was accomplished through comparisons of the language used by each group, comparisons of the discrimination faced by atheists and that faced by gay men and lesbians, and frequent use of coming out stories and the rhetoric of the closet.

As the Brights movement explicitly patterns itself after the gay rights movement by choosing to use the moniker "Bright" instead of "atheist," analogous to "gay" instead of "homosexual," individual Brights frequently talked about the language used to describe both groups:

> I see very little difference in our usage of the word bright, in comparison to homosexual people wanting to use "gay" as their title. We both wanted something positive to show that being an atheist isn't a sad or depressive, or immoral thing. We both do not wish to tell anyone who goes by such a meme that they must follow any rules and that individuality is encouraged. It may mean different things to different people, but

given enough time and exposure people will stop associating the word with the original definition. The word "homosexual" gives off a worse vibe than "gay" does, just like "godless" and "atheist" sound worse than "bright." (21-year-old female from Australia)

Other participants employed this logic quite frequently throughout the forum. There were a few people who questioned the comparison, however. For instance, this forum participant said:

The term "gay" is now becoming (or has become) the biggest insult you can throw at anyone . . . I remember reading the "gay" reference on my first visit to the Brights.net and hoping then, as I hope now, that the same fate does not await the term "Bright/s." But I like the term myself. I call myself a Bright. But I very rarely (seven times to date) tell anyone else I am one. (no personal information given)

Overwhelmingly, though, individual Brights were comfortable viewing the term "bright" as comparable to "gay." Once this comparison was made, it was also noted that, like gays and lesbians making a conscious decision to use the word "gay," Brights also consciously must choose to use "Bright" in everyday conversation:

So why not say Bright? Really! Why not? The reason that the word "gay" worked is that homosexuals used it. They used it proudly, and even defiantly. They **made** the word stick, despite ridicule, and they changed their image in this country. We can do the same, but we have to use the word. We have to **correct** people when they call us atheists and we have to **make** the word stick. **We** have to do it. No one else will do it for us. (40 years old, from the United States)

According to the Brights' movement, and the Brights who post on the forum, by using the term Bright, they can begin to change the way in which atheists are viewed in our society. This can be viewed as a type of identity deployment, which Bernstein defines as "expressing identity such that the terrain of conflict becomes the individual person so that the values, categories, and practices of individuals become subject to debate."[32] The goal here, by confronting people with a new term, is to force the listener to ponder his or her prejudices against atheism. But where the terms "gay" and "queer" (which has been reclaimed by some lesbian and gay activists) already bore some familiarity among the general public, the term "bright" is virtually unknown, making this strategy of identity politics all the more difficult to pursue.

Brights moved beyond these linguistic comparisons to discussions of the stigmatization of atheism and homosexuality. One fifty-three-year-old man from Mexico even cited the Edgell et al. study.[33] Other Brights discussed this stigma as it plays out in their everyday experiences. One forty-one-year-old college student from the United States, for example, felt that a Fundamentalist Christian woman in her class treated her unfairly, as the Christian woman continually made negative comments regarding atheists during class time:

> You know what is funny? We have one gentleman in the classroom who is very obviously gay and the Fundie tolerates him, even though in our gov[ernment] the Religious Reich is forbidding gays from having civil unions and making snide remarks. Not that I want her to pick on the guy, I don't and would not like it, but why can't she have the same toler-ance for me as she does of him? (41-year-old woman from the United States)

A gay man from the United States also compared the stigma surround-ing atheism and homosexuality when giving advice to a sixteen-year-old struggling to tell his parents that he is an atheist:

> I'm gay and grew up in an Episcopalian household with parents who have a few close gay friends. Nonetheless, they have never been tolerant of my life. Your telling your parents that you reject all religion is going to be tantamount to me telling my parents that I don't like girls. I strongly recommend that you wait until you are independent and have NO strings attached before you consider saying anything. By that time, you may find no need to discuss religion at all. I never told my parents that I am atheist. It would finish off what coming out gay didn't kill. (male from the United States)

Edgell and her coauthors claim that atheists are the group most reviled in their sample of Americans.[34] According to these Brights, such survey results prove true in their own lives.

Like the atheists and secular humanists interviewed by Cimino and Smith,[35] Brights discussed the process of coming out of the closet as a way to describe the revelation of their identity, and, also, as a way to begin to overcome some of the stigma surrounding that identity:

> It wasn't calling themselves "gay" that advanced the civil rights of homosexuals—it was coming out of the closet. We have a nice, positive-sounding name to call ourselves, but if we don't come out, we will never achieve anything. . . . The gays proclaimed "we're here and we're queer!" We need to proclaim, **"we're Bright and we're right!"** (55-year-old male from the United States)

On the forum, individual "coming out" stories were extremely preva-lent. They ranged from teenagers struggling to tell their parents that they do not believe in God, to a fifty-year-old woman who "came out" to a friend only to become the target of her friend's evangelism, to a father trying to decide how best to tell his children that while their mother makes them go to church, he does not believe in God. Here are two examples of coming-out stories. We chose the first because it is fairly typical of coming out stories on the forum, while we chose the second because of the striking parallels that can be drawn between it and discussions of coming out among gay men and lesbians:

> So there seems to be a Bright's equivalent to a gay coming out, and I'm kind of having the same problem. I come from a deeply religious family, but I've tried to break free from that. The problem is that I'm also deeply involved in the community, I am a scout leader at the church, I'm also a designer for many church Web sites and am involved in church activities. All my friends are also part of this community, my girlfriend is also involved in church and doesn't really know about my atheism. I've been doing that for years, and now I feel like a sort of hypocrite working for the church when I really don't believe in what they're doing anymore (since about a year ago?). I'm not really sure how to handle this situation. While I can't simply leave, since my whole life is based on my exchange with this community, I can't simply stay and pretend like nothing's going on. (from Canada)
>
> My dad is a reverend, former pastor, and former televangelist. Needless to say, coming out to [my family] wasn't exactly that easy. I held it in for the longest time, and then suddenly decided to tell my Uncle Tommy that I don't believe in god. Big mistake. He tells my parents, and then I get the first, of about a hundred thousand to date, hell/Jesus talks. I get one almost daily, so it's sort of the norm now, but it really makes me think that they're nutcases, as is stereotypical. You know? They're still in denial, I believe. Especially my sister, who is completely awestruck, and my mom who is constantly annoying me with "god did this, god did that" mumbo jumbo. (17 years old)

Like gay and lesbian identities, one's atheist identity is not readily apparent to those with whom one interacts and is something that can be concealed if that person so chooses. Also similar to gay and lesbian identities, once an individual reveals her atheist identity, odds are good it will develop into a master status within her community, affecting all aspects of this person's interactions with those close to her.[36] This leads atheists to consider these moments seminal and explains why it is common to have coming-out stories in their narrative repertoires.[37] However, one possible difference between the two groups is the perceived ability to change one's behavior. Clearly there are many who believe that a refutation of homosexuality is possible, and the ex-gay movement has gained in prominence in recent decades.[38] But just as many consider homosexuality to be inherent and unchangeable (for example, the one time the GSS asked Americans about this issue, in 1994, 52 percent of respondent said sexual orientation could not be changed). As the lesbian and gay rights movement continues to achieve success, these numbers are likely to increase. But for atheists, making the argument for an inherent identity is more difficult. Many social groups engaging in identity politics at least partially base their claims on the inherent nature of the identity: gay men and lesbians, women, racial and ethnic minorities, and people living with disabilities or disease, to name a few. The Brights are attempting something considerably more difficult: engaging in identity politics based on a set of beliefs held by a small minority in the United States.

## CONCLUSION

We often tell our students that sociology's job is to complicate that which seems simple. The understanding of relationships between secularism and homosexuality, as far as we had seen, was vastly oversimplified: of *course* atheists and agnostics support gay men and lesbians; why on earth *wouldn't* they? We hope that this chapter has done its job and that we have added some much needed nuance to these relationships. The first problem we identified is that, too often, atheists and agnostics are equated (or, worse, put into a category of "no religion"). Our GSS research shows that separating them exposes confounding differences between the two groups. Second, even though many atheists offer their support of lesbians and gay men, we use our Brights research to argue that this support is sometimes less than ideal and that these faulty connections between atheists and gay men and lesbians hold the potential for political discord.

We readily admit that our explorations here are just that: preliminary steps toward a better understanding of these connections. We end with suggestions for moving beyond our findings. Undoubtedly, the differences between atheists and agnostics need further attention. As far as we were able to tell, these differences are real and persistent. As with any representative quantitative research on these groups, though, the sample sizes were frustratingly small. There should be attempts to replicate these differences with other sources of data, especially international sources, given that rates of atheism in other countries are markedly higher than in the United States.[39] If the differences do remain, explaining them is the next step. We acknowledge defeat in this respect, and welcome any suggestions for why these differences exist.

Our research on the Brights is enlightening, but admittedly small scale. We hope we have shown enough complexity in their thinking about homosexuality to spawn more expansive research, either through studying a longer period of time on the forum, or studying other atheist groups. We also realize that the study of preexisting Internet discussion forums has its limitations. Though the entries seemed sincere, there is no way to verify this. Our roles as complete observers did not permit us to ask for clarification to some of the arguments Brights made. But one thing was clear: talk of homosexuality conjures many emotions in atheists: respect, sympathy, envy, and hope. A full analysis of these emotions, perhaps through in-depth interviews, would bring us closer toward understanding the complex relationships between sexuality and the secular.

## NOTES

1. Moon, 2004; Linneman, 2003; Hartman, 1996.
2. Erzen, 2006; Wolkomir, 2006.
3. Wolkomir, 2006; Gray and Thumma, 2005; Wilcox, 2003; Rodriguez and Ouellette, 2000; Warner, 1995; Thumma, 1991.
4. Bull and Gallagher, 1996; Herman, 1997.
5. Beit-Hallahami, 2005.
6. Clark, 2004.
7. Zuckerman, 2006.
8. Beit-Hallahami, 2005, 305.
9. Hoffmann and Miller, 1997.
10. Laumann et al., 1994.
11. Hout and Fischer, 2002.
12. Reimer and Park, 2001; Miller, 1996; Ellison and Musick, 1993.
13. Edgell, Gerteis, and Hartmann, 2006.
14. Ibid., 230.
15. Cimino and Smith, 2007.
16. Kurtz, 2000, 6.
17. Cimino and Smith, 2007.
18. Ibid.; www.the-brights.net.
19. D'Emilio, 1983.
20. Taylor and Whittier, 1992.
21. Bayer, 1987.
22. Beit-Hallahmi, 2007.
23. Hout and Fischer, 2002, 165.
24. Loftus, 2001; Yang, 1997.
25. Moon, 2004; Hartman, 1996.
26. Dawkins, 2006.
27. www.the-brights.net.
28. Craig, 2007.
29. Moon, 2004; Hartman, 1996.
30. Moon, 2004, 236.
31. Cimino and Smith, 2007.
32. Bernstein, 1997, 537.
33. Edgell, Gerteis, and Hartmann, 2006.
34. Ibid.
35. Cimino and Smith, 2007.
36. Linneman, 2003.
37. Plummer, 1995.
38. Erzen, 2006.
39. Zuckerman, 2007.

## REFERENCES

Bayer, Ronald. 1987. *Homosexuality and American psychiatry: The politics of diagnosis.* Princeton, NJ: Princeton University Press.

Beit-Hallahmi, Benjamin. 2007. Atheists: A psychological profile. In *The Cambridge companion to atheism,* ed. Michael Martin, 300–17. New York: Cambridge University Press.

Bernstein, Mary. 1997. Celebration and suppression: The strategic use of identity by the lesbian and gay movement. *American Journal of Sociology* 103 (3): 531–565.

Bull, Chris, and John Gallagher. 1996. *Perfect enemies: The religious right, the gay movement, and the politics of the 1990s.* New York: Crown.

Cimino, Richard, and Christopher Smith. 2007. Secular humanism and atheism beyond progressive secularism. *Sociology of Religion* 68 (4): 407–424.

Clark, Thomas. 1994. Secularism and society: The case for gay equality. *The Humanist* 54 (3): 23–29.

Craig, William Lane. 2007. Theistic critiques of atheism. In *The Cambridge companion to atheism,* ed. Michael Martin, 69–85. New York: Cambridge University Press.

Dawkins, Richard. 2006. *The God delusion.* New York: Houghton Mifflin.

D'Emilio, John. 1998. *Sexual politics, sexual communities: The making of a homosexual minority in the United States, 1940–1970.* Chicago: University of Chicago Press.

Edgell, Penny, Joseph Gerteis, and Douglas Hartmann. 2006. Atheists as "other": Moral boundaries and cultural membership in American society. *American Sociological Review* 71 (2): 211–234.

Ellison, Christopher G., and Marc A. Musick. 1993. Southern intolerance: A fundamentalist effect? *Social Forces* 72 (2): 379–398.

Erzen, Tanya. 2006. *Straight to Jesus: Sexual and Christian conversions in the ex-gay movement.* Los Angeles: University of California Press.

Gray, Edward R., and Scott L. Thumma. 2005. *Gay religion: Innovation and tradition in spiritual practice.* Walnut Creek, CA: Altamira Press.

Hartman, Keith. 1996. *Congregations in conflict: The battle over homosexuality.* New Brunswick, NJ: Rutgers University Press.

Herman, Didi. 1997. *The anti-gay agenda: Orthodox vision and the Christian right.* Chicago: University of Chicago Press.

Hoffman, John P., and Alan S. Miller. 1997. Social and political attitudes among religious groups: Convergence and divergence over time. *Journal for the Scientific Study of Religion* 36 (1): 52–70.

Hout, Michael, and Claude S. Fischer. 2002. Why more Americans have no religious preference: Politics and generations. *American Sociological Review* 67 (2): 165–190.

Kurtz, Paul. 2000. Letting atheists come out of the closet. *Free Inquiry* 20 (3): 5–6.

Laumann, Edward O., John H. Gagnon, Robert T. Michael, and Stuart Michaels. 1994. *The social organization of sexuality: Sexual practices in the United States.* Chicago: University of Chicago Press.

Linneman, Thomas J. 2003. *Weathering change: Gays and lesbians, Christian conservatives, and everyday hostilities.* New York: New York University Press.

Loftus, Jeni. 2001. America's liberalization in attitudes toward homosexuality. *American Sociological Review* 66 (5): 62–82.

Miller, Alan S. 1996. The influence of religious affiliation on the clustering of social attitudes. *Review of Religious Research* 37 (3): 123–136.

Moon, Dawne. 2004. *God, sex & politics: Homosexuality and everyday theologies.* Chicago: University of Chicago Press.

Plummer, Ken. 1995. *Telling sexual stories: Power, change, and social worlds.* New York: Routledge.

Reimer, Sam, and Jerry Z. Park. 2001. Tolerant (in)civility? A longitudinal analysis of white conservative protestants' willingness to grant civil liberties. *Journal for the Scientific Study of Religion* 40 (4): 735–745.

Rodriguez, Erin, and Suzanne Ouellette. 2000. Gay and lesbian Christians: Homosexual and religious identity integration in the members and participants of a gay positive church. *Journal for the Scientific Study of Religion* 39 (3): 333–347.

Taylor, Verta, and Nancy E. Whittier. 1992. Collective identity in social movement communities: Lesbian feminist mobilization. In *Frontiers in social movement theory*, ed. Aldon D. Morris and Carol McClurg Mueller, 104–129. New Haven: Yale University Press.

Thumma, Scott. 1991. Negotiating a religious identity: The case of the gay Evangelical. *Sociological Analysis* 52 (4): 333–347.

Warner, R. Stephen. 1995. The Metropolitan community churches and the gay agenda: The power of pentacostalism and essentialism. In *Religion and the social order*, ed. M. Neitz and M. Goldman, 81–107. Greenwich, CT: JAI Press.

Wilcox, Melissa. 2003. *Coming out in Christianity: Religion, identity and community.* Bloomington: IN: University Press.

Wolkomir, Michelle. 2006. *Be not deceived: The sacred and sexual struggles of gay and ex-gay Christian men.* New Brunswick, NJ: Rutgers University Press.

Yang, Alan S. 1997. Trends: Attitudes toward homosexuality. *Public Opinion Quarterly* 61 (2): 477–507.

Zuckerman, Phil. 2007. Atheism: Contemporary numbers and patterns. In *The Cambridge companion to atheism*, ed. Michael Martin, 47–65. New York: Cambridge University Press.

———. 2006. Is faith good for us? *Free Inquiry* 26 (5): 35–38.

## WEB SITES

The Brights. http://www.the-brights.net.
The Brights' Web Forum. http://www.the-brights.net/forums.

# Chapter 5

# Morality and Immorality among the Irreligious

## Benjamin Beit-Hallahmi

The question of morality and immorality among nonbelievers is part of an old, indeed ancient, discourse on the relationship between religion and morality. In the fifth century BCE, Athenian historians asserted that fear of the gods and belief in divine reward and punishment kept humans close to the word of the law, while the absence of such fear and such beliefs led to lawlessness.[1] Later, it was the Roman Cicero, in *De Natura Deorum* (45 BCE), who wondered whether, without fear of the gods, trust and cooperation among humans will be lost and, with them, justice. It has often been claimed that only the expectation of supernatural reward and punishment, meted out by omniscient, but invisible, entities, can cause humans to give up their natural selfishness and recognize the needs of others.

Cicero's concern has been reiterated in the form of two questions:

1. Can the institutions of society survive without their authority believed to originate from the world of the spirits?
2. Could individuals who reject supernaturalism be moral?

With growing secularization and the reality of atheism and atheists, these questions took on some immediacy, or, in some circles, even urgency. "It is one of the oldest of sociological generalizations that any coherent and viable society rests on a common set of moral understandings about good and bad, right and wrong . . . these common moral understandings must also in turn rest upon a common set of religious understandings that provide a picture of the universe in terms of which the moral understandings make sense."[2] If it is indeed religion that provides moral coherence, how can society survive without it? Another interpretation is offered by looking at technological development: "In the technologically developed society authority is freed, to the extent that technology has provided it with coercive instruments, from the constraints imposed by the need to maintain its sanctity."[3] In a technologically advanced society, religion loses its legitimation function, and so the decline of religion should not affect the social order.

## WOULD YOU TRUST AN ATHEIST?

Individuals who reject all supernaturalism have long been considered morally suspect. John Locke stated that nonbelievers should not be trusted, because "promises, covenants, and oaths, which are the bonds of human society, can have no hold upon an atheist."[4] His contemporary, Pierre Bayle (1647–1706), presented an opposite view and argued that morality had nothing to do with religious belief and that a society of atheists could be as moral as or more moral than a society of Christians.[5] He also wrote in 1697 that "who pass through the hangman's hands, there are none found to be Atheists"[6] Bayle was clearly far ahead of his time.

George Washington, echoing John Locke, warned in his Farewell Address (1796): "Where is the security for property, for reputation, for life, if the sense of religious obligation deserts the oaths which are the instruments of investigation in courts of justice? And let us with caution indulge the supposition that morality can be maintained without religion. Whatever may be conceded to the influence of refined education on minds of peculiar structure, reason, and experience both forbid us to expect that national morality can prevail in exclusion of religious principle."[7]

Voltaire, to whom Christianity was an "infamy" that deserved crushing, but was still a deist, found the influence of faith useful among the masses and once silenced a discussion about atheism until he had dismissed the servants, lest in losing their faith they might lose their morality.[8] Voltaire's rhetorical question was "What restraint, after all, could be imposed on covetousness, on the secret transgressions committed with impunity, other than the idea of an eternal master whose eye is upon us and will judge even our most private thoughts?"[9] On another occasion, Voltaire stated this idea forcefully: "I want my attorney, my tailor, my servants, even my wife to believe in God; and I think that I shall then be robbed and cuckolded less often."[10] It seems that Voltaire became worried, realizing that secularity was indeed spreading beyond the elite.

We find the best known and most quoted modern warning about nihilistic, amoral, atheists in Dostoevsky's *The Brothers Karamazov* (1880). Mitya tells Alyosha about a conversation he had with the atheist Rakitin: " 'But what will become of men then?' I asked him, 'without God and immortal life? All things are lawful then, they can do what they like?' 'Didn't you know?' he said laughing, 'a clever man can do what he likes,' he said."[11] Earlier in the book, Father Zossima presents an overview of the contrast between contemporary secular Europe, immoral and revolutionary, and the great popular Russian tradition of faith and obedience: "It is different with the upper classes. They, following science, want to base justice on reason alone, but not with Christ, as before, and they have already proclaimed that there is no crime, that there is no sin. And that's consistent, for if you have no God what is the meaning of crime? In Europe the people are already rising up against the rich with violence, and the leaders of the people are everywhere leading them to bloodshed, and teaching them that their wrath is righteous. But their 'wrath is accursed, for it is cruel.' But God will save Russia as He has saved her many times. Salvation will come from the people, from their faith and their meekness."[12]

William James, writing in 1891, described the difference between a religious and a secular morality in terms of energy, music, and objective power:

> ". . . in a merely human world without a God, the appeal to our moral energy falls short of its maximal stimulating power. Life, to be sure, is even in such a world a genuinely ethical symphony; but it is played in the compass of a couple of poor octaves, and the infinite scale of values fails to open up. . . . When, however, we believe that a God is there, and that he is one of the claimants, the infinite perspective opens out. The scale of the more imperative ideals now begin to speak with an altogether new objectivity and significance, and to utter the penetrating, shattering, tragically challenging note of appeal."[13]

James, an ambivalent but consistent defender of religion,[14] was implying that atheism may be a true risk factor on the road to an immoral symphonic performance.

The sociologist Talcott Parsons stated that ". . . man's relation to the supernatural world is in some way intimately connected with his moral values."[15] Both James and Parsons make claims about psychological processes in individual humans. Such processes must be different in a person who does not believe in the supernatural. Such ideas are still common in the United States today. Surveys have consistently shown that atheists have been the least trusted group, because they are perceived as having rejected the basis of moral solidarity and cultural membership in American society.[16]

## RELIGIOUS AND SECULAR MORAL DOMAINS

If we do just a little bit of introspection, it seems that we all have inside our heads a moral calculator, part of our stream of consciousness, constantly scanning and rating actions as positive or negative, superior, or inferior. The moral calculator does a whole legal proceeding in a split second, judging intentions, consequences, circumstances, and character. It leads to frequent condemnation and rare praise, whether of ourselves or of others. We know that condemning others brings some pleasure and a feeling of superiority, while praising others seems less satisfying. The algorithms behind all these calculations must be based on general principles, intuitions, and ideals, which are known collectively as morality.

A leading researcher defined morality as ". . . prescriptive judgments of justice, rights, and welfare pertaining to how people ought to relate to each other."[17] This definition is designed to steer us away from cultural conventions: "Moral judgments are primarily about welfare, justice, and rights, distinguishable from judgments about conventional uniformities."[18] Shweder[19] and Haidt[20] correctly point out that such definitions are too secularized and Western, because in many cultures some domains of "conventional uniformity" give rise to moral judgments, emotional reactions, and severe condemnation. Thus, in some Indian communities, a widow eating fish may be condemned, as may be parents refusing to sleep in the same bed with children.

Shweder suggested a universal morality triad of Autonomy (harm, rights, and justice, with violation leading to anger), Community (duty, hierarchy, and interdependency, with violation leading to contempt), and Divinity (natural order, sacred order, sanctity, sin, and pollution, with violation leading to disgust). Haidt[21] proposed a division of morality into five domains: harm/care, fairness/reciprocity, in-group/loyalty, authority/respect, and purity/sanctity. If we use Shweder's and Haidt's divisions, what we observe is that the elements of the triad or the five foundations cannot be regarded as having an equal standing in practice, and some domains are underemphasized or absent in specific belief systems. A hierarchy of moral domains is universal. Whatever concerns some individuals may have about purity, we have reason to assume that they do not lead to the same emotional reactions as concerns about harm and fairness.

Purity rules are also about identity. Thus, food taboos serve as identity markers, which are always tied to self-esteem and superiority.[22] Individuals feel superior to members of their caste who choose not to observe the taboos or sometimes to nonmembers who naturally do not observe them. The arbitrary and sometimes symbolic meaning of food taboos can be illustrated with the case of the Nation of Islam in the United States, which expects its followers to avoid cornbread and okra, because they have been identified for so long with Afro-American culture and the history of slavery. The group seeks to renew Afro-American identity, and the rejection of such foods clearly symbolizes that. In this case we know the circumstances that led to the choice of an object as tabooed. In other cases the historical roots are unknown, but the function as an identity marker is clear.

Shweder and Haidt suggest that disgust is a potent moral emotion, but we must tell parochial from universal revulsions. Humans clearly share a capacity for revulsion, culturally conditioned and activated. Individuals may have their own visceral reactions to homosexuals, gypsies, Jews, Africans, menstruating women, or snails, and cultures may have their own parochial revulsions to dog meat or women with an unmodified clitoris. Ideas about death pollution, specific to one culture, may reflect universal fears about death. But the question is whether violations of death pollution customs are judged in the same way as violations of care and fairness rules.

The idea of purity/sanctity is found only in religious traditions, and norms dealing with group loyalty and respect for authority vary greatly in many cultures and settings, religious or secular. Concerns about autonomy (harm and fairness) are universally most salient and universally accompanied by anger. Contempt and disgust are experienced as less morally powerful than anger.

Preoccupation with purity and pollution varies with some religions, such as Hinduism and Judaism investing much in them, but a distinction between purity rules and concerns about justice is always made. In the Old Testament we find several texts, attributed to mythological prophets, which denounce those who follow their ritual obligations but act unjustly toward the weak and helpless. "To what purpose is the multitude of your sacrifices unto me? saith the Lord. . . . Learn to do well; seek judgment, relieve the oppressed, judge the fatherless, plead for the widow." (Isaiah 1:11, 1:17)

Ancient prophetic texts from West Asia teach us that ritual obligations are secondary to justice because rituals are an expression of duties to the gods and are secondary to our duties to other humans. Sayings attributed to the mythological Jesus reflect what must have been an ongoing discourse millennia ago about the moral primacy of justice over any pollution rules. This discourse about moral hierarchy is still evident among Orthodox Jews, the proud successors to the Pharisees denounced in the New Testament.[23]

In South Asian religions, we find a strong historical tradition of an emphasis on purity and on the relationship of status to purity, together with the same primacy of *Ahimsa*, the prohibition on any violence, in Jainism, Hinduism, and Buddhism. If we look at the Five Precepts that are the basis of Buddhist moral ideals, we find a clear hierarchy. The first precept is to avoid killing or harming living beings. The second is to avoid stealing, the third is to avoid sexual misconduct, the fourth is to avoid lying, and the fifth is to avoid intoxication. The descending order of severity is clear. Intoxication may give rise to both contempt and disgust, but is in itself not as much of a sin as violence.

All cultures recognize the limited validity of parochial revulsion and the universal validity of care/fairness norms. Brown's work[24] on universals in human behavior supports the notion of panhuman moral ideals. He lists among the culture components found everywhere: moral sentiments; right and wrong; murder proscribed; rape proscribed; sexual regulation, including incest prevention; redress of wrongs; tabooed foods; and tabooed utterances. It is clear that controlling aggression is foremost and then controlling sex, as well as justice. Food taboos are universally found, but the specific taboos vary from one culture to another and make no sense to outsiders, whereas rules about violence and incest are easy to understand across cultures.

Hauser[25] proposed a universal moral grammar that constrains human behavior, with such ideals as caring for children and the weak; avoiding killing; avoiding adultery and incest; and rules against cheating, stealing, or lying. Systematic research shows that judgments about welfare and justice are consistent across cultures.[26]

We can expect the irreligious to be concerned only about harm/care and fairness/reciprocity, and this is indeed what Haidt[27] reports. If we follow the Shweder triad, the irreligious will be concerned mostly with autonomy, less with community, and never with divinity. Concerns about harm and fairness are universal indeed, and this is a meeting point between atheists and religionists.[28]

### Has Secularization Corrupted Western Society?

Over the past two centuries, anti-Enlightenment polemicists (and others concerned about what secularization might do to individuals) have been treating us to warnings and laments about the dire consequences of the decline in the authority of religion. We are not surprised to read Hegel's observation: "Reverence for God, or for the gods, establishes and preserves individuals, families, states; while contempt of God, or of the gods, loosens the basis of laws and duties, breaks up the ties of the family and of the State, and leads to their destruction."[29] Herbert Spencer asserted that "the control exercised over men's conduct by theological beliefs and priestly agency has been indispensable,"[30] and Charles Darwin wrote: "A man who has no assured and ever present belief in the existence of a personal God or of future existence with retribution and reward, can have for his rule of life, as far as I can see, only to follow those impulses and instincts which are the strongest or which seem to him the best ones."[31]

In the late 1920s, T. S. Eliot stated: "It is doubtful whether civilization can endure without religion,"[32] and in 1933, it was Adolf Hitler who objected to secular schools, in which no character training is possible without religious instruction.[33] Kristol[34] claimed that nothing could replace religion as the vehicle for moral tradition, and Bork[35] argued: "Belief is probably essential to a civilized future." The psychoanalyst Neville Symington wrote: "What is certain is that religion is the guarantor of civilization and without it we collapse into barbarism."[36] The bioethicist Leon Kass has stated: "Western moral teaching, so closely tied to Scripture, is also in peril if any major part of Scripture can be shown to be false."[37] The political struggle against Enlightenment ideals calls for reversing the historical course of secularization and modernity, and recreating a premodern, idealized, past.

Rothman[38] stated that secularization and the rise of secular humanist elites were behind the historical decline of the United States, as its elite lost the confidence that used to be based on the idea of a "sacred mission" and secularists had undermined the spirit that made capitalism great. According to Davies "respectable Britain" which was in existence till the middle of the twentieth century, was maintained thanks to the church, and to Sunday Schools. What made respectability widespread was not "the minority with a strong faith but the majority with some faith."[39]

Those sounding the alarm on the moral apocalypse have suggested that modern society has not reached the level of anarchy expected in the wake of secularization only because it was using up something described as "moral capital."[40] Referring to unnamed "social critics," this view is expressed as follows: ". . . for well over a hundred fifty years now, social critics have been warning us that bourgeois society was living off the accumulated moral capital of traditional religion and traditional moral philosophy, and that once this capital was depleted, bourgeois society would find its legitimacy ever more questionable."[41] Glazer, a well-known sociologist, assures us that in this case Kristol was speaking for him also, as well as for Daniel Bell, another leading sociologist.

According to Himmelfarb[42] it was already the late Victorians (in the 1880s) who were living off the religious capital of their immediate past. This capital has been considerable, because Himmelfarb[43] claimed that her own contemporaries were still living off the religious capital of previous generations, but that only another Great Awakening could replenish the depleted source of social integration and individual integrity.

This view is shared by Robert K. Bork, who states: "We all know persons without religious belief who nevertheless display all the virtues we associate with religious teaching . . . such people are living on the moral capital of prior religious generations . . . that moral capital will be used up eventually, having nothing to replenish it, and we will see a culture such as the one we are entering."[44] One nice thing about the "moral capital" explanation is that it cannot be disproved. We can look forward to a long future ahead of us, in which this elusive substance is going to sustain morality and decency.

## The "Noble Lie" Tradition

Aristotle, in *Politics*, suggested that autocratic rulers should put on a show of religiosity to exploit popular beliefs about divine reward and punishment. In Plato's plan for an ideal state, the lower classes must believe that the social order had supernatural sanction, being unable to consider it a purely human creation and still regard it as binding. This idea became known as the Noble Lie. Defenders of Plato mention that he also hoped that the upper class would believe that lie for the good of the state. That religion was a fraud designed to keep lawlessness at bay was a notion which was being openly expressed 2,500 years ago in Athens.[45]

The idea that the elite can give up religious illusions, but that the spread of unbelief among the masses would lead to anomie, has been expressed and discussed in modern times. Stewart[46] suggested that the philosopher Leibnitz was a closet atheist, who believed that the masses needed religious belief, but Jean-Jaques Rousseau openly suggested that the basis for public order is the belief in a powerful Divinity, to be enforced by the state.[47]

Himmelfarb[48] praised Victorian agnostics, who were ready to hide their own absence of faith in the interest of maintaining public morality. Sigmund Freud did not hide his atheism, but was among those who thought that the elite does not need external authority, whereas the masses will deteriorate into lawlessness without the promises of divine judgment and retribution.[49]

Describing the educated classes in Europe and the United States in the late nineteenth and the early twentieth century, Leuba stated: "There is among us a large number of well-intentioned persons of influence who go to great length to hide their disbelief. The masses, they think, are not able to live decently without the support provided by the religion they profess."[50] Leuba did not hesitate to name names and denounce those, such as G. Stanley Hall, one of the founding fathers of psychology in the United States, who presented a façade of religiosity for the sake of their public image and the benefit of the masses.

Kristol[51] presented a clear rationale for the Noble Lie. "If God does not exist, and if religion is an illusion that the majority of men cannot live without . . . let men believe in the lies of religion since they cannot do without them, and let then a handful of sages, who know the truth and can live with it, keep it among themselves. Men are then divided into the wise and the foolish, the philosophers and the common men, and atheism becomes a guarded, esoteric doctrine—for if the illusions of religion were to be discredited, there is no telling with what madness men would be seized, with what uncontrollable anguish. It would become the duty of the wise to publicly defend and support religion, even to call the police power to its aid, while reserving the truth for themselves and their chosen disciples."[52]

Leo Strauss, one of the great inspirations to US neo-conservatives, was an atheist, but thought the truth known to the educated elite should not be available to the masses, lest it destroy the social order. He proposed a state religion as a way of creating social cohesion and state control.[53] Similarly, Bork,[54] while claiming that religion is vital for the social order, never said that we should believe the claims of religion because they are true.[55]

One clear answer to the Noble Lie argument has been given by George Santayana: "To be boosted by an illusion is not to live better than to live in harmony with the truth; it is not nearly as safe, not nearly as sweet, and not nearly as fruitful."[56]

## THE ATHEIST DICTATORS CLAIM

Over the past half-century, religionists have enjoyed telling us that the historical secularization experiment has been a failure, most decisively proven by the acts of atheist despots in the twentieth century, such as Adolf Hitler, Joseph Stalin, and Mao Zedong.[57] Looking at the record, it should be noted first that Adolf Hitler was a member in good standing of the Roman Catholic Church until his dying day. His official biography as the Reichskanzler of Germany always reflected this fact. The Third Reich was far from being a secular enterprise, and most Nazi leaders made frequent references to the Christian God in their speeches and writings[58] Most Nazis came from Christian homes (in 1933, 95 percent of Germans were Christians), and in Nazi-occupied Europe, the political forces that supported the occupier were always proreligious. Religious polemicists happily ignore the record of official Roman Catholic collaboration with such dictators as Francisco Franco, Antonio Salazar, Jozef Tiso, and Benito Mussolini.

Away from Europe, Shinto religion did play a major role in the rise and fall of the fascist Japanese empire, Nazism's global ally.[59] Japanese Zen Buddhism, widely considered meditative and pacifist, was actually an enthusiastic supporter of the imperial regime and Japan's war policies.[60]

As to Joseph Stalin, Mao Zedong, Pol Pot, and Kim Il-Sung, they were indeed atheists, but their despotic and cruel acts have been matched by the behavior of thousands of rulers in history who were publicly committed to a variety of religions. One wonders what religionists like D'Souza think of the religious regimes that would happily join them in denouncing atheism, such as those in Iran, Saudi Arabia, or Sudan.

Looking at events over the past thirty years, we can still find plenty of examples of horrors sanctioned to various degrees by religious traditions and establishments. A short list would include Rwanda, Afghanistan, Iran, Serbia, Bosnia, Croatia, and Sri Lanka.[61] In the twenty-first century, it is still possible to find religious dictators, claiming divine authority, who have caused millions of deaths, such as Robert Mugabe.[62]

Ferguson[63] argued that the twentieth century, the "age of hatred," was more violent in both relative and absolute terms than any previous era, but then conceded that it was no worse than other ages. In earlier times, the carnage was not less horrifying. The only significant differences between the horrors of the twentieth century and the horrors committed in earlier times were technological capacity and moral outrage, which were not to be found before the coming of the Enlightenment.

Long before modern genocides, there were religious texts reporting and commanding the total annihilation of some human groups. The Old Testament offers us narratives of the extermination of the Midianites and the Canaanites by the Israelites, as ordered by divine authority (see Numbers 31, 1 Samuel 15). These blood-curdling narratives are totally fictitious, but they reflect very real ideals. They were invented to justify and explain prescribed exclusionary attitudes towards non-Israelites. Those who composed them more than two millennia ago were not worried about anybody being outraged by them. Moore[64] claimed that the readiness to persecute and kill people of different religious and political persuasions in the defense of "moral purity" had its origins in Old Testament monotheism, responsible for some of the most virulent forms of intolerance in history. However, we can easily discover that followers of nonmonotheistic religions are just as committed to lethal intolerance.

Traditional religious morality is ethnocentric, which meant that moral compassion ended at the boundary of the religious community. The celebrated "Love thy neighbour" command in the Old Testament quite explicitly covered only members of the tribe. The original verse states: "Thou shalt not avenge, nor bear any grudge against the children of thy people, but thou shalt love thy neighbor as thyself: I am the Lord" (Leviticus 19:18).

Pre-Enlightenment ideals were always close to pre-Enlightenment practices. The Age of Faith was the age of unchecked human cruelty. The Middle Ages were marked by unimaginable barbarities, including many public displays of sadistic violence presented without apologies but with great pride. Torture was considered just one privileged way of discovering truth. Countless millions died in various crusades against heretics and infidels, whether in Europe or in West Asia. When genocide was carried out in the Middle Ages, moral outrage by witnesses was hard to detect, as such behavior was taken for granted. No medieval intellectuals protested the inhumanity of the Crusades. The European sphere was not unique, and we can assume that untold acts of horrific carnage were taking place on other continents.

The reality of European colonialism, starting in 1492, was one of genocidal cruelty, often sanctioned by religious authorities. Christian missionaries were often part of the colonial enterprise which enslaved whole continents. Secular intellectuals were prominent in the global anticolonialist struggle, promoting the rights of non-Europeans, most visibly in the cases of Algeria, Vietnam, and Palestine. Anticolonialist movements were likely to be made up of the least religious. During the years of United States military intervention in Vietnam (1954–1975), studies showed that those with no religious affiliation were most opposed to the war. In the 1960s' civil rights movement in the United States, most of the white activists involved were unaffiliated or secular, and an inverse relationship was found between religiosity and support for the movement.[65]

The apartheid regime in South Africa (1948–1994) was being led and supported by devout Christians and opposed by atheists. Under apartheid, South Africa did not admit atheists or agnostics as immigrants, despite its desperate efforts to increase the white population. This policy was fully justified, because atheists were indeed likely to oppose government policies.[66] Looking at the Jewish community in apartheid South Africa is instructive, as religiosity again correlated with support for the regime. Jews made up fifty percent of all white activists arrested for their opposition to apartheid, despite constituting only 2 percent of the white South African population. But who were these activists? Just like the case of other whites, religious Jews supported the regime. The activists, who made up most of the white members of the African National Congress, were atheists of Jewish descent.[67]

## THE LESSONS OF HISTORY

One answer to the claim that a Golden Age of morality preceded the coming of secular revolutions was given by Mark Twain in 1889: "There were two 'Reigns of Terror,' if we would but remember it and consider it; the one wrought murder in hot passion, the other in heartless cold blood; the one lasted mere months, the other had lasted a thousand years; the one inflicted death upon ten thousand persons, the other upon a hundred millions; but our shudders are all for the 'horrors' of the minor. . . . A city cemetery could contain the coffins filled by that brief Terror which we have all been so diligently taught to shiver at and mourn over; but all France could hardly contain the coffins filled by that older and real Terror—that unspeakably bitter and awful Terror which none of us has been taught to see in its vastness or pity as it deserves."[68]

Honore de Balzac, writing only 40 years after the Revolution, mentions the well known fact that more people were sacrificed in building the aqueduct of Maintenon, designed to supply water to the Versailles palace, than during the revolutionary Reign of Terror.[69] But what does this have to do with religion?

The monarchy, needless to say, enjoyed the active support of the Church, as all tyrannical regimes of yore were all legitimized in terms of some religious doctrine. A well-known critic has described the historical role of Christianity as follows: "It has been, at all times and everywhere, the steady defender of bad governments, bad laws, bad social theories, bad institutions. It was, for centuries, an apologist for slavery, as it was an apologist for the divine right of kings."[70] Smith reminds us that Christianity should not be singled out, as ". . . religion has rarely been a positive, liberal force. Religion is not nice; it has been responsible for more death and suffering than any other human activity."[71]

About the notion of continuity between religious traditions and current political ideals, the following is the judgment of one historian: "Human rights—roughly the idea that all individuals everywhere are entitled to life, liberty and the pursuit of happiness on this earth—is a relatively modern proposition. Political orators like to trace this idea to religious sources, especially to the so-called Judeo-Christian tradition. In fact the great religious ages were notable for their indifference to human rights in the contemporary sense—not only for their acquiescence in poverty, inequality and oppression, but for their addiction to slavery, torture, wartime atrocities and genocide. Christianity, for example, assigned to earthly misery an honored and indispensable role in the drama of salvation. The trials visited on mankind in this world were conceived as ordained by the Almighty in order to test and train sinful mortals. From the religious perspective, nothing that might take place on earth mattered in comparison to what must take place hereafter. The world was but an inn at which humans spent a night on their voyage to eternity, so what difference could it make if the food was poor or the bed uncomfortable?"[72]

## THE TRANSATLANTIC EXPERIMENT

Over the past two centuries, a great social experiment has been taking place on both sides of the North Atlantic Ocean. On the west side of the Atlantic we find the United States, which leads modern nations on all measures of religious commitment and beliefs, whereas Europe, to the east of the Atlantic leads in secularity. Ninety-five percent of Americans say that they believe in God, and 66 percent believe in the devil. Among holders of graduate degrees, the percentage of those believing in the devil is only 55 percent: "Regardless of political belief, religious inclination, education, or region, most Americans believe that the devil exists."[73] On the more benevolent side of U.S. popular theology, a 2001 poll found that 43 percent of Americans thought pets went to heaven, whereas 40 percent held the opinion that heaven is reserved for humans.[74]

When we compare the United States to other nations with the same level of economic development, whether it is to members of the G8 (eight leading world economies) or OECD (the world's 25 leading economies) or the English-speaking world, it becomes clear that all other countries are significantly more secular. If we order nations by the percentage of nonbelievers, European nations are at the top. Sweden is first, Denmark third, and Norway fourth, followed by the Czech

Republic, Finland, France, Estonia, Germany, Russia, Hungary, Netherlands, Britain, and Belgium.[75] Beyond that, "What makes modern Europe unique is that it is the first and only civilization in which atheism is a fully legitimate option, not an obstacle to any public post."[76]

If religiosity guarantees morality, the United States should be a happy place, brimming with the good and virtuous life, but reality is somewhat different. In 1997, Ralph Reed, executive director of the Christian Coalition, stated that the United States was "the most devoutly religious nation in the entire world. . . . America is a nation undergirded by faith, built by faith, and enlivened by faith. It is not a faith in word alone, but an active, transforming faith. Look around today and what you will see are the fruits of our national faith,"[77] and at the same time Reed lamented: "Social pathologies once imagined only in our darkest nightmares are a daily reality."[78] Reed offers a solution to all social problems, and we can all guess what it is: More religion, of course. Like Dostoyevsky's Father Zossima, he is certain that faith will save the American Way.

Compared to other wealthy nations (per capita GNP over $20,000), the United States has the highest rates of violence and incarceration, as well as other social pathologies such as drug addiction, the highest teen pregnancy rate, and sexually transmitted diseases rates among developed nations. What is also quite prominent in the United States is the absence of social solidarity and compassion. Tens of thousands of American families lose their homes every year because of medical expenses. This is inconceivable in other wealthy nations with universal health care systems.

For many American conservatives, the only thing that stands between them and the immoral welfare state is religion,[79] and religion has indeed played a role in that. If in Old Europe it was the monarchy that enjoyed religious sanction, in the United States it has always been capitalism. Leuba[80] wrote about those in the United States who wanted "to preserve at all cost, for the masses, a religion preaching humility, obedience to established authority, and renouncement of earthly possessions in exchange for the imperishable treasures of heaven." We find an echo of that in the words of the Reverend Henry Ward Beecher, a leading abolitionist, who stated in 1875: "no man in this land suffers from poverty unless it be more than his fault, unless it be his sin."[81] In 1877, Beecher preached against the railroad strikers: "the necessities of the great railroad companies demanded that there be a reduction of wages. . . . It was true that $1 a day was not enough to support a man and five children, if a man would insist on smoking and drinking beer. Was not a dollar a day enough to buy bread? Water costs nothing." Beecher's well-fed congregation reportedly laughed in accord.[82]

A great symbiosis between religion and economic enterprise can be observed in the United States today. Thousands of religious entrepreneurs have made great fortunes by selling salvation to the masses. Little has changed since Sinclair Lewis wrote about Elmer Gantry,[83] except the enormous increase in the sums of money involved. New generations of Gantrys, with names like (Dr.) Kreflo A. Dollar, have taken over the mantle.[84]

When all the world's nations are ranked on measures of the quality of life, happiness, and longevity, we find at the top of the list more or less the same names. On the World Map Of Happiness, produced recently, the 10 happiest nations in the world are Denmark, Switzerland, Austria, Iceland, The Bahamas, Finland, Sweden, Bhutan, Brunei, and Canada. East Asia is another region where we can observe the connection between public morals and secularity. Japan and South Korea present a European-like picture of low religiosity, low levels of violence, and much solidarity. Japan holds the world's average life expectancy record. The most secularized nations demonstrate a high level of solidarity and have crime rates that are a fraction of that in the United States. They show no signs of moral anarchy, but some signs of contentment.[85]

## FINDINGS ON RELIGION AND INDIVIDUAL MORALITY

The claim that religion supports impulse control is one of the most common made in its defense, and it has been investigated over the past century, with some interesting results.

### Exemplary Moral Behavior and Moral Rehabilitation

Those extolling the moral benefits of religion can justifiably point to such cases of moral commitment as Roman Catholic nuns, and members of other religions, taking care of terminal patients or the severely retarded; many religious individuals helping the unfortunate all over the world and showing great humanity; and religious pacifists ready to be imprisoned, or die, for their moral objection to war.[86]

Another phenomenon which is almost uniquely religious is that of a dramatic moral transformation in individuals and communities, produced by a religious conversion or revival. The case of the Handsome Lake religion among the Seneca is one dramatic example of moral revitalization.[87] We can point to inspiring cases of converts saved from a life of crime and drug dependence, but although dramatic cases may be found, overall efficacy with criminals and addicts remains to be proven.

On the other side of the ledger, one can point to horrific acts committed with religious sanction. Saradijan and Nobus[88] found religious beliefs held by the clergy offenders removed inhibitions and were instrumental in facilitating offending behavior against children.

Whether it is religious professionals who abuse their power over the helpless and the gullible[89] or genital mutilation and lethal, motivated, medical neglect, helpless children suffer under various religious commandments. Asser and Swan[90] reported on child fatalities caused by medical neglect in twenty-three U.S. religious groups, led by Christian Science, the Church of the First Born, and the Faith Assembly. Cases of death caused by exorcism are still reported in the world media.

## Tolerance and Prejudice

Research on prejudice and intolerance has consistently shown that being more religious was correlated with more prejudice, authoritarianism, intolerance, and punitive attitudes (supporting harsh penalties, including death). In one classical study, the findings were summarized as follows: "it appears that those who reject religion have less ethnocentrism that those who seem to accept it."[91] The prevalence of religious prejudice has been interpreted to show that the moral obligations owed coreligionists do not extend to outsiders.[92] We know that the terror of death, a common religious theme, increases social conformity.[93]

What is socially and politically significant is that a strong religious commitment may interfere with a commitment to religious freedom, as the concern of group members for their own rights does not extend to the rights of others and of other groups.

## Prosocial Behavior

What are the predictors of compassion, altruism, honesty, and readiness to help? Do religious people feel more empathy towards their fellow men and are more likely to provide help to a person in need? According to Duriez,[94] the answer is no.

When college students in the United States were given a chance to cheat and to perform an act of helping, there was no correlation between their eventual behavior and their religiosity level.[95] On the other hand, it has been found that for adults in the United States religiosity was inversely related to a predisposition to cheat on taxes. Findings over many years in the United States indicate that religiosity does predict more generous donations to charity and doing volunteer work with the needy.[96]

Darley and Batson[97] wanted to test whether the parable of the Good Samaritan, taken from the New Testament and presented as a model of true altruism, would affect helping behavior. Christian seminary students, who had just read the parable, some of whom were supposed to give a talk about it, were put in a situation where that could help someone in apparent distress. After meeting the experimenter and being asked to help, they ran across a man who was clearly incapacitated. The results showed that the parable of the Good Samaritan had no effect on the students' readiness to help.

What happens in situation where altruism is literally hazardous to one's life? Oliner and Oliner[98] studied the truly heroic behavior of individuals who saved the lives of Jews in Europe during the Holocaust, but reported that religiosity had no effect in these cases. Varese and Yaish[99] found that "religiosity and altruism are negatively related; the less religious one is, the more likely she is to rescue. A plausible explanation for this negative effect is that a very religious person might be more receptive to anti-Semitism." It seems that the net contribution of religion in the Holocaust in terms of altruism was negative.[100]

## Hedonistic Offenses

Research has consistently shown the effects of religiosity on "sinful" behaviors such as gambling, extramarital intercourse, and illicit drug use. When it comes to psychoactive substances, which are tied to the experience of pleasure and loss of control, religiosity predicts less use, less abuse, and less dependence.

## Serious Crime

Studies in different countries found that some measures of religiosity are negatively correlated with deviance of all kinds. For adolescents who are at risk because of poverty and family history, ritual attendance is a protective factor, reducing the probability of delinquency, drug use, and later maladjustment. Religious commitment reduces delinquency when church membership is the norm, but not where is it unusual. Large-scale surveys of adults find that a wider range of offenses and deviance is affected, including rape and other crimes of violence.[101] However, religiosity appeared to serve as a weaker deterrent on serious crimes such as murder and theft. Jensen[102] found that homicide rates were higher in nations where beliefs in a God and the devil were prevalent, such as the United States.

## EXPLAINING THE EVOLUTION OF RELIGION AND MORALITY

One way of looking at the religion–morality connection has been through the evolutionary lens, with attempts to demonstrate that religion does have evolutionary roots or evolutionary value because of its potential contribution to individual and social integration. Although a variety of psychological explanations have been offered for the evolution of religion over the past three centuries,[103] recent theorizing has focused on brain architecture and universal cognitive mechanisms to account for religious ideas. Although these basic cognitive mechanisms are held to be adaptive, religion itself has been considered a cognitive error, an appendage to more necessary psychological processes.[104]

If this is the case, then religion has survived without being adaptive and without offering believers any real advantage. This seems to be the dominant view among those who have developed evolutionary explanations of religion.

Other researchers hold to a evolutionary logic which assumes that religion could not have survived so successfully among humans without making a real contribution to adaptation, and what could be that contribution if not the presumed privileged connection with morality. In the behavioral sciences today, assertions about the vital role of religion in the survival of the social order are part of a wider discourse of psychological pragmatism. Benton Johnson expressed this view in the following way: "Although religious ideas are not true, there is much in religion that is good."[105] And so the question becomes "Is a belief in the world of the spirits good for you? Is it good even though it is not true? Does it have positive consequences?"

We can find hundreds of books and articles, published over the past few decades, most often in the United States, telling us that religion is a "resource for well being," and specifically for "prevention, healing and empowerment."[106] In other publications, religion is assessed in terms of "costs and benefits."[107] As revelation lost its authority, these arguments emphasize positive consequences of collective and individual religious commitments, rather than assert the truth and authority of a particular religious message.[108] In this instrumentalist line of defense, the references are always to a generic "religion" or "faith," reflecting the reality of secularization. When those seeking a desecularization of culture talk about "faith," they are careful to use the most generic and nebulous language, speaking out of clear weakness.

Claims about religion's role in adaptive individual and social behavior have been made recently by psychologists, anthropologists, and sociologists. Alcorta and Sosis,[109] Bering,[110] Norenzayan and Shariff,[111] and Rossano[112] are among those who suggested that religions facilitate costly prosocial behaviors, primarily where reputational concerns are heightened. One thing religions do is to promote the idea of ever-vigilant spiritual monitors. Believing that the spirits were always watching may have helped reduce the number of noncooperators in human groups. One hypothesis is that the evolution of cooperation could not have proceeded without the support of religious ideas.[113] McCullough and Willoughby[114] present findings relating religiosity to various measures of self-control. They then suggest that religion may have evolved because of its ability to help people exercise self-control. The explicit notion is that the connection between religion and prosociality had evolutionary value in the past and has social value at present.

Several interesting experiments, which measured the behavioral effects of introducing religious ideas into one's consciousness without awareness, have been carried out. Randolph-Seng and Nielsen[115] found that participants who were primed with religious words cheated significantly less than participants who were primed with neutral words. Conscious priming demonstrated a greater effect than the nonconscious priming.

Shariff and Norenzayan[116] reported that priming with religious concepts promoted cooperative behaviors, regardless of personal religiosity. However, similar effects were found when the stimulus words were "jury," "contract," or "police." Randolph-Seng and Nielsen[117] suggested that the Shariff and Norenzayan[118] experiment was flawed because respondents were probably conscious and the religious priming effects were general. When presented with the word "God," respondents, whether believers or not, were responding to the cultural association, just as they did with the word "police." These findings clearly show that religious stimuli do affect behavior even in a secularized culture, but these findings also demonstrate that secular impulse control stimuli, such as "police" or "jury" had the same effect as "God." Historically speaking, the transition from the religious to secular control seems easy, smooth, and well established, despite the powerful legacy of historical religions.

## EXPLAINING THE EVOLUTION OF MORALITY

Over the past five decades, evolutionary researchers have explored the phylogenesis of cooperation, because the phenomenon of altruism initially seemed like a problem for evolutionary theory. What is universally agreed now is that cooperation is a fundamental aspect of all biological systems[119] and there are clear biological imperatives that push organisms to coordinate their activities with those of conspecifics. Cooperation based on reciprocity makes sense for all organisms, from bacteria to primates.[120] Impulse control, and a balance between cooperation and competition, are crucial for individual and species survival. Restraints on individual behavior are necessary for social life and have been naturally selected because of their survival value.[121] The biological forces directing organisms towards cooperation have been in existence long before the appearance of *Homo sapiens*. Pylogenetically, religions cannot be the real source of any moral codes but, at most, social enforcers of evolved moral responses in some cultures, taking on this role in quite recent times.

These conceptions of human evolution are supported by a variety of findings and simulations, and so it is not surprising that more researchers have reached the conclusion that religion is not in any way vital for the maintenance of morality, but may define its (narrow) scope within a particular culture.[122]

Similarly, Bocock[123] acquits religion of any responsibility for human cruelty, because hatred and aggression are innate, and humans learn to direct them as socially prescribed targets. Thus, religion cannot be blamed for an emotion that predates its appearance in the lives of individuals and collectivities. Both religions and nationalisms merely prescribe socially conventional ways of expressing hate.

It seems that evolutionary thinking has not provided the hoped-for support for ideas about the privileged religion–morality connection. If humans are hardwired to cooperate because of particular phylogenetic forces and then also hardwired to develop religious beliefs, because of a separate set of particular phylogenetic forces, then we see two separate and powerful phenomena, which can be combined in history and culture, but in not in evolutionary time, going far into the past to the earliest of humanity.

Looking at the historical record, we do find circumstantial evidence for a cultural–structural connection. Stark[124] found that religion sustains the moral order only when it is based on belief in powerful and morally concerned gods, but in some highly developed societies, the religious basis for morality is missing. Moralizing religion, like the wheel or farming, may be a cultural invention, and moralizing gods appear in large, differentiated groups where religious elites control many resources.[125]

## ONTOGENESIS OF MORALITY

How should we think about the genesis of the internal moral calculator, or the "moral faculty," in any given individual? Children are made into moral agents quite early on in their lives, through socialization and social control mechanisms, as they are assigned blame and learn to blame others and especially themselves. Whatever we call morality is tied to powerful bonds developed between children and caretakers. The panhuman experience is that parents are the carriers of morality, as they convey to their children a fantasy of a world ordered into right and wrong, reward and punishment.

Socialization in all cultures focuses first on impulse control and then on competition–cooperation skills. Ethical reasoning everywhere involves the capacity to transcend self-interest.[126] Morality is an abstraction, while discipline and impulse control are what children and parents experience in all cultures. The universal early experience of every human includes a total dependency on other humans, who create an internalized system of impulse control, as well as heightened sensitivity to external impulse control systems. Parents everywhere teach their children compassion, responsibility, and honesty, values that are promoted via exemplary models. They limit aggression and reinforce altruistic acts among their children.[127] The young are asked to reduce their egocentrism and impulsivity in return for parental love. Erikson[128] stated that "the internalization of the parental voice" creates what he calls "the judicial" in human life and culture.

All cultures have the same ideal of impulse control. Self-control is the master virtue, because it overcomes selfish and antisocial impulses for the sake of what is best for the group.[129] This universal ideal is that of controlling one's body, because maturity equals the ability to set limits on the gratification of physical needs. The newborn baby is pure body and as such is the enemy of culture and society. Its body has to be conquered externally and internally. The ideal we convey to our children is that of rising above bodily needs, conquering the weaknesses of hunger, elimination, disease, sex, and death. Pain, hunger, and desire are experienced as ego-dystonic invaders, which we learn to resist. Surrendering to the body in pleasure or in pain and disease is experienced as a failure, as nature wins over culture and our conscious will. Victory over the body is achieved in asceticism, fasting, celibacy, or athletic feats. Victory over our own body equals victory of spirit and culture over nature in the most direct and decisive way. Both secular and religious individuals share a universal guilt complex in cases of surrender to the body and its weakness. Ontogenetically, the earliest moral intuitions precede any learning about supernatural agents and are unrelated to beliefs about them. Universal socialization towards self-control precedes the use of religious ideation.

Giving up our egocentric perspective is the starting point for sympathy and concern, leading to responses in terms of justice and fairness. Innate empathic arousal and internalized empathy are the motivating force behind moral orientation.[130] Jean Piaget, who pioneered moral development theory, believed that basic discipline is learned from parents, but the ethic of cooperation and justice is learned in interaction with peers.[131] Lawrence Kohlberg thought that justice-based moral reasoning develops out of perspective-taking abilities developed in social interaction.[132]

## THE NEW PUBLIC MORALITY

The disappearance of religious justification for the social order has not brought about the disintegration of society. The secularization of moral discourse has not reduced human kindness. Just the opposite is true. Secularization means that we no longer interpret misfortune as caused by supernatural agents angry at human sins. We cope with natural disasters and disease without tying them to any imaginary moral calculus. What can be and is condemned is human immorality. The Enlightenment means that humans have come to think of injustice and of many forms of suffering as social arrangements, under human consideration. The new public morality means a change from an emphasis on the idea of individual sin to concern about collective injustice and individual rights. It also means that rules may be discussed in the context of power in interpersonal relationships.

Historically, kinship has been the foundation of social solidarity. The Enlightenment morality transcends kin, tribe, and nation. "In the course of human cultural development there has been a gradual though faltering progression toward enlarging the area brought within a single ethical system. The logical (and undoubtedly necessary) end of such an evolutionary process is the establishment of a world community and the permanent elimination of borders that limit the application of basic ethical codes."[133]

The Enlightenment has led to a new, totally secular, public discourse about morality, focusing on justice, rights, equality, and human welfare, and dealing with impulse control as an individual problem. Enlightenment ideals have been translated into the language of human rights, civil liberties, women's rights, children's rights, the right to education and health, national self-determination, and the rights of workers. This language of rights, which today seems natural and familiar, has been created in a secular context, by secular individuals. We know now how many of these ideas have been considered radical and revolutionary when first proposed and are now universally preached, if not practiced.

This sea change in our moral outlook is evident in the Universal Declaration of Human Rights (UNUDHR), adopted by the United Nations on December 10, 1948. This document is both a declaration of the triumph of the Enlightenment and a political program for future action, which is bent on tearing down traditional human divisions. Public declarations are significant, even though we often find them hypocritical. We have to recall that, three hundred years ago, those committed to equality and human rights could not express their views publicly very often.

The new universal morality has led to new forms of global humanitarian action, in such secular groups as Amnesty International (winner of the Nobel Peace Prize in 1977) and Médecins sans Frontières (MSF, winner of the Nobel Peace Prize in 1999), Human Rights Watch, and Greenpeace. Bernard Kouchner, the founder of MSF, can serve as a leading exemplar of the new atheist, humanitarian, morality.[134] It is important to note that the Red Cross (winner of the Nobel Peace Prize in 1917, 1944, and 1963), despite the religious associations of its emblem, was founded in 1863 by Henri Dunant, a militant secularist.

One significant element of the new public morality is its support of religious freedom and tolerance. As has often been observed, religionists are rather intolerant, but the irreligious are likely to defend the rights of religionists. As one observer put it, "Atheism is a European legacy worth fighting for, not least because it creates a safe public space for believers."[135]

We find a rather unexpected view of religion and morality coming from the 14th Dalai Lama, widely revered in the United States as a spokesman for religion, and sometimes even on "religion and science." To the surprise of many among his admirers, it turns out that he does not believe that we need any religion to serve as the source of ethics: "Rather, I am speaking of what I call 'secular ethics,' which embrace the principles we share as human beings: compassion, tolerance, consideration of others, the responsible use of knowledge and power."[136] This statement is another recognition of the historical victory of the Enlightenment and the new public morality.

### Should You Trust an Atheist?

Are atheists more likely to be involved in criminality or deviance? Ever since the field of criminology got started and data were collected of the religious affiliation of criminal offenders, the fact that the unaffiliated and the nonreligious had the lowest crime rates has been noted.[137] According to von Hentig,[138] having no religious affiliation is the best predictor of law-abiding behavior. There is no reason to doubt the validity of this generalization today. We know very well that the prisons are not filled with atheists, and as Bayle noted in the seventeenth century, there are rarely among those punished for capital crimes.

Looking at modern culture, we know quite well that secular public servants could be trusted with our tax money and will be more devoted to the public interest. Transparency International is an organization devoted to monitoring levels of corruption in the world's nations. When the world's nations were ranked from the least to most corrupt in 2008, at the top we find the usual suspects: Denmark, New Zealand, Sweden, Singapore, Finland, Iceland, the Netherlands, Australia, and Canada. It turns out that there is a clear correlation between low religiosity and low corruption.

Could we or should we expect atheists to be morally superior in any way? One answer to that is to embrace the null hypothesis, which denies any relevance of religious commitment to the reality of everyday life. One leading atheist proves that modesty is another virtue of the faithless when she states, "You can't accurately claim that atheists are particularly virtuous or intelligent or even courageous."[139] Atheists may be immoral or moral, but this has little to do with their absence of supernaturalism and more to do with general factors common to them and the rest of humanity.

However, what we hear sometimes, explicitly or implicitly, is that atheists are somehow deficient in their qualifications for public office or social life, because of a lack of moral energy or moral harmony.[140] The claim that atheists are somehow likely to be immoral or dishonest has long been disproved. No one has seriously claimed, by way of presenting historical or statistical data, that atheists or agnostics are more likely to commit immoral acts (with the exception of the "atheist dictators" argument presented above). Although any given atheist may be no better or worse than a next door neighbor, probabilities are that the atheist neighbor is also better educated, which in turn is tied to other positive attributes. Lifelong atheists have been found to be well-socialized, law-abiding, and nonviolent. They are also likely to be less prejudiced and more tolerant than religious individuals.[141]

It has become clear by now that secularization has not created the moral equivalent of the mythological Sodom. We know that secular morality is possible, because we can observe it in action every single day all over the globe.[142] What we have found is that under certain social-historical circumstances, religion is the main source of legitimacy for social order in some societies,[143] but secular legitimation is possible. What is clear is that we can be pro-social without being religious, and that the secular system of social control is just as effective (or ineffective) as the religious one.

If, according to McCullough and Willougby[144] and to Norenzayan and Shariff[145] religion is tied to self-control and to prosocial behavior, what does it imply for those lower in religiosity? If indeed it is claimed that atheists are different in terms of moral behavior, then we must ask for a specification and a detailed description of the psychological processes involved. If the normal process is that which takes place in a religious family, and such families may still represent the global majority, what would the irregular cases in the minority look like?

Growing up in an atheist family means developing inner controls, because those are always internalized because of the parental teaching of self-control. The internalized voice is found in all children because of the interaction between parents and children, regardless of the religious environment surrounding any given family. Atheists obviously go through blaming themselves, and others, and feel guilty. They have gotten all that from their evolved brain architecture and early experience, without the help of any functional religious illusions.

Any claims about the positive contributions of all and any religions to morality and prosocial behavior, either prehistorically or now, has to account for the behavior of atheists and the reality of global secularization. The assumption of a direct connection between one's moral faculty and one's religiosity or religion is challenged by atheists, a growing segment of humanity.

The author thanks Gabriel Bar-Haim, Barry D. Berger, Harvey Chisick, Menachem Kellner, and Richard Schuster for their important help in the preparation of this chapter.

## NOTES

1. A. Powell, *Athens and Sparta: Constructing Greek Political and Social History from 478 BC* (London: Routledge, 2001).

2. R. N. Bellah, *The Broken Covenant* (New York: The Seabury Press, 1975), ix; F. Ferraroti, "The Destiny of Reason and the Paradox of the Sacred," *Social Research* 46 (1975): 648–681.

3. R. A. Rappaport, "Ritual, Sanctity and Cybernetics," *American Anthropologist* 73 (1971): 72.

4. J. Locke, *A Letter Concerning Toleration* (Indianapolis: Hackett Publishing, 1689/1983), 51.

5. E. Labrousse, *Bayle* (Oxford: Oxford University Press, 1983).

6. S. Jenkinson, *Bayle: Political Writings* (New York: Cambridge University Press, 2000), 317.

7. R. H. Horwitz, *The Moral Foundations of the American Republic* (Charlottesville, VA: University of Virginia Press (1986), 213.

8. S. Law, *The War for Children's Minds* (London: Routledge, 2006).

9. Quoted in F. Manuel, *The Changing of the Gods* (London: University Press of New England, 1983), 66.

10. M. B. Borg, "The Problem of Nihilism," *Sociological Analysis* 49 (1988): 6.

11. F. Dostoyevsky, *The Brothers Karamazov* (New York: Penguin Group, 1880/1999), 557.

12. Ibid., 305.

13. W. James, *The Will to Believe* (New York: Dover Publications, 1897/1956), 211, 213.

14. S. T. Joshi, *God's Defenders: What They Believe and Why They are Wrong* (Amherst, NY: Prometheus Books, 2003).

15. T. Parsons, "Religious Perspectives in Sociology and Social Psychology," in *Reader in Comparative Religion: An Anthropological Approach*, ed. W. Lessa and E. Vogt (New York: Harper and Row, 1952/1979), 63.

16. P. Edgell, J. Gerteis, and D. Hartmann, "Atheists as 'Other': Moral Boundaries and Cultural, Membership in American Society," *American Sociological Review* 71 (2006): 211–234.

17. E. Turiel, *The Development of Social Knowledge: Morality and Convention* (New York: Cambridge University Press, 1983), 3.

18. E. Turiel and K. Neff, "Religion, Culture and Beliefs about Reality in Moral Reasoning," in *Imagining the Impossible: Magical Scientific, and Religious Thinking in Children*, ed. K. S. Rosengren, C. N. Johnson, and P. L. Harris (New York: Cambridge University Press, 2000), 279; M. Keller, "The Development of Obligations and Responsibilities in Cultural Context," in *Norms in Human Development*, ed. L. Smith and J. Vonèche (Cambridge: Cambridge University Press, 2006), 169–188.

19. R. A. Shweder, N. C. Much, M. Mahapatra, and L. Park, "The 'Big Three' of Morality (Autonomy, Community, Divinity) and the 'Big Three' of Suffering," in *Morality and Health*, A. Brandt and P. Rozin, eds. (New York: Routledge, 1997), 119–169.

20. J. Haidt, "The New Synthesis in Moral Psychology," *Science* 316 (2007): 998–1002.

21. Ibid.

22. H. Tajfel and J. C. Turner, "The Social Identity Theory of Intergroup Behavior," in *Psychology of Intergroup Relations*, ed. S. Worchel and W. Austin (Chicago: Nelson-Hall, 1986), 7–24.

23. I. Etkes, *Rabbi Israel Salanter and the Mussar Movement* (Philadelphia: Jewish Publications Society, 1993).

24. D. E. Brown, *Human Universals* (New York: McGraw-Hill, 1991).

25. M. D. Hauser, *Moral Minds: How Nature Designed Our Universal Sense of Right and Wrong.* (New York: HarperCollins, 2006).

26. Ibid.; E. Turiel, *The Culture of Morality: Social Development, Context, and Conflict* (Cambridge, England: Cambridge University Press, 2002).

27. J. Haidt, "The New Synthesis."

28. Hauser, *Moral Minds.*

29. G. W. F. Hegel, *Lectures on the Philosophy of Religion* (London: Routledge & Kegan Paul, 1832/1962), 103.

30. J. Offer, ed., *Herbert Spencer: Political Writings* (Cambridge: Cambridge University Press, 1994), 93.

31. C. Darwin, *The Autobiography of Charles Darwin* (New York: Totem Books, 1887/2004), 94.

32. E. Wilson, *Axel's Castle: A Study in the Imaginative Literature of 1870–1930* (New York: Charles Scribner's Sons, 1931), 125.

33. Law, *The War for Children's Minds.*

34. I. Kristol, *Two Cheers for Capitalism* (New York: The Free Press, 1978).

35. R. H. Bork, *Slouching towards Gomorrah: Modern Liberalism and American Decline* (New York: Regan Books, 1997), 295.

36. N. Symington, "Religion: The Guarantor of Civilization," in *Psychoanalysis and Religion in the 21st Century: Competitors or Collaborators?* ed. D. M. Black (London: Routledge, 2006), 200.

37. Quoted in P. R. Ehrlich, *Human Natures: Genes, Cultures and the Human Prospect* (Washington, D.C.: Island Press, 2000), 430.

38. S. Rothman, "The Decline of Bourgeois America," *Society* 33 (1996): 147–201.

39. C. Davies, *The Strange Death of Moral Britain* (Edison, NJ: Transaction Publishers, 2006), 50.

40. I. Kristol, *Two Cheers for Capitalism.*

41. I. Kristol quoted in N. Glazer, "Neoconservative from the Start," *The Public Interest* (Spring 2005): 12–18.

42. G. Himmelfarb, *Poverty and Compassion: The Moral Imagination of the Late Victorians* (New York: Knopf, 1991).

43. G. Himmelfarb, *One Nation, Two Cultures: A Searching Examination of American Society in the Aftermath of Our Cultural Revolution* (New York: Knopf, 1999).

44. Quoted in J. H. Toner, *Morals under the Gun* (Lexington, KY: University Press of Kentucky, 2000), 74.

45. Powell, *Athens and Sparta.*

46. M. Stewart, *The Courtier and the Heretic: Leibnitz, Spinoza, and the Fate of God in the Modern World* (New York: W. W. Norton, 2006).

47. A. Dacey, *The Secular Conscience: Why Belief Belongs in Public Life* (Amherst, NY: Prometheus Books, 2008).

48. G. Himmelfarb, *Darwin and the Darwinian Revolution* (New York: W. W. Norton, 1959).

49. P. Rieff, *Freud, The Mind of the Moralist* (Chicago: University of Chicago Press, 1959).

50. J. H. Leuba, "The Making of a Psychologist of Religion," in *Religion in Transition*, ed. V. Ferm (New York: Macmillan, 1937), 198.

51. I. Kristol, "God and the Psychoanalysts: Can Freud and Religion be Reconciled?" *Commentary* 8 (1949): 443.

52. I. Kristol, *Two Cheers for Capitalism*; I. Kristol, *Neoconservatism: The Autobiography of an Idea* (New York: The Free Press, 1995).

53. S. B. Drury, *Leo Strauss and the American Right* (London: Palgrave Macmillan, 1999); S. B. Drury, *The Political Ideas of Leo Strauss* (London: Palgrave Macmillan, 2005).

54. Bork, *Slouching towards Gomorrah*.

55. P. R. Ehrlich, *Human Natures*.

56. G. Santayana, *Character and Opinion in the U.S.* (New York: Anchor, 1956), 53.

57. D. D'Souza, "Atheism, Not Religion, is the Real Force behind the Mass Murders of History," *Christian Science Monitor* (November 22, 2006): A4.

58. O. Bartov and P. Mack, eds., *In God's Name: Genocide and Religion in the Twentieth Century* (Oxford and New York: Berghahn Books, 2001); G. Lewy, *The Catholic Church and Nazi Germany* (New York: McGraw-Hill, 1964); R. Steigmann-Gall, *The Holy Reich: Nazi Conceptions of Christianity, 1919–1945* (New York: Cambridge University Press, 2003).

59. H. Hardacre, *Shinto and the State, 1868–1988* (Princeton: Princeton University Press, 1991).

60. B. Victoria, *Zen at War* (Lanham, MD: Rowman and Littlefield, 2006).

61. O. Bartov and P. Mack, eds. *In God's Name: Genocide and Religion in the Twentieth Century* (Oxford and New York: Berghahn Books, 2001).

62. D. Morris, "Commentary, Mugabe Plays the God Card" *The Globe and Mail* (June 27, 2008): A13.

63. N. Ferguson, *The War of the World: History's Age of Hatred* (London: Allen Lane, 2006).

64. B. Moore, Jr., *Moral Purity and Persecution in History* (Princeton: Princeton University Press, 2000).

65. B. Beit-Hallahmi and M. Argyle, *The Psychology of Religious Behavior, Belief and Experience* (London: Routledge, 1997).

66. R. Buis, *Religious Beliefs and White Prejudice* (Johannesburg: Raven Press) 1975.

67. G. Shimoni, *Commentary and Conscience: The Jews in Apartheid South Africa* (Waltham, MA: Brandeis University Press, 2003).

68. M. Twain, *A Connecticut Yankee in King Arthur's Court* (Berkeley: University of California Press, 1889/1983), 72.

69. A. Hassall, *Louis the XIV and the Zenith of the French Monarchy* (New York: G. P. Putnam's Sons, 1895).

70. H. L. Mencken, *Treatise on the Gods* (New York: Knopf, 1930), 305–306.

71. J. Z. Smith, *Imagining Religion* (Chicago: University of Chicago Press, 1982), 110.

72. A. M. Schlesinger, Jr. "Human Rights and the American Tradition," *Foreign Affairs* 57 (1978): 503; A. A. An-Na'im, J. D. Gort, H. Jansen and H. Vroom, eds., *Human Rights and Religious Values: An Uneasy Relationship?* (Amsterdam/Grand Rapids: Rodopi/Eerdmans, 1995).

73. C. H. Partridge, *The Re-enchantment of the West: Alternative Spiritualities, Sacralization, Popular Culture, and Occulture* (New York: Continuum International Publishing Group, 2006), 240.

74. R. Morin, "Voters: Take a Chill Pill," *The Washington Post* (October 10, 2004): B05.

75. P. Zuckerman, *Society without God: What the Least Religious Nations Can Tell Us about Contentment* (New York: New York University Press, 2008).

76. S. Zizek, "Defenders of the Faith," *New York Times* (March 12, 2006): A23.

77. R. Reed, "Democracy and Religion are not Compatible," *USA Today* (July 1, 1997): 27.

78. Ibid., 28.

79. Himmelfarb, *Poverty and Compassion*; Himmelfarb, *The De-moralization of Society* (New York: Knopf, 1994).

80. Leuba, "The Making of a Psychologist of Religion," 197.

81. W. G. McLoughlin, *The Meaning of Henry Ward Beecher: An Essay on the Shifting Values of Mid-Victorian America. 1840–1870* (New York: Knopf, 1970), 150.

82. Ibid., 98–99.

83. S. Lewis, *Elmer Gantry* (New York: Harcourt, 1927).

84. L. Martz and G. Carroll, *Ministry of Greed: The Inside Story of the Televangelists and Their Holy War* (New York: Weidenfeld and Nicolson, 1988).

85. P. Zuckerman, "Atheism: Contemporary Rates and Patterns," in *The Cambridge Companion to Atheism*, ed. M. Martin (New York: Cambridge University Press, 2007).

86. A. Colby and W. Damon, *Some Do Care: Contemporary Lives of Moral Commitment* (New York: Free Press, 1992); M. K. Matsuba and L. J. Walker, "Extraordinary Moral Commitment: Young Adults Involved in Social Organizations," *Journal of Personality* 72 (2004): 413–436.

87. A. F. C. Wallace, *The Death and Rebirth of the Seneca* (New York: Alfred A. Knopf, 1970).

88. A. Saradijan and D. Nobus, "Cognitive Distortions of Religious Professionals Who Sexually Abuse Children," *Journal of Interpersonal Violence* 18 (2003): 905–923.

89. W. Rodarmor, "The Secret Life of Swami Muktananda," *Coevolution Quarterly* 40 (1983): 104–11; M. Neilsen, "Appalling Acts in God's Name," *Society* (March/April 2003): 16–19.

90. S. M. Asser and R. Swain, "Child Fatalities from Religion-Motivated Medical Neglect," *Pediatrics* 101 (1998): 625–629.

91. T. W. Adorno, E. Frenkel-Brunswik, D. J. Levinson, and R. N. Sanford, *The Authoritarian Personality* (New York: Harper & Row, 1950), 213.

92. B. Beit-Hallahmi and M. Argyle, *The Psychology of Religious Behavior, Belief and Experience* (London: Routledge, 1997).

93. J. Greenberg, S. Solomon, and T. Pyszfynski, "Terror Management Theory of Self Esteem and Cultural Worldviews: Empirical Assessments and Conceptual Refinements," in *Advances in Experimental Social Psychology*, ed. M. P. Zanna (San Diego, CA: Academic Press, 1997).

94. B. Duriez, "Taking a Closer Look at the Religion-Empathy Relationship: Are Religious People Nicer People?" *Mental Health, Religion & Culture* 7 (2004): 249–254.

95. Beit-Hallahmi and Argyle, *The Psychology of Religious Behavior*.

96. A. C. Brooks, *Who Really Cares; The Surprising Truth about Compassionate Conservatism: America's Charity Divide—Who Gives, Who Doesn't, and Why It Matters* (New York: Basic Books, 2006).

97. J. Darley and C. D. Batson, "From Jerusalem to Jericho: A Study of Situational and Dispositional Variables in Helping Behavior." *Journal of Personality and Social Psychology* 27 (1973): 100–108.

98. S. P. Oliner and P. M. Oliner, *The Altruistic Personality: Rescuers of Jews in Nazi Europe* (New York: Free Press, 1988).

99. F. Varese and M. Yaish, "The Importance of Being Asked. The Rescue of Jews in Nazi Europe," *Rationality and Society* 12 (2000): 320.

100. E. Fogelman, *Conscience and Courage: Rescuers of Jews during the Holocaust* (New York: Anchor Books, 1994).

101. W. S. Bainbridge, "The Religious Ecology of Deviance," *American Sociological Review* 54 (1989): 288–295.

102. G. F. Jensen, "Religious Cosmologies and Homicide Rates among Nations," *The Journal of Religion and Society* 8 (2006): 1–13.

103. B. Beit-Hallahmi, *Prolegomena to the Psychological Study of Religion* (Lewisburg, PA: Bucknell University Press, 1989); Beit-Hallahmi and Argyle, *The Psychology of Religious Behavior*.

104. S. Atran, *In Gods We Trust: The Evolutionary Landscape of Religion* (New York: Oxford University Press, 2002); P. Boyer, *Religion Explained* (New York: Basic Books, 2001); S. Guthrie, *Faces in the Clouds* (Oxford: Oxford University Press, 1993).

105. B. Johnson, "Sociological Theory and Religious Truth," *Sociological Analysis* 38 (1977): 368–388.

106. For example, K. I. Maton and B. Wells, "Religion as a Resource for Well-being: Prevention, Healing and Empowerment Pathways," *Journal of Social Issues* 51 (1988): 177–193.

107. For example, K. I. Pargament, "The Bitter and the Sweet: An Evaluation of the Costs and Benefits of Religiousness," *Psychological Inquiry* 13 (2002): 168–181.

108. R. Stark and C. Y. Glock, "Will Ethics Be the Death of Christianity?" *Transaction* 5 (1968): 7–14.

109. C. Alcorta and R. Sosis, "Ritual, Emotion and Sacred Symbols: The Evolution of Religion as an Adaptive Complex," *Human Nature* 16 (2005): 323–359.

110. J. M. Bering, "The Folk Psychology of Souls," *Behavioral and Brain Sciences* 29 (2006): 453–462.

111. A. Norenzayan and A. F. Shariff, "The Origin and Evolution of Religious Prosociality," *Science* 322 (2008): 58–62.

112. M. J. Rossano, "Supernaturalizing Social Life: Religion and the Evolution of Human Cooperation," *Human Nature* 18 (2007): 272–294.

113. Bering, "The Folk Psychology of Souls."

114. M. E. McCullough and B. L. B. Willoughby, "Religion, Self-Regulation, and Self-Control: Associations, Explanations, and Implications," *Psychological Bulletin* 135 (2009): 69–93.

115. B. Randolph-Seng and M. E. Nielsen, "Honesty: One Effect of Primed Religious Representations," *The International Journal for the Psychology of Religion* 17 (2007): 303–315.

116. A. F. Shariff and A. Norenzayan, "God is Watching You: Priming God Concepts Increases Prosocial Behavior in an Anonymous Economic Game," *Psychological Science* 18 (2007): 803–809.

117. B. Randolph-Seng and M. E. Nielsen, "Is God Really Watching You? A Response to Sharif and Norenzayan (2007)," *The International Journal for the Psychology of Religion* 18 (2008): 119–122.

118. Shariff and Norenzayan, "God Is Watching You."

119. H. Ohtsuki, C. Hauert, E. Lieberman, and M. A. Nowak, "A Simple Rule for the Evolution of Cooperation on Graphs and Social Networks," *Nature* 441 (2006): 502–505.

120. R. Alexander, *The Biology of Moral Systems* (New York: Aldine De Gruier, 1987); R. Axelrod and W. D. Hamilton, "The Evolution of Cooperation," *Science* 211 (1981): 1390–96; A. Field, *Altruistically Inclined? The Behavioral Sciences, Evolutionary Theory, and the Origins of Reciprocity* (Ann Arbor, MI: University of Michigan Press, 2001); N. S. Henrich and H. Henrich, *Why Humans Cooperate: A Cultural and Evolutionary Explanation* (Oxford: Oxford University Press, 2007); E. Sober and D. S. Wilson, *Unto Others: The Evolution and Psychology of Unselfish Behavior* (Cambridge, MA: Harvard University Press, 1999); R. Trivers, "The Evolution of Reciprocal Altruism," *Quarterly Review of Biology* 46 (1971): 35–37.

121. M. D. Hauser, *Moral Minds*.

122. P. J. Richerson and L. Newson, "Is Religion Adaptive? Yes, No, Neutral, But Mostly We Don't Know," (short version), in *The Evolution of Religion: Studies, Theories, and Critiques*, ed. J Bulbulia, R. Sosis, E. Harris, R. Genet, and K. Wyman (Collins Foundation Press, 2008), 73–78.

123. R. Bocock, "Religion, Hatred and Children," in *How and Why Children Hate: A Study of Conscious and Unconscious Sources*, ed. V. Varma (London: Jessica Kingsley Publishers, 1993).

124. R. Stark, "God, Rituals and the Moral Order," *Journal for the Scientific Study of Religion* 40 (2002); 619–636.

125. F. L. Roes and M. Raymond, "Belief in Moralizing Gods," *Evolution and Human Behavior* 24 (2003): 126–135.

126. P. Singer, *The Expanding Circle: Ethics and Sociobiology* (New York: Farrar, Straus and Giroux, 1981).

127. A. Field, *Altruistically Inclined? The Behavioral Sciences, Evolutionary Theory, and the Origins of Reciprocity* (Ann Arbor, MI: University of Michigan Press, 2001).

128. E. H. Erikson, "Ontogeny of Ritualization," in *Psychoanalysis: A General Psychology*, ed. R. M. Lowenstein (New York: International Universities Press, 1966), 614.

129. R. F. Baumeister and J. J. Exline, "Virtue, Personality, and Social Relations: Self-Control as the Moral Muscle," *Journal of Personality* 67 (1999): 1165–1194.

130. M. L. Hoffman, *Empathy and Moral Development: Implications for Caring and Justice* (Cambridge, England: Cambridge University Press, 2000); J. Decety and C. D. Batson, "Empathy and Morality: Integrating Social and Neurosciences Approaches," in *The Moral Brain*, ed. J. Braeckman, J. Verplaetse, and J. De Schrijver (Berlin: Springer Verlag, 2009).

131. J. Piaget, *The Moral Judgment of the Child* (New York: The Free Press, 1932/1965).

132. L. Kohlberg, *Essays on Moral Development, Vol. 1: The Philosophy of Moral Development. Moral Sages and the Idea of Justice* (San Francisco: Harper & Row, 1981).

133. W. R. Goldschmidt, *Ways of Mankind: Thirteen Dramas of Peoples of the World and How They Live* (Boston: Beacon Press, 1954), 107.

134. P. Redfield, "Doctors, Borders and Life in Crisis," *Cultural Anthropology* 20 (2005): 328–361.

135. Zizek, "Defenders of the Faith," A23.

136. T. Gyatso, "Our Faith in Science," *The New York Times*, November 12 (2005): A21.

137. W. A. Bonger, *Race and Crime* (New York: NY: Columbia University Press, 1943).

138. H. von Hentig, *The Criminal and His Victim* (New Haven, CT: Yale University Press, 1948).

139. W. Kaminer, "The Last Taboo: Why America Needs Atheism," *The New Republic*, October 14 (1996): 27.

140. James, *The Will to Believe.*

141. B. Beit-Hallahmi, "Atheists: A Psychological Profile" in *The Cambridge Companion to Atheism*, ed. M. Martin (New York: Cambridge University Press, 2007).

142. Martin, *Atheism, Morality and Meaning.*

143. Stark, "Gods, Rituals, and the Moral Order."

144. McCullough and Willoughby, "Religion, Self-Regulation, and Self-Control."

145. Norenzayan and Shariff, "The Origin and Evolution of Religious Prosociality."

## REFERENCES

Adorno, T. W., E. Frenkel-Brunswick, D. J. Levinson, and R. N. Sanford. *The Authoritarian Personality*. New York: Harper & Row, 1950.

Alcorta, C. S., and R. Sosis, "Ritual, Emotion, and Sacred Symbols: The Evolution of Religion as an Adaptive Complex." *Human Nature*, 16 (2005): 323–359.

Alexander, R. *The Biology of Moral Systems*. New York, Aldine De Gruier, 1987.

An-Na'im, A. A., J. D. Gort, H. Jansen, and H. Vroom, eds. *Human Rights and Religious Values: An Uneasy Relationship?* Amsterdam/Grand Rapids: Rodopi/Eerdmans, 1995.

Asser, S. M., and R. Swan, "Child Fatalities from Religion-Motivated Medical Neglect." *Pediatrics*, 101 (1998): 625–629.

Atran, S. *In Gods We Trust: The Evolutionary Landscape of Religion*. New York: Oxford University Press, 2002.

Axelrod, R., and W. D. Hamilton. "The Evolution of Cooperation." *Science* 211 (1981): 1390–1396.

Bainbridge, W. S. "The Religious Ecology of Deviance." *American Sociological Review* 54 (1989): 288–295.

Balzac, H. de. *La Peau de Chagrin*. Paris: Editions Rencontre, 1831/1962.

Bartov, O., and P. Mack, eds. *In God's Name: Genocide and Religion in the Twentieth Century*. Oxford and New York: Berghahn Books, 2001.

Baumeister, R. F., and J. J. Exline. "Virtue, Personality, and Social Relations: Self-Control as the Moral Muscle." *Journal of Personality* 67 (1999): 1165–1194.

Beit-Hallahmi, B. "Atheists: A Psychological Profile." In *The Cambridge Companion to Atheism*, edited by M. Martin. New York: Cambridge University Press, 2007.

———. *Prolegomena to the Psychological Study of Religion*. Lewisburg, PA: Bucknell University Press, 1989.

Beit-Hallahmi, B., and M. Argyle. *The Psychology of Religious Behavior, Belief and Experience*. London: Routledge, 1997.

Bellah, R. N. *The Broken Covenant*. New York: The Seabury Press, 1975.

Bering, J. M. "The Folk Psychology of Souls." *Behavioral and Brain Sciences* 29 (2006): 453–462

Bocock, R. "Religion, Hatred and Children." In *How and Why Children Hate: A Study of Conscious and Unconscious Sources*, edited by V. Varma. London: Jessica Kingsley Publishers, 1993.

Bonger, W. A. *Race and Crime*. New York, NY: Columbia University Press, 1943.

Borg, M. B. "The Problem of Nihilism." *Sociological Analysis* 49 (1988): 1–16.

Bork, R. H. *Slouching Towards Gomorrah: Modern Liberalism and American Decline*. New York: Regan Books, 1997.

Boyer, P. *Religion Explained*. New York: Basic Books, 2001.

Brooks, A. C. *Who Really Cares; The Surprising Truth About Compassionate Conservatism: America's Charity Divide—Who Gives, Who Doesn't, and Why it Matters*. New York: Basic Books, 2006.

Brown, D. E. *Human Universals*. New York, McGraw-Hill, 1991.

Buis, R. *Religious Beliefs and White Prejudice*. Johannesburg: Ravan Press, 1975.

Colby, A., and W. Damon. *Some Do Care: Contemporary Lives of Moral Commitment*. New York: Free Press, 1992.

Dacey, A. *The Secular Conscience: Why Belief Belongs in Public Life*. Amherst, NY: Prometheus Books, 2008.

Darley, J., and C. D. Batson. "From Jerusalem to Jericho: A Study of the Situational and Dispositional Variables in Helping Behavior." *Journal of Personality and Social Psychology* 27 (1973):100–108.

Darwin, C. *The Autobiography of Charles Darwin*. New York: Totem Books, 1887/2004.

Davies, C. *The Strange Death of Moral Britain*. Edison, NJ: Transaction Publishers, 2006.

Decety, J., and C. D. Batson. "Empathy and Morality: Integrating Social and Neuroscience Approaches." In *The Moral Brain*, edited by J. Braeckman, J. Verplaetse, and J. De Schrijver. Berlin: Springer Verlag, in press.

Dostoyevsky, F. *The Brothers Karamazov*. New York: Penguin Group USA, 1880/1999.

Drury, S. B. *Leo Strauss and the American Right*. London: Palgrave Macmillan, 1999.

Drury, S. B. *The Political Ideas of Leo Strauss*. London: Palgrave Macmillan, 2005.

D'Souza, D. "Atheism, Not Religion, Is the Real Force behind the Mass Murders of History." *Christian Science Monitor*, November 22, 2006.

Duriez, B. "Taking a Closer Look at the Religion-Empathy Relationship: Are Religious People Nicer People?" *Mental Health, Religion and Culture* 7 (2004): 249–254.

Duriez, B., and Soenens, B. "Religiosity, Moral Attitudes and Moral Competence: A Critical Investigation of the Religiosity-Morality Relation." *International Journal of Behavioral Development* 30 (2006): 76–83.

Durkheim, E. *The Division of Labor in Society*. New York: The Free Press, 1893/1964.

Edgell, P., J. Gerteis, and D. Hartmann. "Atheists as 'Other': Moral Boundaries and Cultural Membership in American Society." *American Sociological Review* 71 (2006): 211–234.

Ehrlich, P. R. *Human Natures: Genes, Cultures, and the Human Prospect*. Washington, D.C.: Island Press, 2000.

Erikson, E. H. "Ontogeny of Ritualization." In *Psychoanalysis: A General Psychology*, edited by R. M. Lowenstein. New York: International Universities Press, 1966.

Etkes, I. *Rabbi Israel Salanter and the Mussar Movement*. Philadelphia: Jewish Publications Society, 1993.

Ferguson, N. *The War of the World: History's Age of Hatred*. London: Allen Lane, 2006.

Ferrarotti, F. "The Destiny of Reason and the Paradox of the Sacred." *Social Research* 46 (1979): 648–681.

Field, A. *Altruistically Inclined? The Behavioral Sciences, Evolutionary Theory, and the Origins of Reciprocity*. Ann Arbor, MI: University of Michigan Press. 2001.

Fogelman, E. *Conscience and Courage: Rescuers of Jews during the Holocaust*. New York: Anchor Books, 1994.

Glazer, N. "Neoconservative from the Start." *The Public Interest*, Spring (2005): 12–18.

Goldschmidt, W. R. *Ways of Mankind: Thirteen Dramas of Peoples of the World and How They Live*. Boston: Beacon Press, 1954.

Greenberg, J., S. Solomon, and T. Pyszcynski. "Terror Management Theory of Self-Esteem and Cultural Worldviews: Empirical Assessments and Conceptual Refinements." In *Advances in Experimental Social Psychology*, edited by M. P. Zanna, 61–139. San Diego, CA: Academic Press, 1997.

Guthrie, S. *Faces in the Clouds*. Oxford: Oxford University Press, 1993.

Gyatso, T. "Our Faith in Science." *The New York Times*, November 12 (2005): A 21.

Haidt, J. "The New Synthesis in Moral Psychology." *Science*, 316 (2007): 998–1002.

Hardacre, H. *Shinto and the State, 1868–1988*. Princeton: Princeton University Press, 1991.

Hassall, A. *Louis XIV and the Zenith of the French Monarchy*. New York: G. P. Putnam's Sons, 1895.

Hauser, M. D. *Moral Minds: How Nature Designed Our Universal Sense of Right and Wrong*. HarperCollins, New York, 2006.

Hegel, G. W. F. *Lectures on the Philosophy of Religion*. London: Routledge and Kegan Paul, 1832/1962.

Henrich, N. S., and J. Henrich. *Why Humans Cooperate: A Cultural and Evolutionary Explanation*. Oxford: Oxford University Press, 2007.

Himmelfarb, G. *Darwin and the Darwinian Revolution*. New York: W. W. Norton, 1959.

Himmelfarb, G. *Poverty and Compassion: The Moral Imagination of the Late Victorians*. New York: Knopf, 1991.

Himmelfarb, G. *The De-Moralization of Society: From Victorian Virtues to Modern Values*. New York: Knopf, 1994.

Himmelfarb, G. *One Nation, Two Cultures: A Searching Examination of American Society in the Aftermath of Our Cultural Revolution*. New York: Knopf, 1999.

Hoffman, M. L. *Empathy and Moral Development: Implications for Caring and Justice*. Cambridge, England: Cambridge University Press, 2000.

Horwitz, R. H. *The Moral Foundations of the American Republic*. Charlottesville, VA: University of Virginia Press, 1986.

James, W. *The Will to Believe*. New York: Dover Publications, 1897/1956.

Jenkinson, S. *Bayle: Political Writings*. New York: Cambridge University Press, 2000.

Jensen, G. F. "Religious Cosmologies and Homicide Rates among Nations." *The Journal of Religion and Society* 8 (2006): 1–13.

Johnson, B. "Sociological Theory and Religious Truth." *Sociological Analysis* 38 (1977): 368–388.

Johnson, D. D. P., and J. M. Bering. "Hand of God, Mind of Man: Punishment and Cognition in the Evolution of Cooperation." *Evolutionary Psychology* 4 (2006): 219–233.

Joshi, S. T. *God's Defenders: What They Believe and Why They Are Wrong*. Amherst NY: Prometheus Books, 2003.

Kaminer, W. "The Last Taboo: Why America Needs Atheism." *The New Republic*, October 14, 1996, 26–29.

Keller, M. "The Development of Obligations and Responsibilities in Cultural Context." In *Norms in Human Development*, edited by L. Smith and J. Vonèche, 169–88. Cambridge: Cambridge University Press, 2006.

Kohlberg, L. *Essays on Moral Development, Vol. 1: The Philosophy of Moral Development. Moral Stages and the Idea of Justice*. San Francisco: Harper and Row, 1981.

Kristol, I. "God and the Psychoanalysts: Can Freud and Religion be Reconciled?" *Commentary* 8 (1949): 434–443.

———. *Two Cheers for Capitalism*. New York: The Free Press, 1978.

———. *Neoconservatism: The Autobiography of an Idea*. New York: The Free Press, 1995.

Labrousse, E. *Bayle*. Oxford: Oxford University Press.

Law, S. *The War for Children's Minds*. London: Routledge. 2006.

Leuba, J. H. "The Making of a Psychologist of Religion. In *Religion in Transition*, edited by V. Ferm. New York: Macmillan, 1937.

Lewis, S. *Elmer Gantry*. New York: Harcourt, 1927.

Lewy, G. *The Catholic Church and Nazi Germany*. New York: McGraw-Hill, 1964.

Locke, J. *A Letter Concerning Toleration*. Indianapolis: Hackett Publishing, 1689/1983.

Manuel, F. *The Changing of the Gods*. London: University Press of New England, 1983.

Martin, M. *Atheism, Morality and Meaning*. Amherst, NY: Prometheus, 2002.

Martz, L., and G. Carroll. *Ministry of Greed: The Inside Story of the Televangelists and Their Holy War*. New York: Weidenfeld and Nicolson, 1988.

Maton, K. I., and B. Wells. "Religion as a Resource for Well-Being: Prevention, Healing and Empowerment Pathways. *Journal of Social Issues* 51 (1995): 177–193.

Matsuba, M. K., and L. J. Walker. "Extraordinary Moral Commitment: Young Adults Involved in Social Organizations." *Journal of Personality* 72 (2004): 413–436.

McCullough, M. E., and B. L. B. Willoughby. "Religion, Self-Regulation, and Self-Control: Associations, Explanations, and Implications." *Psychological Bulletin* (in press).

McLoughlin, W. G. *The Meaning of Henry Ward Beecher: An Essay on the Shifting Values of Mid-Victorian America. 1840–1870*. New York: Knopf. 1970.

Mencken, H. L. *Treatise on the Gods.* New York: Knopf. 1930.

Moore, B., Jr. *Moral Purity and Persecution in History.* Princeton: Princeton University Press, 2000.

Morin, R. "Voters: Take a Chill Pill." *The Washington Post,* October 10, 2004.

Morris, D. "Commentary: Mugabe Plays the God Card." *The Globe and Mail,* June 27, 2008.

Neilsen, M. "Appalling acts in God's name." *Society* (March/April 2003): 16–19.

Norenzayan, A., and A. F. Shariff. "The Origin and Evolution of Religious Prosociality." *Science* 322 (2008): 58–62.

Offer, J., ed., *Herbert Spencer: Political Writings.* Cambridge: Cambridge University Press, 1994.

Ohtsuki, H., C. Hauert, E. Lieberman, and M. A. Nowak. "A Simple Rule for the Evolution of Cooperation on Graphs and Social Networks." *Nature* 441(2006): 502–505.

Oliner, S. P., and P. M. Oliner. *The Altruistic Personality: Rescuers of Jews in Nazi Europe.* New York: Free Press, 1988.

Pargament, K. I. "The Bitter and the Sweet: An Evaluation of the Costs and Benefits of Religiousness." *Psychological Inquiry* 13 (2002): 168–181.

Parsons, T. "Religious Perspectives in Sociology and Social Psychology." In *Reader in Comparative Religion: An Anthropological Approach,* edited by W. Lessa and E. Vogt. New York: Harper and Row, 1952/1979.

Partridge, C. H. *The Re-enchantment of the West: Alternative Spiritualities, Sacralization, Popular Culture, and Occulture.* New York: Continuum International Publishing Group, 2006.

Piaget, J. *The Moral Judgment of the Child.* New York: The Free Press, 1932/1965.

Powell, A. *Athens and Sparta: Constructing Greek Political and Social History from 478 BC.* London: Routledge, 2001.

Randolph-Seng, B., and M. E. Nielsen. "Honesty: One Effect of Primed Religious Representations." *The International Journal for the Psychology of Religion* 17 (2007): 303–315.

Randolph-Seng, B., and M. E. Nielsen. "Is God Really Watching You? A Response to Sharif and Norenzayan (2007)." *The International Journal for the Psychology of Religion* 18 (2008): 119–122.

Rappaport, R. A. "Ritual, Sanctity and Cybernetics." *American Anthropologist* 73 (1971): 59–76.

Redfield, P. "Doctors, Borders and Life in Crisis." *Cultural Anthropology* 20 (2005): 328–361.

Reed, R. "Democracy and religion are not incompatible." *USA Today,* July 1, 1997.

Richerson, P. J., and L. Newson. "Is Religion Adaptive? Yes, No, Neutral, But Mostly We Don't Know" (short version). In *The Evolution of Religion: Studies, Theories, and Critiques,* edited by J. Bulbulia, R. Sosis, E. Harris, R. Genet, and K. Wyman, 73–78. Collins Foundation Press, 2008.

Rieff, P. *Freud: The Mind of the Moralist.* Chicago: University of Chicago Press, 1959.

Rodarmor, W. "The Secret Life of Swami Muktananda." *Coevolution Quarterly* 40 (1983): 104–111.

Roes, F. L., and M. Raymond. "Belief in Moralizing Gods." *Evolution and Human Behavior* 24 (2003): 126–135.

Rossano, M. J. "Supernaturalizing Social Life: Religion and the Evolution of Human Cooperation." *Human Nature* 18 (2007): 272–294.

Rothman, S. "The Decline of Bourgeois America." *Society* 33 (1996): 147–201.

Santayana, G. *Character and Opinion in the U.S.* New York: Anchor, 1956.

Saradjian, A., and D. Nobus. "Cognitive Distortions of Religious Professionals Who Sexually Abuse Children." *Journal of Interpersonal Violence*, 18 (2003): 905–923.

Schlesinger, A. M., Jr. "Human Rights and the American Tradition." *Foreign Affairs* 57 (1978): 503–526.

Shariff, A. F., and A. Norenzayan. "God is Watching You: Priming God Concepts Increases Prosocial Behavior in an Anonymous Economic Game." *Psychological Science* 18 (2007): 803–89.

Shimoni, G. *Community and Conscience: The Jews in Apartheid South Africa.* Waltham, MA: Brandeis University Press, 2003.

Shweder, R. A., N. C. Much, M. Mahapatra, and L. Park, "The 'Big Three' of Morality (Autonomy, Community, Divinity) and the 'Big Three' of Suffering." In *Morality and Health*, edited by A. Brandt and P. Rozin, 119–169. New York: Routledge, 1997.

Singer, P. *The Expanding Circle: Ethics and Sociobiology.* New York: Farrar, Straus and Giroux, 1981.

Smith, J. Z. *Imagining Religion.* Chicago: University of Chicago Press, 1982.

Sober, E., and D. S. Wilson. *Unto Others: The Evolution and Psychology of Unselfish Behavior.* Cambridge, MA: Harvard University Press, 1999.

Stark, R. "Gods, Rituals, and the Moral Order." *Journal for the Scientific Study of Religion* 40 (2002): 619–636.

Stark, R., and C. Y. Glock. "Will Ethics be the Death of Christianity?" *Transaction* 5, (1968): 7–14.

Steigmann-Gall, R. *The Holy Reich: Nazi Conceptions of Christianity, 1919–1945.* New York: Cambridge University Press, 2003.

Stewart, M. *The Courtier and the Heretic: Leibnitz, Spinoza, and the Fate of God in the Modern World.* New York: W. W. Norton, 2006.

Symington, N. "Religion: The Guarantor of Civilization." In *Psychoanalysis and Religion in the 21st Century: Competitors or Collaborators?* edited by D.M. Black, London: Routledge, 2006.

Tajfel, H., and J. C. Turner. "The Social Identity Theory of Intergroup Behavior." In *Psychology of Intergroup Relations*, edited by S. Worchel and W. Austin, 7–24. Chicago: Nelson-Hall, 1986.

Toner, J. H. *Morals Under the Gun.* Lexington, KY: University Press of Kentucky, 2000.

Trivers, R. "The Evolution of Reciprocal Altruism. *Quarterly Review of Biology* 46 (1971): 35–37.

Turiel, E. *The Development of Social Knowledge: Morality and Convention.* New York: Cambridge University Press, 1983.

———. *The Culture of Morality: Social Development, Context, and Conflict.* Cambridge, England: Cambridge University Press, 2002.

Turiel, E., and K. Neff. "Religion, Culture, and Beliefs about Reality in Moral Reasoning." In *Imagining the Impossible: Magical, Scientific, and Religious Thinking in Children*, edited by K. S. Rosengren, C. N. Johnson, and P. L. Harris, 269–304. New York: Cambridge University Press, 2000.

Twain, M. *A Connecticut Yankee in King Arthur's Court*. Berkeley: University of California Press, 1889/1983.

Varese, F., and M. Yaish. "The Importance of Being Asked. The Rescue of Jews in Nazi Europe." *Rationality and Society* 12 (2000): 307–334.

Victoria, B. *Zen at War*. Lanham, MD: Rowman and Littlefield, 2006.

von Hentig, H. *The Criminal and His Victim*. New Haven, CT: Yale University Press, 1948.

Wallace, A. F. C. *The Death and Rebirth of the Seneca*. New York Alfred A. Knopf, 1970.

Wilson, E. *Axel's Castle: A Study in the Imaginative Literature of 1870–1930*. New York: Charles Scribner's Sons, 1931.

Zizek, S. "Defenders of the Faith." *The New York Times*, March 12, 2006.

Zuckerman, P. "Atheism: Contemporary Rates and Patterns." In *The Cambridge Companion to Atheism*, edited by M. Martin. New York: Cambridge University Press, 2007.

Zuckerman, P. *Society Without God: What the Least Religious Nations Can Tell Us about Contentment*. New York: New York University Press, 2008.

# Chapter 6

# The Evolution of Popular Religiosity and Secularism: How First World Statistics Reveal Why Religion Exists, Why It Has Been Popular, and Why the Most Successful Democracies Are the Most Secular

*Gregory S. Paul*

For the first time since modern humans evolved democratic modernity has confronted popular religiosity with a set of scientific and socioeconomic pressures and threats of a scope it has not previously faced. As a result theism has been effectively ruined in some first world nations in favor of popular nontheism. In turn, the data generated by this fast and voluntary loss of mass first world theosupernaturalism has produced the statistical information that provides the key to finally answering some of the most fundamental and perplexing questions of why the majority of the world believes in deities whose objective reality is as plausible as that of other supernatural entities such as ghosts, gremlins, and fairies.[1] Based on the sociological analysis conducted by a number of researchers in recent years, this new synthesis of popular religion and secularism explains the fundamental questions of mass religion, including why theofaith appeared, why it has been so popular around the world for most of history, why belief in and worship of a creator has suddenly and strongly contracted in the western democracies while remaining relatively high, conservative, and procreationist in the United States,[2] and why only those First World nations that have seen historically unprecedented declines in mass religiosity are enjoying the best socioeconomic circumstances yet seen. These in turn allow the fundamental nature of religious opinion in most people to be described.

This work focuses on long-term trends in large populations with an emphasis on majority opinions that have led to high levels of religious activity, and/or serious belief in the existence of one or more supernatural deities versus the lower levels associated with popular secularism. Because the emphasis is on popular trends, terms such as *religious* and *secular* are used to characterize and contrast the views of national populations, rather than the configuration of governments. For a hypothesis regarding mass theism or nontheism to be verified it must be plausible, it must be compatible with rather than contradicted by the observed statistical data, and there cannot be an alternative that is superior in these regards; these obvious criteria are outlined because many common explanations for popular opinion on these matters do not meet these requirements.[3] Little attention is paid in this chapter to presently or formerly communist states because popular opinion has been skewed by government suppression. The methods for estimating the level of popular theism and nontheism and their relationship to socioeconomic conditions in First World democracies is detailed in Appendix 1. The data is used to construct the exclusively extensive Popular Religiosity Versus Secularism Scale (PRVSS), and the uniquely comprehensive Successful Societies Scale (SSS).

## THE NONUNIVERSALITY OF RELIGION

If all national societies retained high levels of popular religiosity, then the resulting uniformity would render it impossible to determine its actual causes and effects. Such homogeneity would also be compatible with, but would not prove, the widely held belief that theosupernaturalism is a universal human condition inherent to most if not all human minds. Some researchers have proposed that mass secularization of national populations has not occurred in the first place (Finke and Stark 1993; Stark and Finke 2000; Stark 2008), and others contend that most of the world is experiencing a resurgence of popular religiosity (Lester 2002; Longman 2006; Mead 2006; Shah and Toft 2006), especially of the conservative variety; fortunately for optimal scientific analysis these propositions are flawed.

Barrett et al. (2001), Bruce (2002), Paul (2002, 2005, 2008a, 2009c), Pew (2002, 2007, 2008), Groeneman and Tobin (2004), Norris and Inglehart (2004), Smith and Kim (2004), Gallup (2005b, 2006a–c, 2007a, b), Savage et al. (2006), Times/Harris (2006), Zuckerman (2006, 2008),

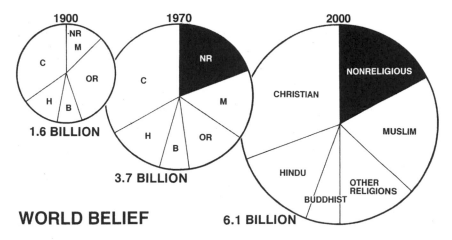

WORLD BELIEF

**Figure 6.1.** World Belief

Barna (2007a, b), Rainer (2007), and Paul and Zuckerman (2007) describe the past and current status of theism and nontheism around the globe and in the First World that forms the core of the discussion in the next few paragraphs. At the end of the 1800s popular theism was still nearly universal, with nontheists probably less than a percent (Figure 6.1). Although making some gains in particular regions, Africa especially, Christianity has remained stable at a third of the total. Despite the exceptional population growth of the population of India Hinduism has experienced minimal growth and remains limited to one ethnic group. Then an eight and now a fifth of the population, Islam is the only major faith to enjoy significant growth, but mainly through rapid reproduction. Paganism has drastically declined in spite of the appearance of New Ageism. None of the chief religions is growing via large-scale conversion. Mass religiosity, often of an increasingly fundamentalist nature, remains the norm in the rest of the Third and Second Worlds, but secularism is rising in some Latin American countries. Over the last century the nonreligious have ballooned to about a sixth of the population. The recovery of mass theosupernaturalism in formerly communistic states has been exaggerated.

The most historically radical, and for the purposes of this inquiry, the most scientifically informative circumstances have arisen in the First World. In eighteen of nineteen of the most prosperous democracies—Western Europe, Canada, Australia, New Zealand, and Japan—only a few percent to at most half absolutely believe in the gods, and in some examples two thirds or more qualify as atheists and agnostics. Levels of religious activity are correspondingly suppressed, and majorities—up to and more than 80 percent in some cases—accept human descent from animals.

The de-Christianization has not been filled by a corresponding rise in alternative forms of spirituality including neopaganism, and Muslims make up only 4 percent of western Europeans. Religion is not, therefore, nearly as universal as language that is very well developed in all mentally healthy adults (contra Bloom 2007; also contra Dennett 2006; Boyer 2008).

Equally important to solving the religion question is the major exception to western popular secularism, the American Anomaly, where two-thirds absolutely believe in God, and religious practice and socio-political activism remain strong to the point that even Democrats are playing the religion card.[4] American Exceptionalism extends to opinion on human origins, only half accept human descent from animals, almost as many think God invented humans a few thousand years ago, and the new Answers in Genesis Museum draws in big crowds.

The seven indicators that form the PRVSS confirm that the United States is over all the most religious and creationist First World nation, followed by Ireland, which retained exceptional levels of religious activity even though belief is below American levels at the time of the ISSP survey, and more distantly Italy. Sweden, Japan, Denmark, and France are the most secular, with the other nations falling in between (see Figure 6.5 and Appendix 2). That no nation scores a 10 on the PRVSS signals that none are entirely atheistic, but the reality of First World secularization is affirmed. Those First World nations where half or less absolutely believe in God and a solid majority accept human descent from animals—which are always the same—are tagged secular, hypotheistic, and proevolution (Paul 2005). Jensen (2006) criticized this secular label, and Stark (2008) cites one survey as denying large numbers of European nonbelievers, but multiple surveys indicate that some secular nations have large nontheistic majorities (Times/Harris 2006; Zuckerman 2006, 2008). The one First World country where a solid majority have no doubt there is at least one god exists, almost a third take the Bible literally, and a solid majority support for evolution is absent, the United States, is tagged as religious or theistic, theoconservative, and procreationist or creationist.

The cumulative long-term longitudinal evidence indicates that religiosity is failing to recover in any secular democracy as the post-WWII secularization generally continues. The relatively robust level of Amero-faith has inspired the conventional wisdom that faith is so integral to the national character that the United States will always remain pious, but indicators show that even the states are rapidly secularizing, as suspected by Hitchens (2007). The results of consistently worded Gallup surveys indicate that those who accept evolution have been edging up, whereas those who think the Bible is built on legends and fables rose from one in ten to nearly one in four in just three decades (Figure 6.2; Paul 2008a).[5] The number of atheists and agnostics rose

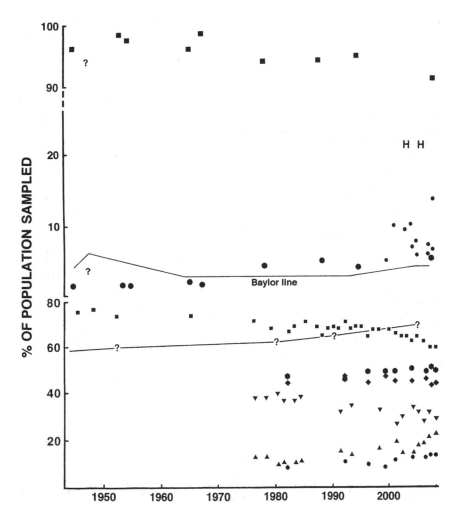

**Figure 6.2.**   Percent of Population Sampled

from about 2 million in the 1950s to as much as 60 million, a fifth of
the population according to two Harris polls designed to overcome
American's reluctance to admit nonbelief (Figure 6.2; Taylor 2003,
Times/Harris 2006).[6] The nonreligious doubled in the last decade and
half alone (Figure 6.3; providing the market base for recent atheist
best-selling books, Dawkins 2006; Dennett 2006; Harris 2006; Hitchens
2007). In comparison the fast-reproducing Mormons expanded from 2
to just 6 million over the same period, and their growth is slowing.
   The 2008 Pew survey finds that only half the population now absolutely believes in a personal God,[7] a striking drop from probable historical levels and well below some Second and Third World countries,

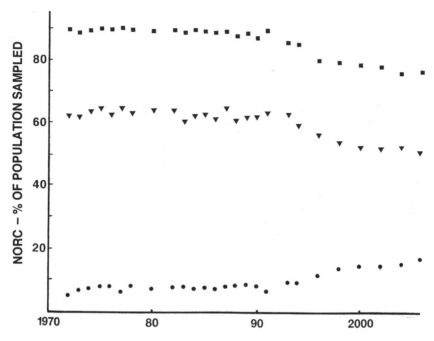

**Figure 6.3.** NORC: Percent of Population Sampled

and shows that American religiosity is unstable in that large numbers switch allegiances. Church membership has steadily declined over the last half century, and if anything, the drop sped up after 9/11 (Figure 6.2). Only a fifth of the population is in church on a typical Sunday. Once making up almost the entire population, Christians are down to three quarters, the Catholic fifth of the population remains steady only because of massive Hispanic immigration, and the formerly dominant Protestants are close to being a minority for the first time (Figure 6.3) and may already be if the heretical Mormons are subtracted. Until recently liberal and "mainline" churches were understood to be dwindling, but Bible literalists have sunk steadily and spectacularly from four in ten to less than a third over thirty years—contradicting the impression of a numerically resurgent religious right—and if the consistent trends continue literalists should be matched and then outnumbered by Bible skeptics in a decade or two (Figure 6.2). Other Biblical worldviews are also waning (Barna 2007a), whereas a bastion of theoconservative creationism, the Southern Baptist Church, is shrinking as a portion of the population because of a failure to sustain sufficient baptism rates (Banks 2005a, b; Rainer 2005; Salmon 2008). Following the pattern of failing western churches, American Christianity is feminizing as men become increasingly reluctant to spend time attending religious services, and children are strongly prone toward picking up their non/religiosity from their fathers (Haug and Warner 2000). A given generation retains its level of religiosity through life, and young Americans are the least theistic and most socially tolerant generation in the nation's history; even the nation's deeply entrenched antiatheist bigotry is easing as gays become widely tolerated and often popular (Edgell 2006; Mendenhall 2006; Anonymous 2007; Grossman 2007; Rainer 2007; Paul 2008b; Zogby 2008). Some regions of the United States are already as nonreligious and proevolution as some secularized western nations, and once red, theoconservative states are turning a more secular purple and even blue (Judis and Texeira 2002; Sager 2006).

It is crucial to this investigation that the loss of First World belief is largely a casual, voluntary conversion within which hundreds of millions have spontaneously lost interest in religious beliefs and practices despite the absence of an organized atheistic movement comparable in scale to the churches that work against secularization. In most developed nations the historical contraction of religion since WWII has been a notably quiet affair eliciting remarkably little popular controversy, and only American society is experiencing a culture war. Only disbelief in the supernatural has proven able to achieve significant growth by organic conversion: that this is occurring despite the low rate of reproduction of secularists makes their success at conversion all that more impressive.

## HYPOTHESES PLAUSIBLE BUT FAILED

### It's Not Internal

The thesis that there is a compulsive "desire for God" in most or all humans is falsified by the nonuniversality of the longing (Paul 2009d). The absence of a consistent drive to be religious or spiritual in turn falsifies a large number of potential hypotheses for why religion appeared and is often popular. We first consider internal mental processes.

Secular or natural explanations commonly offered as primary causes of mass religiosity include the following: fear of death or hell and a desire for an enjoyable eternal life, fear of societal chaos if a society is not godly, desire for an uber father figure or a universal companion, an explanation for the meaning of life or the existence of the universe, a social primate's desire for community and need for practical social support, a means to achieve political power, the excessive tendency to perceive patterns where they do not exist, the retention of childhood patterns of gullible thinking into adulthood, a deep set psychological need for spirituality, a "God gene" in which religious belief and/or prosociality somehow imparts a survival or reproductive benefit to individuals or related groups, left brain hemisphere function, the euphoria often associated with intense theistic beliefs and activities, and memes that spread religious ideas like viral infections even if religious devotion is maladaptive to a given individual or group.

The supernatural hypothesis contends that faith is popular because it is part of the human mental condition to believe in their creator; the exact mechanism of this speculative connection is obscure because of a lack of reliable scientific data.

No predominantly internal mental causes, either natural or supernatural, survive the test of large-scale First World secularization for the simple reason that if any or all were crucial to mass belief then all populations would be strongly religious unless subject to severe coercion by an antireligious ruling elite. If fear of death and hope for a never-ending paradise are primary driving forces behind mass belief, then why have the great majority of the French, Swedes, and Japanese spontaneously abandoned religion even though they face the same lethal fate as faithful Americans? Likewise, if need for social community is so compelling, then why are western Europeans and Australians not flocking to the churches? Political ambitions are not crucial because public expressions of deep piety have become an electoral detriment in the strongly secular democracies. Nor is the highly skeptical French population genetically or neurologically distinct from highly religious ones, so factors that potentially involve selective forces, including excessive pattern recognition and gullibility, are not predominant. There a no reason to think that the brains of the French and Canadians are more or less resistant to infectious memes.

The nonhomogeneity of faith that has resulted from the spontaneous loss of theofaith among large populations falsifies the hypothesis that belief and worship of supernatural entities is inherent to most much less all human brains. The forces most responsible for generating and deconstructing large-scale religiosity must be environmental. To the extent that internal mental causes of religion and nonreligion are real, they can contribute to the level of religiosity only when environmental conditions are suitable for high levels of popular theosupernaturalistic opinion (Paul 2009d).

## Inadequate External Factors

The free market explanation for why America is unusually theistic by First World standards (Stark and Finke 2000; Bruce 2002) has been so thoroughly falsified (Voas et al. 2002; Norris and Inglehart 2004; McCleary and Barro 2006a; Zuckerman 2006; Paul and Zuckerman 2007) that there is no need to consider it in detail. The failure of European churches to prevent the continent from sinking into mass war and their complicity in fascism and the Holocaust (Goldhagen 2002; Paul 2003/4; Heckenes 2004; Dawkins 2006) may help explain the continent's postwar lack of religious enthusiasm, but does not *adequately* explain why faith has since declined much more sharply in Canada, Australia, and New Zealand than the United States. There is one modern democracy where a specific WWII-related event helped spark a failure of mass faith. Shortly after the conflict Emperor Hirohito admitted he was not divine, and the Japanese majority has been leery of supernaturalistic claims ever since. The Cold War against atheistic communism seemed to inspire a pro-God reaction in the United States, but this does not explain why Christianity was already imploding in postwar Europe, even though they were subject to direct invasion by the Soviet alliance. The comparison of the PRVSS to levels of immigration, and ethnocultural diversity failed to demonstrate statistically significant relationships. Other factors must explain the American Anomaly.

## THE TRIPLE THREAT TO WESTERN FAITH

The same population trend data that has allowed both the internal and some external causes of popular opinion on religion to be rejected allows the environmental reasons—which form three major factors—why religion is in dire trouble in the First World to be determined.[8]

### Modern Science, Evolution, and Education

For millennia religious explanations of the existence of a universe containing humans encountered little competition because scientific research hardly existed, and in recent centuries the emerging sciences seemed to verify the need for a hyperintelligent creator. If modern science confirmed the existence of a designer—if geologists, paleontologists and geneticists showed that there is not consistent order to the appearance of organisms and for example, that they are too genetically different to be related to one another, then belief in some form of creator would remain prevalent even among well-educated Westerners. Instead, Darwinian and related sciences have refuted even Paleyian intelligent design, much less the Genesis story, leaving belief in supernatural gods at best an intellectual stretch. As Dawkins (2006) observes, the scientific environment that Westerners dwell within permits and encourages nontheism. It is not necessary for nonscientists to be well informed on the details of the matter; simply living in a society where the mainstream scientific paradigm does not demand belief in a supernatural designer is sufficient for large-scale disbelief to arise, just as the opposite will occur if the reigning paradigm favors a creator. Higher levels of education correspond to lower rates of religiosity and creationism on a personal and national basis; every year of college suppresses average religiosity by about 7 percent, and scientists, especially elite researchers, are exceptionally nontheistic (Leuba 1916; Larson and Witham 1999; Norris and Inglehart 2004; Gallup 2005b, 2006a, b). This

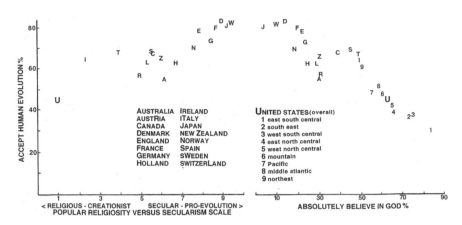

**Figure 6.4.**   Popular Reliousity versus Secularism Scale

is in accord with the experimental psychological evidence that acceptance of scientific explanations is automatically antagonistic to the acceptance of religious explanations for the same phenomenon in most human minds (Preston and Epley 2009). In First World countries lower levels of popular religiosity logically are associated with lower levels of creationism because the latter cannot thrive outside the context of a strongly pro-God population; there are no major exceptions to the progressive and statistically strong and very strong correlations that continue into regions of the United States (Figure 6.4, Appendix 3; Paul 2002, 2005, 2008a).

Because the rise of mass disbelief in a creator would not be possible if not for the materialist results of modern science and popular knowledge of the same, the Naturalistic Science Contribution to Democratic Secularization is the first leg in the triad of popular secularism. However, the science and education factor does not explain why the United States, whose mass science knowledge base is, aside from evolution, similar to that of other First World nations (NORC 2008), remains more religious than other advanced democracies.

## Societal and Economic Security

As popular as the proposition that religion is a universal human drive is the moral-creator socioeconomic hypothesis that proposes that mass belief in and worship of creator deity is essential if a national society is to enjoy benevolent social and economic circumstances (Appendix 3; Paul 2005, 2009d), forming in turn the concept of "spiritual capital."[9] Many current theoconservatives maintain that a laissez-faire capitalist economy combined with high levels of mass religiosity and faith-based charity are more effective at producing a benevolent and healthy socioeconomic environment than is secular democracy that modulates free market capitalism with government-based assistance to produce more equitable results (Brooks 2006). The hypothesis includes the antievolution or creationist version that contends that popular acceptance of Darwinian science contributes to the irreligiosity that dooms societies to chaos, and the proevolution version in which the basic existence of a creator, not its mode of creation, alone is considered critical. If any version of the moral-creator socioeconomic hypothesis is correct then the socioeconomic environment has little impact on the level of popular religiosity because the latter can be high regardless of whether the former is positive or negative. If the countervailing secular-democratic socioeconomic hypothesis (Appendix 3) is accurate, then benevolent national circumstances are not compatible with high levels of popular religiosity, either because the latter suppresses the former, or the reverse, or because the two factors are mutually antagonistic.[10] If pathological socioeconomic conditions encourage popular religiosity and improving circumstances curb the same, then this major environmental factor is operative.

How the First World countries perform in each of the 25 socioeconomic and environmental indicators is detailed in Appendix 1. The United States scores the worst in fourteen and by a very large margin in eight, very poorly in two, average in four, well or very in four, and the best in one. Specifically, the United States, scores the most dysfunctional in homicide, incarceration, juvenile mortality, gonorrhea and syphilis infections, abortions, adolescent pregnancies, marriage duration, income disparity, poverty, work hours, and resource exploitation base (Appendix 2). The level of relative and absolute societal pathology in the United States is frequently so severe that it is repeatedly an outlier that strongly reinforces the correlation between high levels of popular religiosity and poor societal conditions; because it performs so poorly relative to more secure democracies, the status of the United States as an advanced First World nation is marginal. That none of the nations scores a perfect 10 on the cumulative SSS affirms that even the best performing examples are not close to being ideal utopias (Figure 6.5; Paul 2009d). The top-scoring countries are the three Scandinavian countries, which sampled between 7 and 8, with Norway at the latter value, and Holland a little lower than these three. Most countries are in a fairly narrow middle zone from about 5 to over 6. The United States is again an outlier: with a cumulative score of only 2.9, it is so far below the other advanced democracies that some researchers have described it as "sick" (Sapolsky 2005; Wilkinson 2005).[11] The depth of the poor performance of the United States makes it all the more difficult to explain its level of pathology vis-à-vis more secular democracies, especially considering its exceptional wealth and power. On the other hand, the position of the United States as the most competitive

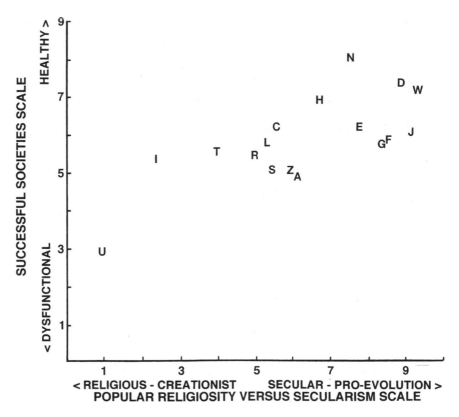

**Figure 6.5.** SSS versus PRVSS. See Figure 6.4 for country letter key.

economy is tentative (WEF 2007) as more secular democracies contend for the status, and no other First World country is as inefficient at transforming its assets and resources into societal health (Sapolsky 2005; Marks et al. 2006; Rosnick and Weisbrot 2006).[12] The next question is what factors best explain the observed pattern: are they largely or entirely nonreligious in nature, or is religiosity strongly interrelated?

The relationship between gross per capita income and the SSS is not consistent (Appendix 3). The 10 percent of the U.S. population that is foreign born is too small to dramatically alter its socioeconomic characteristics, and a number of the moderately secular nations exhibit a much higher proportion of aliens. The cultural fractionalization of the United States is somewhat high, but is likewise exceeded in some moderately secular democracies. Insular Japan is at the other extreme in both attributes. The Pearson correlations (*r*) between these population factors and societal conditions are too weak to explain the divergence in First World conditions (Appendix 3; Neapolitan 1997; Beeghley 2003). Nor does a violence and sex saturated media offer a primary causal explanation because the American popular culture has spread across the First World (Tomlinson 1991; Neapolitan 1997; Beeghley 2003; Paul 2008c). America's frontier heritage cannot be a critical contributor to its exceptional violence and related issues because markedly less dysfunctional Canada and Australia also have large frontiers (Neapolitan 1997; Beeghley 2003). The major nonreligious factors do not adequately explain America's failings.

Other potential contributing factors are more religious than they may first appear. America's heritage of mass racial slavery and Jim Crow apartheid may play a role in the nation's current ills. Discriminatory slavery and the chronic societal terror required to suppress human rights is endorsed at length in the Old and New Testaments, including the Jesus figure, and routine brutal treatment of blacks as inferiors by white Christians, often with the tacit or explicit complicity of the regional churches, began in the colonies in the 1620s and did not cease until the 1960s (Dray 2003; Harris 2006, Jaspin 2007; Blackman 2008; Budiansky 2008).[13]

The relationship between non/religiosity and socioeconomic problems is not ambiguous. When the United States is included all specific indicators of religiosity and secularism show strong to very strong correlations with SSS, higher levels of secularism as measured by nontheism and acceptance of secularism being associated with superior overall socioeconomic conditions (Figure 6.5, Appendix 3). With the U.S. outlier removed the correlations are moderate to good.[14] The very strongest and most progressive correlation is absolute belief in God with the religious United States at the dysfunctional end of the SSS and only highly secular democracies at the other. The most comprehensive single correlation in this study, the comparison of the cumulative PRVSS and SSS scores (Figure 6.5), produces a robust progressive relationship with the religious and creationist United States easily the most pathological, none of the secular democracies below 4.8, and only the most secular and proevolution democracies above 6.5. The very strong $r$ correlation of ~0.7 (Appendix 3) means that about half of the variation in PRVSS scores can be explained by the variation in the SSS scores and vice versa. With the U.S. outlier excluded the correlation is still strong, with about a quarter of the variation of one axis explained by the other.

The results of the cross-national comparison abjectly falsify both the creationist and proevolution versions of the moral-creator socioeconomic hypothesis, which qualifies as an unsubstantiated urban legend that has never been supported by a large-scale cross-national or cross-regional study. The democratic-secular socioeconomic hypothesis is robustly verified. This outcome is highly compatible with and strongly supports the socioeconomic security hypothesis of democratic secularization detailed in the seminal work by Norris and Inglehart (2004) and discussed by Zuckerman 2006, 2008) and Paul and Zuckerman (2007).

This is true because it is improbable that the tendency of levels of opinion regarding the existence or nonexistence of a creator to so strongly correlate with a large number of societal circumstances and vice versa is an accident. Either socioeconomic conditions are strongly influencing popular religiosity and secularism, or the reverse, or both effects are occurring. The social environmental based hypothesis rests on a large body of research that is used in the next paragraphs to describe the political, social, and economic policy differences between the United States and other prosperous democracies that appear to be driving their respective national conditions and hence their popular opinion on non/religion (including Lane 1997; Neapolitan 1997; American Academy of Pediatrics 1998, 2000; Zimring and Hawkins 1999; Panchaud et al. 2000; Singh and Darroch 2000; Messner and Rosenfeld 2001; Kawachi and Kennedy 2002; Pew 2002; Beeghley 2003; Pratt and Godsey 2003; Marmot 2004; Norris and Inglehart 2004; Reid 2004; Gallup 2005b, 2006a, b; Himmelstein et al. 2005; Sapolsky 2005; Schoen et al. 2005; Wilkinson 2005; Anderson et al. 2006; Banks et al. 2006; Wellings 2006; Winkleby et al. 2006; Zuckerman 2006, 2008; Finer 2007; Paul and Zuckerman 2007; Trenholm 2007; Kaiser 2008; Rosenbaum 2009).

Among nations as a whole, and on a personal basis, levels of popular religiosity and creationism tend to decline as income levels rise (Pew 2002; Norris and Inglehart 2004; Gallup 2005b, 2006a, b). But among First World nations the correlations between per capita income on the one hand and the SSS and PRVSS are weak, with the two most religious and exceptionally dysfunctional countries exhibiting among the highest levels of wealth, the high income yet theistic and creationist United States a partial outlier; simple prosperity cannot, however, explain the existing situation.[15]

There are strong to very strong and progressive correlations between income disparity and poverty on one hand relative to the SSS and PRVSS on the other, with the inequitable and theistic United States at the dysfunctional end of the SSS and only the most egalitarian strongly secular democracies at the other (Appendix 3). Up to half of the variation between these factors is attributable to the other. Removing the outlier United States from the statistical processing leaves the two correlations somewhat less strong. The existence of a major connection between levels of popular non/theism and economic conditions, particularly those pertaining to levels of security and insecurity, is robustly supported.

The basic causal mechanism of the socioeconomic security hypothesis of democratic secularization is as follows. Among the prosperous democracies, all but the United States have adopted most or all of a set of pragmatic secular policies that have elevated these nations' societal efficiency, success, and security while reducing personal levels of stress and anxiety. These include reduced socioeconomic disparity and competition via targeted tax and welfare strategies, handgun control, anticorporal punishment and antibullying policies, protection for women in abusive relationships, intensive sex education that emphasizes condom use, rehabilitative incarceration, increased leisure time that can be dedicated to family needs, and perhaps most importantly job security and universal health care that make it difficult for ordinary citizens to suffer catastrophic financial failure. As a result the middle-class majorities of western Europe, Canada, Austro-Zealand, and Japan feel sufficiently secure in their lives so that increasingly few citizens feel a need to seek the aid and protection of a supernatural creator, resulting in dramatic drops in religious belief and activity. The displacement of faith-based charities with governmental assistance further hinders the ability of the churches to influence the lay community. The increasing number of nonreligious presumably make the automatic psychological flip from preferring religious explanations to scientific alternatives, further suppressing religiosity in general, as well as fundamentalist worldviews. Although the popular secularization induced by pragmatic policies is accidental, the effect is apparently so efficacious that it has occurred in every progressive western democracy despite the absence of a large-scale organized atheistic movement and has yet to be reversed by a major religious revival. Although the time frame needed to inspire dramatic shifts in popular religiosity is decadal rather than a few years, the speed of change can be startling.[16] The universality of the effect is supported by Asian Japan experiencing the same basic secularization process as formerly Euro-Christian democracies.

As a member of the First World the United States is as anomalous in social, economic, and political policies as it is in its non/religiosity. Provided with comparatively low levels of government support and protection, members of even the middle class are at serious risk of financial and personal ruin if they lose their job or private health insurance; millions go bankrupt in a given year, many because of overwhelming medical bills. The need to acquire wealth as a protective buffer encourages an intense competitive race to the top, which contributes to income inequality. These high-risk circumstances and the strong variation in economic circumstances help elevate rates of social pathology and strongly contribute to high levels of personal stress and anxiety. The majority are left feeling sufficiently insecure that they perceive a need to seek the aid and protection of a supernatural creator, boosting levels of religious opinion and participation. The nation's good score in life satisfaction and happiness is compatible with a large segment of the population using religion to psychologically self-medicate against high levels of apprehension.[17] The ultimate expression of this social phenomenon is the large minority who adhere to the evangelical Prosperity Christianity and Rapture cultures, whose Bible-based worldview encourages belief in the Genesis creation story. This antirationalist effect is encouraged by the psychological exclusion of scientific explanations by the widespread preference for religious alternatives.

Not only does popular theism apparently depend on adverse socioeconomic circumstances, conservative religion appears to contribute to the latter. Politically powerful elements of the American religious right have preferred to focus on promoting a series of ideology based and socioeconomically problematic wedge issues rather than addressing social ills (Weisman and Cooperman 2006). These forces favor the deregulated, reduced taxation especially for the wealthy, free market economy that raises personal risk. As an adjunct to privatization, theoconservatives are promoting the displacement of government services with faith-based charities that increase outreach into the general population, even though data showing that faith-based charities are more effective than government alternatives has not been produced (Johnson et al. 2002), and charities lack the enormous financial resources and infrastructure needed to provide the comprehensive assistance that the government can (contra Brooks 2006). America's high levels of adult and especially juvenile mortality are probably partly due to the lack of the comprehensive medical system that is opposed by most elements of the creationist right (Kawachi and Kennedy 2002; Schoen et al. 2005; Anderson et al. 2006; Banks et al. 2006; Winkleby et al. 2006). The Bible-based juvenile corporal punishment advocated by theoconservatives (Dobson 2007a, b) may contribute to a tendency toward violence in adult years (American Academy of Pediatrics 1998, 2000). The claim that the Biblical God is the best if not sole source of morality is suspect because the testaments justify the use of extreme personal and mass violence and theft to address various problems and can produce "honor cultures" that demand extreme retribution for even trivial slights (Grasmick et al. 1992; Niditch 1993; Neapolitan 1997; Nisbett and Cohen 1999; Dray 2003; Ellison et al. 2003; Messner and Zevenbergen 2005; Dawkins 2006; Harris 2006; Hitchens 2007). The extent of natural evil is so extensive that it falsifies the existence of a benign god (Paul 2009b), so the continual effort to justify the unethical acts of the proposed creator potentially degrades the moral values of believers. Gun control is opposed by many religious traditionalists. Hood et al. (1986), Scheepers et al. (2002), and Sider (2005) observe that higher levels of conservative religious practice are associated with elevated levels of racial and ethnic prejudice, examples of which can be found in contemporary creationist literature (Morris 1991, 147–48). The patriarchal nature of traditional evangelical marriage may contribute to its instability (Bennett 2007). Extensive research, *including this study*, indicates that the Biblically inspired abstinence only sex education programs are not as efficacious in reducing adverse consequences of sexual activity to the degree seen in better educated Euroyouth (Panchaud et al. 2000;

Singh and Darroch 2000; Wellings et al. 2006; Finer 2007; Trenholm 2007; Paul 2009a; Rosenbaum 2009).

Patterns within the United States support the proposition that high levels of societal dysfunction are associated with high levels of religiosity, especially when traditionalist in nature. Levels of homicide, STD infections, abortion, and teen pregnancy are especially high in the pro-creationist Bible Belt, which is also the primary location of the rise in mortality that is already unusually high in the region (Aral and Holmes 1996, Nisbett and Cohen 1999; Doyle 2000, 2002; Beeghley 2003; Ellison et al. 2003; Messner et al. 2005; Ezzati et al. 2008). One reason America has a high level of divorce is because of the excessive rates characteristic of born-again married couples (Barna 2004; Sider 2005; Bennett 2007).[18] Keister (2008) explores how conservative Protestantism can hinder personal finances. The longitudinal investigation in Appendix 1 finds that the United States did not enjoy markedly superior conditions prior to its recent secularization, the same applies to once Christian Europe, and much of the recent improvements the United States occurred in parallel with the national secularization.[19]

Not only does the validity of the secular-democratic socioeconomic and the socioeconomic security hypotheses fail to substantiate the reality of spiritual capital, the verification is sociologically intriguing because, as Shermer (2006) and Bloom (2008) note, they appear to contradict the proposal that Americans often benefit from participating in religious activities (Putman 2000; Powell et al. 2003; Norris and Inglehart 2004; Brooks 2006; Gillum et al. 2008; Norenzayan and Shariff 2008; Pew 2008; McClullough and Willoughby 2009), although this effect is not consistent (Powell et al. 2003; Blumenthal et al. 2007; Keister 2008; Paul 2008d). Individuals frequently profit from being members of one or more connected groups (Sampson et al. 1997; Putman 2000; McNeely et al. 2002; CASA 2003; Eisenberg et al. 2004); the last two citations show that salutary group activities can be as simple as regular family dinners. Such social "clubs" can be private or governmental, religious or secular; in other words Putman's "social capital" is more efficacious than "spiritual capital." This is particularly true in a nation like the United States where government support systems are relatively weak in favor of private alternatives, belonging to religious "clubs" can provide benefits not available to those who are unable (often due to cost) or unwilling to join secular private cooperatives. In the secular democracies people belong to critical support groups, including the health care club, simply by being citizens, boosting overall general societal health to higher levels. It is therefore proposed that "secular capital" is a significant contributor to the success of irreligious democracies.

The empirical patterns and theoretical analysis indicate that the relationship between popular religiosity and societal circumstances is both passive and active—a positive socioeconomic environment indirectly negatively influences the level of mass theism and creationism; meanwhile high levels of conservative theism directly contribute to the poor societal circumstances and faith-based charitable work that encourage popular religiosity and creationist opinion. The socioeconomic security contribution to democratic secularization is the second in the three-legged stool of Western secularization.

## The Corporate–Consumer Popular Culture

Although modern science provides the matrix for Western disbelief, and socioeconomic circumstances have severely degraded faith in progressive democracies, the growing secularization of the United States is not fully explained.

Religious traditionalists dominated the Western mainstream culture until the Great War. Starting in the 1920s, only partly reversed during the Great Depression, reinitiating during and after WWII, and accelerating in the 1960s, the popular culture has become increasingly radicalized until it is unrecognizable by historical norms (Paul 2008b). A primary driving force behind cultural secularization is private enterprise. At first resistant to the initially antiestablishment counterculture as it began to appear more than four decades ago, the corporations quickly realized it is to their advantage to capture and exploit the "me generation" portion of the secularized popular culture. This is because the long-term fiduciary aim of capital is to persuade citizens to become materialistic, hedonistic, and youth-, sports-, violence-, sex-, celebrity-, and status-obsessed consumers whose values and life goals are antagonistic to those associated with traditional culture and piety. Although business interests are careful to not overly offend their many religious customers, religious activity and charity do not contribute to the mercantile bottom line. Capital prefers a calm, tolerant society whose main life goal is to acquire as much personal material goods and services as possible.

The effect is measurable. A contributing factor to the slippage of church activity is the retailers' victorious campaign to repeal the once widespread puritanical Blue Laws (Gruber and Hungerman 2006; Paul 2008c). The gay-friendly policies of corporations vex their theoconservative elite allies, but capitalists must put priority into tapping into the same-sex cohort's disposable cash (Paul 2008b).[20] The theoconservative Coors family sells light beers that fuel college binge drinking. The Catholic Church and Protestant allies used to control Hollywood via the Hayes Code. Today the irreligious entertainment offered by the corporate media is a major contributor to cultural secularism. Rupert Murdoch's FOX entertainment empire offers a wide array of theologically incorrect TV and film product that fuels secularization, and his FOX News presents conservative pundits who denounce secular liberals for de-Christianizing the culture. No entertainment program promoting traditional religious values appears on any major television network, largely because past shows failed to garner sufficiently high ratings. The detraditionalization effect of mass consumerism is so powerful that the formerly prevailing traditionalist society has been driven into a parallel culture that, for all its power and influence, remains a minority cohort whose persistent attempts to recapture the majority culture over the last half century have just as persistently failed in the face of the stimulating enticements of the free-wheeling culture offered by the corporations (contra Gilbert 2007).[21]

The liberating consumer culture created by the often contentious yet highly popular collaboration between the material demands of the public and their corporate suppliers forms the third leg of the triad of Western nontheism, the corporate-consumer culture contribution to democratic secularization.[22]

## Synopsis of the Triple Threat

To review and join the three hypotheses into a coherent whole, the first threat to mass faith is the modern science, especially evolutionary theory, that made mass disbelief in the gods both possible and probable in those nations where the socioeconomic environment is favorable to widespread nontheism. The second threat is the social and financial security associated with historically benign conditions featuring long lifespans, a middle-class majority whose financial status is ensured by universal medical coverage, job protection, and an extensive safety net combined with low levels of societal dysfunction that has grievously injured faith in the strongly secular democracies. This effect is so powerful because democratic secularization of the population tends to be associated with, and encourages, the adoption of the progressive, secular socioeconomic policies that encourage further secularization in a classic sociological feedback loop. In the secular democracies socioeconomic security has combined with the third threat, the mass consumer culture—in part imported from Christian America (Tomlinson 1991)—to radically reform eighteen of the nineteen wealthiest nations away from religious devotion. Although socioeconomic circumstances remain sufficiently primitive in the United States to encourage correspondingly primitive levels of popular religiosity, the nation's exceptionally aggressive corporate–consumer mainstream culture is sufficient to push a delayed, Americanized version of the secularization process.

Religion is proving able to thrive only in populations where conditions are sufficiently defective to cause the majority to resort to petitioning speculative supernatural powers to come to their aid. The mere act of running a society in a competent manner causes most of the population to lose interest in church and God. That a sufficiently benevolent national environment is automatically antagonistic to mass faith is a core reason why a highly religious country never has been, and probably cannot be, socially healthy and vice versa. The tendency of conservative theists to oppose effective policies is a contributing factor to the poor performance of nations of faith. Can a more science friendly, liberally religious national society better cope with modernity? Although liberal and moderate, proevolution churches tend to support progressive social policies and values that converge with those of secularists (Wallis 2005; Weisman and Cooperman 2006), the progressive values characteristic of these seem too secular to inspire widespread devotion, and improving social conditions and economic security degrades religiosity from liberal to conservative. It follows that only voluntarily secular cultures, not religious ones of any type, can enjoy historically low levels of dysfunction because the beneficent environment suppresses religion and because secularists favor the policies that create that environment. This pattern explains the lack of any example of such a country.

The Naturalistic Science, Socioeconomic Security, and Corporate–Consumer Culture Contributions combine to form the Triple-Threat Hypothesis of Democratic Secularization. Falsification of the hypothesis requires demonstration of the existence of a highly religious and creationist prosperous democracy that enjoys low income disparity, high security for the middle-class majority, and low levels of societal dysfunction or the existence of a strongly secular, proevolution prosperous democracy that suffers from high income disparity, low security for the middle-class majority, and high levels of societal dysfunction. To demonstrate that other factors are important contributors, it must be shown that they provide effective explanations for the disparate levels of religiosity in modern nations.

A thought experiment further reveals the central role played by the human environment in setting the level of majority non/religiosity and the nonuniversality of faith, while helping discern why theofaith arose in the first place. Assume that from the very beginning of humanity that every person enjoyed secure, middle class, well educated lives broadly similar to those experienced by today's western Europeans. Also assume that scientific evidence for the supernatural was absent. Considering how these circumstances have consistently suppressed popular religiosity, it is hardly likely that extensive supernaturalism would have ever evolved if these conditions prevailed from the start.

## THE BEGINNING OF RELIGION AND THE SOCIOECONOMIC INSECURITY HYPOTHESIS OF FAITH

That most people's religious opinions flow primarily from benign environmental rather than internal causes allows the origins of faith-based supernaturalism to be broadly reconstructed. Although the details will always be obscure because of a gross deficiency in data, the probable basic cause of the human invention of the supernatural is not particularly mysterious or complicated[23]—considering the unfavorable circumstances they lived within it would be remarkable if early humans never devised numinous entities. At some point in human evolution, perhaps a few hundred thousand years ago and no later than circa 40,000 BP (before Paleolithic), our ancestors evolved the selectively advantageous mutations that genetically code for a high-level imagination and the capacity to invent abstract concepts. In addition humans do two things that other animals do: dream and use mind-altering drugs. Ancient hunter-gatherers understandably assumed that the bizarre experiences associated with dreams and natural hallucinogens were real and that they represented a genuine connection with other realms. The early humans lived under impoverished conditions in which over half the children died and few made it to old age. Effective health care was not available. Nor could early humans explain how the world came into existence or how it worked, and they were awed by the power of storms and natural disasters. It certainly appeared that some terrible power was easily angered and needed appeasing. This Paleolithic stew was bound to inspire early humans, perhaps led by drug using shamans and to invent fictional entities that ancient peoples hoped would help them survive in, and explain, a brutal world. It is plausible that internal mental factors such as fear of death, improved group bonding, power accumulation, a neurological bias toward seemingly transcendent thinking played subsidiary roles in the origin of faith, but this was possible only because the archaic environment was ideal for popular supernaturalism (Paul 2009d).

Impecunious, high-risk conditions have since been the norm for most people. As a result organized supernaturalism developed along with civilization as religious elites exploited its popularity among the masses to consolidate power, and persists in the Second and Third Worlds where conditions are sufficiently dysfunctional to support popular faith. The proposition that adverse environmental conditions encourage mass religiosity may be compatible with the hypothesis that high parasite loads promote higher levels of religious diversity (Fincher and Thornhill 2009). Ergo, religion is a superficial primitive and dysfunctional condition, and popular rejection of fictional supernaturalism is the advanced and less pathological human state. The theory of why religion arose and has been popular is the Socioeconomic Insecurity Hypothesis of Faith.

## MATERIALISM: THE UNIVERSAL HUMAN CONDITION

The primary selective advantage of the high level cognition that incidentally invented religion on the side is that it gives humans the capacity to conceive the real world material tools and goods that are truly genetically integral to the human mind, i.e., materialism. Although nongenetically coded religion can and has disappeared as a majority opinion in a number of societies, materialism is so core to the human mind that it is a feature of every major population. Stone Age peoples went to great effort to produce and accumulate items of value and adornment that satisfied both practical needs and vanity and enhanced status. The fascination with material goods characterizes all civilizations, which are a means to expand, acquire, and display worldly possessions. Small groups that choose impoverishment are scarce fringe elements, and societies that even partly reject materialism are even rarer. Those that do, such as the Mennonites, not only must resort to heavy societal pressure to enforce conformity, but they remain significantly materialistic: the Amish own, operate, produce, and sell high-quality goods, clothes, livestock, farms, and small factories. Although there has always been an ideological struggle between the forces of the material and the spiritual, even much religious activity is actually an excuse for more materialism, from countless religious trinkets to mega-structures. Atheistic communism tried to redistribute wealth, not eliminate it, and the key reason it imploded was a failure to better satisfy material desires. The materialist compulsion has been taken to an extreme by religiously neutral industrial capitalism, but the genetic predisposition is proving so strong that many are unable to resist the compulsion to devote entire lives accumulating wealth far beyond logical needs; it is the DNA-ingrained desire for the material that has made the corporate project to promote the consumer culture at the expense of religion so successful. Because materialism is about as ubiquitous as language, the great percentage of humans spend much more time dealing with material than religious matters.

## THE NATURES OF POPULAR THEISM, NONTHEISM, AND THE CULTURE WAR

The popularity of faith in all dysfunctional nations never religiously cleansed by communism, the casual ease with which hundreds of millions of financially secure, well-educated Westerners have cast off religious devotion, and the much greater genetic predisposition for the material rather than the spiritual, establish the following. For the majority religiosity is a superficial, fear-driven psychological means to alleviate the chronic stress and anxiety created by an adverse or insecure societal environment and is readily and normally cast off when socio-economic conditions are sufficiently benign. To put it another way, most persons are religious only when their financial situation is defective enough for them to look for help from the beyond. So theosupernaturalism is predominantly self-aggrandization rather than a self-sacrifice either noble as doctrines propose or as contraadaptive as Dawkins (2006), Dennett (2006), and Dunbar (2006) proffer. Nor is religion generally as deeply held as Dennett (2005), Bloom (2007), and Boyer (2008) presume. The mundane quality of mass theofaith makes sociological and psychological sense. What most people are really interested in are not erudite concepts and doctrine or in spending extended segments of their time communing with the gods for the sake of some cosmic connection, but how their daily lives are going and what can be done to improve the situation if necessary. When their situation is deficient or insecure, the mental and social pressure to seek relief by imagining that one has magical friends on one's side can be overwhelming. So, far from being either universal or integral to human minds, most religious faith is a casual opinion of convenience. The popular premise that faith in a creator represents a deep, transcendent connection with supernatural reality is correspondingly refuted; it is a paranormal creation of the human mind broadly similar to belief in ghosts and other spirits.[24]

The yawning gap between the more than four in ten Americans who profess to believe in the Genesis story and the now less than a third who claim to be Bible literalists exposes that for tens of millions popular young earth creationism is not a firmly held belief, but has the characteristics of a superficially held protest opinion.[25] The American rise of right-wing religious political activism since the 1960s has been a reactionary protest against the secularization of the culture (Numbers 2005; Lienesch 2007). It began with the introduction of evolution into public education following the Sputnik scare, gained speed with the ban of official school prayer, accelerated in angry reaction to the emergence of the counterculture, and has been sustained by the evolution of the latter into the extreme consumer culture developed by the theoconservative's corporate allies. The religious elite perpetually complain that the religiosity of followers is generally shallow (Barna 2003; Sider 2005; Prothero 2007). This superficiality is not limited to theoliberals. Only a small percentage of theoconservatives bother to live a strict Biblical lifestyle (Barna 2003), half their marriages fail, and although polls show that the theoconservative third of the population disapproves of premarital sex, surveys reveal that more than eight in ten theoconservatives engage in it (Finer 2007).[26]

Even though popular nontheism involves a high level of conversion from theism, the former is no more integral to the human condition than is the latter. Nor is it likely that most atheists and agnostics base their decision to not believe in the gods on a careful, rational analysis of the pertinent philosophical and scientific arguments. As noted earlier Europeans score about as poorly on tests of scientific knowledge as do the more religious American population. The common perplexment of rationalists that so many people are superstitious is psychosociologically naïve; most people do not care all that much about scientific rationalism, which explains why three quarters of Americans and many other Westerners believe in something paranormal aside from gods (Sjodin 2002; Gallup 2005a). A growing body of research indicates that humans are not a predominantly rational species; intuitive thinking based on inadequate information being the norm (Pinker 2002; Marcus 2008), this mental limitation is in accord with the tendency of human minds to automatically prefer either religious or scientific explanations (Preston and Epley 2009). It seems that most nonreligious Westerners raised in religious surroundings simply lost interest in the supernatural when their lives became sufficiently pleasant and ensured and drifted away from church with relatively little thought about the matter (in accord with the results of Zuckerman 2008).

The casual nature of both religious and nonreligious opinion accords with the quiet, laissez-faire nature of the reduction of the popularity of religion in most Western countries. This reality leads to the fact that the cultural war for popular opinion between faith and secularism is not what many think it is: a grand ideological battle of ideas in which the side that does the best job convincing the body politic wins. The philosophical struggle is largely limited to partisan activists and the intellectual elite. The United States is the sole Western democracy where the theocultural war involves a major portion of the population, only because the socioeconomic environment inspires a large minority to be religious militants. Because popular opinion on religion is actually a more humdrum side effect of the scientific, social, economic, and commercial environment a population happens to dwell in over a period of decades, it is difficult for partisans on either side to mold popular opinion in the manner they desire, in which case educational and propaganda efforts *should* always have limited impact.

## LIMITATIONS OF THE HYPOTHESES HEREIN

Even though the environment centered Socioeconomic Insecurity Hypothesis portion of the New Synthesis of Popular Religion and Secularism explains the core questions concerning popular non/religion, its explanatory power is not universal because it does not apply to all aspects of religiosity, some of which may stem from internal mental factors. The hypothesis does not cover the competition between faiths within the context of a human environment that favors mass religiosity, such as why Christianity and Islam have become the most successful theofaiths at the expense of polytheistic alternatives. It is plausible that the eternal paradise promised by Christo-Islam is operative. Nor does the socioeconomic hypothesis deal with many individual circumstances, including the continuing religious devotion that persists among a minority of those who enjoy secure prosperity, including the minority of scientists who publicly proclaim their unverified belief faith in the supernatural. The hope for perpetual life may be operative here as well. Unfortunately these questions are difficult to test and in some cases may require a deeper understanding of brain function. Nor is it yet known just how antisupernaturalist an advanced society can become.

## PREDICTIONS

Because materialism is a much deeper part of the human psyche and a more stable feature of human societies than is religion, the perpetual hope by theists that a profound human need for spirituality inevitably forces a revival of faith is unsubstantiated. The Triple Threat to Hypothesis of Democratic Secularization predicts that the future course of religion versus secularism will continue to be determined mainly by the scientific, social, economic, and commercial environmental conditions populations live in. Organized religion has never faced anything as hazardous as the Triple Threat before, and their ability to directly challenge the forces of modernity appears to be minimal.

That evolutionary science makes disbelief in creator deities possible explains why the theoconservative elites are desperate to destroy evolutionary science, but they lack realistic prospects of doing so since advanced research is likely to only reinforce the theory.[27] If the gap between Genesis literalists and Bible literalists continues to grow—and considering the consistent decline of the former for the last three decades this is likely, then the erosion of the Bible literalist base will apply growing pressure that should undermine young youth creationism, leaving it increasingly vulnerable to sudden collapse.

Although the half-century-old alliance of the religious right with corporate powers under the umbrella of the Republican Party has increased the theoconservative's political power (Frank 2004; Phillips 2006; Hedges 2007; Paul 2008c), the cultural secularization effect of the corporate consumer culture is so extensive that the alliance is doing the cause of faith more harm than good while capital gets the better results from this arrangement (Frank 2004). The concern of some (Gilbert 2007; Hedges 2007) that the conservative church–corporate alliance is conspiring to impose a theocracy is incorrect in view of the mercantile forces preference for an irreligious, materialistic citizenry.[28] The theoconservative leadership is boxed in; if they abandon their collaboration with the corporations they lose most of what political power they have, and—being dependent on member charity and other revenue streams that amount to only tens of billions a year—the churches cannot hope to match the tens of trillions commerce wields to promote the exciting "hip" and "cool" aspects of modern consumerism that persistently trump the dull, "square" values associated with cultural traditionalism.

The American theoconservative movement as a whole has been badly damaged by its inevitable inability to run the government, the incompetence stemming from the inherently impractical nature of faith-based ideology, one that believes it is not possible for government to be run well in the first place, mixed with unavoidable rampant corruption. As a result the ability of the right to convince the majority that they will use godly morality to reform American society has disappeared. Surveys indicate that the increasingly secular American population increasingly favors the pragmatic programs, including universal health care, that spur the socio-economic secularization feedback loop that once underway is so difficult to stop that has yet to be reversed (Judis and Texeira 2002; Sager 2006; Pew 2007; Zogby 2008). Even large segments of born-agains are shifting from ide-ological wedge issues toward more centrist social, economic, and political policies, and much of their youth cohort is socially tolerant (Mendenhall 2006; Pew 2007; Mead 2008; Paul 2008b; Rossi 2008)—further evidence that conservative Christianity as a sociopolitical force is weakening.

It follows that American secularization should continue, and may accelerate, until America is much less religious, perhaps no more than other advanced nations. Nor is there compelling evidence that secularism will not hold its ground and even make gains in the latter countries; Euroyouth is especially nonspiritual (Bruce 2002; Norris and Inglehart 2004; Savage et al. 2006). If correct then the thesis that religiosity and poli-tics are strongly cyclical as theistic traditionalism and secular modernity alternately gain the upper hand is inflated; as long as socioeconomic con-ditions remain reasonably good it is unlikely that First World nations will return to the more conservative social mores of the 1950s or even the late 1900s, when the idea of gay marriage was barely imaginable rather than legal as it increasingly is in parts of the West (Paul 2008b). The theists' best and probably only hope for a massive Western religious revival is a long-term economic reversal that degrades the majority's sense of comfort and security to the point that most abandon rationalism in favor of irra-tionalism. The Great Depression partly reversed the cultural revolution that began in the booming 1920s and resumed during the subsequent Great Prosperity, but Western culture was markedly less traditionalist even in the late 1930s than it had been prior to the '20s. The failure of re-ligion to make great strides in most formally communist states suggests that once a population has become highly nontheistic it may be resistant to returning to the primitive level of supernaturalism.

On a planetary scale, if the majority of the planet's inhabitants achieve a degree of secure, middle-class prosperity characteristic of strongly secular democracies, then global religion should deteriorate to the same magnitude already seen in the West. If the bulk of humanity remains mired in inadequate socioeconomic circumstances, then reli-gious supernaturalism will continue to enjoy considerable success.

## CONCLUSIONS

Combining past research with the analysis contained in this chapter, the following conclusions ensue.

Determining the primary causes of popular religiosity versus secularism is predominantly a scientific sociological procedure based on quantitative analysis of population statistics on opinion and socioeconomic conditions.

Over the last century no major religion has been able to achieve significant growth as a portion of the global population via conversion from another theofaith or nontheism.

The Popular Religiosity Versus Secularism Scale confirms that the secularization of the First World is a real phenomenon in which spontaneous conversion has strongly favored popular nontheism over mass theism and creationism. Although the most religious and creationist First World country, the United States is undergoing a delayed and rapid secularization, and the rise of the nonreligious incorporates a surge in nontheists supplemented by unchurched believers. The historically unprecedented organic secularization of hundreds of millions provides the statistical data needed to solve the problems of majority opinion on theosupernaturalism.

The casual abandonment of theofaith by a large portion of the First World population, up to majorities in some nations, falsifies natural or supernatural causes internal to the human brain whether they be adaptative or pathological as leading causes of mass religiosity, although this may apply to a minority of humans. The primary causes of belief and disbelief in the gods are environmental.

By removing the need for a creator modern science has allowed and encouraged the appearance of widespread nontheism when other environmental conditions are also favorable to popular secularism.

The Successful Societies Scale demonstrates that there is a strong and progressive correlation between socioeconomic conditions and non/theism in the advanced democracies. The results falsify all versions of the moral-creator socioeconomic hypothesis in favor of the secular-democratic socioeconomic hypothesis, as well as the socioeconomic security hypothesis of democratic secularization.

Unless valid studies confirming the validity of the moral-creator socioeconomic hypothesis in the context of First World nations appear in the legitimate scientific literature, continuing to promote to the public the unsubstantiated hypothesis that religion is critical to individual and societal health constitutes manipulative propaganda and is intellectually and ethically fraudulent.

Rather than being a godly "Shining City on the Hill," the United States is the only First World nation to retain primitive Second and Third World levels of popular religiosity because it is the only one to retain the primitive Second and Third World levels of socioeconomic dysfunction that are needed to sustain mass theism. Conversely, it is not a coincidence that religiosity is low in every First World nation with universal health coverage: there is a direct cause and effect mechanism in which pragmatic secular progressive socioeconomic policies that use government assistance to modulate capitalism suppress mass faith by suppressing the economic and societal disparity and insecurity that mass religion depends on. As a result the least socioeconomically dysfunctional nations in history are consistently the most secular First World nations in history.

Because the faith-based American socioeconomic system produces inferior overall conditions and because nontheists suffer from discriminatory national attitudes, those who do not belong to religious organizations providing compensating services may suffer poorer outcomes. The superior general circumstances extant in secular progressive democracies reduce the advantages of religiosity.

The traditional, dogma based socioeconomic policies favored by the Religious Right directly contribute to an array of societal ills, so the theoconservative ideology that a democracy can have it all in terms of using economic liberty and high levels of faith-based activity and charity to achieve socioeconomic success is incorrect. The theoliberal premise that a progressively religious nation can be socioeconomically successful is also errant because the latter suppresses theofaith across the sociopolitical spectrum. This explains why no socioeconomically healthy theistic country has ever existed and why it is probably not possible for one to appear.

The concept of socioeconomic spiritual capital is falsified; secular capital appears to be operative.

Contrary to widespread hope and opinion, the sociological and psychological evidence indicate that scientific and religious opinions are normally antagonistic in minds and societies. Evolutionary science, for example, does not encourage theism, and because levels of creator belief are consistently low in socioeconomically healthy nations, high rates of acceptance of bioevolution are not compatible with elevated levels of religiosity in the First World even if the latter is proevolution. (Whether this always applies to noncommunist Second and Third World nations is not clear since they never have the socioeconomic security needed to suppress mass faith, nor is sufficiently reliable data on opinion on evolution available.)

The core original and sustaining cause of high levels of mass belief in and worship of supernatural deities has been the sufficiently dysfunctional and insecure socioeconomic environments that have existed since the Paleolithic and still dominate most of the globe including the United States. Popular secularism has suddenly appeared only because sufficiently healthy and secure socioeconomic environments have recently evolved in the rest of First World nations. Simply put, insecurity breeds religion and creationism, and security promotes casual rationalism.

Because theofaith is usually a psychological coping mechanism used to alleviate stress and anxiety ensuing from insecure and pathological socioeconomic conditions, for most persons religion is a casual and superficial form of self-aggrandizement in which alleged supernatural entities are called on to provide services regarding aid and protection concerning earthly matters in exchange for following sets of rules that demonstrate loyalty. It follows that for most theists their faith is not a form of self-sacrifice, and theism is readily cast off by large numbers of people when circumstances favor the adoption of the alternative. Likewise being a result of environmental conditions in most cases, nontheism typically is not based on careful, rational analysis either. It is not yet known how readily people will abandon nontheism under the pressure of an increasingly dysfunctional socioeconomic environment.

Because the majority chose to be religious or nonreligious on casual grounds driven by environmental conditions the culture war is not primarily an ideological struggle between competing worldviews ardently held by most citizens, so the ability of partisans on either side to influence popular opinion is limited. The introduction of universal health coverage should do more to further drive secularization and acceptance of evolution in the United States than any level of advocacy; conversely retention of highly inequitable health care is vital to slowing the pace of de-Christianization.

The lack of truly intense popular interest in either theism or nontheism helps explain why the Western churches have not succeeded in stopping much less reversing the slide in faith and creationism despite their efforts and why a large grass roots organized atheistic movement never has and probably never will emerge.

Materialism is far more integral to human nature, probably via genetic influence on the function of the mind, than are spirituality and religiosity.

The evolution of the mass corporate consumer culture made possible by modern science and technology has exploited the human propensity toward materialism to the detriment of popular theofaith. A probable secondary contributor to nontheism in the secular democracies, it is powerful enough in the United States to overcome socioeconomic insecurity and initiated a sharp decline in American religious devotion and activity.

Having effectively lost the culture war, the theoconservative alliance with the corporations is correspondingly self-defeating in the long term, but the churches lack a superior alternative strategy. Dependent on member charity and other revenue streams that amount to only tens of billions a year, the churches cannot hope to match the tens of trillions commerce wields to promote the popular counterculture, which is popular because it enjoys greater majority appeal.

The secularization feedback loop appears to be continuing to operate in the First World, including the United States, so religion should continue to lose ground despite the occasional minirevival of theosupernaturalism. If so then a major Schlesingerian cycle[29] back toward theism is unlikely. The Karl Rovian project to play the political margins to establish a faith-based permanent Republican majority was correspondingly as sociologically and politically naïve as it was doomed.[30] Because the churches lack workable mechanisms to defeat the Triple Threat to First World theofaith as long as egalitarian democratic prosperity remains extant. The best hope for a Great Revival in the West is a similarly great economic reversal, but corporate interests are likely to continue to promote cultural secularization. Religion should continue to thrive in the faith-friendly dysfunctional environment of Second and Third World nations.[31]

The statistical analyses presented herein were conducted by Peter Nardi. Special thanks also are given to Phil Zuckerman for discussions on the subject and the invitation to contribute this chapter.

## NOTES

1. Four in ten Americans believe in haunted houses (Gallup 2005a), and the occultist Arthur Conan Doyle wrote *The Coming of the Fairies*.

2. Creationism includes all forms of belief that disfavors natural explanations of the origins and evolution of the universe and its contents (Paul 2005).

3. The widely held fear of death, free market of religion, and socioeconomic hypotheses are all plausible, but only the last is compatible with the available data.

4. However, the Republican 2008 presidential nominee was not particularly religiously active nor creationist.

5. The seeming jump of support to majority status for special creation in a Gallup survey (2006b) was due to a one-time change in wording.

6. Stark (2008) selected a very small portion of available survey data since WWII to claim that nonbelievers have remained a consistently small minority. He included only two Gallup surveys from the 1940s, ignoring the 1950s data showing extremely few nonbelievers, and all recent Gallup or Harris results showing much higher rates of disbelief (see Figure 6.2; Paul 2009c). The poorly documented conclusion by Finke and Stark (1993) and Stark (2008) that U.S. church membership has risen since the 1950s is likewise contradicted by consistently gathered Gallup results (see Figure 6.2, Paul 2009c).

7. Even this may be somewhat elevated considering the disinclination to admit nontheism to pollsters (Taylor 2003). Note that absolute belief in a personal God is not the same and is a subset of absolute belief in a God whose characteristics are not defined by the pollster. Also note that almost all those who express absolute belief in a personal God must include the nearly equal number who believe in the recent creation of humans.

8. Dawkins (2006) is an example of the many who remain mystified by this novel event.

9. Since the discussion of the history of this hypothesis in Paul (2005), recent proponents of the moral-creator socioeconomic hypothesis include the best selling Boyle (2005), Coulter (2006), O'Reilly (2006), and D'Souza (2007), the widely released (but not highly successful, Paul 2008a) 2008 intelligent design documentary film *Expelled: No Intelligence Allowed*, the TV program

*Darwin's Deadly Legacy* broadcast in 2006 on a nationwide Christian cable channel and about 200 hundred broadcast stations, the new and successful fundamentalist Answers in Genesis Museum near Cincinnati, and Gruber and Hungerman (2006). Proponents of spiritual capital are Fogel (2000), Malloch (2003), Barro (2004), Templeton Foundation (2004). Although these polemics contribute to making atheism a societal fear factor in America (Edgell 2006), the moral-creator socioeconomic hypothesis has yet to be supported by the necessary comprehensive technical assay (that Paul 2005 set a challenge for).

10. New advocates of the prosecular hypothesis include Harris (2006), Dawkins (2006), and Hitchens (2007).

11. Note that the United States scores so poorly even though it scores well in factors that were included even though their ability to establish dysfunction is dubious, such as fertility and marriage (see Appendix 1).

12. With ~5 percent of the world's population, the United States possesses a quarter of the global financial assets and uses a similar portion of the planet's energy production. No other First World country has such a financially inefficient health care system, which wastes as much as a trillion dollars or $3,000/person each year (Paul 2008e).

13. The tendency to attribute slavery and the apartheid lynching culture at least in part to a virulent expression of racist social Darwinism (Dray 2003) is misplaced because of the late appearance of the philosophy, which itself was founded on a heritage of Christian bigotry.

14. With the exception that the Bible literalism correlation is no longer significant with the United States excluded, a reflection of the consistent lack of significant conservative theism in the secular democracies.

15. In scientific terms it is therefore fortunate that the American Anomaly exists: if the United States were not so religious we would not have the means to realize that a simple rise in prosperity does not automatically suppress mass religiosity in favor of popular nontheism.

16. As late as the 1970s Ireland and Spain were impoverished bastions of Catholicism. Nowadays the hi-tech boom "Celtic Tiger" and progressive Spain are typically Eurosecular. Spain has become so progressive that divorce and even same sex marriage are legal.

17. America's apparently high level of mental illness (Bijl et al. 2003) may reinforce this suggestion.

18. It is pertinent that the covenant marriage promoted by conservative evangelicals in three states has attracted only a few thousand couples over the last few years.

19. Although there has been a recent tendency for gains to plateau out (Paul 2005, 2008d).

20. Hence the spokesperson for American Express is the nation's most popular lesbian, Ellen Degeneres, whose popular talk show hosted presidential candidate John McCain who was looking for the socially tolerant youth vote and was followed by Laura and Jenna Bush, promoting the latter's book.

21. That Gibson's hyperviolent *Passion of the Christ*, a film that could not have been produced under the Hayes Code that many traditionalists laud, was so popular with Christian theoconservatives exposes how they fail to realize the depth of their defeat in the culture war or their accommodation to the triumphant counterculture.

22. It is ironic that capitalism is a major contributor to the loss of mass faith that Marx predicted would result from antisocially Darwinistic egalitarian communism.

23. The speculative and overly elaborate explanations by Dennett (2006), Dunbar (2006), and King (2007) do not incorporate the primary roles played by the prehistoric socioeconomic environment. The multimillion Templeton/Oxford University collaboration to investigate the origin and popularity of theofaith (www.ox.ac.uk/media/news_stories/2008/000219.html) appears redundant.

24. The common opinion expressed by Chris Hedges (on Book TV) that "those who fail to fully explore the religious impulse, the ability to connect with those transcendent forces, are not fully human" is correspondingly exposed as both inaccurate and casually bigoted.

25. This effect is supported by the highly inconsistent response of Americans to questions on evolution and creationism depending on whether they are framed in scientific or religious terms (NORC 2008).

26. A large portion of the population switches religions (Pew 2008) in a manner that suggests it is more a cursory consumer product subject to being dropped than a deep set and unshakeable devotion.

27. It is ironic that the faith-based traditionalist opponents of Darwinian science have allied with the Darwinian social economic powers, the latter being a radical and crucial part of modernity that constitute the greatest force ever seen for radically transforming First Worlders into hypermaterialist members of the cultural revolution that theoconservatives despise.

28. The architect of the wedge strategy to make intelligent design a part of mainstream academe, Phillip Johnson, has lamented the project is not proceeding as envisioned (Apsell 2007).

29. Schlesinger (1986).

30. Judis and Texeira (2002) appear more prescient.

31. Lester (2002), Longman (2006), Shah and Toft (2006), and Griswold (2008) observe that the flourishing of faith in unstable nations can be pathological.

## REFERENCES

American Academy of Pediatrics. 1998. Policy statement: Guidance for effective discipline. *Pediatrics* 101:723–728.

———. 2000. Policy statement: Corporal punishment in schools. *Pediatrics* 106:343.

Anderson, G., B. Frogner, R. Johns, and U. Reinhardt. 2006. Health care spending and use of information technology in OECD countries. *Health Affairs* 25:819–831.

Anonymous. 2007. Lifeway Research uncovers reasons 18- to 22-year-olds drop out of church. Lifeway Research. www.lifeway.com.

Apsell, P. 2007. *Judgment Day: Intelligent design on trial. NOVA.* PBS. http://www.pbs.org/wgbh/nova/id/program.html/ (accessed August 23, 2009).

Aral, S., and K. Holmes. 1996. Social and behavioral determinants of the epidemiology of STDs: Industrialized and developing countries. In *Sexually transmitted diseases*, 3rd ed., ed. K. Holmes et al., 39–76. New York: McGraw-Hill.

Banks, A. 2005a. Southern Baptists address drop in baptism numbers. *The Washington Post,* June 18, 2009.

———. 2005b. Southern Baptist evangelism has "discernable deterioration." Beliefnet. www.beliefnet.com/story/166/story_16648_1.html.

Banks, J., M. Marmot, Z. Oldfield, and J. Smith. 2006. Disease and disadvantage in the United States and in England. *JAMA* 295:2037–2045.

Barclay, G., and C. Taveres. 2002. International comparisons of criminal justice statistics 2000. *Research Development and Statistics Publications.* May 2002: 20 pp. www.homeoffice.gov.uk/rds/pdfs2/hosb502.pdf.

———. 2003. International Comparisons of Criminal Justice Statistics 2001. *Research Development and Statistics Publications* December 2003: 24 pp. www.csdp.org/research/hosb1203.pdf.

Barna, G. 2003. A Biblical worldview has a radical effect on a person's life. Barna Research Online. http://www.barna.org/barna-update/article/5-barna-update/131-a-biblical-worldview-has-a-radical-effect-on-a-persons-life (accessed August 23, 2009).

———. 2004. Born again Christians just as likely to divorce as are non-Christians. Barna Research Online. http://www.barna.org/barna-update/article/5-barna-update/194-born-again-christians-just-as-likely-to-divorce-as-are-non-christians (accessed August 23, 2009).

———. 2007a. Barna's annual tracking study show Americans stay spiritually active, but biblical views wane. Barna Research Online. http://www.barna.org/barna-update/article/18-congregations/103-barnas-annual-tracking-study-shows-americans-stay-spiritually-active-but-biblical-views-wane (accessed August 23, 2009).

———. 2007b. Atheists and agnostics take aim at Christians. Barna Research Online. http://www.barna.org/barna-update/article/12-faithspirituality/102-atheists-and-agnostics-take-aim-at-christians (accessed August 23, 2009).

Barrett, D., G. Kurian, and T. Johnson, eds. 2001. *World Christian encyclopedia.* Oxford: Oxford University Press.

Barro, R. 2004. Spirit of capitalism: Religion and economic development. *Harvard International Review* 25(4).

———, and R. McCleary. 2003. Religion and economic growth across countries. *American Sociological Review* 68:760–781.

Beeghley, L. 2003. *Homicide: A sociological explanation.* Lanham: Rowman & Littlefield Publishing Group.

Bennetts, L. 2007. *The feminine mistake.* New York: Voice/Hyperion.

Bijl, R. et al. 2003. Prevalence of treated and untreated mental disorders in five countries. *Health Affairs* 22:122–133.

Blackman, D. 2008. *Slavery by another name: The reenslavement of black Americans from the Civil War to World War II.* New York: Doubleday.

Bloom, P. 2007. Religion is natural. *Developmental Science* 10:147–151.

———. 2008. Does religion make you nice? Does atheism make you mean? *Slate* November 7, 2008. www.slate.com/toolbar.aspx?action=print&id=2203614.

Bloss, W. 2005. Comparative European and American drug control policy. *ERCES Online Quarterly Review* 2 (2):1–18. Erces.com/journal/articles.archives/volume2/v02/v06.htm.

Blumenthal, J. et al. 2007. Spirituality, religion, and clinical outcomes in patients recovering from an acute myocardial infarction. *Psychosomatic Medicine* 69:501–8.

Boyer, P. 2008. Religion: Bound to believe? *Nature* 455:1038–1039.

Boyle, D. 2005. *Vile France*. New York: Encounter Books.

Brandt, A. 1987. *No magic bulletin: A social history of venereal disease in the United States since 1880.* Oxford: Oxford University Press.

Brooks, A. 2006. *Who really cares?* New York: Basic Books.

Bruce, S. 2002. *God is dead: Secularization in the West.* Oxford: Blackwell.

Budiansky, S. 2008. *The bloody shirt: Terror after Appomattox.* New York: Viking.

CASA. 2003. The importance of family dinners. *Reports of the National Center for Addiction and Substance Abuse at Columbia University.* www.Casacolumbia. org/pdshopprov/shop/item.asp?itemid=35.

Coulter, A. 2006. *Godless: The church of liberalism.* New York: Crown Forum.

Dawkins, R. 2006. *The God delusion.* New York: Houghton Mifflin.

Dennett, D. 2006. *Breaking the spell: Religion as a natural phenomenon.* New York: Viking.

De Tocqueville, A. 1835. *Democracy in America.*

Diener, E., E. Suh, R. Lucas, and H. Smith. 1999. Subjective well-being: Three decades of progress. *Psychological Bulletin* 125:276–302.

Divorce Reform. 2002. www.divorceform.org/gul.html.

Dobson, J. 2007a. *Does spanking work for all kids?* Focus on the Family. www. family.org/parenting/A000001547.cfm.

———. 2007b. To spank or not to spank. Focus on the Family. www.family. org/parenting/A000001548.cfm.

Doyle, R. 2000. The roots of homicide. *Scientific American* 283(3):22.

———. 2002. Quality of life. *Scientific American* 286(4):32.

Dray, P. 2003. *At the hands of persons unknown: The lynching of black America.* New York: Random House.

D'Souza, D. 2007. *What's so great about Christianity.* Washington, DC: Regenery Publishing.

Dunbar, R. 2006. We believe. *New Scientist* 189(2536):30–33.

Edgell, P., J. Gerteis, and D. Hartmann. 2006. Atheists as "other": Moral boundaries and cultural membership in American society. *American Sociological Review* 71:211–234.

Eisenberg, M. et al. 2004. Correlations between family meals and psychological well-being among adolescents. *Archives of Pediatrics and Adolescent Medicine* 158:792–96.

Ellison, C., J. Burr, and P. McCall. 2003. The enduring puzzle of Southern homicide: Is regional religious culture the missing piece? *Homicide Studies* 7:326–352.

Ezzati, M. et al. 2008. The reversal of fortunes: Trends in county mortality and cross-country mortality disparities in the United States. *PLoS Medicine* 5:e66.

Farrington, D., P. Langan, and M. Tonry, eds. 2004. Cross-national studies in crime and justice. Bureau of Justice Statistics. www.ojp.usdoj.gov/bjs/ pub/pdf/cnscj.pdf.

Fearon, J. 2003. Ethnic and cultural diversity by country. *Journal of Economic Growth* 8:195–222.

Fincher, C., and R. Thornhill. 2008. Assertative sociality, limited dispersal, infectious disease and the genesis of the global pattern of religious diversity. *Proceedings of the Royal Society of London, B* 295:2587–2594.

Finer, L. 2007. Trends in premarital sex in the United States, 1954–2003. *Public Health Reports* 122:73–78.

Finke, R., and R. Stark. 1993. *The churching of America, 1776–1990: Winners and losers in our religious economy*. New Brunswick: Rutgers University Press.

Fogel, R. 2000. *The fourth great awakening and the future of egalitarianism*. Chicago: University of Chicago Press.

Gallinger, P. 2003. *Illegal drugs: A complete guide to their history, chemistry, use and abuse*. New York: Plume.

Gallup. 2005a. Three in four Americans believe in the paranormal. Gallup Brain.

———. 2005b. Religion in America: Who has none? Gallup Brain.

———. 2006a. Who believes in God and who doesn't? Gallup Brain.

———. 2006b. American beliefs: Evolution vs. Bible's explanation of human origins. Gallup Brain.

———. 2006c. Twenty-eight percent believe Bible is actual word of God. Gallup Brain.

———. 2007a. One-third of Americans believe the Bible is literally true. Gallup Brain.

———. 2007b. Majority of Republicans doubt theory of evolution. Gallup Brain.

Gartner, R. 1995. Methodological issues in cross-national large-survey research. In *Interpersonal violent behaviors: Social and cultural aspects*, ed. B. Ruback and N. Weiner, 7–24. New York: Springer-Verlag.

Gately, I. 2008. *Drink: A cultural history of alcohol*. New York: Gotham.

Gilbert, D. 2007. *The Jesus machine: How James Dobson, Focus on the Family, and evangelical Americans are winning the culture war*. New York: St. Martin's Press.

Gillum, R., D. King, T. Obisesan, and H. Koenig. 2008. Frequency of attendance at religious services and mortality in a U.S. national cohort. *Annals of Epidemiology* 18:124–129.

Goldhagen, D. 2002. *A moral reckoning: The role of the Catholic Church in the Holocaust and its unfulfilled duty of repair*. New York: Alfred A Knopf.

Grasmick, H., G. Davenport, M. Chamblin, and R. Bursick. 1992. Protestant fundamentalism and the retributive doctrine of punishment. *Criminology* 30:21–45.

Griswold, E. 2008. God's country. *The Atlantic Monthly* 301(2):40–55.

Groeneman, S., and G. Tobin. 2004. The decline of religious identity in the United States. *Institute for Jewish and Community Research*. www.Jewish research.org/PDFs/religion.pdf.

Grossman, C. L. 2007. Young adults aren't sticking with church. *USA Today*, August 8. www.usatoday.com/news/religion/2007-08-06-church-dropouts_N.htm.

Gruber, J., and Hungerman. D. M. 2006. The Church vs. the mall: What happens when religion faces increased secular competition? National Bureau of Economic Research, August, 2006. www.papers.nber.org/papers/w12410.pdf.

Hall, J. 2008. School associated violent deaths. Center For Disease Control. www.cdc.gov/ncipe/sch-shooting.htm?loc=interstitialship.

Harris, S. 2006. *Letter to a Christian nation*. New York: Alfred A. Knopf.

Haug, W., and P. Warner. 2000. The demographic characteristics of the linguistic and religious groups in Switzerland. *Population Studies* 31.

Heckenes, M. 2004. *A church divided: German Protestants confront the past*. Bloomington: Indiana University Press.

Hedges, C. 2007. *American fascists: The Christian right and the war on America*. New York: Free Press.

Himmelstein, D., E. Warren, D. Thorne, and S. Wollhander. 2005. Illness and injury as contributors to bankruptcy. *Health Affairs* February 2, 2005. http://content.healthaffairs.org/cgi/content/short/hlthaff.w5.63v1/ (accessed August 23, 2005).

Hitchens, C. 2007. *God is not great: How religion poisons everything*. New York: Twelve Books.

Hood, R., S. Bernard, B. Hunsberger, and R. Gorsuch. 1986. *The psychology of religion, an empirical approach*. New York: The Guilford Press.

ICPS. 2006. International Centre for Prison Studies. www.kcl.ac.uk/depsta/rel/icps/worldbrief/highest_to_lowest_rates.php.

Inglehart, R., and H. Klingemann. 2000. *Genes, culture, democracy and happiness*. Cambridge: MIT Press.

Jaspin, E. 2007. *Buried in the bitter waters: The hidden history of racial cleansing in America*. New York: Basic Books.

Jay, J. 2004. Cross-national comparisons of rape rates: Problems and issues. Joint UNECE-UNODC Meeting on Crime Statistics. www.unece.org/stats/documents/2004/11/crime/wp.18.e.pdf.

Jensen, G. 2006. Religious cosmologies and homicide rates among nations: A closer look. *Journal of Religion and Society* Vol. 8. www.moses.creighton.edu/JRS/2006/2006-7.html (accessed August 23, 2009).

Johnson, B., R. Tompkins, and D. Webb. 2002. Objective hope: Assessing the effectiveness of faith-based organizations: A review of the literature. www.manhattan-institute.org/pdf/crrucs_objective_hope.pdf.

Jowell, R. 1998. How comparative is comparative research? *American Behavioral Scientist* 42:168–177.

Judis, J., and Texeira, R. 2002. *The emerging democratic majority*. New York: Lisa Drew Books.

Kaiser. 2008. Economic problems facing families. www.kff.org/kaiserpolls/upland/7773.pdf.

Kawachi, I., and B. Kennedy. 2002. *The health of nations: Why inequality is harmful to your health*. New York: New Press.

Keister, L. 2008. Conservative Protestants and wealth: How religion perpetuates asset poverty. *American Journal of Sociology* 113:1237–1271.

King, B. 2007. *Evolving God: A provocative view on the origins of religion*. New York: Doubleday.

Komlos, J., and B. Lauderdale. 2007. Underperformance in affluence: The remarkable relative decline in U.S. heights in the second half of the 20th century. *Social Science Quarterly* 88:283–305.

Lane, R. 1997. *Murder in America: A history*. Columbus: Ohio State University Press.

Larson, E., and L. Witham. 1999. Scientists and religion in America. *Scientific American* 281(3):88–93.

Lester, T. 2002. Oh, gods! *Atlantic Monthly* 289(3):37–45.

Leuba, J. 1916. *The belief in God and immortality: A psychological, anthropological and statistical study.* Boston: Sherman, French.

Lienesch, M. 2007. *In the beginning: Fundamentalism, the Scopes trial, and the making of the antievolution movement.* Chapel Hill: University of North Carolina Press.

Longman, P. 2006. The Return of patriarchy. *Foreign Policy* July/Aug: 56–65.

Malloch, T. 2003. Social, human and spiritual capital in economic development. Spiritual Capital Project. www.metanexus.net/spiritual_capital/pdf/malloch.pdf.

Marcus, G. 2008. *Kluge: The haphazard construction of the human mind.* New York: Houghton Mifflin.

Marks, N., S. Abdallah, A. Sims, and S. Thompson. 2006. The happy planet index. New Economics Foundation. www.happyplanetindex.org.

Marmot, M. 2004. *The status syndrome.* London: Bloomsburg Publishing.

MASA. 2003. Occurrence of rape. www.sa.Rochester.edu/masa/stats.php.

McCleary, R., and R. Barro. 2006a. Religion and political economy in an international panel. *Journal for the Scientific Study of Religion* 45:149–175.

———. 2006b. Religion and economy. *Journal of Economic Perspectives* 20(2): 49–72.

McClullough, M., and B. Willoughby. 2009. Religion, self-regulation, and self control: Associations, explanations, and implication. *Psychology Bulletin* 135:69–93.

Mead, W. 2006. God's country. *Foreign Affairs* 85(5):24–43.

———. 2008. Born again. *The Atlantic Monthly* 301(2):21–22.

Mendenhall, V. 2006. Generation next. *PBS News Hour.* www.pbs.org?newshour/generation-next/demogrpahics/religion3_11-21.html.

Messner, S., and R. Rosenfeld. 2001. *Crime and the American dream.* Belmont, CA: Wadsworth/Thomson Learning.

Messner, S., and M. Zevenbergen. 2005. The legacy of lynching and Southern homicide. *American Sociological Review* 70:633–655.

Moreno-Riano, G., M. C. Smith, and T. Mach. 2006. Religiosity, secularism and social health. *Journal of Religion and Society* Vol. 8:10 pp. www.moses.creighton.edu/JRS/2006/2006-1.html (accesssed August 23, 2009).

Morris, H. 1991. *The beginning of the world.* Phoenix: Master Books.

Neapolitan, J. 1997. *Cross-national crime.* Westport: Greenwood Press.

Nettle, D. 2005. *Happiness: The science behind your smile.* Oxford: Oxford University Press.

Niditch, S. 1993. *War in the Hebrew Bible: A study in the ethics of violence.* Oxford: Oxford University Press.

Nisbett, R., and D. Cohen. 1999. *Culture of honor: The psychology of violence in the South.* Boulder: West View Press.

NORC. 2008. Science and engineering indicators. www.nsf.gov/statistics/seind08/c7/c7h.htm & c7s2htm.

Norenzayan, A., and A. Shariff. 2008. The origin and evolution of religious prosociality. *Science* 322:58–62.

Norris, P., and R. Inglehart. 2004. *Sacred and secular.* Cambridge: Cambridge University Press.

Numbers, R. 2005. *The creationists: From scientific creationism to intelligent design.* Cambridge: Harvard University Press.

OECD. 2001. *Society at a glance*. Paris, Organization for Economic Co-operation and Development.

———. 2007. *Health at a glance*. Paris, Organization for Economic Co-operation and Development.

O'Reilly, B. 2006. *Culture warrior*. New York: Broadway.

Panchaud, C., S. Singh, D. Darroch, and J. Darroch. 2000. Sexually transmitted diseases among adolescents in developed countries. *Family Planning Perspectives* 32:24–32.

Paul, G. 2002. The secular revolution of the West. *Free Inquiry* 22(3):28–34.

———. 2003/4. The great scandal: Christianity's role in the rise of the Nazis. *Free Inquiry* 23(4):20–28/24(1):28–33.

———. 2005. Cross-national correlations of quantifiable societal health with popular religiosity and secularism in the prosperous democracies. *Journal of Religion and Society* Vol. 7:17 pp. www.moses.creighton.edu/JRS/2005/2005-11.html.

———. 2008a. Expelled expired: Creationism is not winning. *EnergyGrid, May 2008*. www.energygrid.com/society/2008/05gp-creationists.html (accessed August 23, 2009).

———. 2008b. The gays are winning: Why that spells doom for the religious right. *OpEdNews,* June 24. www.opednews.com/articles/The-Gays-Are-Winning—Why—by-Gregory-Paul-080624-910.html.

———. 2008c. Buckley's big mistake, *Dissident Voice*, March 5, 2008. www.dissidentvoice.org/2008/03/buckleys-big-mistake.

———. 2008d. The remote prayer delusion: Clinical trials that attempt to detect supernatural intervention are as futile as they are unethical. *Journal of Medical Ethics* 34:e18.

———. 2008e. If socialized medicine is such a bad thing, then why not privatize the police and fire departments? *Dissident Voice* www.dissidentvoice.org/2008/04/if-socialized-medicine-is-such-a-bad-thing-then-why-not-privatize-the-police-and-fire-departments.

———. 2009a. How are other 1st world nations suppressing the adverse consequences of violence and youth sex in the modern media environment? *Pediatrics* (in press).

———. 2009b. Theodicy's problem: A statistical look at the Holocaust of the children, and the implications of natural evil for the free will and best of all world's hypotheses. *Philosophy and Theology* (in press).

———. 2009c. Is the Baylor religion study reliable? www.secularhumanism.org/greg-paul-baylor.pdf and www.secularhumanism.org/reply-to-rodney-stark.pdf.

———. 2009d. The Successful Societies Scale: The first broad based statistical tool for comparing prosperous nations' socioeconomic conditions reveals how dysfunctional psychosociological conditions underlie the origin and evolution of high levels of popular religious belief and worship. *Evolutionary Psychology* 7 (in press). www.epjournal.net/filestore/ep.pdf.

Paul, G., and P. Zuckerman. 2007. Why the gods are not winning. *Edge* www.edge.org/3rd_culture/paul07/paul07_index.html.

Pew. 2002. Among wealthy nations US stands alone in its embrace of religion. Pew Global Attitudes Project. www.pewglobal.org/reports/display.php?reported=167.

———. 2007. Pew trends in political values and core attitudes: 1987–2007. www.people- press.org/reports/display.php3?Report ID=312.

———. 2008. U.S. Religious Landscape Survey. www.religions.pewforum.org/ pdf/report2religious-landscape-study-full.pdf.

Phillips, K. 2006. *American theocracy.* New York: Viking.

Pinker, S. 2002. *The blank slate.* New York: Viking.

Powell, L., L. Shahabi, and C. Thoresen. 2003 Religion and spirituality: Linkages to physical health. *American Psychologist* 58:36–52.

Pratt, T., and T. Godsey. 2003. Social support, inequality and homicide: A cross-national test of an integrated theoretical model. *Criminology* 41:611–643.

Preston, J., and N. Epley. 2009. Science and God: An automatic opposition between ultimate explanations. *Journal of Experimental Social Psychology* 45:238–241.

Prothero, S. 2007. *Religious illiteracy: What every American needs to know—and doesn't.* New York: Harper One.

Putman, R. 2000. *Bowling alone: The collapse and revival of American community.* New York: Simon & Schuster.

Rainer, T. 2005. A resurgence not yet realized: Evangelistic effectiveness in the Southern Baptist convention since 1979. *The Southern Baptist Journal of Theology* 9(1):54–69.

Reid, T. 2004. *The United States of Europe.* New York: Penguin Press.

Rosenbaum, E. 2009. Patient teenagers? A comparison of the sexual behavior of virginity pledgers and matched nonpledgers. *Pediatrics* 123:e110–e120.

Rosnick, D., and M. Weisbrot. 2006. Are shorter work hours good for the environment? Center for Economic and Policy Research. www.repr.net/ documents/publications/energy_2006_12.pdf.

Rossi, H. 2008. Evangelicals embrace new global priorities. *Beliefnet* www. beliefnet.com/story/168_16822_1.html.

Sager, R. 2006. Purple mountains. *The Atlantic Monthly* 298(1):37–41.

Salmon, J. 2008. Southern Baptists struggle to maintain flock. *The Washington Post,* June 8.

Sampson, R., S. Raudenbush, and F. Earls. 1997. Neighborhoods and violent crime: a multilevel study of collective efficacy. *Science* 277:918–924.

Sapolsky, R. 2005. Sick of poverty. *Scientific American* 293(6):92–99.

Savage, S., S. Collins-Mayo, B. Mayo, and G. Gray. 2006. *Making sense of generation Y: The world-view of 16–25 year olds.* London: Church House Publishing.

Scheepers, P., M. Gijsberts, and E. Hello. 2002. Religiosity and prejudice against ethnic minorities in Europe: Cross-national tests on a controversial relationship. *Review of Religious Research* 43:242–265.

Schlesinger, A. 1986. *The cycles of American history.* New York: Houghton Mifflin.

Schoen, C. et al. 2005. Taking the pulse of health care systems: Experiences of patients with health problems in six countries. *Health Affairs,* November 3, 2005. http://content.healthaffairs.org/cgi/content/full/hlthaff.w5.509/DC1? maxtoshow=&HITS=10&hits=10&RESULTFORMAT=&author1=Schoen& fulltext=health+care&andorexactfulltext=and&searchid=1&FIRSTINDEX= 0&resourcetype=HWCIT (acessed August 23, 2009).

Sedgh, G. et al. 2007. Induced abortion: Estimated rates and trends worldwide. *The Lancet* 370:1338–1345.

Shah, T., and Toft, M. 2006. Why God is winning. *Foreign Policy* March/April:38–43.

Shermer, M. 2006. Bowling for God. *Scientific American* 295(6):44.

Sider, R. 2005. The scandal of the evangelical conscience: Why are Christians living just like the rest of the world? Grand Rapids: Baker Books.

Siegal, R. 2005. Intoxication: The universal drive for mind-altering substances. Montpelier, VT: Park Street Press.

Singh, S., and J. Darroch. 2000. Adolescent pregnancy and childbearing: Levels and trends in developed countries. *Family Planning Perspectives* 32:14–23.

Sjodin, U. 2002. The Swedes and the paranormal. *Journal of Contemporary Religion* 17:75–85.

Smith, T., and S. Kim. 2004 The vanishing Protestant majority. *GSS Social Change Report* 14:1–22. www.norc.uchicago.edu/issues/PROTSG08.pdf.

Stark, R. 2008. *What America really believes.* Waco: Baylor University Press.

Stark, R., and R. Finke. 2000. *Acts of faith.* Berkeley: University of California Press.

Taylor, H. 2003. While most Americans believe in God, only 36% attend a religious service once a month or more often. Harris Interactive. www.harrisinteractive.com/harris_poll/index.asp?PID=408.

Templeton Foundation. 2004. Spiritual capital. www.templeton.org/capabilities_2004/horiz03.html.

Times/Harris. 2006. Religious views and beliefs vary greatly by country, according to the latest Financial Times/Harris poll. www.harrisinteractive.com/NEWS/allnewsbydate.asp?NewsID=1130.

Tomlinson, J. 1991. *Cultural imperialism: A critical introduction.* Baltimore: Johns Hopkins University Press.

Transparency International. 2000. Corruption perceptions index. www.transparency.org/cpi/2000/cpi2000.

Trenholm, B. 2007. Impacts of four Title V Section 510 abstinence education programs (report to Congress). www.mathematica-mpr.com/publications?PDFs/impactabstinence.pdf.

United Nations. 2000. *Human Development Report 2000.* Oxford: Oxford University Press.

———. 2001. *Monthly Bulletin on Statistics April 2001.* Oxford: Oxford University Press.

———. 2004. *Human Development Report 2004.* Oxford: Oxford University Press.

———. 2005. *Human Development Report 2005.* Oxford: Oxford University Press. www.harrisinteractive.com/NEWS/allnewsbydate.asp?NewsID=1130 (accessed August 23, 2009).

Voas, D., V. D. Olson, and A. Crockett. 2002. Religious pluralism and participation: Why previous research is wrong. *American Sociological Review* 67:212–230.

Wallis, J. 2005. *God's politics: Why the Right gets it wrong and the Left doesn't get it.* New York: Harper One.

WEF. 2007. Global Competitiveness Report 2006–2007. www.weforum.org/en/initiatives/gcp/Global%20Competitiveness%20Report/index.html.

Weisman, J., and A. Cooperman. 2006. A religious protest largely from the Left: Conservative Christians say fighting cuts in poverty programs is not a priority. *The Washington Post,* December 14.

Wellings, K. et al. 2006. Sexual behavior in context: A global perspective. *Lancet* 368:1706–1728.

WHO. 2001. www.who.int/mental.health/Topic.Suicide.

———. 2004. Global Status Report on Alcohol. www.who.int/substance_a-buse/publications/global_status_report_2004_overview.pdf (accessed August 23, 2009).

Wilkinson, R. 2005. *The impact of inequality: How to make sick societies healthier.* New York: New Press.

Winkleby, M., C. Cubbin, and D. Ahn. 2006. Individual socioeconomic status, neighborhood socioeconomic status, and adult mortality. *American Journal of Public Health* 96:2145–2153.

Wuthnow, R. 2007. *After the baby boomers: How twenty- and thirty-somethings are shaping the future of American religion.* Princeton: Princeton University Press.

Zimring, F., and G. Hawkins. 1999. *Crime is not the problem: Lethal violence in America.* Oxford: Oxford University Press.

Zogby, J. 2008. *The way we'll be: The Zogby report on the transformation of the American dream.* New York: Random House.

Zuckerman, P. 2006. Atheism: Contemporary rates and patterns. In *The Cambridge companion to atheism,* ed. M. Martin, 47–68. Cambridge: Cambridge University Press.

———. 2008. *Society without God: What the least religious nations can tell us about contentment.* New York: New York University Press.

## APPENDIX 1

## Measuring Popular Religion versus Secularism and Socioeconomic Conditions in the First World

The nations sampled are seventeen of the nineteen most prosperous First World democracies (per capita income at least $23,000 circa 2000) with a population of about 4 million or more that have not recently experienced systemic ethnic violence such as Northern Ireland; Belgium and Finland are excluded as explained below, and their absence is unlikely to significantly alter the results. This sample limitation is similar to that of other studies (such as Panchaud et al., 2000; Singh and Darroch, 2000) and is a recommended procedure because it minimizes extraneous variables that are associated with dramatic differences in education and income levels as well as political systems (Neapolitan 1997; Jowell 1998; Paul 2005, 2009d), contra Jensen (2006). Because all but Japan are share Western cultures with a predominantly Euro-Christian heritage this variable is also minimized, whereas the inclusion of the Asian Japanese culture adds a potentially informative variation. The limitation to advanced nations also maximizes the size and quality of the data set; sociological statistics from Second and Third World nations are often unreliable if they are available at all (Gartner 1995; Neapolitan 1997; Jowell 1998; Paul 2005, 2009d). The next most comprehensive measure of national conditions is limited to only three variables because quality statistics are not available for most of the large number of countries included in their sample (Marks et al. 2006). Also, by definition only First World nations have the potential for the great majority to be socio-economically healthy in critical factors such as life spans and financial prosperity. Nor is it advisable for an advanced democracy like America to look to Second and Third World nations, many of which are not democratic, as examples for the highest standards of societal success yet reached. The prosperous democracies comprise a mass epidemiological experiment consisting of 800 million citizens.

Because the competing hypotheses center on popular opinion regarding religiosity on the one hand as opposed to secularism on the other, relations between church and state are not pertinent to this type of analysis (contra Moreno-Riano et al. 2006).[1] Mass opinion is measured by absolute belief in a supernatural creator deity, which is a superior measure of religious devotion than general belief in God because the latter includes the following: partial doubters; Bible literalism, which is a proxy for the conservatism of mass faith; frequent attendance at religious services and frequency of prayer that measure religious activity; belief in an afterlife; agnostics and atheists; and acceptance of human descent from animals, which is also a measure of creationist opinion (Appendix 2). In order to maximize data uniformity, most plotted data for popular religiosity is from the International Social Survey Program (ISSP) 1998 Religion II poll. The ISSP statistics for western and eastern Germany were combined in accord with their respective populations. That the ISSP sampled absolute belief in a creator is another reason it forms the database for this study, although this excludes Belgium and Finland because they are not members of the consortium. Because the ISSP did not ask the Japanese their opinion on the Bible, the nation's small percentage of Christians was divided by two to arrive at an approximation of the probable figure. The high rates of church activity for the Swiss reported by the ISSP are anomalous compared to other indicators and are excluded. To test the hypothesis examined by Jensen (2006) that "benevolent" versus "malevolent" religious cosmologies impact societal conditions, ISSP sampling on absolute belief in heaven and hell is analyzed separately. International data on acceptance of human descent from animals is from the ISSP 1993, and values from the Eurobarometer Europeans and Science and Technology of 2005 surveys are averaged when the same country was sampled by both polls. That polling on evolution is very limited outside the First World is another reason to focus on the prosperous democracies. Data on opinion on evolution in regions of the United States is from the National Opinion Research Center General Social Survey.

In order to approximately measure the overall cumulative level of popular religiosity and secularism, the absolute data values for each indicator that are available for each nation are normalized by scoring them on a 0–10 scale, with zero being applied to the most religious value present in a given sample of prosperous democracies and 10 to the most secular value. The average score on the 0–10 scale is then calculated for each nation, less any data gaps, creating its cumulative Popular Religiosity Versus Secularism Score for each nation that are used to construct the Popular Religiosity Versus Secularism Scale (PRVSS) for First World nations.[2]

Because the ISSP Religion II poll was conducted around the turn of the century, social indicators from the same time period were favored over more recent data sets, which differ little from the former because there has not been sufficient time for major change. The indicators chosen provide a broad overall measure of societal and economic conditions in each nation because they include the major categories that are based on sufficiently reliable data. The primary indicators examined are homicide, incarceration, juvenile mortality, lifespan, adolescent and all age gonorrhea and syphilis infections, adolescent abortion, adolescent births, youth and all age suicide, fertility, marriage, marriage duration, divorce, life satisfaction, alcohol consumption, corruption, income, income disparity, poverty, employment, work hours and resource exploitation base (Appendix 2). This totals 25 specific factors within 21 primary socioeconomic indicators; four of the primary indicators include two specific factors. It will be difficult to build a significantly broader data set that more comprehensively measures socioeconomic conditions. Of the 10 indicators also used in Paul (2005) the same data sets are used except for homicide. Scatter plots for some of the correlations not included here are in Paul (2005, 2009d). The indicator comparisons were statistically analyzed with Pearson correlations (Appendix 3). Because the United States is often a strong outlier, the correlations were run both with all 17 nations sampled and also with the United States excluded. To add a historical perspective some longitudinal information is included.

Homicide data (from the rigorous tallying by Barclay and Taveres 2003) is reliable because it is based on forensic analysis and body counts. A comparison of nonlethal crime data is more a comparison of rates of inconsistent reportage by victims and recording of crime according to differing official criteria rather than of actual acts and should not be used for direct quantitative assessments (as per Paul 2005, 2009d, contra Jensen 2006).[3] As Neapolitan (1997) states, homicide "is generally regarded as the most valid and reliable of official cross-national crime indicators. . . . In general, violent crimes other than homicides—such as rapes, assaults, and robberies—*should probably not be compared cross-nationally, unless there is substantial improvement in the quality of the data* [italic emphasis added]. Indications are that definitional, reporting, and recording differences are too great for these crimes to be suitable for analysis. This is particularly true for sexual offenses and rapes. Thus, cross-national comparisons of violent crime should probably be restricted to homicides."[4] Barclay and Taveres (2002), who calculate criminal act rates only for homicide, agree that "comparisons between the recorded [nonviolent and nonlethal violent] crime levels in different countries may be misleading. . . . [S]ince the definition of homicide is similar in most countries, absolute comparisons are possible." (Also see Zimring and Hawkins 1999, OECD 2001, Beeghley 2003, and Farrington et al. 2004). That using nonlethal crime data for cross-national purposes would garner severe criticism from criminologists is fortuitous in that murder is the most extreme crime and contributes to societal fear and insecurity more than any other (Neapolitan 1997; Zimring and Hawkins 1999; OECD 2001; Beeghley 2003; Paul 2005; Jensen 2006).

Murder was astonishingly common in crime-rampant medieval Christian Europe (Lane 1997; Neapolitan 1997). Homicide levels in the United States have always been elevated well above the rates in the more secular democracies where murder rates have long been low and relatively stable, perhaps representing the minimum practically possible (Lane 1997; Neapolitan 1997; Beeghley 2003). During the Jim Crow era public spectacles featuring brutal vigilante murders were events common to the strongly religious culture (Dray 2003; Messner and Zevenbergen 2005; Budiansky 2008). Despite a recent decline from an extreme peak in the 1980s, homicide rates are still many multiples higher in the United States than in any other First World nation (Lane 1997; Neapolitan 1997; Doyle 2000; Barclay and Taveres 2003; Beeghley 2003; Paul 2005; Jensen 2006). In some locations 10 percent of American males are murdered before age 35, and street crime–ridden cities like Detroit, Baltimore, Washington, D.C., Atlanta, and New Orleans are not found in the other advanced nations (Barclay and Taveres 2003).[5] Even when U.S. white-only rates are considered homicide remains above the general secular democracy levels (Lane 1997; Neapolitan 1997; Zimring and Hawkins 1999; Doyle 2000; OECD 2001; Barclay and Taveres 2003; Beeghley 2003; Paul 2005). The United States suffers from an unusually high level of school shootings (Hall 2008). The correlation is very strong in favor of secularism entirely because the theistic and creationist United States is a strong outlier. Among the hypotheistic democracies homicide levels are consistently low, and with the United States removed there is no significant correlation. However, the lowest homicide levels are found among some of the most secular democracies; it may be impractical to achieve lower rates. The Interpol and International Crime Victims Survey data suggests that the United States is a high-crime nation and is not superior to other First World nations in terms of nonlethal transgressions (Neapolitan 1997; OCED 2001; Barclay and Taveres 2003), so inclusion of the latter would probably not significantly alter the cumulative SSS results in favor of the United States.

Incarceration levels are reliably recorded (ICPS 2006). No other country, even much more populous China, has so many inmates as does the United States, more than 2 million. Following a steep climb in recent decades, the theoconservative United States has half a dozen times more inmates per capita than the Western norm. The correlation of more than 0.6 in favor of secularism is strong entirely because the United States is a strong outlier. With the United States removed there is no significant correlation because incarceration rates are consistently low in the rest of the countries sampled, although the lowest incarceration levels are found among some of the most secular democracies.

Suicide data is robust because it is based on forensic analysis and body counts (WHO 2001). Despite the reservations about including all age suicide cited in Paul (2005), these statistics are included in order to test whether inclusion of the data significantly improves the societal status of the United States as suggested by Jensen (2006). The theoconservative United States is fairly typical in youth suicide, but most of the highly secular democracies perform even better, and the correlations marginally favor secularism whether the United States is included or not. The United States performs better in all-age suicide, and the correlations moderately favor religious countries in this case whether or not the United States is included. Note that the belief that the non-religious Scandinavian nations exhibit exceptional levels of suicide is exaggerated, nor is Japan particularly extreme.

The implication by Jensen (2006) that it is appropriate to compare a number of specific causes of death is incorrect because this leads to an arbitrary competition between the multitude of lethal mistakes humans are vulnerable to; therefore, basic levels of juvenile and adult mortality are examined (UN 2000). Historical juvenile mortality rates were 50 percent or more and average lifespans were just 20 years in Christian Europe and America (Paul 2008d). Since then enormous science- and technology-driven gains in reducing mortality have been achieved, but no prosperous democracy loses children as rapidly as the United States, whose mortality in infants and young children is almost twice as high as achieved by some of the most secular countries. It may not be possible to further reduce mortality rates with current technologies. Some Second World nations have juvenile mortality rates little above the U.S. level (UN 2000). Being above 0.7 whether the United States is included or not, the $r$ correlation in favor of secularism is remarkably strong. The strength of the relationship is reinforced by the progressive nature of the correlation in which higher religiosity is associated with higher losses of children and vice versa. The theoconservative United States has among the lowest life expectancy among the sample, whereas highly secular Japan enjoys the longest. Even though the differential is not very large in total years, the situation for the United States is actually more serious than it seems. Although national life expectancy continues to rise, the United States is not keeping up with the general Western pace and now suffers from the lowest life expectancy in the First World (OECD 2007). This slippage is attributable to an actual decline in average lifespans in some regions (Ezzati et al. 2008), a disturbing failure occurring in none of the secular democracies.[6] With hypotheistic Denmark exhibiting low life expectancy, the correlation in favor of secularism is modest with the United States included and not significant with the United States excluded. Nor is there a compelling historical, mass epidemiological or clinical evidence that high rates of prayer are associated with lower levels of mortality and illness; if anything, the reverse may be true (Paul 2005, 2008e; Blumenthal et al. 2007).

Gonorrhea and syphilis infections are recorded sufficiently well to be compared cross-nationally, albeit only in a limited number of Western nations according to the source utilized herein (Panchaud et al. 2000); information for HIV, chlamydia, genital herpes, and human papilloma virus is grossly inadequate for quantitative cross-national comparisons. STDs ravaged old Europe, and high infection rates promoted national campaigns to suppress rampant prostitution in America in the later 1800s and early 1900s (Brandt 1987; Aral and Holmes 1996). After being suppressed by post-WWII campaigns, STDs became epidemic in the 1970s in the First World. Since then there has been a general decrease in Western nations, but syphilis and especially gonorrhea remain at epidemic levels in the theoconservative United States, including middle-class whites for the latter (Aral and Holmes 1996; Panchaud et al. 2000). Teen gonorrhea infection rates, for example, are dozens to literally hundreds of times higher in the United States than in secular western Europe and Canada, and gonorrhea and syphilis have been nearly exterminated in the highly secular Nordic countries and France. The correlations are very strong in favor of secularism with the United States included in all cases. They are strong in favor of secularism with the United States excluded for gonorrhea. For syphilis the correlation is not significant for youth and is moderate in favor of religiosity in the all age case. Because the sample size is limited some caution is necessary, but it is unlikely that addition of additional prosperous democracies will markedly alter the results. The data that are available suggest that the infection rates of other STDs are not lower in the United States relative to more secular prosperous democracies (Aral and Holmes 1996; Panchaud et al. 2000), so inclusion of the latter would probably not significantly alter the SSS results in favor of the United States.

The degree to which abortion is a societal problem is controversial, but it often signals a failure to use contraceptives. Sufficiently robust adolescent abortion rates are available for only a portion of the nations examined (Singh and Darroch 2000). Abortion rates are persistently high even when illegal (Sedgh et al. 2007). After a modest reduction over time, youth abortion rates remain markedly higher, up to a factor of two, in the religious and creationist United States than in the more secular advanced democracies. The correlation favoring secularism is very strong whether or not the United States is included, and the correlation is strongly progressive in either case.

Youth birthrate data is generally well recorded (Singh and Darroch 2000); this indicator is compared in an age cohort where marriage is infrequent. Despite previous declines, birth rates among teens who are not married are two to dozens of times lower in the secular democracies than in the United States. The correlation is very strong in favor of secularism with the United States outlier included, it remains moderate with the United States excluded.

Low national birth rates may in part reflect a high perception of personal security and may be a societal positive in nations that lack adequate habitable land area and at a time when the global population is rapidly approaching 7 billion. Because this reliably recorded indicator (UN 2005) is often cited by advocates of the moral-creator socioeconomic hypothesis as important to societal health, it is included to discover whether it substantially improves the cumulative status of the United States. The theoconservative United States is matched in fertility only by moderately secular New Zealand, but highly secular France in not far behind. Strongly secular Japan and Germany have very low fertility rates, but so do the four most religious western European nations. The Pearson correlation is not significant with the United States included and is even less so with it removed.

Marriage versus cohabitation is a lifestyle choice, and there is little evidence that the much lower rates of marriage in secular democracies is adversely impacting the children of unmarried couples (Reid 2004). Because this dependably recorded indicator (UN 2001) is often cited by proponents of the moral-creator socioeconomic hypothesis, it too is included.

The marriage rate in the religious and creationist United States is so high that it is a strong outlier compared to the more secular countries. With the United States included, the correlation is moderate in favor of religiosity; with the United States excluded the correlation is not significant. Divorce laws are inconsistent between democracies, so the statistics on marriage duration before divorces among married couples reflect both legal as well as social differences (Divorce Reform 2002; OECD 2001). The United States performs poorly in marriage duration and divorce, being uniquely low in the former and edged out in the latter only by highly secular Sweden. With the United States included, the correlations are not significant. With the United States excluded the correlation for marriage duration is moderate in favor of more religious democracies, and for divorces this correlation is strong; but these results may be skewed by restrictive divorce laws in some of the more religious examples.

After the massive use of opiates to alleviate pain in wounded Civil War soldiers, the United States developed a mass drug culture that the legal war on drugs initiated in the early 1900s has never succeeded in suppressing (Gallinger 2003; Siegal 2005). Data for illegal drug use is not sufficiently dependable to statistically analyze (Bloss 2005). Because alcohol is usually sold under government regulation, levels of consumption are reasonably well recorded (WHO 2004), and use of this drug is included following the suggestion by Jensen (2006). De Tocqueville (1835) observed that alcohol consumption rates were extraordinarily high in the new American nation, inspiring the Prohibition Movement that after backfiring lead to a new wave of excessive consumption well into the post-WWII era (Gately 2008). Currently the theistic and creationist United States has fairly low levels of alcohol consumption, but the next most religious nation Ireland has very high levels of consumption, whereas some of the most secular examples are below the United States level. With the United States included the correlation is insignificant, and with it excluded the correlation marginally favors secularism.

Corruption statistics are estimated with reasonable albeit inexact reliability by Transparency International (2000). The level of corruption is fairly typical in the theistic United States as well as Ireland, is very high in less theistic Italy, and is both high and very low in the least theistic democracies. Regardless of whether the correlations include the United States, the trend very marginally favors secularism.

Comparing societal contentment is valuable since the moral-creator social hypothesis predicts that those who do not believe in a creator are at risk of suffering from the chronic malaise of living a meaningless life terminated by final death. Life satisfaction (Marks et al. 2006) is considered a more robust measure of this factor than is happiness because it is somewhat less subjective, reflecting long-term fulfillment rather than transitory feelings of the respondent (Diener et al. 1999; Inglehart and Klingemann 2000; Marks et al. 2006; Nettle 2005). The theoconservative United States is typical in life satisfaction, as is somewhat less religious Ireland, and the factor is both very high and very low in the most secular examples. The statistical correlation is insignificant both with and without the United States included.

Economic statistics are generally robust. Adjusted per capita gross national product, poverty statistics, and GINI income equality coefficient are from UN (2004). Because unemployment figures often do not include those who are out of but not searching for work, employment as a percentage of the working age population is the superior measure of this indicator (OECD 2001). Average hours worked by each civilian in a year are included because the more free time a person has the more potential they have to engage in parenting and other family and neighborhood activities, to reduce stress through leisure activities, and because the combination of hours worked and per capita income is a measure of worker productivity (Rosnick and Weisbrot 2006). Resource exploitation base or ecological footprint, the average planetary surface area needed to support each citizen within a nation, can be used to gauge the efficiency at which a nation transforms resources into beneficent societal conditions (Marks et al. 2006).

The overall, cumulative socioeconomic conditions of the First World nations were calculated using the same basic procedures for the PRVSS, with zero being applied to the most dysfunctional value present in a given sample of prosperous democracies and 10 to the healthiest, creating its cumulative Societal Success Score for each nation.[7] The latter were used to construct the Successful Societies Scale (SSS) for First World nations. No attempt was made to differentially weigh the various indicators for the SSS or PRVSS. In part this is because of the difficulty of assessing their relative value. Is homicide, for example, twice on an order of magnitude as important than fertility levels? Also, the absence of other crime statistics suggests that giving extra weight to homicide alone is not appropriate, and the same applies to the STDs included when others could not be included. In any case the results are sufficiently robust that weighing the indicators would not significantly alter the outcome.

The number of foreign born is sufficiently determinable (OECD 2001). Measuring the diversity of a national population is much more difficult due to inherent definitional problems, the sole recent attempt to assay this dynamic is Fearon (2003), who tabulated both ethnic and cultural fractionalization. The two factors parallel one another, and cultural fractionalization was utilized in this inquiry in accord with the advice of Fearon (2003).

Because there is no significant difference in the correlations, the hypothesis that levels of belief in heaven and hell have differing impacts on socioeconomic conditions (Barro and McLeary 2003; Jensen 2006) is not supported by this examination of First World nations.

## APPENDIX 1: NOTES

1. The authors of this criticism of Paul (2005) are faculty at Cedarville University, a fundamentalist institution that hosted a research conference promoting the belief that the Genesis creation story that the earth is a few thousand years old is literally true (www.cedarville.edu/departments/er/geology).

2. When scores for more than one country differ slightly when the original values listed are the same is because the latter were rounded off during tabulation.

3. Interpol merely gathers and reports nonlethal crime statistics provided by member nations without standardizing or vetting them (Neapolitan 1997; Barclay and Taveres 2002, 2003). For example, assaults are reported at a rate about six times higher in Australia and Sweden than in Canada and France, but this level of disparity is suspect. Rates of theft are reported to be twice as high in Sweden as in France. Are the former actually twice as larcenous as the French,

or are the latter twice as unlikely to file a report, or is the reality somewhere in-between? Similarly suspicious discrepancies exist in International Crime Victims Survey results.

4. Reported rates of rape are two to twenty times higher in the United States than in other First World nations (Jay 2004; MASA 2003), but this only means that American females report being raped at far higher rates, not that American males are more prone to committing sexual assaults.

5. Seemingly very high homicide rates for some European cities in UN (2000) are inflated by the inappropriate inclusion of attempted homicides (Barclay and Taveres 2003; Barclay, personal communication).

6. The United States has lost its stature as a nation of exceptionally tall citizens, a probable reflection of problems in providing health care (Komlos and Lauderdale 2007).

7. See Note 2.

**APPENDIX 2**
**Cross-national data sets and scores**

| Country | PRVSS score[b] | Absolutely believe in God[a] | | Bible literalists[a] | | Religious services[a] | | Prayer[a] | |
|---|---|---|---|---|---|---|---|---|---|
| | | % | Score | % | Score | % | Score | % | Score |
| Sweden (W) | 9.3 | 12 | 8.6 | 5 | 9.0 | 7 | 9.5 | 14 | 9.7 |
| Japan (J) | 9.2 | 4 | 10 | 2 | 10 | 4 | 10 | 11 | 6.9 |
| Denmark (D) | 8.8 | 14 | 8.4 | 8 | 8.0 | 7 | 9.5 | 17 | 9.1 |
| France (F) | 8.5 | 20 | 7.3 | 4 | 9.2 | 13 | 8.6 | 21 | 8.3 |
| Germany (G) | 8.3 | 19 | 7.4 | 8 | 7.7 | 17 | 8.1 | 13 | 10 |
| Great Britain (E) | 7.6 | 23 | 6.9 | 5 | 8.9 | 17 | 8.0 | 24 | 7.6 |
| Norway (N) | 7.5 | 18 | 7.6 | 11 | 7.0 | 9 | 9.6 | 20 | 8.5 |
| Holland (H) | 6.6 | 26 | 6.2 | 9 | 7.4 | 18 | 7.9 | 30 | 6.4 |
| Australia (A) | 6.1 | 29 | 5.8 | 6 | 8.5 | 21 | 7.4 | 31 | 6.1 |
| New Zealand (N) | 5.9 | 31 | 5.4 | 10 | 7.1 | 21 | 7.5 | 28 | 6.8 |
| Canada (C) | 5.5 | 39 | 4.1 | 10 | 7.3 | 29 | 6.4 | 30 | 6.4 |
| Spain (S) | 5.4 | 46 | 2.9 | 13 | 5.9 | 36 | 6.7 | 29 | 6.5 |
| Switzerland (L) | 5.2 | 28 | 5.9 | 11 | 6.9 | — | — | 35 | 5.2 |
| Austria (R) | 4.9 | 32 | 5.2 | 14 | 5.6 | 33 | 5.8 | 31 | 6.1 |
| Italy (T) | 3.9 | 48 | 2.5 | 26 | 1.6 | 44 | 6.3 | 34 | 5.5 |
| Ireland (I) | 2.3 | 50 | 2.2 | 23 | 2.7 | 73 | 0 | 45 | 3.1 |
| United States (U) | 0.9 | 63 | 0 | 30 | 0 | 39 | 4.9 | 60 | 0 |

# APPENDIX 2 (*continued*)

| Country | Absolutely believe in afterlife[b] | | Absolutely believe in heaven (%)[b] | Absolutely believe in hell (%)[b] | Agnostics and atheists[b] | | Acceptance of evolution[c] | |
| --- | --- | --- | --- | --- | --- | --- | --- | --- |
| | % | Score | | | % | Score | % | Score |
| W | 22 | 9.2 | 12 | 7 | 35 | 9.1 | 82 | 9.7 |
| J | 9 | 10 | 7 | 6 | 31 | 8.3 | 81 | 9.5 |
| D | 16 | 8.6 | 14 | 8 | 31 | 7.8 | 83 | 10 |
| F | 26 | 6.7 | 14 | 10 | 37 | 10 | 80 | 9.2 |
| G | 17 | 8.4 | 15 | 9 | 36 | 9.6 | 73 | 7.4 |
| E | 25 | 6.8 | 23 | 14 | 25 | 6.1 | 78 | 8.8 |
| N | 24 | 7.0 | 18 | 10 | 24 | 5.7 | 70 | 6.7 |
| H | 31 | 5.6 | 23 | 13 | 29 | 7.5 | 63 | 4.9 |
| A | | — | — | — | 24 | 5.7 | 55 | 2.8 |
| Z | 37 | 4.4 | 33 | 23 | 20 | 4.3 | 66 | 5.6 |
| C | 38 | 4.3 | 36 | 26 | 17 | 3.5 | 68 | 6.2 |
| S | 28 | 6.3 | 25 | 18 | 16 | 3.0 | 69 | 6.4 |
| L | 32 | 5.3 | 22 | 14 | 16 | 3.2 | 62 | 4.6 |
| R | 30 | 5.8 | 19 | 13 | 15 | 2.8 | 57 | 3.3 |
| T | 41 | 3.6 | 34 | 30 | 9 | 1.9 | 67 | 5.9 |
| I | 44 | 2.9 | 50 | 27 | 6 | 0 | 64 | 5.1 |
| L | 59 | 0 | 67 | 55 | 8 | 1.6 | 44 | 0 |

| Country | SSS score | Homicides[d] Per 100K | Score | Incarceration[e] Per 100K | Score | Suicide, age 15—24 years[f] Per 100K | Score | Suicide all ages[f] Per 100K | Score | Mortality, under 5 years[g] Per 1000 | Score | Lifespan[f] Years | Score |
|---|---|---|---|---|---|---|---|---|---|---|---|---|---|
| W | 7.1 | 1.11 | 9.7 | 78 | 9.7 | 8.3 | 7.7 | 14.2 | 4.7 | 4 | 10 | 78.6 | 6.7 |
| J | 6.0 | 1.05 | 9.8 | 60 | 10 | 8.5 | 7.5 | 18.8 | 1.1 | 4 | 10 | 80.0 | 10 |
| D | 7.3 | 1.02 | 9.8 | 77 | 9.7 | 7.9 | 8.0 | 17.5 | 2.1 | 5 | 7.5 | 75.7 | 0 |
| F | 5.8 | 1.73 | 8.3 | 88 | 9.6 | 8.9 | 7.2 | 19 | 0.9 | 5 | 7.5 | 78.1 | 0.6 |
| G | 5.7 | 1.15 | 9.7 | 97 | 9.4 | 8.2 | 7.7 | 14.2 | 4.7 | 5 | 7.5 | 77.2 | 3.5 |
| E | 6.2 | 1.61 | 8.6 | 141 | 8.8 | 6.7 | 8.9 | 7.4 | 10 | 6 | 5.0 | 77.2 | 3.5 |
| N | 8.0 | 0.95 | 10 | 68 | 9.9 | 12.6 | 4.4 | 12.1 | 6.3 | 4 | 10 | 78.1 | 5.6 |
| H | 6.9 | 1.51 | 8.8 | 127 | 9.0 | 7.9 | 8.0 | 7.9 | 9.6 | 5 | 7.5 | 77.9 | 5.1 |
| A | 4.8 | 1.87 | 8.2 | 120 | 9.1 | 18.5 | 0 | 14.3 | 4.6 | 5 | 7.5 | 78.3 | 6.0 |
| Z | 5.0 | 2.5 | 6.6 | 181 | 8.2 | 15.1 | 2.6 | 15.3 | 3.8 | 6 | 5.0 | 76.9 | 2.8 |
| C | 6.2 | 1.77 | 8.3 | 107 | 9.3 | 13.7 | 3.6 | 12.3 | 6.2 | 6 | 5.0 | 79.0 | 7.7 |
| S | 5.0 | 1.12 | 9.7 | 140 | 8.8 | 5.3 | 9.9 | 8.6 | 9.1 | 6 | 5.0 | 78.0 | 2.4 |
| L | 5.7 | 1.12 | 9.7 | 81 | 9.7 | 15.3 | 2.4 | 20.2 | 0 | 5 | 7.5 | 78.7 | 7.0 |
| R | 5.4 | 1.23 | 9.4 | 108 | 9.3 | 12.9 | 9.3 | 19.2 | 0.8 | 5 | 7.5 | 77.0 | 3.0 |
| T | 5.6 | 1.50 | 8.8 | 97 | 9.4 | 5.2 | 10 | 8.2 | 9.4 | 6 | 5.0 | 78.2 | 5.8 |
| I | 5.3 | 1.42 | 9.0 | 85 | 9.6 | 15.2 | 2.5 | 11.3 | 7 | 7 | 2.5 | 76.4 | 1.6 |
| U | 2.9 | 5.56 | 0 | 724 | 0 | 11.1 | 5.6 | 11.3 | 7 | 8 | 0 | 76.7 | 2.3 |

| Country | Gonorrhea, 15–19 years[h] | | Gonorrhea, all ages[h] | | Syphilis, 15–19 years[h] | | Syphilis, all ages[h] | | Abortions, 15–19 years[i] | | Births, 15–17 years[i] | |
|---|---|---|---|---|---|---|---|---|---|---|---|---|
| | Per 100K | Score | Per 100K | Score | Per 100K | Score | Per 100K | Score | Per 1000 | Score | Per 1000 | Score |
| W | 1.8 | 10 | 2.8 | 10 | 0.6 | 9.0 | 0.8 | 8.3 | 17.2 | 8.1 | 2.7 | 9.5 |
| J | — | — | — | — | — | — | — | — | — | — | 1.1 | 10 |
| D | 5.0 | 9.9 | 3.4 | 9.9 | 0.8 | 8.8 | 0.4 | 9.3 | 14.4 | 10 | 2.2 | 9.7 |
| F | 7.7 | 9.9 | 8.4 | 9.6 | — | — | — | — | — | — | 3.5 | 9.3 |
| G | — | — | — | — | — | — | — | — | — | — | 4.4 | 9.0 |
| E | 77 | 8.7 | 22 | 8.4 | 0.2 | 9.7 | 0.2 | 9.8 | 18.6 | 7.2 | 14.6 | 5.9 |
| N | 6.7 | 9.9 | 4 | 9.9 | 0 | 10 | 0.1 | 10 | 18.7 | 7.1 | 4 | 9.1 |
| H | — | — | — | — | — | — | — | — | — | — | — | — |
| A | — | — | — | — | — | — | — | — | 23.8 | 3.6 | 10.6 | 7.1 |
| Z | — | — | — | — | — | — | — | — | 20 | 6.2 | 19.2 | 4.5 |
| C | 59 | 9.0 | 17 | 9 | 0.6 | 9.0 | 0.3 | 9.5 | 21.2 | 5.4 | 13.6 | 6.1 |
| S | — | — | — | — | — | — | — | — | — | — | — | — |
| L | — | — | — | — | — | — | — | — | — | — | — | — |
| R | — | — | — | — | — | — | — | — | — | — | 5.8 | 8.5 |
| T | — | — | — | — | — | — | — | — | — | — | — | — |
| I | — | — | — | — | — | — | — | — | — | — | 6.6 | 8.3 |
| U | 57 | 20 | 125 | 0 | 6.4 | 0 | 4.3 | 0 | 29.2 | 0 | 33.8 | 0 |

| Country | Fertility[j] | | Marriages[k] | | Marriage duration[l] | | Divorces[m] | | Alcohol consumption[n] | | Life satisfaction[o] | |
|---|---|---|---|---|---|---|---|---|---|---|---|---|
| | Rate | Score | Per 1000 | Score | Years | Score | Per 1000 | Score | Liters/year | Score | Value | Score |
| W | 1.6 | 4.3 | 4.0 | 0 | 12 | 4.8 | 55 | 0 | 6.9 | 8.7 | 7.7 | 7.5 |
| J | 1.3 | 0 | 6.3 | 5.3 | 10 | 3.1 | 30 | 5.5 | 7.4 | 8.2 | 6.2 | 0 |
| D | 1.8 | 7.1 | 6.6 | 6.0 | 11.5 | 4.3 | 45 | 2.3 | 11.9 | 3.0 | 8.2 | 10 |
| F | 1.9 | 9.3 | 4.8 | 1.9 | 13 | 5.8 | 38 | 3.7 | 13.5 | 1.1 | 6.6 | 2.0 |
| G | 1.3 | 0 | 5.2 | 2.8 | 12 | 4.4 | 39 | 3.5 | 12.9 | 1.8 | 7.2 | 5.0 |
| E | 1.7 | 5.7 | 5.1 | 2.6 | 11.5 | 4.3 | 43 | 2.7 | 10.4 | 4.7 | 7.1 | 4.5 |
| N | 1.8 | 7.1 | 5.3 | 3.0 | 13 | 5.5 | 40 | 3.2 | 5.8 | 10 | 7.4 | 6.0 |
| H | 1.7 | 5.7 | 5.6 | 3.7 | 11.5 | 4.3 | 38 | 3.7 | 9.7 | 5.5 | 7.5 | 6.5 |
| A | 1.7 | 5.7 | 6.0 | 4.7 | 7.5 | 0.3 | 43 | 2.7 | 9.2 | 6.4 | 7.3 | 5.5 |
| N | 2.0 | 10 | 5.3 | 3.0 | 14 | 6.8 | 50 | 1.1 | 9.8 | 5.4 | 7.4 | 6.0 |
| C | 1.5 | 2.9 | 5.0 | 2.3 | 13.5 | 6.3 | 37 | 4.0 | 8.3 | 7.1 | 7.6 | 7.0 |
| S | 1.3 | 0 | 6.3 | 5.3 | — | — | 15 | 8.8 | 12.3 | 2.5 | 7.0 | 4.0 |
| L | 1.4 | 1.4 | 4.9 | 2.1 | 12 | 5.1 | 26 | 6.5 | 11.5 | 3.4 | 8.2 | 10 |
| R | 1.4 | 1.4 | 4.8 | 1.9 | 11 | 3.5 | 42 | 2.6 | 12.6 | 2.2 | 7.8 | 8.0 |
| T | 1.3 | 0 | 4.7 | 1.6 | 17 | 10 | 10 | 10 | 9.1 | 5.8 | 6.9 | 3.5 |
| I | 1.9 | 8.6 | 4.9 | 2.1 | — | — | 15 | 8.9 | 14.5 | 0 | 7.6 | 7.0 |
| U | 2.0 | 10 | 8.3 | 10 | 7 | 0 | 54 | 0.1 | 8.5 | 6.9 | 7.4 | 6.0 |

**APPENDIX 2** *(continued)*

| Country | Corruption[p] Value | Corruption[p] Score | Per capita Income[q] U.S., $K | Per capita Income[q] Score | Income inequality[q] Index | Income inequality[q] Score | Poverty index[q] Score | Poverty index[q] Value | Employment levels[l] % | Employment levels[l] Score |
|---|---|---|---|---|---|---|---|---|---|---|
| W | 9.4 | 9.2 | 26.1 | 3.0 | 25 | 9.9 | 6.5 | 10 | 73 | 7.5 |
| J | 6.4 | 3.5 | 26.9 | 3.6 | 24.9 | 9.9 | 11.1 | 5.1 | 69 | 6.0 |
| D | 9.8 | 10 | 30.9 | 6.2 | 24.7 | 10 | 9.1 | 7.2 | 7 | 8.8 |
| F | 6.7 | 4.0 | 26.9 | 3.6 | 32.7 | 6.3 | 10.8 | 5.4 | 60 | 2.7 |
| G | 7.6 | 5.8 | 27.1 | 3.7 | 28.3 | 8.4 | 10.3 | 5.9 | 65 | 4.6 |
| E | 8.7 | 7.9 | 26.2 | 3.1 | 36 | 4.8 | 14.8 | 1.1 | 72 | 7.1 |
| N | 9.1 | 8.7 | 36.6 | 10 | 25.8 | 9.5 | 7.1 | 9.4 | 78 | 9.4 |
| H | 8.9 | 8.3 | 29.1 | 5.0 | 30.9 | 7.2 | 8.2 | 8.2 | 71 | 6.8 |
| A | 8.3 | 7.1 | 28.3 | 4.5 | 35.2 | 5.2 | 12.9 | 3.1 | 68 | 5.8 |
| N | 9.4 | 9.2 | 21.7 | 0.2 | 36. | 4.7 | — | — | 70 | 6.4 |
| C | 9.2 | 8.8 | 29.5 | 5.3 | 33.1 | 6.2 | 12. | 3.9 | 70 | 6.5 |
| S | 7.0 | 4.6 | 21.5 | 0 | 32.5 | 6.4 | 11 | 5.2 | 54 | 0.5 |
| L | 8.6 | 7.7 | 30.0 | 5.6 | 33.1 | 6.2 | — | — | 78 | 10 |
| R | 7.7 | 6.0 | 29.2 | 5.1 | 30 | 7.6 | — | — | 68 | 5.8 |
| T | 4.6 | 0 | 26.5 | 3.3 | 36 | 4.8 | 11.6 | 4.5 | 53 | 0 |
| I | 7.2 | 5.0 | 36.4 | 9.8 | 35.9 | 4.9 | 15.3 | 0.5 | 63 | 3.7 |
| U | 7.8 | 6.2 | 35.8 | 9.4 | 46.6 | 0 | 15.0 | 8 | 74 | 7.9 |

| | Average hours worked[r] | | Resource exploitation bases | | Foreign born (%)[l] | Cultural fractionalization[t] |
| | Hours/year | Score | Hectares/person | Score | | |
|---|---|---|---|---|---|---|
| W | 1550 | 5.6 | 7.0 | 4.4 | 5.7 | 0.189 |
| J | 1760 | 1.3 | 4.3 | 9.1 | 1.5 | 0.012 |
| D | 1520 | 6.3 | 6.4 | 5.4 | 4.9 | 0.128 |
| F | 1430 | 8.1 | 5.8 | 6.5 | 6.5 | 0.251 |
| G | 1440 | 7.9 | 4.8 | 8.2 | 8.5 | 0.09 |
| E | 1620 | 4.2 | 5.4 | 7.2 | 4.0 | 0.184 |
| N | 1340 | 10 | 6.2 | 5.8 | 3.9 | 0.098 |
| H | 1350 | 9.8 | 4.7 | 8.4 | 4.4 | 0.077 |
| A | 1760 | 1.3 | 7.7 | 3.2 | 23 | 0.147 |
| Z | 1750 | 1.5 | 5.5 | 7.0 | 20 | 0.363 |
| C | 1760 | 1.3 | 6.4 | 5.4 | 17.5 | 0.499 |
| S | 1800 | 0.4 | 4.8 | 8.2 | 2.0 | 0.263 |
| L | 1540 | 5.8 | 5.3 | 7.4 | 19 | 0.418 |
| R | 1500 | 6.7 | 4.6 | 8.6 | 9.0 | 0.1 |
| T | 1610 | 4.4 | 3.8 | 10 | 2.3 | 0.04 |
| I | 1650 | 3.5 | 6.2 | 5.8 | 3.0 | 0.157 |
| U | 1820 | 0 | 9.5 | 0 | 9.9 | 0.271 |

— = not available.

Source: [a]ISSP; [b]PRVSS; [c]ISSP/Eurobarometer; [d]Barcley and Taveres 2002; [e]ICPS 2006; [f]WHO 2001; [g]UN 2000; [h]Panchaud et al. 2000; [i]Singh and Darroch 2000; [j]UN 2005; [k]UN 2001; [l]OECD 2001; [m]Divorce Reform 2002; [n]WHO 2004; [o]Marks et al. 2006; [p]Transparency International 2000; [q]UN 2004; [r]Rosnick and Weisbrot 2006; [s]Marks et al. 2006; [t]Fearon 2003.

**APPENDIX 3**

**Pearson correlation coefficients for correlation of secularism with social and economic circumstances**

| | +U.S.* | −U.S.† | N = (+U.S.) |
|---|---|---|---|
| PRVSS compared to | | | |
| SSS | **0.705** | **0.534** | 17 |
| Homicides | −**0.611** | −0.262 | 17 |
| Incarceration | −**0.606** | −0.273 | 17 |
| Suicides, 15–24 years old | **0.326** | **0.379** | 17 |
| Suicides, all age | 0.322 | 0.297 | 17 |
| Mortality, under 5 years old | −**0.835** | −**0.746** | 17 |
| Life expectancy | **0.304** | **0.198** | 17 |
| Gonorrhea infections, 15–19 years old | −**0.937** | −**0.676** | 7 |
| Gonorrhea infections, all age | −**0.938** | −**0.643** | 7 |
| Syphilis infections, 15–19 years old | −**0.886** | 0.213 | 6 |
| Syphilis infections, all age | −**0.856** | 0.596 | 6 |
| Abortions 15–19 years old | −**0.938** | −**0.825** | 8 |
| Births, 15–17 years old | −**0.716** | −**0.443** | 13 |
| Fertility | −**0.188** | 0.038 | 17 |
| Marriages | −0.310 | **0.197** | 17 |
| Marriage duration at divorce | **0.148** | −0.354 | 15 |
| Divorces among married couples | 0.298 | 0.639 | 17 |
| Alcohol consumption | −0.174 | −**0.345** | 17 |
| Life satisfaction | −0.202 | −0.233 | 17 |
| Corruption indices | **0.280** | **0.312** | 17 |
| Adjusted per capita income | −0.390 | −0.205 | 17 |
| GINI income inequality | −**0.813** | −**0.707** | 17 |
| Human poverty index | −**0.682** | −**0.572** | 14 |
| Employment levels | **0.205** | **0.392** | 17 |
| Average hours worked | −**0.422** | −0.283 | 17 |
| Resource exploitation base | −0.299 | 0.157 | 17 |
| % of population who are foreign born | −0.174 | −0.178 | 17 |
| Cultural fractionalization | −0.296 | −0.257 | 17 |
| Accept human descent from animals | **0.837** | **0.754** | 16 |
| Accept human descent from animals compared to absolutely believe in God | −**0.739** | −**0.612** | 16 |
| SSS compared to | | | |
| Absolutely believe in God | −**0.709** | −**0.551** | 17 |
| Bible literalists | −**0.549** | −0.256 | 16 |
| Attend religious services at least several times a month | −**0.536** | −**0.530** | 17 |
| Pray at least several times a week | −**0.711** | −**0.484** | 16 |
| Absolutely believe in an afterlife | −**0.669** | −**0.417** | 16 |
| Absolutely believe in heaven | −**0.725** | −**0.447** | 16 |

| | | | |
|---|---|---|---|
| Absolutely believe in hell | −**0.706** | −**0.429** | 16 |
| Agnostics and atheists | **0.547** | **0.434** | 17 |
| Accept human evolution from animals | **0.690** | **0.501** | 17 |
| Adjusted per capita income | **0.053** | **0.464** | 17 |
| GINI income inequality | −**0.822** | −**0.688** | 17 |
| Human poverty index | −**0.778** | −**0.717** | 14 |
| Foreign born | −0.333 | −0.395 | 17 |
| Cultural fractionalization | −0.308 | −0.278 | 17 |

+U.S. = United States included; −U.S. = United States excluded. N = number of countries. PRVSS, Popular Religiosity versus Secularism Scale; SSS, Successful Societies Scale. Pearson *r* correlations are represented by the following typefaces: boldface when socio-economic conditions or other factors improve or rise with increasing secularism, regular type when factors deteriorate or decrease with increasing secularism. Significance of correlations is represented by the following underlines: no underline = correlation not significant, single underline = correlation moderate, double underline = correlation strong, and single or double boldface underline = correlation very strong.

# Chapter 7

# Atheism, Secularity, and Gender

## *Inger Furseth*

Issues of feminism, gender, and religion have received a great amount of scholarly attention during the past three to four decades.[1] However, little research has been conducted on atheism, secularity, and gender. This is surprising given the fact that women's roles in the Western world have changed drastically during the same period. Indeed, in this part of the world women have entered the labor force in great numbers and stayed there, thus, challenging traditional perceptions of feminine and masculine roles and identities. In addition, the advent of feminism and the liberalization in sexual attitudes and behavior have posed major challenges for Christian religiosity.[2]

During the modern era up until the late 1960s, traditional gender roles tended to link religiosity with femininity and the work sphere with masculinity. Because women's primary roles were in the domestic sphere as housewives and mothers, they were also seen as the main carriers of religion. In contrast, men's primary roles were in the work sphere as providers, and religion and work were often seen as two more or less mutually exclusive categories.[3] Therefore, men were often perceived to be somewhat more secular or reluctant to religion than women were. The cultural and religious changes of the 1960s and '70s challenged these notions. As a growing number of women began to participate in the labor force, the location of their identities expanded to include more than home and religion, and as men took on more responsibilities in the home and for their children, the representations of their identities became more flexible. The sexual revolution also led many women to challenge traditional moral restrictions on women, often religiously legitimated. They wanted to make their own choices about their lives and their bodies and desired more egalitarian sexual relationships inside and outside marriage.

In addition, second-wave feminism posed challenges to the traditional link between religion and femininity. One common theme was the focus on patriarchy as a concept or theory on gender power and gender difference. Many feminists viewed traditional religion to be patriarchal and oppressive.[4] Some decided to stay in their religious communities while they redefined and renegotiated their religious traditions. Indeed, several feminist theologians criticized Christianity and attempted to form a feminist spirituality and theology.[5] Other women joined new religious movements and alternative spiritual communities. Some feminist theologians rejected traditional religion and turned to feminized versions of spiritualities, such as the Goddess movement and Wicca.[6] Yet, other feminists rejected all forms of religion, left religious institutions, and became secular. These women were often involved in full-time and professional careers. Leaving could be due to profound disagreements with traditional religion, especially when it came to its teachings on sexual piety, abortion, and homosexuality and its focus on marriage and women's role as caretakers. Many feminist women found it hard to remain within traditional religion.[7] Leaving religion was, however, not a phenomenon that only took place among women. The radicalism of the 1960s and '70s also led to disaffiliation from traditional forms of religion among men.

In general, the sociological research on atheism and secularity has been slim. In the 1960s and '70s, some sociologists of religion attempted to analyze irreligion as a social phenomenon. During the first *International Symposium on Unbelief*, held in Rome in 1969, sociological programs for the study of nonbelief were outlined.[8] Later, British sociologist Colin Campbell proposed a more systematic sociology of irreligion.[9] More recently, this body of research has been growing.[10] Nevertheless, social scientific studies of irreligion tend to focus on the secular society[11] or secular movements[12] rather than affirmatively irreligious individuals. They also tend to ignore gender. In contrast, this chapter will address the subject of women and men who have moved away from religion and see themselves as nonreligious.

## ATHEISM AND GENDER IN GERMANY, GREAT BRITAIN, THE NETHERLANDS, AND SWEDEN

Social scientific studies on gender and worldviews show that women score higher than men on most measures of religiosity, such as interest in religion, religious faith, and church attendance. This pattern tends to be consistent for different phases of life, various types of religious organization, and in several parts of the Western world.[13] Findings from the European Value Studies and the International Social Survey

Program (ISSP): Religion, 1992, confirm a higher score on religious values among women than men in Great Britain, Germany, Norway, and Denmark.[14]

Conversely, data from the International Social Survey Program (ISSP): Religion, 1998, show that men in Germany, Great Britain, the Netherlands, and Sweden tend to be more irreligious than women are (see Table 7.1). This study distinguishes between West and East Germany, in spite of the fact that Germany was united in 1990. Although the East German respondents are far more secular than the West German respondents in 1998, there is a tendency for men to be more irreligious than women in both places.

When we first take a look at atheist views, we find that more men than women agree with the statement "Do not believe in God" in West Germany (15 versus 10 percent), East Germany (61 versus 50 percent), Great Britain (14 versus 8 percent), the Netherlands (22 versus 13 percent), and Sweden (23 versus 11 percent).

Likewise, when we look at the percentages who reply "No, definitely not" when they are asked if they believe in the afterlife, more men express this view than women do in West Germany (21 versus 18 percent), East Germany (75 versus 63 percent), Great Britain (25 versus 13 percent), the Netherlands (30 versus 20 percent), and Sweden (29 versus 14 percent).

So far, we have looked at atheist values. By turning our attention to a common religious practice, namely praying, we see that the two genders continue to be different. More men report that they never pray than women do in West Germany (39 versus 24 percent), East Germany (78 versus 64 percent), Great Britain (45 versus 24 percent), the Netherlands (48 versus 38 percent), and Sweden (48 versus 29 percent). These

## Table 7.1
### Secular beliefs and practices according to gender

| | West Germany | | East Germany | | Great Britain | | Netherlands | | Sweden | |
|---|---|---|---|---|---|---|---|---|---|---|
| | M | F | M | F | M | F | M | F | M | F |
| Don't believe in God | 15 | 10 | 61 | 50 | 14 | 8 | 22 | 13 | 23 | 11 |
| Definitely no faith in the afterlife | 31 | 18 | 74 | 63 | 25 | 13 | 30 | 20 | 29 | 14 |
| Never pray | 39 | 24 | 78 | 64 | 45 | 24 | 48 | 38 | 56 | 37 |

Values are percentages. M, male; F, female.
Source: International Social Survey Program: Religion, 1998.

data show that there is a relatively wide pattern at play where men tend to score higher than women on atheist values and practice in several European countries.

## THE CASE OF NORWAY

In order to explore the issue of gender and secularity further, we will take a more detailed look at one country located in what has often been termed "the secular Northern Europe,"[15] namely Norway. Here, the data from the same survey as mentioned above, ISSP: Religion, 1998, will be combined with a more detailed narrative analysis of the life stories of two Norwegian secular humanists, one woman and one man. Both informants are in their forties and represent the well-educated Norwegian baby-boomer generation. The woman is a member of the Norwegian Humanist Association (Human-Etisk Forbund), whereas the man is nonaffiliated. The article examines the situation of these two informants' lives and the diversity of their views. In particular, it analyzes the gender difference between them.

During the 1960s and '70s, Norway underwent similar changes to those that took place in other countries in the West. Large groups of high school graduates were able to enter colleges and universities, largely due to free public education and state subsidized loans. Many young couples decided not to marry but to live together. Married and nonmarried women with young children began to enter the labor market, taking part-time unskilled jobs or jobs within the health and social services. In the 1980s, the number of working women with young children (ages 3–6) increased from 47 to 74 percent. The majority of these women were well educated and worked full-time.[16]

From the early 1970s to the late '90s, the religious landscape changed, as the membership rate of the Church of Norway dropped from 92 percent of the population to 86 percent. There was a growing defection from the Church, and several defectors joined the Norwegian Humanist Association (formed in 1956). This organization first arranged secular confirmations in 1951, and it grew from 10,000 members in 1981 to almost 80,000 in 2007.[17] Parts of these changes implied a turning away from traditional religion to secular humanism.

Just as the surveys from West Germany, East Germany, Great Britain, the Netherlands, and Sweden show that secularity is gendered, the question remains whether this is true for Norway as well. In addition, we want to explore how men and women organize their discourse on secularity. Do their secular worldviews play the same role in their lives? Also, as women and men turn toward secular humanism, are their roads in this direction the same? We want to know if gender identities are related to secular identities. For example, how important are the feminist movement and new roles for women in defining women's secular outlook on life? These are some of the issues analyzed here. The turn toward secularity can be a turn toward an identity as "a skeptic," or it can be a totalizing attempt at "creating my own life." It is the issue of how gender informs our understanding of secularity that we want to discuss further.

## RESEARCH QUESTIONS AND METHODS

The following analysis is divided into two parts. The first part consists of a brief overview of the major findings from the analysis of the survey ISSP Norway: Religion, 1998, regarding gender and secularity. Here, we will look at gender differences regarding atheist beliefs. The second part consists of an in-depth analysis of the life stories of two professed humanists, one woman and one man. The following questions are asked: (1) What types of secular worldview do they present? (2) What images of self are found in their stories?

The data for this study were collected in two stages: (1) general survey and (2) life story interviews. The general survey ISSP Norway: Religion was conducted in 1998.[18] This sample included 2,500 persons from across the country. On the instructions of KIFO Centre for Church Research, an additional sample of 1,500 persons was drawn, 500 from each of the counties Vest-Agder, Oppland, and Troms, which were selected to maximize regional variation. These respondents were asked if they would consider taking part in an additional study based on life story interviews. The overall response rate of the main sample of 2,500 persons was 61.3 percent. The results of the main survey are, thereby, based on a net sample of 1,532 persons between the age of 18 and 79.[19] The response rate for the additional sample, consisting of 1,500 persons, was 56.5 percent, which resulted in a net sample of 848 persons. The second phase, an in-depth life story interview, was conducted with 72 of the respondents from the additional sample. The selection of these cases was not made on any strictly random basis, but in such a way that it would be practical to conduct the interviews.

The two humanists selected for in-depth analysis took part in the quantitative and the qualitative study. The man, here called Jan, lives in Troms County in Northern Norway and the woman, Bente, lives in Vest-Agder County in Southern Norway. Although both informants are professed humanists, Bente is a member of the Norwegian Humanist Association, whereas Jan is not. Both informants were in their forties at the time of the interview. They attended either college or university in Southern Norway and today they work in the educational sector. Here, we treat them as representatives of the baby-boomer generation in Norway, who grew up during times of economic growth and attended college and university during the radical 1970s. As members of the same generation who share "a common location" in the social process[20] and have common, unifying social experiences, it is of particular interest for us to see if and how gender shapes their secular worldviews.

The selection of two informants for in-depth analysis raises questions about generalizations. A common strategy in life story analysis is to interview people until the field is filled, meaning that interviews are conducted until no new information is acquired. In presenting and analyzing specific cases, the idea is to present typical cases, which are viewed as representative of other cases.[21] Following these considerations, Bente and Jan were selected on the basis of their gender, age, and worldview. In a Norwegian context, the narratives of the well-educated, middle-aged educators who are professed humanists seem familiar. In this way, they represent typical cases when it comes to secular people in their generation, and the analysis of their stories locates them in historical and social contexts that are not unique for them.

Life stories are often unreliable as factual reproductions of the past.[22] A life story is subject to the individual's selection of events, and there is a tendency to produce continuity through a selective memory. Rather than being a weakness, however, this might also be their strength, because the errors, myths, and inventions lead us beyond facts to their meanings. Therefore, life stories are particularly useful in studies of worldviews, including secular ones.[23]

In the following, I will first present the major findings in the survey, before we turn to Jan and Bente's life stories. Toward the end, I will look at the similarities and differences between these two humanists and attempt to detect what their stories reveal about gender difference and secularity.

## ATHEISM AND GENDER

The data from 1998 show that only a minority of Norwegians can be labeled "atheists." Of the total sample, 12 percent report that they "Do not believe in God," and 12 percent say that they "Can't find out." In contrast, three of four say that they believe in God or a higher power.[24] Nevertheless, consistent with the findings from Germany, Great Britain, the Netherlands, and Sweden, Norwegian men also score higher than women on atheist beliefs. For example, more men agree with the statement "Do not believe in God" than women do (17 versus 8 percent). More men also harbor doubt and agree with the statement "Can't find out" than women do (16 versus 9 percent).

Men also score consistently lower than women on various forms of religious beliefs. Table 7.2 shows that the gender difference is somewhat smaller when it comes to beliefs in hell and miracles and beliefs in the Bible as the word of God or inspired by God. Although men score lower than women on all of these measures of religious beliefs, the gender difference is most drastic when it comes to the view of the

**Table 7.2**
**Religious beliefs according to gender**

| Religious beliefs | Women | Men |
| --- | --- | --- |
| Life after death | 52 | 35[a] |
| Heaven | 41 | 27[a] |
| Hell | 18 | 15 |
| Miracles | 32 | 28[a] |
| The Bible is the word of God/inspired by God | 41 | 36[a] |
| No. of respondents | 829 | 703 |

Values are percentage of all ("Yes, absolutely" and "Yes, probably").
[a]The difference between women and men is significant at the 0.05 level.
*Source*: International Social Survey Program: Religion, 1998.

afterlife, where 27 percent of men believe in heaven and 41 percent of women do so. When it comes to religious practice, 50 percent of Norwegians report that they never pray or pray less than once per year. Although the data show that men pray less than women do on an annual, monthly, weekly, and daily basis, the most drastic gender difference is among those who are the most secular. Altogether 60 percent of men report that they never pray or pray less than once a year, whereas 40 percent of women do so.

Empirical studies of New Age beliefs in the Nordic countries show that there is a smaller representation of men who support these values than women.[25] By looking at one indicator of New Age beliefs, faith in reincarnation, we see that only 14 percent of Norwegians respond "yes, quite certain" and "yes, but uncertain" to the statement that "people have lived before and will get a new life." Again, gender makes a difference as more women respond this way (respectively, 17 versus 9 percent), whereas more men respond "no, quite certain" than women do (53 versus 41 percent). One may assume that men's lower score on most measures of religiosity can be explained by their level of education. However, the data show that men consistently score lower than women on beliefs in God, frequency of prayers, and church attendance even when education is controlled for.

The data from this study show that atheists constitute a minority in the Norwegian population, but that more men harbor secular values than women do. It is to the topic of gender difference regarding secularity that we now turn as we take a closer look at the life stories of Jan and Bente.

## I AM A SKEPTIC: JAN'S LIFE STORY

Jan lives by himself in his childhood home in a small coastal village in the northern region. The area gives the impression of desolate remoteness with small, poor farms scattered far away from each other. Jan's story portraits a baby boomer born in the early 1950s who grew up in the post-World War II era. His narrative contains information about the historical context of his life and its impact upon his life course. Jan grew up in the rural periphery as one of three children of parents who only had elementary school educations. Yet, he could look at higher education as a matter of course. He attended the country's largest university in Oslo during the 1970s and '80s. This was a time of political activism and a growing skepticism toward church and religion, which became shaping influences in his life. After obtaining a Master's degree, he decided to move back to his childhood home in the North, where he works as a high school teacher.

During Jan's childhood, no one in his family demonstrated much interest in religion. His parents were members of the Church of Norway, but they only went there if there was a confirmation or other types of ritual events. Today, Jan is not affiliated with any church or worldview organization. He marks in the questionnaire that he does not know whether God exists and that he does not believe that there is any way to find out, which 16 percent of the men report. He used to have a religious faith, but not anymore. Jan does not believe in life after death, although he is not quite sure, which 21 percent of the sample and 25 percent of the men state. He absolutely does not believe in heaven, hell, or in miracles. For him, the Bible consists of old legends, an answer given by 45 percent of the sample and 50 percent of the men.

Jan has a negative view of religion. He defected from the Church of Norway when he was a teenager and today he characterizes himself as "strongly nonreligious," a response 11 percent of the men gave in the quantitative study. He believes that religious people tend to be intolerant and that the world would be a better place if religion had less influence. Jan never prays and he never attends church, except during rites of passage. He is quite sure that he does not believe in reincarnation, horoscopes, or that people can foresee the future or have contact with those who have gone before us. He is somewhat open to alternative medicine, although he has doubts. By looking at the percentages of the total sample and the men who give the same response as Jan does in the questionnaire, we find that Jan is more secular than the majority of the total sample as well as the men, but that his lack of religious practice is similar to that of the majority.

Jan belongs to the leftists and votes for the Left Socialists (SV). Consistent with his political orientation, he has "relatively high trust" in the parliament, the judicial system, and the educational system, but less so in the Church of Norway and religious organizations, and hardly any in private enterprise. As the large majority in this study, Jan believes that sex before marriage is not at all wrong. Indeed, he thinks that it is a good idea for people to live together before they get married. He does not see sex between two people of the same sex as wrong, a view found among 38 percent of the total sample and 32 percent of the men. However, Jan has a strict view on abortion. For him, abortion is almost always wrong, including the situation where the woman does not want to have a child. Jan is relatively supportive of gender equality. He strongly disagrees with the statement that "men should work and women should stay home with the family." Only 28 percent of the men share his view on this issue. Yet, he is not sure whether he should agree or disagree with the statement that "the family suffers when women have full-time work."

There is a tension in Jan's narrative between the rural boy who succeeded in obtaining an academic degree and returning to his home community as a high school teacher and the outsider and the reclusive man who seeks gratification and meaning in solitude. In many ways, this tension has to do with tension between consistency and skepticism, involvement and distance.

## Atheism, Agnosticism, Secular Pietism, and an Ambiguous Self

Jan marks in the questionnaire that he used to have a religious faith, which he also tells us in the interview. He describes his childhood faith as "the type of faith people grew up with, a little simple, perhaps a naive, nonreflective faith. It's based on God as a creator, and the content of Christianity." By describing his childhood faith as "the type of faith people grew up with," he generalizes his faith to become a universal type of faith that all people have during childhood. In this way, he paints the picture of himself as person who is a member of a larger group, with which he identifies himself. As an adult looking back, he is quick to say that this came to a halt as soon as he entered puberty.

Jan was confirmed: "I was fourteen years old and it was perhaps a border phase, but perhaps there was still some faith left. I was not confirmed because I believed in renewing the baptism covenant, but because the others got confirmed, and I was not so critical that I chose to break away when it came to confirmation." In the late 1960s confirmation was no longer solely a matter of tradition in this northern, rural community, but it had become a matter of choice. Some of Jan's friends decided not to be confirmed, but being part of the group was important for him, so he did as most of "the others." In doing so, he demonstrated that he was part of the majority group. Indeed, it was a group setting that led him to change his worldview. When we ask him when and how he developed his worldview, he replies:

> It must have been during the period when I began in high school and studied at the university. I developed an antipathy to the propaganda I heard, and I became quite anti-Church, anti-Christian in many ways,

but that was partly because I thought the Christianity I heard in school was so extreme. I actually think it was during junior high school when I took a standpoint, under the influence of friends who were not Christian.

His move away from faith was not a process where he as an individual broke away from the group and opposed the views accepted by those around him. Instead, he refers to his group of friends and claims that their views affected him. Once again, he demonstrates that he was part of the group by adopting its accepted views.

Although Jan seemed to be group-oriented in his approach to religion, this was not so when it came to education. He finished high school and decided to attend the University of Oslo. This was not a common path for a boy in rural northern Norway, who usually "went to sea." In this area, Jan broke away from the group and went out on his own. Yet, in his narrative he presents the picture of a young man who more or less passively follows the opportunities laid before him. He says: "I sort of continued in school; it was that which existed. I applied to the University of Oslo without any conscious decision to become a teacher." The educational opportunities were just there, and as doors opened, Jan entered.

Nevertheless, compared to a commonly expected life course for baby boomers, Jan is atypical. Upon finishing his Master's degree, he decided to return to his home village and work there. At the time of the interview, he is divorced and not involved in any long-term relationship, and he has no children. Jan seems to live at the margins of social life. He gives little information about friends or people with whom he interacts. His professional life is also a topic that is almost absent in his narrative. This is atypical for a male life story, which tends to focus on the work life career.[26] One possible explanation is found toward the end of the interview when Jan reveals that he has been on sick leave for one year without a diagnosis. He believes he has chronic fatigue syndrome, characterized by headaches, dizziness, and general fatigue. Being unable to work may pose a threat to Jan's masculine identity, especially because his illness is one associated with women more so than men. The picture of the man suffering from a typical "women's illness" represents a breach with the picture of the successful male high school teacher.

As most men of his generation, Jan believes that both women and men should pursue their careers. Yet, he has a notion of women as more emotional and easily misled than men. When asked about alternative medicine, he says: "persons of the opposite sex, whom I have the impression act more and believe in such, whereas I shake my head and fret." Jan is a professed rationalist, who states in the questionnaire that he strongly disagrees with the statement that "we do not trust faith and emotions enough." For him, rationality is masculine, whereas emotionality is feminine. He affirms his masculinity through his belief in rationality and his nonemotional approach to life.

In the questionnaire, Jan reports that he characterizes himself as "strongly nonreligious." He compares himself with "other people," whom he sees as more religious than himself, and he defines himself as "not Christian." He explains: "I think that many people in Norway attend Church without thinking anything about it. If a person says that "I'm a Christian," it must mean something for them personally, because it's a way of life, that's what I demand of a personal Christian." Jan believes that rituals are empty. This is not surprising, given the lasting influence of Pietism upon Norwegian culture. Pietism argued against "meaningless rituals" and emphasized individual Christian piety and practice. For him, rituals belong to the sphere of external action, and are irrelevant. In contrast, he exalts the inner experience and the internal states of mind in combination with everyday practice. In this way, Jan represents a type of Pietism devoid of its original religious content.

Jan sees himself as "either an atheist or an agnostic." He continues

> I don't believe, but I can't say that there's no form of god. I don't believe in the god described in the Bible, but I can't exclude the existence of the creative power of god, although I don't see any evidence that there's something that rules, I can't see that there is a god who personally intervenes in people's lives.

Over the years, he has changed:

> During one phase of my life, as a student, I looked at myself as an atheist, anti-Christian, and I'm still skeptical towards religion. However, I no longer believe in absolutes. I can't be the only person who has found the truth. There are many views. I don't believe that the sole truth can be found in one religion.

Jan describes a transition in his life from being a hard-core atheist to becoming more of an agnostic. In spite of his change of heart, it is difficult for him to leave his absolutism behind. He attaches great importance to consistent belief systems, which fits his ideal of "the true believer." This is evident when he discusses gay clergy. Although he supports their right to be clergy, he sympathizes with those who oppose them: "If they find out that the Bible doesn't accept it [homosexuality], why should one accept that they [gay clergy], as teachers of the Church, should live in something the Bible possibly says is sinful?" Because he believes that consistency of beliefs is more important than the issue itself, he concludes that the view voiced by the opponents of gay clergy is "quite reasonable."

The continuing dialogue and conflict Jan expresses between consistency and content of beliefs produce a type of ambivalence that does not easily fit into the political and religious landscape of Norway. His anti-Christian position would initially lead one to expect that was a member of the Norwegian Humanist Association, which he is not. He explains

> I felt that this [joining] would replace one congregation with another congregation who is a competitor to Christianity. Without doubt, I sympathize with their views, but I don't care much for being a member of such permanent movements, neither political nor religious.

He sees the humanist association as one type of community, comparable to that of a Christian one. With his notions of "the true believer" and the emphasis he places on consistency of beliefs, Jan could only have joined this association if he fully supported their program and participated in their organizational activities. Although he supports their program, a membership will not provide the type of space needed for his ambivalence. Because he cannot be a "true believer" in this community, he chooses to remain outside.

Jan has a somewhat ambiguous view of life. He reports in the questionnaire that he is "relatively happy." When we ask him if there is anything in his life he wants change, he says: "I'm fairly skeptical towards everything. One can ridicule and become ironic and cynical." He admits that he has a negative view of life. By shifting from the personal "I" to the general "one," he describes his emotions as typical, which gives him a basis to formulate a morality, namely that skepticism leads to cynicism. There is a conflict in Jan's narrative between his skepticism and his demand for being a true believer. Whereas he has an admiration for the believer who is willing to make sacrifices in order to be true to one's beliefs, Jan chooses the stand of the skeptic: one who keeps his distance and does not get involved.

Jan's life story operates on two levels. On one level, it is a linear narrative about his social mobility: from being a rural boy from the periphery to becoming a high school teacher. On another level, the narrative is about the tension between his longing for consistency and a realization of the dilemmas that aiming for consistency involves. His move back to the village is an example of how he is trying to create and maintain continuity and consistency in his life. He expresses a modern self, who defines himself in relation to others, but at the same time he sees himself as an observer who lives on the margins of social life. Thus, there is a tension between his group orientation and his individualism.

Jan's concept of self embodies a sharp distinction between the inside and the outside with a desire to harmonize the two. His life story reveals distinct categories of people who are outsiders and insiders, "us" and "them." His claim for consistency and moral integrity is demonstrated in his discussion of religious categories. By demanding harmony between consistency and content of one's beliefs, he ends in a type of absolutism, which creates an unresolved ambivalence. On the one hand, Jan gives the impression of a man who is in control of his life. He paints the picture of himself as a man characterized by masculine, nonemotional rationality. On the other hand, Jan struggles with his distance and cynicism, as he is unable to live up to his demands of others to be true believers. Therefore, he resolves his own ambivalence by keeping a distance from other people.

## CREATING MY OWN LIFE: BENTE'S LIFE STORY

Bente is about the same age as Jan, but she lives in a town in southern Norway. Unlike her mother, she could look at higher education as a matter of course. She attended a teacher's training college during the 1970s, a period of new consciousness for women, which impacted her life profoundly. It was during her student years that she met her partner. As many students at the time, they opposed the institution of marriage and decided to live together. By now, they have been together for almost twenty years and have two teenage girls. Bente has always combined family obligations with work. As she and her partner are struggling with careers, raising teenagers, and incipient middle age, their relationship is going through a difficult time.

Bente and her partner are members of the Norwegian Humanist Association. In her childhood home, her parents attended the Church of Norway less than once a year. Bente marks in the questionnaire that she does not believe in God and has never done so, a view she shares with only 20 percent of the sample and 15 percent of the women. She has never participated in any religious organization, and she left the Church in her late teens. She characterizes herself "strongly nonreligious," which only 9 percent of the sample and 7 percent of the women do. She also believes that there is little truth to be found in any of the world religions.

However, Bente reports that she is quite sure that some people are able to foresee the future, a view she shares with 16 percent of the sample and 19 percent of the women. She also believes with some uncertainties that it is possible to have contact with those who went before us, which 12 percent of the sample and 13 percent of the women state. Bente says she never prays, although she would like to practice yoga and meditation. Altogether, Bente has a more negative view of traditional religion than the majority in the sample and the women. Yet, she is open to some aspects commonly associated with New Age, which are views found among more women than men.

Bente is a woman of strong moral convictions. She supports the Labor Party, and she agrees with Jan that it is more important to protect the environment than developing new industry. She voices trust in the government, the legal system, the public school system, but less so in the Church, and not in private enterprise. She also agrees with Jan that sex before marriage is not at all wrong, and neither is sex between two persons of the same sex. However, sex with someone else than your spouse is almost always wrong. Although she strongly supports free choice, she believes that abortion, in many instances, is morally wrong.

Bente's life story is characterized by her belief that human beings create their own lives. According to her, life has meaning, not because of the existence of a god, but because human beings are part of the life cycle. She has a positive view of life and she believes that people have choices in life. Nevertheless, there is a tension in Bente's story between her hopefulness toward others and her own unhappiness. As she grapples with adult life, she attempts to create consistency between her life experiences and her fundamental beliefs.

## Agnosticism, Humanism, the Life Cycle, and Harmony with Her Inner True Self

Bente relates childhood religion to her paternal grandparents, who were actively involved in the Church. "One had to go to church when one visited their place," she recalls, "because that was proper." She admits that it was her father who put pressure on the rest of the family to attend church when they visited his parents. Indeed, conflicts over religion in Bente's childhood and early adolescence seem to appear in her relationship to her father. In her early teens, Bente mentioned at home that she "really did not want to be confirmed in the Church." This was totally unacceptable to her father. Bente resolved the conflict by agreeing to be confirmed there. As an adult looking back, she does not interpret her adaptation as a passive act, but an active choice. "I was the one who chose to let myself be influenced by that pressure," meaning the pressure to be confirmed.

Conflicts over religion also appeared in Bente's life when she was around 11 years old. Her family moved from the more tolerant eastern region to the Bible belt in the South, where people were perceived as either very religious or very secular. Bente sees herself as belonging to a group that perceive themselves to be "in the middle." She says: "For me it's ok that people believe in a god of some sort, but I didn't recognize myself in that." When Bente reflects upon acceptance and rejection of religious beliefs, she uses the expression "to recognize herself," implying that she has an authentic self. Acceptance or rejection of religion is not related to its claim for truth, but it is related to a harmony between her authentic self and the religious worldview offered to her. For her, the acceptance of new ideas was based upon their quality of fitting in with her authentic self.

In the 1970s, when Bente was still in high school, she and other women took the initiative to form a local women's liberation group, Kvinnefronten (The Women's Front), a political left-wing group that worked to extend the rights of women. She says: "I wanted very much to do something. Not just to think or have ideas, but to demonstrate how it could be done, or what could be changed. I wanted to participate and have an effect." For her, ideals or theories were viewed as negatives, unless they were demonstrated in everyday life. She also joined the protests against the European Union. The fact that the grass root mobilization actually affected the end result of the referendum in 1972, where the opponents won, became a sort of evidence to her that it was *action* and not *ideas* that changed the world.

When we ask her about her perceptions of the meaning of life in her youth, Bente recalls that her high school years "were a time when I had a need to put things together. I knew my own views, but I wanted to see if I could find a larger ideological or moral frame around them. When I made up my mind that I will leave the Church, I was 17." Bente actively searched to create and formulate her own individual worldview, where she could "recognize herself" and "feel at home." In many ways, her worldview is similar to the one Jan harbors. However, her approach is strikingly different. Rather than seeking to formulate an individual meaning system, which Jan largely attempts to do, Bente searches for a ready formulated meaning system where she can "fit in." In her attempt to integrate her view of life within a larger frame, she tries to make a system whereby she harmonizes different aspects of her life.

At the time of the interview, Bente works within the school system. It is a striking feature in her story that she directs very little attention to her career. In spite of the fact that she is a full-time professional, she gives little information about her professional life. It becomes obvious that her identity is to a very small degree connected to work and career. Instead, her story centers on her family, friends, and close relationships.

Bente's two children are not baptized. At the time when they were born, it was not yet common to arrange secular "name-giving" ceremonies among irreligious couples. Therefore, Bente and her husband had no rituals or ceremonies that celebrated the birth of their children, which Bente misses. Because the children were not baptized, they were not members of the Church of Norway and would therefore, not normally be confirmed there. However, Bente's oldest daughter chose to be baptized and confirmed in the Church two years ago. Bente admires her daughter's independence in this matter, resisting the tradition of her secular family. In many ways, she seems to fulfill Bente's ideal of the independent person.

Bente's identity is related to her definition of herself as a humanist. She does not see herself as an atheist, which she defines as "one who denies that there's something beyond oneself, meaning that there's nothing religious or a divinity beyond." Instead, she sees herself as an agnostic:

> I do perceive things that are beyond, meaning I do have connections with others whom I can't see. I register that things are happening, and I've

experienced this in relatively specific ways, that there are some communications or some presence. I don't believe in something religious or a
god or anything, but I can't prove that it doesn't exist.

When Bente is trying to formulate and elaborate upon her perceptions
of herself as a humanist, she says: "I believe more in people." For her,
life is a cycle, consisting of a beginning and an end, that gives life
meaning. When we ask her about the most important events in her life,
Bente's answer is "to give birth to my children." She explains: "It's
related to being able to create. It is fantastic to be able to create human
beings, that in itself." Because the life cycle gives life meaning, giving
birth was one of the most important events of her life. Her life is part
of a greater life cycle, which bestows her individual life with meaning.
Bente attempts to create a view of life where she harmonizes her ideas
of humanness, meaning, and love.

However, there is a tension in her story between her view of life
and her life experiences. She and her partner are going through a difficult time in their relationship at the time of the interview. She has also
experienced that a close relative committed suicide. These experiences
challenge her positive outlook on life.

On one level, Bente's life story is a narrative of a woman with a positive view of life, where she perceives herself and others as having
choices in life. On another level, the story is about the experiences in
her life that make her unhappy. Her story can be interpreted as a way
of striving for consistency between her life experiences and her fundamental beliefs. Bente's self is typically modern, as she celebrates her
individual self. Yet, she does not admire fragmentation or multiple
identities. In contrast to Jan, who attempts to formulate an individual
worldview, she strives for a larger frame of reference where different
ideas fit together in wholeness. She defines herself in relation to other
people, but she is at the same time the individual who leaves the group
to create her own life.

Bente's life story illustrates the conflict between conformity and individualism or between self-realization and community. She attempts to
define her own space and form her own life. When doing so, she is not
purely individual. Instead, she operates within the frames of Norwegian culture, and she consciously seeks other existing ideologies that
she finds there, within which she attempts to fit her own. In this way,
she has a collective orientation where she tries to conform her individual interpretation of life to parts of the larger culture.

Bente's discussion of her family life expresses both a longing for a
consistency and a realization of the dilemmas that aiming for consistency implies. On the one hand, she chose her partner and formed a
family. She cannot blame others for her choice; it is her responsibility.
On the other hand, as a mother, her choices no longer affect only

herself, but also her children. As she strives to save her family, she has to put herself aside. And as she attempts to create her own life, she is also dependent on the lives of those with whom she interacts, and their choices. There is, thereby, a celebration of consistency as well as a realization that consistency between ideals and life experiences is not always possible.

## CONCLUSION

The fact that secularity is gendered in Norway is expressed in several different ways. Our analysis of the data from ISSP Norway: Religion, 1998, shows that Norwegian men score higher than women on several measures of secularity. Norwegian women and men reveal a similar pattern to the ones found in Germany, Great Britain, the Netherlands, and Sweden. The two life stories confirm the picture of gendered worldviews, and they provide information about some of the ways in which gender structures these worldviews.

Jan and Bente organize their discourse on secularity in different ways. As Bente describes her worldview, she focuses on the meaning that it provides in her life. This is revealed in her language of "finding a larger ideological frame." Bente's search for meaning led her to the humanist association. In contrast, Jan's discourse centers on morality. He focuses on the behavior that he believes religious people should have. For him, meaning does not constitute a major theme, but morality does.

Bente and Jan also speak about their experiences differently. Bente's worldview reflects her position as a woman and mother of two. For her, it is a direct connection between giving birth and her idea of being part of the great cycle of life. Bente emphasizes issues relating to personal relationships and emotions. She speaks of her worldview as a search for "an ideological frame" that harmonizes with her inner, true self. Her quest is not to find some sort of truth, but to find something to which she can "relate" or "recognize" herself. The emotional and relational aspects are also evident in her perceptions of some sort of unexplainable reality. She uses words such as "connections" or "communications." In contrast, Jan as a single man attempts to formulate his worldview by picking and choosing from different theoretical traditions. When he describes his beliefs, he speaks about truth and a "creative power." For him, his secular worldview is not discussed in terms of emotional fulfillment or personal relationships, but in terms of its truth and power.

In complex ways, the secular identities of Jan and Bente are related to their gender identities. Even if Jan's story shows that his male identity does not lie in the work sphere, it is located in his education or status as an "academic." His story points to the importance of higher education in personal and intellectual fulfillment. For him, gender is also related to his secular worldview. It is his identity as an academic with his emphasis on masculine rationality that led him away from religion. For him, a male identity excludes a religious identity. Bente's story suggests that the feminist movement and new roles for women lead to changes in the role that religion plays in women's lives. Bente's aim to find wholeness brought her on a quest for a worldview that would combine the different aspects of her life. Her search led her away from religion to secular humanism. Here, she found a worldview that brings together her identity as a mother, partner, working woman, and political activist.

This study has attempted to show that Norwegian women and men not only differ on measures of secularity, but that gender structures the ways in which they speak about their secular worldviews and the role that secularity plays in their lives. The analysis is tentative and more studies are needed in the study on gender and secularity.

## NOTES

1. See for example, Young, Serinity, ed. 1999. *Encyclopedia of women and World religion*, Vol. I–II. New York: Macmillan Reference; Aune, Kristin, Sonya Sharma, and Giselle Vincette, eds. 2008. *Women and religion in the West. Challenging secularization.* Aldershot: Ashgate.

2. Vincett, Giselle, Sonya Sharma, and Kristin Aune. 2008. Introduction: Women, religion and secularization: One size does not fit all. In *Women and religion in the West. Challenging secularization*, ed. Kristin Aune et al., 1–19. Aldershot: Ashgate.

3. Furseth, Inger. 2006. *From quest for truth to being oneself. Religious change in life stories.* Frankfurt am Main: Peter Lang.

4. See Woodhead, Linda. 2003. Feminism and the sociology of religion: From gender-blindness to gendered difference. In *The Blackwell companion to sociology of religion*, ed. Richard K. Fenn, 67–84. Oxford: Blackwell.

5. Daly, Mary. 1978. *Gyn/ecology. The metaethics of radical feminism.* Boston: Beacon Press; Ruether, Rosemary Radford, ed. 1974. *Religion and sexism. Images of women in the Jewish and Christian traditions.* New York: Simon and Schuster.

6. Berger, Helen A. 1998. *A community of witches: Contemporary neo-Paganism and witchcraft in the United States.* Columbia: University of South Carolina Press; Finley, Nancy J. 1994. Political activism and feminist spirituality. In *Gender and Religion*, ed. William H. Swatos, Jr., 159–172. New Brunswick and London: Transaction; Salomonsen, Jone. 2002. *Enchanted feminism: Ritual, gender and divinity among the reclaiming witches of San Francisco.* New York: Routledge.

7. Aune, Kristin. 2008. Singleness and secularization: British evangelical women and church (dis)affiliation. In *Women and religion in the West. Challenging secularization*, ed. Kristin Aune et al., 57–70. Aldershot: Ashgate; Furseth. *From quest for truth to being oneself*; Sharma, Soya 2008. When young women say "yes": Exploring the sexual selves of young Canadian women in Protestant churches. In *Women and religion in the West. Challenging secularization*, ed. Kristin Aune et al., 71–82. Aldershot: Ashgate.

8. Caporale, Rocco, and Antonio Grumelli, eds. 1971. *The culture of unbelief.* Berkeley: University of California Press.

9. Campbell, Colin. 1971. *Toward a sociology of irreligion*. London: Macmillan.

10. Flynn, Tom, ed. 2007. *The new encyclopedia of unbelief*. Amherst, NY: Prometheus Books.

11. Fenn, Richard K. 2001. *Beyond idols. The shape of a secular society*. Oxford: Oxford University Press.

12. Cimino, Richard, and Christopher Smith. 2007. Secular humanism and atheism beyond progressive secularism. *Sociology of Religion* 68: 407–424.

13. Aune et al. 2008. Ibid.; Furseth. *From quest for truth to being oneself*; Miller, Alan S., and John P. Hoffman. 1995. Risk and religion: An explanation of gender differences in religiosity. *Journal for the Scientific Study of Religion* 34(1): 63–75; Ozorak, Elizabeth Weiss. 1996. The power, but not the glory: How women empower themselves through religion. *Journal for the Scientific Study of Religion* 35(1): 17–29.

14. Botvar, Pål Ketil. 1993. *Religion uten kirke* [*Religion without church*]. Oslo: Diakonhjemmets høgskolesenter; Gundelach, Peter, and Ole Riis. 1992. *Danskernes Værdier* [*The values of the Danes*]. København: Forlaget sociologi.

15. Zuckerman, Phil. 2008. *Samfund uden Gud. En amerikaner ser på religion i Danmark og Sverige* (*Society without God. An American looks at religion in Denmark and Sweden*). Højbjerg: Univers.

16. Benum, Edgeir. 1998. Overflod og fremtidsfrykt: 1970–. In *Aschehougs Norgeshistorie* (*Aschehoug's history of Norway*), Vol. 12, ed. Knut Helle, Knut Kjeldstadli, Even Lange, and Sølvi Sogner. Oslo: Aschehoug.

17. Ormestad, Solveig Bonde. 1981–1982. *Human-Etisk Forbund 1956–1981* (*The Norwegian Humanist Association 1956–81*). Oslo: Human-Etisk Forbund; Statistics Norway. 2007. *Kulturstatistikk* (Cultural statistics) [online]. Iski: Statistisk sentralbyrå. Available from: www.ssb.no/trosamf/tab-2008-01-07-01.html (in Norwegian; accessed 1 September 2008).

18. *Undersøkelse om religion* 1998 is part of an international survey, *Religiion II*, initiated by the International Social Survey Program (ISSP). *Norsk Samfunnsvitenskapelig datatjeneste* (NSD) had the overall responsibility for the Norwegian survey. NSD bears no responsibility for the analyses and interpretations in this article.

19. Lund, Monica. 1998. *Undersøkelse om religion 1998* (*Study on religion 1998*). Bergen: Norsk samfunnsvitenskapelig datatjeneste.

20. Mannheim, Karl. 1952. *Essays on the sociology of knowledge*, ed. Paul Kecskemeti. London: Routledge and Kegan Paul.

21. Plummer, Ken. 1990. *Documents of life*. London: Unwin Hyman.

22. Ibid.

23. Furseth. *From quest for truth to being oneself*.

24. Furseth. *From quest for truth to being oneself*, 59–60.

25. Gundelach, Peter, and Ole Riis. 1992. *Danskernes værdier* (*Values among Danes*). København: Forlaget Sociologi; Lunestad, Jorun. 1999. Nyreligiøsitet—konkurrent eller supplement? Religion 1998 om nyreligiøsitet. In *Tallenes tale 1999* (*Numbers speaking 1999*), Rapport nr. 12, ed. Ole Gunnar Winsnes, 27–42. Trondheim: Tapir.

26. Vilkko, Anni. 1992. "Att skaka med hanskar på." Kvinneliga självbiografier och tolkarens position. In *Självbiografi, Kultur, Liv* (*Autobiography, culture, life*), ed. Christoffer Tigerstedt et al., 107–126. Stockholm: Brutus Östlings Borkförlag Symposion.

# Chapter 8

# Freethinkers and Hell Raisers: The Brief History of American Atheism and Secularism

## *Daniel Cady*

American history has not been kind to atheists, agnostics, and secularists. To examine the unfolding of the country's history through the standard accounts of nontheists in American history textbooks is to present a very short study indeed. In fact, from a student's point of view, the narrative simply does not exist. Due in large part to the overwhelming success of the Christian establishment to both formally and informally censure the act of history writing, the traditions of atheism, agnosticism, and secularism in America have been generally supplanted by myth, mischaracterized by historical revision, and silenced through scholarly omission.

In this chapter I will attempt to unearth the hidden history of American atheism, agnosticism, and secularism from its burial under the weight of popular myth and its obstruction at the hands of historical censors. From era to era, persona to persona, America has been home to countless nonbelievers who have faced relentless persecution from theists, particularly Protestant theists. Sometimes the attacks originated with the state and other times they flowed from an agitated populous. More often than not, antiatheist activity came from a combination of state-sponsored scapegoating and reactionary populist hysteria. At different times these forces targeted nonwhites, nonconformists, intellectuals, socialists, and scientists. Atheists—or those accused of atheism—found themselves imprisoned, ostracized, and in some cases exterminated. Yet, within this continuum of unabashed hostility reside pockets of tolerance and the flowering of freethought. By excavating elements of Colonial and Revolutionary America, nineteenth-century intellectuals, and twentieth-century nonconformists (and regressive trends), I will illustrate how an oft-hidden nontheistic world impacted the development of American history. The bulk of this chapter will be devoted to the grand American myth of national religiosity and fabled origins. That battle begins with the Pilgrims and ends with the death of the founders, and its details deserve special attention.

In 1987, President George H. W. Bush proclaimed his unofficial doctrine on the issue of atheists in American culture. When posed with a question on the atheists' civil rights, he retorted, "I don't know that atheists should be considered as citizens, nor should they be considered patriots. This is one nation under God." Such marginalization has been standard fare for atheists as evidenced in some of the earliest written histories of North America. More of a criminal charge than a description of one's belief, the accusation of atheism was as misused in early America as "communist" and "terrorist" have been in the last sixty years. Now, historically speaking, one must be clear about what constituted atheism before the mid-nineteenth century. As James Turner argues in *Without God, Without Creed*, atheism in America before the Civil War was essentially unheard of. Much of the worldview of preindustrial people was anchored in the notion that the earth was the product of a creator.[1] With the influence of rational Enlightenment thought in the eighteenth century, this view shifted towards a god of nature and away from a Christian god, but was usually confined to an educated elite. That true atheists were as common as unicorns in early America hardly stopped accusations of disbelief. These charges also illustrate the limited spectrum of acceptable religious expression and suggest the often dire consequences of such pronouncements.

## COLONIAL AMERICA

Christian European America was initially sown in the native soil of disbelief. From the founding of Jamestown in 1607 to the turn of the eighteenth century, only a handful of European Christians lived among hundreds of thousands of non-Christian Natives.[2] In a world where even slight deviations from Christian denominational orthodoxy would result in cries of atheism, American Indians presented a special challenge to the Protestant English. Even before the first permanent English colonies took root, Anglo writers identified the profound religious deficit of the continent's natives. In early Virginia colony booster Richard Hakluyt's *Discourse on Western Planting* (1584), he warned potential settlers that North America was bursting with "infidells," and that English Christians needed to work for

> the gayninge of the soules of millions of those wretched people, the reducinge of from darkenes to lighte, from falsehoodde to truthe, from

the dombe idols to the lyvinge God, from the depe pitt of hell to the highest heaven.[3]

Often characterizing themselves and their colonization of America in Old Testament terms, many of the English settles landed in "New Canaan" with a profound sense of mission and an even greater sense of superiority. Some scholars have argued that the melding of English nationalism and religion before the eighteenth century served to characterize the English as the apex of civilization looking down on all others. At the nadir of this model resided Indians (and Africans), who the English oft referred to as *savages, heathens,* or *pagans.* This designation proved vital to the both the English looking to convert Indians and to those bent on enslaving or killing the native population.[4] True to the biblical story of the Israelites in Canaan, invaders with a divine contract occupied a new territory and subjugated its people and did so because of the vanquished "detestable practices" (Deut. 18:9–13). In early America, as in later periods, the charge of atheism became a rationalization for the denial of basic human rights.

Nowhere in the course of early American history did piety and intolerance play a greater role than in colonial New England. Despite the uncritical acceptance of the national holiday Thanksgiving, when English newcomers allegedly broke bread with natives on equal terms, the relationship between Anglo immigrants and indigenous peoples was rife with conflict. Again, the incapacity of the English to understand Indians beyond a rigid Christian worldview led the newcomers to characterize Indians as either evil or under the spell of evil. In 1660, English theologian William Hubbard argued that the atheistic condition of New England's Indians was rooted in their evil origins:

> His conceit is, that when the devil was put out of his throne in the other parts of the world, and that the mouth of all his oracles was stopped in Europe, Asia, and Africa, he seduced a company of silly wretches to follow his conduct into this unknown part of the world, here he might lie hid and not be disturbed in the idolatrous and abominable, or rather diabolical service he expected from his followers; for here are no footsteps of any religion before the English came, but merely diabolical.[5]

As wretches controlled by Satan, native New Englanders found themselves in the unenviable position of enemies of the new Anglo theocracy. Puritans developed a policy for dealing with the Indians based on the model of the Israelites in Canaan—with the natives playing the role of Canaanites. Fearing the contamination of their saintly souls and bodies by native influences, Puritans actively fought to occupy Indian land not merely for purposes of personal enrichment, but as a bulwark against contamination.[6] Additionally, within this particular cosmology, the near extermination of the natives, like the conquest of the Canaanites, was seen as a gift from God to his chosen people. For instance, as natives died in mass after exposure to smallpox, Puritan leader John Winthrop thanked the creator for more free land. Reading the pox as a providential sign, Winthrop penned, "God hath consumed the Natives with a great Plauge in those partes, soe as there be few Inhabitants lefte."[7] All things beneficial to the Puritans were deemed "providential," while acts against them were often characterized as tied to the influence of accused nonbelievers.

Natives were not the only ones, however, to suffer because of their visible heterodoxy in the face of Puritanism. Scores of European immigrants among the America's self-proclaimed saints found themselves open to punishment at the hands of Puritan authorities. Stocks, branding, whipping, and dunking were common forms of remediation for religious transgressions. Those beyond repair were either cast out or executed. In both lethal and non lethal cases, charges of atheism were as common as they were imprecise. In the Puritan worldview, atheism described all religious expressions incompatible with Puritanism. Thus, Quakers, Catholics, and Jews fell into the same general category as Indians and witches.

One of the earliest accusations of atheism was levied within a decade after the Pilgrims first arrived. The accused, Thomas Morton, considered himself an aristocratic bon vivant, with little in common with Puritans other than English birth. Morton arrived in New England in New England 1624 and soon found himself at odds with the Puritan authorities. Establishing an outpost outside of the established English perimeter, Morton infuriated Puritans by undercutting established trade, fraternizing with Indians, and erecting a Maypole in the middle of his compound. A literate and adventurous man, Morton rejected Puritan rule and instead established his Indian trading post and christened it Merry Mount. There, Morton, his Anglo comrades, and Indian men and women imbibed, danced, and sang bawdy songs—much to the chagrin of local, town-dwelling leaders. In 1628, Massachusetts Bay Colony Governor William Bradford had Merry Mount sacked and eventually burned to the ground. In his *History of Plymouth Plantation*, Bradford recounts the "the beastly practices of mad Bachanalism" at play in Morton's compound and claimed that Morton was the "lord of misrule, and maintained (as it were) a schoole of Athisme."[8] Morton was arrested, held, and eventually deported to England.

Perhaps the most significant element in New England's role in the history of religion, secularism, and atheism in America is the near universal acceptance of the region's place in the founding of America. This ahistorical account posits the notion that religious principles motivated the colonization of America's eastern seaboard. The tale is often enacted in the public sphere in two ways: the Thanksgiving story and the metaphor of America as a "city on the hill." Both of these narratives place Puritan New England at the forefront of American history, and both are imbued with a sense of divine intentionality. The feast of Thanksgiving was a singular rather than annual event from 1621 when English separatists from the Church of England (later named Pilgrims) shared in an autumn festival with local Wampanoag Indians. Evidence shows that for the next 200 years the tradition remained fairly—but informally—rooted in the Massachusetts area. Not until the mid-nineteenth century did Americans suggest that this regional New England tradition become an official American holiday. Only after the Union Army's victory at Gettysburg—and the confidence that the Confederacy would eventually rejoin the Union—did Abraham Lincoln designate a national day of thanksgiving in November (though evidence suggests that he did not author the piece). In his 1863 "Proclamation of Thanksgiving," Lincoln attempted to fashion a unifying myth based on the presumed belief that God had chosen and blessed America despite the 620,000 war dead. For another seventy-eight years the holiday's observance depended on a yearly presidential proclamation. Finally, Franklin Delano Roosevelt made it permanent two weeks after the bombing of Pearl Harbor in December 1941. Thus, the history of Thanksgiving shows how an informal and often unrecognized holiday based on the temporary convergence of Anglo-Indian cultures was manipulated to create a sense of American social unity in times of crisis. The result of this has been the perpetuation of the myth of America's New England origins and a highlighting of that region's religiosity.[9]

The other great New England myth used to promote America's special relationship with a Christian god to contemporary citizenry deficient in historical literacy is the city on a hill model. Found in John Winthrop's sermon, "Modell of Christian Charity," the image of early New England, and a later United States, as a city on a hill permeates the American consciousness. Simply, the city on a hill concept has been used to promote the idea that America has been chosen by God and granted a covenant similar to one that bound the creator to the ancient Israelites. In its own time, the sermon was understood as a call for obedience to religious and social authority, as well as a reminder of the Puritan mandate to cleanse the Church of England of all things Catholic. Hence when Winthrop penned "wee shall be as a citty upon a hill," and that "the eies of all people are uppon us," he assumed an exclusive contract with God (not even open to the vast majority of Christians) dependent on strict social control. He in no way intended his sermon as a metaphor for a socially mobile, pluralistic society grasping for a unifying theme.[10]

In Ronald Reagan's tenure as California's governor and later as the president of the United States, he often employed Winthrop's metaphor, but within a presentist's context. In his "Farewell Address" of 1989, Reagan's city on a hill transformed from a haven for socially static religious separatists to a "city built on rocks stronger than oceans, wind-swept, God-blessed, and teeming with people of all kinds living in harmony and peace, a city with free ports that hummed with commerce and creativity." Besides expanding Winthrop's model city beyond the spirit of its original meaning, Reagan took even greater liberties with Winthrop himself. According to Reagan, Winthrop was "an early freedom man" who came to America "looking for a home that would be free." Characterizing Winthrop as a man bent on an egalitarian sense of freedom misrepresents America's past and further exaggerates the importance of Puritanism to development of the United States.[11]

The constant invocation of the Thanksgiving story and the city on a hill by politicians and traditionalist historians serves to perpetuate the myth of America's religiously inspired founding. Yet if one looks back to the first permanent English settlement in America, one could not begin with religiously intolerant Pilgrims. That designation belongs to the entrepreneurs of the Jamestown settlement. Established in 1607 by the Virginia Company of London, Jamestown began not as a refuge for religious zealots, but a profit-making venture. Religiously, the residents of Jamestown identified themselves as members of the Church of England, but according to one notable American historian, religious concerns were "never at the forefront of the Virginia enterprise," and all piety was "thoroughly overridden by the race for tobacco profits."[12] In many ways Virginia rather than Massachusetts serves as a model of development for the country that followed. The Virginians were more secular, individualistic, and materialistic, experienced more social fluidity, and willingly exploited people and resources to a greater degree. Virginia also looms large in the history of the American Revolution. The writing of the Declaration of Independence and the American Constitution were dominated by Virginians; four of the first five presidents came from the colony. Only in the nineteenth century during the rise of sectional conflict did Massachusetts supplant Virginia as America's birthplace. By the early twentieth century and the surge of immigration, the unifying myth of the city on a hill in place of a shared historical experience most efficiently emblematized the American past.

In popular American colonial history, the story of American secularism and nontheism has been effectively removed. The New England experience, though an anomaly in the world of British colonial development in the Americas, still dominates the discourse. Every November, school children sit at long tables, facing each other and masquerading as Pilgrims or Indians. There, they relive an origin myth divorced from both fact and geography. The consequences of that theater and its message of providence has been the empowerment of conservative religious forces to shape the basic history of the United States. As Ronald Reagan said as he left office, "we've got to teach history based not on what's in fashion but what's important: why the Pilgrims came here."[13] This false history and imaginative context also frames current views of revolutionary history, the motives of the founders, and the meaning of the U.S. Constitution.

## REVOLUTIONARY AMERICA

Americans still rage over the presumed beliefs of the founders. Pseudohistorian David Barton typifies the nonacademics who have attempted to recast American history as the history of Christians in America. Asking his audience to "discover our nation's godly history," Barton has recast the country's founders as a cohort of evangelicals attempting to forge a modern state from a premodern religious text. In his mind, the course of American history has been steered by orthodox religion from the first moment Europeans made land.[14] In this context, the fact that the American political system's founders intentionally and systematically strayed from religious orthodoxy rings of falsehood. How could the most influential people of their time and the paragons of elite society reject religion amid a populous of dogmatic believers? The answer, of course, is that they were not anomalies, but representative of their time and status. The principle founders of the constitutional government of the United States were not atheists, but they were not Christians either. They were Deists. Jefferson, Adams, Franklin, and Madison all tended to understand religion in its pragmatic application in social control and rejected supernaturalism, but held to the notion of a creative force in society. They believed, though some to a greater degree than others, in an unobtrusive supreme being who created the universe, but paid scant attention to earth's occupants. In their views, this "clock-maker" did not suspend natural law, answer prayers, or magically procreate with virgins.

Thomas Jefferson towers above all other early political figures as the most secular and perhaps the most influential. Jefferson, the author of the Declaration of Independence, the third U.S. president (and in that capacity refused to proclaim a day of thanksgiving), and the founder of the University of Virginia, rejected "demoralizing dogmas of Calvin" in favor of a natural religion based on reason and charitable human interaction.[15] Jefferson, who wrote knowing that his words would later be scrutinized, left a clear paper trail on his unorthodox religious beliefs. Though somewhat reticent in his official writings, his correspondences and library shelves paint a picture of a man with a distain for dogma, orthodoxy, and superstition. In his letters to John Adams, Jefferson disputed the Trinity, bashed Protestantism, and mocked the apostles. In spiritual matters, Jefferson aligned himself with pre-Christian Greeks such as Epicurus, who believed in the existence of gods, but insisted that divine beings ignored the humans altogether. To his friend and mentee, William Short, Jefferson identified himself as an "Epicurean," persuaded by the "moral philosophy which Greece and Rome have left us." Jefferson broke his official silence on the topic of religion in his only published book, *Notes on Virginia*. Here, he argued against a singular tradition within a narrative highly critical of Christian proselytizing:

> Millions of innocent men women and children, since the introduction of Christianity, have been burnt, tortured, fined, imprisoned; yet we have not advanced one inch towards uniformity.[16]

Unlike the majority of living Americans, Thomas Jefferson was not biblically illiterate. According to a recent Gallup poll, over half of American adults and two-thirds of American teenagers are unfamiliar with the Bible (even though the majority believes it to be the true word of God). Jefferson had the opposite problem: he mastered the Bible and could read it in Latin and Greek, but rejected the text's divinity. In order to highlight the teachings of Jesus—within whom Jefferson recognized a model of civility—divorced of superstition, Jefferson rewrote the New Testament. In his *The Life and Morals of Jesus of Nazareth*, or "Jefferson Bible," he attempted to expunge all miracles and superfluous details from the story of Jesus. In doing so he reduced the voluminous text to a handful of pages; for without miracles, really very little remains. For instance, the twenty verses of recounting Jesus' previously miraculous birth were reduced to two verses:

> And so it was, that, while they were there, the days were accomplished that she should be delivered. And she brought forth her firstborn son, and wrapped him in swaddling clothes, and laid him in a manger; because there was no room for them in the inn.[17]

No angels coming and going from heaven, no unexplainable lights, and no sheepherding interlopers. The Jefferson Bible was soon suppressed by his offspring and only introduced publically at the beginning of the twentieth century.

Jefferson's most lasting achievement in the history American secularism comes from his efforts to reduce the influence of clerics on the state and the limit the state's authority on matters of faith. Inasmuch, he showed no religious preferences. Jefferson fought for the rights of all religious minorities as well as all Christian denominations. In his 1802 letter to the Danbury Baptists, Jefferson established the "wall of separation" between church and state, and further clarified the religious clause of the First Amendment to the Constitution. Thus, when the founders penned "Congress shall make no law respecting an establishment of religion, or prohibiting the free exercise thereof," they did not presuppose that the government and its people were of one common Christian mind, if Christian at all.

Although some scholars have refashioned Jefferson as a more or less normative Christian, other founders have been simply erased from the record. For instance, how is it that the most prolific writer of the revolutionary period is still a virtual stranger to American students? Thomas Paine not only wrote *Common Sense*—the single most influential text of the American Revolution—but was also among the first to argue in print against slavery, against cruelty to animals, for women's rights, and the first to ever pen the name "United States of America."[18] Through *Common Sense* (a pamphlet which sold 500,000 copies in the 1770s), Paine was able to galvanize support for the American Revolution among a previously ambivalent population. In his time, Paine's contribution to the founding of the country was universally recognized. Washington, Jefferson, and Monroe personally interceded in Paine's affairs during times of crises on account of the pamphleteer's essential "services to this county."[19] Yet by twentieth century, Paine had been relegated to the dustbin of history or characterized as aberrant. Far from the accolades of the first cadre of presidents, Teddy Roosevelt referred to Paine as a "filthy little atheist."[20]

Paine's path from patriotic icon to filthy atheist is marked by religious intolerance. Although *Common Sense* established Paine as an American hero during the Revolution, his later works inspired a conservative backlash. At the dawn of the twentieth century, American poet Ella Wheeler Wilcox observed that Paine had been effectively removed from the national narrative. "For a century," she wrote, "the world has ignored his brilliant mind. Indeed, Paine's name has been branded by bigots and fanatics with all imaginable obloquy."[21] Paine first published his antimonarchical *Rights of Man* (1791), which defended the French Revolution and made little impact in America. His next book, *The Age of Reason* (1794, 1795, 1807), infuriated the increasingly religious American populous. Written in France during the "Great Terror," *The Age of Reason* was seen as a straightforward defense of deism by educated American elites—who had, in great part, adopted the natural religion of deism over the supernaturalism of Christianity—and as an attack against Christianity by clergymen and commoners. Forever the gadfly, Paine disputed the central tenets of Christian mythology and mocked the very notion of belief in "fables" of the Bible. Upon arrival Paine found the once receptive American public suddenly truculent. In 1802, shortly after Paine's return to the county he named, a Philadelphia journalist referred to "loathsome" Paine as "a drunken atheist and the scavenger of faction."[22] Friends abandoned him for reputation's sake, strangers cursed him as an infidel, and one passerby even took a shot at him.

When Paine died in 1809, only a handful of mourners attended his funeral. Much of the inattention to his death was the public's repayment for attempting to introduce Deism to a general audience in a time of nonelite religious revival. The democratic nature of American religion provided a movement for the masses. Though some historians of the subject emphasize the link between the religiosity of the early nineteenth century and the advent of reform movements, one cannot forget the role of religious revival as a call for order during periods of vast changes. Americans witnessed a bloody revolution, broke with the logic of monarchical deference, and found themselves increasingly mobile and subject to the whim of advancing industrialization. Hence, it was not only a conspiracy of the intolerant who moved Paine to the margins, but also the mere circumstances of the early republic's social development. In other words, not only did the market for the Jefferson Bible and *The Age of Reason* dry up, but the mere mention of the texts would incite cries of "infidel!"

Buried under the weight of revivalism and 200 years of revisionism lies the real beliefs of the founding generation. Washington, Franklin, Adams, Jefferson, Paine, and Madison all defy easy religious categorization, and their collective views would certainly be seen as blasphemous by many contemporary Americans. Rather than creating a "godly" country based on ancient Hebrew laws or within a Calvinistic system of election and providence, the most influential founders actually laid the foundation for American disbelief. Much of the secular narrative was lost in the first few generations of the nineteenth century, due in large part to the post-Revolution conservatism and the revival of emotional Christianity during the Second Great Awakening.[23] The people that once made heroes of Jefferson and Paine either vilified them or recast them as traditional believers. One need look no further than the Treaty of Tripoli, as signed by John Adams and ratified by the United States Senate, as evidence of the secularism of the early republic:

> As the Government of the United States is not, in any sense, founded on the Christian religion; as it has in itself no character of enmity against the law, religion or tranquility of Musselmen; and as the states never have entered into any war or act of hostility against any Mohometan nation, it is declared by the parties that no pretext arising from religious opinion shall ever produce an interruption of harmony existing between the two countries.[24]

## THE NINETEENTH CENTURY

Arguments concerning the beliefs of the founders continue to rage. Yet on issues of religion and public memory in nineteenth century, one hears very little. Like the myth of the Pilgrims and founders, the principle figures of the nineteenth century are often spoken of imbued with a nostalgic sense of religiosity. The age itself has been characterized as the movement of religious revivalism running headlong into Victorianism. In this narrative, the evangelism of the first half of the century settled into the normative, disciplined piety of the latter. On the first end of this equation, this early evangelism has profoundly imprinted American religious consciousness. During the Second Great Awakening (1790–1840) Americans discarded strict Calvinism in favor of a more democratic form of religious expression. Though uneven and chronologically staggered, the era's revivalism stressed personal faith as key to salvation coupled with anti-intellectual emotionalism. Denominations battled for souls, and new religions arose while established traditions accommodated those who cried for change. The result was a complex mix of sometimes reformist, sometimes otherworldly churches with the innate ability to transform during times of crises and always to appeal to one's heart rather than head.[25]

From the vulgar to the urbane, America's nineteenth century then shifted—in the public imagination—to Victorianism and the rise of the middle class. According to scholars, Americans increasingly retreated into the privacy of their own homes during a period of accelerating industrialization. Gender roles became more defined as men engaged in a competitive business world and women settled into the domestic realm. Within the walls of the Victorian home women found a new identity as homemakers. Purity, submissiveness, and piety defined the house-bound woman, and within this role she bore the responsibility of maintaining a religious household and raising the next generation of spiritually devout children. Although this "cult of domesticity" and "self-made man" model only serves as a limited conceptual framework for the study of the nineteenth century, it remains a powerful paradigm for the "traditional" family as advocated by contemporary American conservatives.[26]

When taken together as the singular dominant paradigm for understanding the nineteenth century, revival to Victorianism (while a bit prude) allows theistic historians the opportunity to claim the era's progressive social movements. For instance, it is commonly understood that social reform emerged as the byproduct of the Second Great Awakening and found its greatest advocates amongst the emerging middle class. In this context, abolitionism and women's rights are thus seen as the result of the era's religiosity and millennial zeal. Americans can look back to the age of Garrison, Lincoln, and Susan B. Anthony and illustrate how religious belief inspired these few but important generations to expand the rights of marginalized people while secularists and atheists (if they even existed in the period) sat on the sidelines. However, the people and events of the nineteenth century defy such simple categorization. The people we now celebrate as orthodox then were less so, and many who would be considered infidels now (if we considered them at all) then were among America's most popular figures.

As Susan Jacoby has shown in *Freethinkers*, some nineteenth-century American icons adopted by the current religious right were suspiciously unorthodox. Chief among them is Abraham Lincoln. No doubt, the view that Lincoln led his life as an archetypical frontier Christian is axiomatic among believers, but evidence shows that his religiosity has been perhaps overstated.[27] Lincoln never joined a church, did not believe in revealed truth, and saw no reason for prayer in his own life.[28] Biographers have strongly disputed the characterization of Lincoln as a Christian. Soon after Lincoln's death his long-time friend and personal security guard, Ward Hill Lamon, presented *The Life of Abraham Lincoln* to an unreceptive American reading public. In it, Lamon asserted that Lincoln was a man of great conviction and spiritual want, but alas, a man of little faith. "Mr. Lincoln" he wrote, "was never a member of any church, nor did he believe in the divinity of Christ, or the inspiration of the Scriptures in the sense understood by evangelical Christians." Lamon even quotes Mary Todd as stating, "Mr. Lincoln had no hope, and no faith, in the usual acceptance of those words." In the 1880s, one of Lincoln's long-term associates opened up to the *Louisville Times* on the subject of the former president's beliefs:

> He went to church a few times with his family while he was President, but so far as I have been able to find he remained an unbeliever. . . . I asked him once about his fervent Thanksgiving Message and twittered him about being an unbeliever in what was published. "Oh," said he, "that is some of [secretary of state] Seward's nonsense, and it pleases the fools."[29]

Yet the myth persists as to Lincoln's religiosity. Due to the myth of the "Great Emancipator" and Lincoln's status as the country's most beloved leader, many Americans refuse to accept Lincoln's ambivalence towards religion.

Like Jefferson and Paine, one can either recast significant Americans or erase them. The same can be said of Lincoln (the most popularly recognizable figure in abolitionism) and Elisabeth Cady Stanton, the forgotten mother of women's suffrage. Schooled by Lucretia Mott while fighting for the abolition of American slavery, Stanton, by the 1840s, redirected her energy away from abolitionism and devoted herself (as did Mott) to women's suffrage. Though she did not live to see the Nineteenth Amendment, her contributions to the cause are unparalleled. She was the principal author of the first popular call for women's rights in America, the *Declaration of Sentiments*. Modeled after Jefferson's Declaration of Independence, the document was signed in 1848 at the first women's rights convention at Seneca Falls, New York. In 1869, she founded the National Women's Suffrage Association with Susan B. Anthony. Stanton argued not only for women's suffrage, but more broadly for women's rights. Many of her radical views, including a call to liberalize divorce laws and her acceptance of interracial marriage, ultimately caused fissures in the women's movement. But Stanton truly raised the ire of conservatives when she criticized Christianity. She made the mistake, it appears, of letting her private views influence her public discourse. In 1880, she summed up her view of Christianity in a letter to her son: "How anyone in view of the protracted sufferings of the race," she penned, "can invest the laws of the universe with a tender loving fatherly intelligence, watching, guiding and protecting humanity, is to me amazing."[30] Like the other historical figures, Stanton retained some loose sense of faith, but rejected organized religions altogether.

In 1895 Stanton published the *Women's Bible*, a text that amounted, according to one historian, to a "sustained ideological assault on religious orthodoxy."[31] Stanton had already earned a grand measure of hostility by supporting resolutions before suffrage organizations condemning all religions, but by focusing her gaze on the structural sexism of Christianity, she found herself marginalized from the movement she helped found. Such utterances as "[T]he Bible and the Church have been the greatest stumbling blocks in the way of women's emancipation" alienated Christian suffragettes.[32] As the women's movement gathered steam at the beginning of the twentieth century, the next generation of suffragettes distanced themselves from Stanton. Christian and pious, these women argued that their presence would bring morality to politics. They cared little for full equality and even less for irreligious criticism. The result of this shift to the new generation was the virtual disappearance of Stanton from the pantheon of women's rights.

That the only consequence of Stanton's public lambasting of Christianity was marginalization rather than demonization speaks to the insurgent trend of American freethinking in the latter half of the nineteenth century. Figures like Mark Twain, William James, and Stanton's compatriot Susan B. Anthony all questioned the existence of a Christian god to some degree and suffered little public scorn. But what had changed? Because of a series of scientific discoveries, a generation of post-Civil War freethinkers and unbelievers joined the public discourse on religious subjects. Pointedly, after the publication of Darwin's *Origin of Species* (1859) all things in nature that had once only been explainable through the model of a divine hand now fell within a the realm of science. Science intruded into a space previously reserved for the creator. Although this somewhat complicated the Deist (or later transcendentalist) notions of divine nature, it directly contradicted the static world of the Bible. Before the popular release of *Origin of a Species*, the musing of the educated elite as to the process of human development was rarely a concern of the general public. Darwin, however, wrote lucidly enough for a general audience to comprehend his theory, thus ensuring its popularity, dissemination, and even tacit acceptance. The country, it appeared, was moving toward a tentative embrace of freethought.

In American history, the first popular anti-Christian figure arrived in the form of a Civil War veteran and Midwestern lawyer with a flair for public speaking. Robert Ingersoll was the son of a Presbyterian preacher who honed his nontheism by reading the works of Voltaire and Paine and reliving the long hours spent sitting through his father's monotonous Sunday sermons.[33] By adulthood, Ingersoll had become one of Illinois' leading Republican figures and one of the most sought after public speakers. His list of speeches reveals varied interests from Shakespeare to farming to currency debates, but he is best remembered for his talks on agnosticism—earning him the title of "the Pagan Prophet." Ingersoll referred to himself as an agnostic, then a recent term, coined in 1869.[34] He profitably toured the country gently mocking the Bible and proclaiming the absurdity of faith and doing so to venues packed with curious middle-class Americans. Ingersoll's oratorical skills kept his audience in their seats for hours, and his message compelled the listening public towards greater skepticism. In one lecture, "On Gods," Ingersoll ridiculed the politically sanctified marriage between religion and nationalism:

> Each nation has created a god, and the god has always resembled his creators. He hated and loved what they hated and loved, and was inevitably found on the side of those in power. Each god was intensely patriotic, and detested all nations but his own. All of these gods demanded praise, flattery and worship. Most of them were pleased with sacrifice, and the smell of innocent blood has ever been considered the divine perfume.[35]

Ingersoll's work, however, cannot be reduced to the insightful cynicism of Ambrose Bierce or "Scopes era" H. L Mencken. Like Paine and Jefferson, Ingersoll never suggested an empty deicide, but a rational replacement of a tradition of superstition with what we now commonly call *secular humanism*. Ingersoll provoked the religious, but did so in the advancement of human liberty.[36] He believed that America was progressively moving away from the faith based on ignorance and fear, toward a rational understanding of the world based on the scientific method. He saw an America where those who occupied the church pews held a greater understanding of the world than those at the pulpit. "The idea is abroad," he wrote, "that they who know the most of nature believe the least about theology. . . . The pulpit is losing because the people are growing."[37]

The growth of the people is evident in the diverse voices of agnosticism within this window of freethinking. From Ingersoll's late nineteenth-century lectures, to the early twentieth-century calls for human rights in place of the rigid authority with a religious cover, public figures boldly subverted tradition. In the African American community, W. E. B. DuBois eschewed the spiritualism of the era's major black churches and studied religion as a sociological pursuit. Looking to its transformative power rather than its spiritual mandate, DuBois was the perpetual outsider within the walls of the church—more ethnographer than participant. Arguably the most important intellectual figure in African American history, DuBois saw black religion as an important element in the quest for civil rights. In his personal life, however, he had jettisoned his belief in its spiritual power and occupied himself with its organizational potential. In one instance he clinically described a "Southern Negro revival" replete with the holy spirit passing over his vessel and entering the woman next to him. While watching a preacher who "swayed and quivered," a "gaunt-cheeked brown woman beside me suddenly leaped straight into the air and shrieked like a lost soul . . . a scene of human passion such as I had never conceived before."[38] Like many, DuBois had been educated out of his religion during his time at Harvard and the University of Berlin. By the end of his days he openly labeled religion as oppressive and Christianity as creating "moral disaster" through the perpetuation of "fairy tales."[39]

Jewish immigrant and devout anarchist Emma Goldman also proves that there was an audience for the message of unbelief in an era of Victorian piety. Denouncing religion and advocating free love, Goldman remained a popular lecturer from the economic Panic of 1893 to her deportation to Russia in 1918. Far from being universally shunned, in 1910 she spoke 120 times, in thirty-seven cities to 25,000 listeners.[40] Unlike the gently prodding Ingersoll or the scholarly DuBois, Goldman was a fierce revolutionary who rarely minced words. Like both Ingersoll and DuBois, she viewed all religions as most often the tool of the powerful. The distribution of that power, she believed, would only be possible after the dismantling of the religious order. "Atheism," she said in 1916, "in its negation of the gods is at the same time the strongest affirmation of man, and through man, the eternal yea to life, purpose, and beauty."[41] She also believed, again like Ingersoll, that the march of science would eventually crush superstition under the weight of its rational methods. God as a concept, she claimed, "or whatever term the essence of Theism may have found expression, has become more indefinite and obscure in the course of time and progress."[42] Thus, the human mind would soon outgrow its need for fairy tales.

Scholars of American atheism, secularism, and agnosticism characterize this era as the calm before the storm of government oppression (i.e., Comstock law and Palmer raids). Though true, the battle over theology originated not in the statehouse, but at the very pulpits that Ingersoll saw crumbling. There is a sociotheological explanation as to why Stanton, DuBois, Ingersoll, and Goldman could speak and write with relative impunity in years between Reconstruction and World War I. This is also the period of time that historians of American religion call "the Great Reversal." Around the turn of the century, scholars argue, American evangelicals left the public sphere of worldly politics and focused instead on personal salvation. Much of this shift was the consequence of popular but overtly liberal "Social Gospel" theology

(Christian do-gooders) and the desire of conservative Christians to distance themselves from their progressive brethren. The relative silence by the historically vocal revivalists, allowed for only a temporary flowering of freethought.

## TWENTIETH CENTURY

In a variety of public venues, atheists, agnostics, and secularists made great gains in the twentieth century. In court, cases for the strict separation of church and state and against the reciting of Bible verses in public schools opened the door for greater atheistic expression. The century also witnessed the emergence of atheist organizations such as the American Atheist Association founded by Madalyn Murray O'Hair in 1963. After launching the lawsuit that ended the practice of Christian prayer in public schools, O'Hair established a cable television program and subsequently saw her organization's mailing list reach 50,000.[43] Yet the marginalization of unbelievers continued throughout the century, and at some points the fight against the "enemies of God" reached a near hysterical pitch. The story of atheism, secularism, and agnosticism in the last century is less about the personas of freethinkers and more the tidal wave of religious intolerance and government complicity. The sleeping giant of fundamentalism, being somewhat inactive during the first two decades, stirred during the Scopes trail, awakened with the Cold War, and became fully animated with the rise of the New Right.

During the Great Reversal (1900–1930), American religion dramatically changed. Social reformers such as Jane Addams still applied the social gospel to modern problems, but concurrently another—and eventually stronger—movement took shape in southern tent revivals and northern Bible colleges. Antimodern fundamentalism made its way from the academic realm and into northern congregations. Churches subsequently split along liberal versus conservative theological lines in most major denominations. In many ways this new religious expression in the North resembled white southern religiosity: an emphasis on personal salvation, belief in the inerrancy of the Bible, and a distrust of modernism. Melded together as a national religious bloc, the marriage of northern fundamentalism and dominant southern revivalism served as a potentially powerful counterbalance to the trend towards unbelief.[44]

The fundamentalist-inspired backlash of the 1920s presaged the role of the New Right in the latter part of the twentieth century. Most pointedly, proponents of traditionalism boldly attacked science—the very thing that Ingersoll and Goldman believed would lift humans out of the dark ages of superstition. The Scopes trial in Dayton, Tennessee, gave Americans the first real inkling of what to come. Waking from their slumber, fundamentalists reentered the political realm in an effort to block the teaching of evolution in public schools. High school teacher

John Scopes defied the state of Tennessee by knowingly teaching a theory that denies the story of the Divine Creation of man as taught in the Bible . . . [or] that man has descended from a lower order of animals."[45] The American Civil Liberties Union supplied vocal agnostic Clarence Darrow to defend Scopes, while the eminent and deeply religious William Jennings Bryan grabbed the chance to prosecute. At the time, Darrow was the most famous agnostic in the United States. Bryan, the champion of the underclass, was a perennial Democratic presidential candidate and served in Woodrow Wilson's cabinet. In the minds of participants and spectators, the trail served as a venue for a national referendum on science, religion, and the place of God in public life. It pitted the educated against the uneducated and believers against skeptics, or, as H. L. Mencken said of the trial, "The so-called religious organizations which now lead the war against the teaching of evolution are nothing more, at bottom, than conspiracies of the inferior man against his betters."[46] Perhaps the most famous moment of the trial came when Darrow called Bryan to the witness stand as an expert on the Bible. In his line of questioning, Darrow exposed Bryan as biblically literate but pedantic and entirely ignorant to the world of scientific thought. In the process he also revealed the inherent absurdity of biblical inerrancy and divine creation.

At the time, liberals—particularly in the North—viewed the trial as the last gasp of a backwardly religious rural proletariat. The yokels had been humiliated, defeated, and dismissed. H. L. Mencken, however, warned the learned that "Neanderthal man is organizing in these forlorn backwaters of the land" waiting to attack civilization like Huns at the gates.[47] Some prematurely pronounced the victory of reason over superstition, only to see the latter gain strength as the century wore on. The consequences of the Scopes trial have profoundly impacted the American assessment and acceptance of atheism. Coming at the end of freethought's "golden age," the seeming defeat of fundamentalists was actually a strategic victory for the forces of conservative religion. Quiet but for a moment, fundamentalists reorganized through a network of religious schools, Bible colleges, youth groups, radio programs, and highly mobile ministers. Unwilling to jump into the national spotlight over science, by the 1950s these entities coalesced around anticommunist crusades.

Many of the organizations born of antievolution rematerialized during the Cold War. Like science in the 1920s, the Godless communism of the 1950s threatened to undermine the traditional foundations of American culture. The United States had officially battled communism from the end of World War I, and it was this initial push that sent Emma Goldman to the Soviet Union. The stakes grew higher with the beginning of the atomic age. On August 29, 1949, the Soviets detonated an atomic bomb at Semipalatinsk, Kazakhstan, and dashed the hopes of an open dialogue for American atheists. McCarthyism and the new

Red Scare crept into every facet of American life and solidly linked communism and atheism in the American mind. Communism, it was argued, extolled collectivism and atheism as the logical objective of all modern societies. The Soviet Union for its part, would invade all free countries by force or subterfuge in order to crush capitalism, freedom, and religion. Thus, those adhering to liberal and secular principles was deemed suspect. In 1954 the government inserted "under God" into the flag salute (originally written by a nineteenth Christian socialist) and in 1957 placed "In God We Trust" on American paper currency. In an age of paranoia, an allegiance to the American Christian God became a patriotic litmus test.

Evangelical minister Billy Graham in particular pitted American Christian nationalism against foreign atheistic communism. Arguably the most influential American clergyman of the twentieth century, Graham cut his teeth on anticommunism. In 1951 Graham argued for a more militant approach towards godless communists. A 1962 advertisement for an essay called "Billy Graham Speaks" reads:

> A controversial movement is picking up steam. If it succeeds the Bible will be removed from courtrooms. Public-school prayers will be banned. And IN GOD WE TRUST will be taken off our coins. Billy Graham speaks out against this trend—and tells why he thinks atheists play into Communist hands.[48]

Other ministers propagated postmillennial notion of the battle between communism and America as the precursor to "end times." Viewing the world through the lens of Revelation, a number of ministers declared Russia the "antichrist," and placed non-Christians under the spell of evil and the light of suspicion.[49]

The ebb and flow of American history is undeniable. After the humiliation of Joseph McCarthy and Barry Goldwater's trouncing in 1964, America witnessed a creative explosion in the arts, an explosive civil rights movement, and loosening of the authoritarian structures crafted during the early Cold War. But as the hippies walked through Golden Gate Park and entertainers pushed the boundaries of obscenity laws in metropolitan nightclubs, a new movement emerged from the ashes of McCarthyism and in the suburbs of the Sunbelt. White suburbanites embraced antistatism, feared for America's moral integrity, and flocked to what would later be labeled "mega-churches." The New Right lifted arch-conservatives to the White House and did so with the support of a younger generation of fundamentalists. Jerry Falwell, Pat Robertson, and James Dobson urged religious Americans to battle the agents of secularism in the statehouse, in the streets, and in public memory.

In 1980, the New Right helped place one of their own—Ronald Reagan—into the White House. Taking his words about teaching the

Pilgrims to students of American history, the grassroots Right took it upon themselves to scrutinize public school textbooks and purge American history "of all materials that they consider antifamily, anti-American and anti-God." The most successful textbook reviewers, Texas's Mel and Norman Gabler stopped major textbook publishers from selling objectionable history books to some of the nation's largest school districts. According to the *New York Times*, "The trouble with most of the textbooks, the Gablers contend, is that they are written from the perspective of people who do not believe in God or an absolute value system. This perspective, they say, is a religion called secular humanism, which permeates every aspect of contemporary society and teaches youngsters to lie, cheat and steal."[50] By the 1990s, this ilk of social activism anchored the New Right's "culture war" battle plan. Atheists, agnostics, and secularists were the first targets for engagement.

In the 2008 North Carolina senate race, incumbent Elizabeth Dole accused her Democratic opponent Kay Hagen of being an atheist. This last ditch effort, however, failed to persuade voters to abandon Hagen, the contest's eventual winner. Like the residents in the union's other states, North Carolinians simply could not conceive of a nonreligious public figure and scoffed at the allegation. Hagen quickly responded with a proclamation of faith and a libel suit. She then charged Dole of willfully breaking the ninth commandment (thou shall not bear false witness). Few people considered the fact that unbelief is not a crime, and despite what former presidents have uttered, atheism is not implicitly unpatriotic. In eighteenth-century New England, women confessed to cavorting with the devil in order to avoid execution on charges of witchcraft; in twentieth-century America, charges and countercharges of "communist" destroyed careers and ruined lives. With the rise of the Christian Right in the post-Cold War world, the accusation of atheism holds the same power as these earlier scare tactics in its ability to send public figures scrambling for religious cover. Despite a shared past filled with the good words and deeds of nonbelievers, Americans cling to a myth of unimpeachable religiously from the first colony to the "end times." To question the veracity of this myth is tantamount to resigning from public life. Those who do not heed this advice, such as Thomas Morton, Thomas Paine, Elizabeth Cady Stanton, and Robert Ingersoll, find themselves in the dustbin of history.

## NOTES

1. James Turner, *Without God, Without Creed: The Origins of Unbelief in America* (Baltimore: Johns Hopkins University Press, 1985), 2–4.

2. Michael R. Haines and Richard Hall Steckel, *A Population History of North America* (New York: Cambridge University Press, 2000), 23–24.

3. Richard Hakluyt, *Discourse on Western Planting* (1584), quoted in Avihu Zakai, *Exile and Kingdom: History and Apocalypse in the Puritan Migration to America* (New York: Cambridge University Press, 2002), 97.

4. Winthrop D. Jordon, *White over Black: American Attitudes Toward the Negro, 1550–1812* (Chapel Hill: University of North Carolina Press, 1968), 44–98.

5. William Hubbard, *General History of New England from Discovery to MDCLXXX*, 2nd ed. (Boston: Charles C. Little and James Brown, 1848), 26.

6. John Canup, *Out of the Wilderness: The Emergence of an American Identity in Colonial New England* (Middletown: Wesleyan Press, 1990), 79–85.

7. John Winthrop, "Reasons to be considered for justifying the undertakers of the intended Plantation in New England, and for encouraging such whose hearts God shall move to join with them in it," reprinted in Alan Heimert and Andrew Delbanco, *The Puritans in America: A Narrative Anthology* (Cambridge: Harvard University Press, 1985), 73.

8. William Bradford, *History of Plymouth Plantation* (Boston: Massachusetts Historical Society, 1856). Also see: William Heath, "Thomas Morton: Form Merry Old England to New England," *Journal of American Studies* 41 (April, 2007): 135–68.

9. Elizabeth Pleck, "Making the Domestic Occasion: The History of Thanksgiving in the United States," *Journal of Social History* 32 (Summer 1999): 773–789.

10. Edmund S. Morgan, "John Winthrop's 'Modell of Christian Charity' in a Wider Context," *Huntington Library Quarterly* 2 (Spring 1987): 145–151.

11. Ronald Reagan, "Farewell Address," January 11, 1989. http://www.ronaldreagan.com/sp_21.html.

12. Jack P. Green, *Pursuits of Happiness: The Social Development of Early Modern British Colonies and the Formation of American Culture* (Chapel Hill: University of North Carolina Press, 1988), 11.

13. Reagan, "Farewell Address."

14. David Barton, *America's Godly Heritage* (Aledo Texas: Wallbuilder Press, 1993).

15. Thomas Jefferson to Dr. Benjamin Waterhouse, June 16, 1822.

16. Thomas Jefferson, *Notes on the State of Virginia* (Boston: Lilly and Wait, 1832), 167–168.

17. ———, *The Life and Morals of Jesus of Nazareth* (New York: N. D. Thomas Publishing Co., 1902), 20.

18. C. P. Farrell, ed., *The Works of Robert Ingersoll*, Dresden Edition, Volume III (New York: Dresden Publishing, 1901), 389.

19. George Washington to Thomas Paine, September 10, 1783; quoted in Thomas Paine, *The Rights of Man* (London: Watts & Company, 1906), 119.

20. Theodore Roosevelt, *Gouverneur Morris* (New York: Houghton Mifflin, 1888), 289.

21. Ella Wheeler Wilcox, "Lest We Forget: A Tribute To Thomas Paine," *The Story of Thomas Paine and the Nation's Debt to His Memory* (New York: Thomas Paine National Historical Association, 1914).

22. Quoted in Susan Jacoby, *Freethinkers: A History of American Secularism* (New York: Owl Books, 2004), 60.

23. See Donald G. Mathews, "The Second Great Awakening as an Organizing Process, 1780–1830: An Hypothesis," *American Quarterly*, 21 (Spring 1969), 23–43.

24. Quoted in Peter M. Rinaldo, *Athesits, Agnostics, and Deists in America: A Brief History* (New York: DorPete Press, 2000), 42–43.

25. See Nathan O. Hatch, *The Democratization of American Christianity* (New Haven: Yale University Press, 1991); Mark A. Noll, *America's God: From Jonathan Edwards to Abraham Lincoln* (New York: Oxford University Press, 2005).

26. Carol Smith-Rosenberg, *Disorderly Conduct: Visions of Gender in Victorian America* (New York: Oxford University Press, 1985), 129–163; Mary P. Ryan, *Cradle of the Middle Class: The Family in Oneida County, New York, 1790–1865* (New York: Cambridge University Press, 1981).

27. Joe Wheeler, *Abraham Lincoln: A Man of Faith and Courage: Stories of Our Most Admired President* (New York: Howard Books, 2008).

28. Jacoby, *Freethinkers*, 104–124.

29. Quoted in John E. Remsberg, *Tom Paine: The Apostle of Liberty* (New York: The Truth Seeker Co., 1917), 110–112.

30. Quoted in Turner, *Without God Without Creed*, 207.

31. Maureen Fitzgerald, "The Religious Is Personal Is Political," forward to the 1993 Edition of *The Women's Bible*, in Elizabeth Cady Stanton, *The Woman's Bible* (Boston: Northeastern University Press, 1993), viii.

32. Elizabeth Cady Stanton, *Free Thought Magazine* (September, 1896).

33. Ingersoll fought at the battle of Shiloh and was later captured by future Ku Klux Klan founder, Nathan Bedford Forrest.

34. Rinaldo, *Athesits, Agnostics, and Deists in America*, 80–94.

35. C. P. Farrell ed., *The Works of Robert Ingersoll*, Dresden Edition, Volume I, (New York: Dresden Publishing, 1901), 7.

36. Jacoby, *Freethinkers*, 173.

37. C. P. Farrell ed., *The Works of Robert Ingersoll*, Dresden Edition, Volume VI, (New York: Dresden Publishing, 1901), 8.

38. W. E. B. DuBois, *The Souls of Black Folk* (New York: Penguin Books, 1989 [1903]): 154–155.

39. ———, *The Autobiography of W. E. B. DuBois: A Soliloquy on Viewing my Life from the Last Decade of Its First Century* (New York: International Publishers, 1968), 43.

40. Alix Kates Shulman, ed., *Red Emma Speaks: Selected Writings and Speeches by Emma Goldman* (New York: Random House, 1972), 15.

41. Emma Goldman, "The Philosophy of Atheism," in *Red Emma Speaks*, 202.

42. Ibid., 195.

43. Rinaldo, *Athesits, Agnostics, and Deists in America*, 133–134.

44. George M. Marsden, *Fundamentalism and American Culture* (New York: Oxford University Press, 2006): 164–195.

45. Quoted in Arthur McCalla, *The Creationist Debate: The Encounter Between the Bible and the Historical Mind* (New York: Continuum International Publishing Group, 2006), 161.

46. *The Baltimore Evening Sun*, June 29, 1925.

47. ———, July 18, 1925.

48. *Los Angeles Times*, February 13, 1962.

49. Paul Boyer, *When Time Shall Be No More: Prophecy Belief in Modern American Culture* (Cambridge: Harvard University Press, 1992), 157–166.

50. *New York Times*, July 14, 1981.

# Chapter 9

# Defining Religion and Modifying Religious "Bodies:" Secularizing the Sacred and Sacralizing the Secular

## *Jay Demerath III*

Over the years, most of the real action in church–state matters has involved members of the judiciary. Even those few academics who are interested tend to be relegated to the sidelines and that is almost always the case with those of us who profess disciplines other than the law itself. Occasionally, however, opportunities arise for scholars in the academic hinterland to play a role in the judicial spotlight. One such role involves that of an expert witness in a court proceeding. Here I want to report on my first and only experience in this capacity. After describing the case in question, I shall share my written testimony and its response, describe the results of the case, and then discuss further the major issues involved in developing a definition of religion that bears up under both judicial and social scientific scrutiny and does not veer too far toward either secularizing the sacred or sacralizing the secular.

But first consider the following self-description drawn from a branch of the religious organization on which I was asked to pass judgment:

> [This church] is a non-denominational congregation that teaches ownership over our own . . . [selves]. The Church's purpose is . . . to harmoniously return to . . . spiritual roots that have been forgotten. We are not here to offer spirituality to you as much as we are here because of the spirituality that is already in all of us. . . . [This] is an inter-faith church

whose members practice an assortment of ancient . . . rites which we
believe are essential to our spirituality. . . . It is our belief that by . . .
engaging in rituals . . . we strengthen the bond between mind, body, and
soul, and ensure that we live as spiritually complete and healthy individuals. . . . [The Church] is the spiritual hub in which modified individuals
around the world will find strength, and procure the respect from society
as equal, intelligent, feeling human beings. . . . [and] no longer be dismissed as a minority in our world. . . . This is our birthright.

Does anything seem amiss? I suspect not. But after briefly describing
the case, I shall fill in the ellipses and ask again.

The case involved a young woman, Kimberly Cloutier, who began
working in September 1997, for a Costco retail outlet, where her duties
ranged from food handling in the deli to "front-end" duties as a cash-
ier. In March 2001, she was informed of the company's new dress code,
which banned employees from displaying any form of facial adornment
such as tattoos, scarification, piercings, or jewelry other than earrings.
Although her clothing covered several hours of bodily tattoos (hours
are the preferred measure of quantity because tattoos are often covered
over), Ms. Cloutier's one offending adornment was a small, thin gold
ring through a pierced eyebrow. Once personally confronted with the
store's new policy, she declined to remove the ring but volunteered to
cover it with a Band-Aid. The store declared this unacceptable and soon
acted to terminate her employment. Ms. Cloutier indicated for the first
time that this would violate her freedom of religion. When the store
manager asked what religion that might be, she replied that she was a
member of the Church of Body Modification (CBM).

At this point in my oral accounts of the case, a pause for laughter is
required. (Even during the case's initial court hearing, the judge made
light of the CBM with joking references to the body in both senses of
the term.) Once the guffaws subside, it is necessary to explain that such
an organization is both very real and quite serious, though one of its
many Web sites does refer to it as the "blingdom of God." Here it is
worth reconsidering the CBM's earlier self-description with the missing
material replaced:

The Church of Body Modification is a non-denominational congregation
that teaches ownership over our own bodies. The Church's purpose is
for our modified bodies to harmoniously return to their spiritual roots
that have been forgotten. We are not here to offer spirituality to you as
much as we are here because of the spirituality that is already in all of
us; often expressed through what we do to our own bodies . . . The
Church of Body Modification is an inter-faith church whose members
practice an assortment of ancient body modification rites which we
believe are essential to our spirituality. . . . It is our belief that by practic-
ing body modification and by engaging in rituals of body manipulation

we strengthen the bond between mind, body, and soul, and ensure that we live as spiritually complete and healthy individuals. . . . The Church of Body Modification is the spiritual hub in which modified individuals around the world will find strength, and procure the respect from society as equal, intelligent, feeling human beings, modified individuals will no longer be dismissed as a minority in our world. . . . This is our birthright.

Not long after the events described above I received a call from Michael Shea, an attorney who had agreed to represent the young woman and take her case to U.S. District Court following affirmation by the Equal Employment Opportunity Commission on May 8, 2002. He asked me to serve as an expert witness in support of the Church of Body Modification's status as a constitutionally legitimate "religion." As the affidavit attests, I agreed to serve, but only after some exploration of the matter (and after a younger brother who is the head of litigation for a major law firm in a large Midwestern city warned that questions asked of me were not invitations for fifty-minute lectures). In any case, my first obligation as a witness was to prepare an "Expert Witness Report" (see Appendix 1) to alert the judge and opposing counsel to my *bona fides* and my position on the issues in question.

Frankly, I was proud of this first dip into legal waters, and I confess that I was expecting compliments. Certainly I was not prepared for the onslaught that ensued. Much to my surprise, I had violated a basic rule of the witness role by presuming to instruct the court on matters of law rather than remaining within the narrow confines of my nonlegal expertise.

The judge was so unhappy that he leaked word to court bystanders and the press that I was likely to be disqualified. Opposing counsel described me as "an affront to the Court," and formally moved "to strike" me as a witness. However, the plaintiff's attorney was able to persuade the judge to consider a second memo from me in response to his concerns and those of opposing counsel. Chastened, I went back to work and produced *Affidavit of N. J. Demerath III in Response to COSTCO's Motion to Strike Plaintiff's Expert Witness Designation and as Supplemental Report* (see Appendix 2).

For whatever reason, the judge relented. In the aggressive language of the court, I narrowly avoided being "struck," and now I was to be "deposed." On September 22, 2003, Lynn A. Kappelman, a lawyer from the opposing law firm, made the two-hour drive from Boston to examine, test, and challenge me as a witness with the plaintiff's attorney, Michael Shea, also present in a conference room that he provided.

Once I was sworn in, the deposition took more than three hours. Attorney Kappelman apparently did her job well; she took the offensive from the start and was alternately combative and dismissive throughout.

She began by tempting me to reclaim the kind of legal expertise that had landed me in trouble earlier; later she challenged my written statement that behavior could be deemed "religious" even if not formally required by a religious body, though she later backed down when "my" lawyer showed her a copy of the pertinent 1997 Commonwealth of Massachusetts statute and volunteered to make a copy for her. She questioned my scholarly credentials and sought rifts within the consensus I claimed among other social scientists. When she asked about my own religion, I suspect I told her more than she really wanted to know about the considerable diversity within my extended family.

After deriding my investigation of the Church of Body Modification, Attorney Kappelman spent the lion's share of the deposition testing how far I was willing to go in extending the mantel of "religion" to a range of hypothetical groups and behaviors: "What about a Church of Naked Persons" or "a Church of People in Black Clothes?" "What if the body modification involved [various grotesque extremes of mutilation, such as suspending oneself by transdermal or subcutaneously implanted hooks and then pulling]?" I repeatedly answered yes on the condition that my three-pronged criteria were satisfied. Apparently frustrated, she rose from her seat at two junctures and strode dramatically towards the door while declaring, "Alright! This witness is being uncooperative and I am going to call the judge." In each instance, she returned to her chair after plaintiff's attorney Shea came to my defense and charged her with misleading and badgering his witness.

Following the deposition, I returned home to await the trial, but as so often happens in legal dramas, the trial never came. Opposing counsel asked the judge for a Summary Judgment to dismiss the case, and on March 4, 2004, the judge allowed it. However, it was allowed not on grounds that the Church of Body Modification had no religious standing or that Ms. Cloutier's religious convictions were not sincere. The judge held that at least a *prima facie* case had been made on both these problematic matters. He then allowed counsel's motion for reasons stemming from conventional employment law. After considerable to-ing and fro-ing and a delay of some three weeks after termination, Costco had informed Ms. Cloutier that she could cover her eyebrow ring with either a Band-Aid or a clear plastic retainer and return to work. Even though she refused the concession, the Judge deemed it a "reasonable accommodation."

Not yet finished, the plaintiff's attorney Shea appealed the District Court decision to the U.S. 1st Circuit Court of Appeals. On December 1, 2004, the Court affirmed the summary judgment requested by the Costco counsel, but not on the same grounds as the District Court judge. Although the Court of Appeals made an even stronger point of fully accepting the religious claims in the case, it argued that "reasonable accommodation" was unnecessary because the plaintiff's request for dispensation—however well grounded—would constitute an "undue hardship" on Costco, and in these matters employer hardships trump employee privileges, although both seem to be more preferable grounds for judicial decisions than religion with all of its ambiguity. Finally, this Appellate Court's decision was referred to the U.S. Supreme Court, where it was denied *certiorari,* hence affirmed.

*Costco v. Cloutier* is the kind of judicial acorn from which mighty oaks may grow—or not. Even though the case proved infecund here, it does introduce a range of issues that have long plagued judicial treatments of American religion. While the case is now moot and it is likely that the Church of Body Modification's religious status and Ms. Cloutier's religious claims would have been accepted even without my inexpert testimony, in the final analysis, it also seems clear that at neither the U.S. District nor Appellate levels was there any inclination to join a religious fight. This is especially so when the very definition of religion continues to be left to *de facto* diffusion and confusion as opposed to *de jure* specificity. In what follows, I discuss some of the implications and alternatives.

## ESCAPING THE DEFINITIONAL QUANDARY

The United States is hardly the only country in which judicial or legislative definitions of religion have been scarce and elusive. After reviewing international law on the topic, Jeremy Gunn (2003) characterizes the "quest for a legal definition of 'religion'" as "understandable, but misguided." While I am more sanguine, I am certainly not oblivious to the problems, especially as revealed in a brief history of the American situation (Wilson 1987; Adams and Emmerich 1990).

For its first 175 years, the religion clauses of the U.S. First Amendment had only moderate impact. For one thing, the meaning of its "establishment clause" ("Congress shall make no law respecting an establishment of religion") now appears to have had a very different original meaning as essentially assurance to the eight remaining original states with established religions of their own that the new federal government would not interfere (Stepan 2000). Indeed, it was not until 1940 that the Bill of Rights applied to the states. And if religion sometimes seemed to require a definition, as it did in *Davis v. Beason* in 1890, the result came perilously close to Mr. Thwackum's oft-quoted formulation in Henry Fielding's (1749) English novel, *Tom Jones*: "When I mention Religion, I mean the Christian Religion, and not only the Christian Religion but the Protestant Religion; and not only the Protestant Religion, but the Church of England." More than two hundred years later, U.S. jurists still took it for granted that at least a belief in the supernatural was essential.

As in so many other facets of American life, change came in a rush in the 1960s. As described briefly in my Witness Report, *U.S. v. Seeger* (1965) grabbed the definitional issue by its neck and shook hard.

Pressured during the very unpopular Vietnam War by candidates for conscientious objector status "without a belief in God, except in the remotest sense" and convinced that the Establishment clause forbids granting authority to established religions or their beliefs, the *Seeger* court noted that "while the 'truth' of a belief is not open to question, there remains the significant question whether it is 'truly held.'" It held that a satisfactory equivalent to religious belief was "sincerely held" moral convictions that occupied "a parallel place" in the life of the holder that is occupied by God in the life of the religious believer. The boundaries of such a definition were at best uncertain, but according to Claborn (2007, 37), "That diversity would find its limit in 1968, in *U.S. v. Kuch* as the Neo-American Church, whose church key is a bottle opener and whose motto is 'Victory Over Horseshit,' was denied the same tax immunities as other religious traditions."

The *Seeger* decision was upheld by *U.S. v. Welsh* (1970), and "sincerely held beliefs" began to gain influence as an alternative criterion, albeit slowly and often implicitly. The federal courts have been loathe to confront or grapple with the definition or even cite it. This is also true of the two most important legislative actions concerning religion over the past twenty years. After *Employment Division v. Smith, 494 U.S. 872* (1990) lifted the burden on government to justify limits placed on the free exercise of religion by presumably religiously neutral laws, a broad religious movement succeeded in generating massive congressional support for quick passage of the Religious Freedom Restoration Act (RFRA) in 1993. And yet the act basically deferred the question as what "religion" or "religious exercise" might entail: "the term 'exercise of religion' means the exercise of religion under the First Amendment to the Constitution." Nor was the matter much amplified in the bill that followed after RFRA had been struck down by the Supreme Court for exceeding Congressional powers relative to the Court. However, the Religious Land Use and Institutionalized Persons Act of 2000 did take at least a small leaf from the Seeger book by specifying that, "The term 'religious exercise' includes any exercise of religion, whether or not compelled by, or central to, a system of religious belief."

Clearly the *Seeger* departure had not gone unnoticed. For example, as noted in my earlier expert witness report, at least a version of it became a matter of Massachusetts state law in 1997, though largely for political reasons. When two Catholic women employees of a greyhound racing track refused to work on Christmas Day despite earlier notice that this was the track's busiest day of the year and were therefore fired, the largely Catholic state legislature sought to rescue them and elude the establishment clause by giving each individual the "religious holiday" of their choice and their definition. More recently Hammond et al. (2004) have even proclaimed the advantages of replacing the freedom of religion altogether with freedom of conscience.

The definitional changes experienced over the past forty years have been major. But they also leave major questions in their wake. There is no doubt that constraints on free exercise have been substantially loosened, and this can only be a gain for adherents of movements such as the Church of Body Modification. But beyond my allegiance as an expert witness, I have a gnawing sense of solutions begetting problems. Accordingly, I want to conclude by considering three potential problem areas involving first, a looming reassessment of the relationship between establishment and free exercise clauses; second, a needed shift from a psychological to a more sociological conception of the sacred; and third, the implications of moving not only from "religion" to the "sacred" but ultimately from the sacred to the "secular."

## Establishment vs. Free Exercise Redux

Not long ago an often-mentioned but never tapped candidate for the U.S. Supreme Court was asked after concluding his after-dinner remarks before a small faculty gathering what would happen if members of his faith achieved sufficient power in Congress and the Executive Branch to make their faith the nation's official religion. "Well, this is a democracy, and in a democracy majority rules." Rolling eyes were almost as audible as the coughing. Wasn't the judiciary the one branch of government intended to serve the Constitution and protect minorities against such majorities? And even if a majority is entitled to exercise its religious freedom politically, doesn't the (anti) establishment clause set limits?

Although the United States is known worldwide for its "separation of church and state," the First Amendment's initial establishment clause remains little known and little duplicated around the globe even though its second clause concerning religious free exercise is a constitutional staple even among countries who honor it more as a rhetorical nod than a matter of policy (Demerath 2001; Krislov 1985). Even in the United States, it is the second clause that dominates the amendment in the public's mind. Nor is this surprising, because there has always been a latent conflict between the two clauses (Drackman 1991). When taking on a religious case, the first decision a lawyer must often make is whether to treat it as an establishment issue or a free exercise matter. And as the example at hand suggests, the free exercise of religion may easily challenge establishment constraints, just as these same constraints have been portrayed as violations of religious freedom.

The latent conflict is now becoming manifest. We have yet to reach the point where a constitutional guarantee of the free exercise of religion is itself unconstitutional as a violation of the establishment clause because of the unique standing it gives religion in comparison with other institutions. But there may come a time when simply treating religion as a special case is ipso facto a constitutional violation. As the definitional quandary itself suggests, concerns about conferring establishment legitimacy and official entanglement to any form of existing religion—or to religion generally—requires a definition of religion that is neither proreligious nor antireligious but essentially a-religious—as Gunn (2003) puts it, more "polythetic" than "essentialist," and in more sociological terms, more "functional" than "substantive," i.e., more a matter of what is done than what does it.

## Psychological vs. Sociological Models

The currently reigning (if still implicit) definition of "religion" traces back to *U.S. v. Seeger* (1965) and casts the widest possible net by leaving the choice of religion, if any, up to the "sincerely held beliefs" of an individual. It basically endorses a psychological conception of religion, one that is consistent with the philosopher Alfred North Whitehead's (1926) dictum that "religion is what the individual does with his own solitariness." In fact, it has applied particularly to prison inmates, including those experiencing solitary confinement, hence the title of the aforementioned 1997 U.S. statute: Religious Land Use and Institutionalized Persons Act. In recent decades, judges at every level have been plagued by inmate petitions claiming religious justifications for everything from culinary preferences to conjugal sex.

As important as individual sensibilities are to religion, it is also important to note that these occur in social contexts. The psychology and sociology of religion are complementary rather than mutually exclusive. This is the reason why as a witness I offered and defended not a simple one-dimensional conception of religion, but rather a three-pronged model involving "any shared sense of sacred meaning that is ritually enacted and communally reinforced through a like-minded group or organization." The model includes the current standard of a "sincerely held . . . belief," though it substitutes "sacred" for "religious" belief and it specifies that the belief must be shared with others rather than concocted on one's own. In addition, the model requires that there be a ritual enactment of that belief that is presumably also shared and that it adds the critical communal dimension involving a "like-minded group or organization." However, this need not include formal membership; just a sense of affiliational identity will suffice. After all, the most common form of religion itself is what has been called "cultural religion" on the part of people who don't believe the doctrine or practice most of the rituals of their faith but still feel a kinship to it as the legacy of their forbears. (Demerath 2001).

This is not the place to provide the scholarly development of such a model, though my second affidavit (Appendix 2) to the court provides some of the obligatory references, not including the last two lines of a bit of personal rhyming: "Perhaps what is sacred—as well as our hatred—has little to do with re-ligion; the real source of it all—including our fall—may instead be our we-ligion." But scholarship (and doggerel) aside, the model also helps the judiciary avoid two major problems. On the one hand, the threefold model avoids crossing the establishment line because it does not insist on the legitimacy or exemplar of conventional religion. On the other hand, it also avoids the problem of individuals manufacturing their own beliefs opportunistically in response to their circumstances of the moment. The requirement of shared beliefs, collective rituals, and a communal attachment not only gives the definition the critical social dimension it has recently lacked but should cut down on the self-serving petitions that have been so difficult to process because they often seem so arbitrary. And yet this would fall short of obviating all problematic claims and decisions. It should serve as a well-justified filter for the more egregious cases, but it will hardly rule out the need to draw lines between the serious, the visionary, the whimsical, and the outrageous.

## Secularizing the Sacred and Sacralizing the Secular

It was the turn-of-the-20th-century French sociologist, Emile Durkheim, who first suggested a difference not just between the sacred and the secular, but between religion and the sacred, noting that the former is only one form of the latter and that neither necessarily qualifies as the other. In 1912, he asked: "What basic difference is there between Christians celebrating the principal dates of Christ's life . . . and a citizen's meeting commemorating the advent of a new charter or some other great event of national life?" Durkheim went on to aver that old forms of both religion and the sacred often lose their urgency and are replaced by new forms: "In a word, the old gods are growing old or already dead, and others are not yet born. . . . It is life itself and not a dead past which can produce a living cult." (Durkheim 1912, 429). Of course, Durkheim was aware that religion generally concerns some form of transcendence (though not necessarily to the supernatural) and other forms of the sacred do not. But precisely because religion is therefore a special case of the sacred given special constitutional standing and boundaries, it must steer clear of receiving establishment endorsement in a way that need not concern sacredness as a whole. However, it seems unlikely that we can expect a change in the wording of the First Amendment to "the free exercise of the sacred."

Over the past forty years American history has followed Durkheim's logic. Old forms of religion have been subject to continual change, and many adherents have moved away from religion altogether, thus confirming the long standing post-Enlightenment theory of secularization. But that theory predicted only part of the Durkheimian story and its prophecy ultimately left people normatively depleted and gasping for meaning. It made little room for what has been called "sacralization" (Demerath 2007) whereby people find new sacred commitments in secular spheres ranging from politics and civic causes to musical groups and sports teams, to name but a few possibilities. Nor did secularization theory make sufficient allowance for the return to some religions, the intensification of other religions, and the development of new religions—all other forms of sacralization.

As American history has gone, so has the history of the American First Amendment where religion, the sacred, and the secular are concerned. Beginning with a sense of religion that virtually ignored the establishment clause, decisions since the 1960s have gradually come to embrace the clause. They have not only shifted from a narrow conception of religion to a broad view of the sacred, but they have even made more than ample room for the secular in sacred guise. In the process, the free exercise of religion threatens to become a hard workout if courts continue to honor the judicial theory and definitions now in vogue. But of course, that is a big "if." Theory and definitions are only one of many influences affecting judicial decision-making (Claborn 2007).

## CONCLUSION

This chapter began with the confessions of an inexperienced expert witness in a case involving an employee who claimed a violation of her freedom of religion because she was required to remove a facial adornment despite her involvement in the Church of Body Modification. I agreed to testify that the CBM qualified as a religion despite its seeming unconventionality. As it happened, both the church's and the plaintiff's religious status were accepted, though the defense was ultimately granted summary judgment by the First Circuit Court of Appeals on the grounds that the accommodation requested of the employer would have constituted an "undue hardship." A further appeal to the U.S. Supreme Court was not heard.

In reflecting on the case and its implications, my conclusions as an analyst differ somewhat from my position as a witness. In both roles, I find that the CBM qualifies for free exercise. But as an analyst I have reservations about the definitions that have guided the courts over the past forty years. Although I certainly approve of the increasing respect granted the First Amendment's establishment clause, I have two reservations about the extent to which the door has been opened to free exercise: one, because the implicit psychological model of "sincerely held belief" needs to be placed in social—and dare I say it, sociological—context; the other because decisions may soon be reaching not only beyond narrow religion to the broader category of the deserving sacred but also beyond the genuinely sacred to the still broader but much less deserving category of the secular. At the end of the day and the end of this chapter, I should declare my grudging respect for the courts' apparent determination to leave definitions implicit. Judicial discretion can be an important precondition for wise decisions.

## REFERENCES

Adams, Arlin M., and Charles Emmerich. 1990. *A nation dedicated to religious liberty: The constitutional heritage of the religious clauses.* Philadelphia: University of Pennsylvania Press.

Berger, Peter. 1967. *The sacred canopy.* Garden City, NY: Doubleday.

Christiano, Kevin, William Swatos, and Peter Kevisto. 2002. *The Sociology of religion: Contemporary developments.* Walnut Creek, CA: Alta Mira.

Claborn, David. 2007. *Can the states increase religious freedom if they try? Judicial and legislative effects on religious actor success in the state courts.* Ph.D. Dissertation. Dept. Of Political Science, University of Massachusetts, Amherst.

Demerath, N. J., III. 1965. *Social class in American protestantism.* Chicago: Rand McNally.

———. 1992. *A bridging of faiths: Religion and politics in a New England city.* Princeton: Princeton University Press.

———. 2001. *Crossing the Gods: World religions and wordly politics.* New Brunswick, NJ: Rutgers University Press.

———. 2007. Secularization and sacralization deconstructed and reconstructed. In *Handbook for the sociology of religion.* eds. James Beckford and N. J. Demerath, III. London: Sage Publishing.

Demerath, N. J., III., and Phillip E. Hammond. 1976. *Religion in social context.* New York: Random House.

Demerath, N. J., III., and Rhys Williams. 1984. "The separation of church and state: Notes on a mythical past and an uncertain future." *Society* 21/4 (June-July): 3–10.

Drackman, Donald L. 1991. *Church-state constitutional issues: Making sense of the establishment clause.* New York: Greenwood Press.

Durkheim, Emile. 1912 (1995). *The elementary forms of the religious life.* Trans. by Karen Fields. New York: Free Press.

Farnsley, Arthur E., III, N. J. Demerath, III, *et al.* 2004. *Sacred circles and public squares: The multicentering of American Religion.* Bloomington: Indiana University Press.

Glock, Charles Y., and Rodney Stark. 1967. *Religion and society in tension.* Chicago: Rand McNally.

Gunn, T. Jeremy. 2003. The complexity of religion and the definition of "religion" in international law." *Harvard Human Rights Journal* 16:189–215.

Hammond, Phillip E., David Machacek, and Eric Mazur. 2004. *Religion on trial: How Supreme Court trends threaten the freedom of conscience in America.* Walnut Creek, CA: Alta Mira Press.

Hargrove, Barbara. 1979. *The sociology of religion.* Belmont, CA: Wadsworth Publishing.

Krislov, Samuel. 1985. Alternatives to the separation of church and state in countries outside the United States. In *Religion and the state: Essays in honor of Leo Pfeffe*, ed. James E. Wood, Jr., Waco, TX: Baylor University Press.

McGuire, Meredith. 2002. *Religion: The social context.* Belmont, CA: Wadsworth Publishing.

Robbins, Thomas. 1988. *Cults, converts, and charisma.* London: Sage Publishing.

Robbins, Thomas, and Dick Anthony, eds. 1981. *In gods we trust.* New Brunswick, NJ: Transaction Books.

Stark, Rodney, and William Bainbridge. 1985. *The future of religion.* Berkeley: University of California Press.

Stepan, Alfred. 2000. Religion, democracy, and the "twin tolerations." *Journal of Democracy* 11 (4): 37–57.

Whitehead, Alfred North. 1926. *Religion in the making: The Lowell lectures.* New York: Macmillan.

Wilson, John F., ed. 1987. *Church and state in America: A bibliographic guide.* 2 vols. Westport, CT: Greenwood Press.

Yinger, J. Milton. 1970. *The scientific study of religion.* New York: Macmillan.

## APPENDIX 1

### Expert Witness Report

On May 1, (2003), attorney Michael Shea contacted me about the possibility of serving as an expert witness in the case of *Kimberly Cloutier vs. COSTCO.* He needed to know more about my experience and credentials, and I briefly reviewed them for him. I was unaware of the case, and he briefly reviewed it for me. Subsequently, I sent him a copy of my curriculum vitae (c.v.). He sent me materials bearing on the case, including pertinent documents from the Church of Body Modification, U.S. District Court, and the Massachusetts Commission against Discrimination, plus a letter and motions from the defendant's attorneys Seyfarth and Shaw dated 9/20/01, 1/17/03, and 1/21/03; Kimberly Cloutier's letter to the U.S. EEOC as of 10/16/2001 (and the EEOC's determination of 5/8/02) and her plaintiff's affidavit to U.S. District Court of 1/28/03.

On Wednesday, May 7, we agreed that I would join the case for a fee of $100 per hour, and I have not billed or received a retainer on this case to date (n.b. nor did I ever collect a fee). In what follows, I shall briefly review my experience and expertise in the area, indicate my acquaintance with the Church of Body Modification and the principals involved, and state my position on the matters at issue. In addition to attaching my c.v., I should also note that I have not served as an expert witness in this or any other area during the last four years.

*Personal Qualifications:* For the past 40 years, I have been an active scholar and teacher in the field of sociology. My publications include several scores of published articles, and I have been author or co-author— editor or co-editor—of some eleven books with another due next year.

I have served two terms as chair of my department. I have also been an active leader in various scholarly associations, serving three as president.

Most of my scholarly research has been concentrated in the sociology of religion. Here I have focused especially on religion's relation to its wider secular, political, and legal contexts and how religion might be viewed in a way that bears scrutiny from these various perspectives and holds up to cross-cultural variation around the world. Over the past 20 years, I have given special attention to what Americans call "First Amendment issues" and the interface between religion and the state. I have investigated these issues not only close to home (my 1992 book on religion and politics in New England) but far afield (my 2001 book on "world religions and worldly politics" in some fourteen countries around the globe).

In preparing for this assignment, I have examined the Church of Body Modification and the plaintiff's involvement in it. I have read the CBM's "Presentation of Church Planning" from 6/29/2001. I have also consulted its voluminous Web site. The Web site contains a wealth of information including a general account of "Who Are We?," an overall mission statement, rosters of leaders, a lengthy list of answers to frequently asked questions, news of past and future meetings, brief summaries of pertinent information in the media about various forms of modification, a modest catalog of items from the church "store," and a financial presentation. In addition, I have had telephone conversations with both the president of the Church of Body Modification, Rev. Richard Frueh of Medora, Illinois, and the plaintiff, Ms. Cloutier.

*Opinions to Be Expressed:* In defining religion, the courts have generally sought to steer a course between an undue dependence on the specifics of particular faiths, on the one hand, and an unanchored vagueness when religion is left to the individual's private and sometimes opportunistic choice, on the other hand. In framing the U.S. Constitution's First Amendment, the nation's founding fathers understood the problem and went a long way towards solving it. The amendment's first clause that "Congress shall make no law respecting an establishment of religion," indicates a sense of impartial neutrality that avoids entanglements with present faith traditions while leaving the future open to new and different faiths. They also saw the state as a level playing field for the more philosophical competition between religion and non-religion. Meanwhile, the amendment's second clause held that Congress shall make no law "prohibiting the free exercise" of religion. This indicated their commitment to a widespread religious tolerance in keeping with the country's new democracy. But here a loose end was left dangling. Without being able to rely upon the conventional churches of the day as examples and exemplars lest they confer an established status upon them, it gradually became easier to understand what is "free exercise" than what is "religion." Over time, the boundaries of acceptable religion expanded and changed. While the courts seemed to know intuitively that there had to be some limits, it was difficult to know where to draw them, and there was no clear legal definition of religion on which to lean.

Recently a solution has emerged from social scientific research on religion. In emphasizing what religions "do" rather than what religions "are," it asks about the chief functions that all religions fulfill for their followers and what binds followers to the practices and traditions that compel them. Reflecting a consensus among social scientists in this area, religion may be defined as "any shared sense of sacred meaning that is ritually enacted and communally reinforced through a like-minded group or organization." Clearly this describes more than a purely individual conviction. It places individuals within a community whose commitments are shared and whose sense of mutual support offers important affirmation. The criteria of sacred meaning, ritual activity, and communal belonging can be found in every faith, ranging from the most traditional and familiar churches to less conventional forms that are no less saliently sacred for their members.

On the basis of the evidence at hand and based on my education and experience, I find to a reasonable degree of social scientific certainty that the Church of Body Modification qualifies as a religion. Like many other non-conventional religions, CBM does indeed nurture shared sacred meanings that depend upon members' participation in common rituals such as body piercing and tattooing. Although formally only some four years old, the national organization and its local groups now have approximately 1,000 members. According to its president, its members often voice two common sentiments. The first reports a "spiritual inner peace" provided by experiencing the modification process and displaying its results; the second expresses a sense of "strong personal support" that comes from involvement in the church itself. It is also important to note that Ms. Cloutier's membership in the CBM pre-dates her employment termination and subsequent events.

Still, it is not unusual for outsiders to find the practices of religious groups strange and even threatening. In fact, this is more the rule than the exception for new religious movements. It certainly characterized the struggles of the first Christian sect at the hands of generally hostile bystanders. Moreover, the physical body is commonly implicated in religious rituals, and bodily modification itself has taken myriad forms in various religions. These forms may include the long-term effects of extreme fasting and sensory deprivation, circumcision (both male and female), celibacy and its various techniques, ritual hair and beard stylings, body building, hook swinging, flagellation, scarification, amputations, and even suicide, including memetic crucifixions.

Although it may seem difficult to imagine that a U.S. legislative body might have a group like the CBM in mind when crafting statutes concerning religion, both the First Amendment's establishment clause noted above and current Massachusetts law [*G.L.c.151B & 4(1A)*] prohibit using such conventional and "established" religious imagination as a criterion. The same is true of traditional dictionary definitions of religion that specify a belief in the supernatural. Such beliefs are by no means universal among the great faiths such as Buddhism or Confucianism. There are also exceptions within the Judeo-Christian fold such as Unitarianism, and it has become increasingly clear that there are members (and clergy) within many conventional churches who remain in good standing despite either considerable doubt about or actual disbelief in the supernatural even though other aspects of their traditions remain sacred. As noted in *U.S. v. Welsh* (1970) re: conscientious objector status during the Vietnam War, a wide range of beliefs may qualify as religious so long as they ". . . occupy in the life of that individual 'a place parallel to that filled . . . by God' (cf. *U.S. v Seeger*, 1965) in traditional religious persons." Thus, any form of religion should meet the "sincerely held . . . belief" standard stipulated by the Massachusetts legislature in 1997. And although the social scientific definition goes further to include some form of communal group or organization, this surely need not be "an established church or other religious institution" of the sort proscribed as a model by the same law.

Meanwhile, it is important to understand what constitutes discrimination against "religious free exercise" in employment law. Two conditions apply. First, there must be a satisfactory demonstration that the behavior in question is genuinely religious. Until the 1997 statute referred to above, Massachusetts had an unusual stipulation that discrimination could only occur when it involved denying behavior formally "required" by a plaintiff's religion. But the requirement restriction was both vague and overly demanding. Not only did the term "religion" imply an establishment model, but the term "required" was unclear about just how stringent an expected or desirable mode of conduct must be to qualify. Virtually every faith provides exemptions for circumstances that make religious practices impossible. Worship and ritual are generally most fulfilling when they are "freely exercised"—a phrase whose meaning resonates both legally and theologically. Some religious behavior is gratifying in its public display, such as the wearing of certain garments or jewelry. Moreover, some types of sacred body modification such as tattoos and body piercings are not easily donned and doffed from one day (or part of the day) to the next. Although the plaintiff in this case initially volunteered to use Band-aids to cover her eye ring while at work, the offer was refused.

Fortunately, the operative terms "religion" and "required" were replaced in the 1997 statute by a definition of religious belief (and implicitly behavior) that stipulates, ". . . without regard to whether such beliefs are approved, espoused, prescribed or required by an established church or other religious institution or organization."

[*G.L.c.151B & 4(1A)*]. With this discussion in mind, a claim of violated religious rights appears warranted.

Meanwhile, a second condition of religious discrimination is that the religious behavior in question precludes the employer from making a "reasonable accommodation" without "undue hardship." Here it is important to note that the case at hand differs from most of the cases that have required adjudication in this area. The most common scenario involves an employee's request for dispensation to be absent from work in order to participate in a religious observance. By contrast, the current situation began with no request for dispensation, and the employer initiated the chain of action rather than reacting to events already underway. There appears to be little recent case law for such situations in Massachusetts. But when an employer makes no attempt at an accommodation and yet claims no undue hardship in maintaining the services of an employee terminated for reasons that interfere with the plaintiff's religious freedom, the law suggests that religious discrimination has occurred.

In sum, I respectfully submit my findings that a) the Church of Body Modifications fits within a definition of religion that is in accord with both the law and social science research, b) the plaintiff has been a member of the church in good standing since before her employment was terminated.

Date

N. J. Demerath III
Professor of Sociology
UMass, Amherst

## APPENDIX 2

### Affidavit of N. J. Demerath III in Response to COSTCO's Motion to Strike Plaintiff's Expert Witness Designation and as Supplemental Report

I, N. J. Demerath III, do depose and say the following, based on my personal knowledge, information, and belief, which I believe to be true. Specifically, I respectfully disagree with all four basic premises on which the motion rests; namely, questions of fact, of methodology, of law, and of prejudice.

1. *Questions of Fact:* The defense asserts that any expertise I might have would be unnecessary because whether a practice is religious is a matter of "common sense" and "nearly every citizen . . . [is] familiar with the concept of religion and is readily able to determine whether a given set of beliefs constitutes a religion." With all due respect, I disagree on three counts. First, religion is not just a matter of "beliefs" as the quote indicates. Adherents often hold to patterns of meaning even

without the kind of cognitive conviction that the term "belief" implies. Moreover, belief is only one aspect of religion, and understanding religion requires an appreciation of how its several dimensions relate to each other, as in the core social science definition provided in my initial report and repeated below. Second, in assessing such matters, common sense alone can be more of a problem than a solution. Most citizens have a view of religion that is highly colored by the types of religions to which they have been exposed—for example, Christians by Christianity, Protestants by Protestantism, and even particular sect and cult members by the particular sects and cults they have experienced. Third, assuming that a social scientifically grounded knowledge of the rich variety of experiences that are genuinely "religious" is preferable to a conception of religion that is constrained by a layman's familiarity, I offer assistance based on forty years of research and scholarship in the field. I have studied a wide breadth of American faiths and practices, including some that are new and some that are old, some that are large and some that are small, and some that originated in this nation and some that have come from elsewhere to find a home here. In addition to analyzing various forms of both Catholics and Protestants in the U.S., I have devoted special research to groups ranging from the American Ethical Culture Society to the Buddhist Soka Gokai Movement that began in Japan and spread westward.

2. *Questions of Methodology:* The defense suggests that any claim I might have to expertise is obviated by my lack of any scientific methodology and that my interpretations are purely matters of personal option "premised not on any sociological principle, but on a 1997 amendment to *M.G.L. c. 151B.*" Here too I respectfully disagree. First, as I was at pains to indicate in my earlier report, my judgment rests on well-established sociological principles, including a consensual definition of religion that emphasizes what religions "do" rather than what religions "are." This definition invokes three basic criteria that constitute a methodology of assessment, and I went on to show how sacred meanings, ritual enactment, and communal support are all present in the Church of Body Modification. It is important to understand that my definition and its criteria represent a summary statement of a very large body of social scientific work on religion that has converged upon such a "functional" definition over the past half-century. I myself contributed to the development in my 1976 co-authored text, "Religion in Social Context." But there are many works worth citing, some of which I drew upon in the work above, others which I have benefitted from more recently, most of which begin with a discussion of definitions, and all of which reflect general agreement on the basic conception of religion at issue. A representative list would include Charles Glock and Rodney Stark, *Religion and Society in Tension* (Rand McNally, 1967); Peter Berger, *Sacred Canopy* (Doubleday, 1967); J. Milton Yinger, *The Scientific Study of Religion*

(Macmillan, 1970); Barbara Hargrove, *The Sociology of Religion* (AHM Publishing, 1979); Thomas Robbins and Dick Anthony, eds., *In Gods We Trust* (Transaction Books, 1981); Rodney Stark and William Bainbridge, *The Future of Religion* (California, 1985); Thomas Robbins, *Cults, Converts, and Charisma* (Sage, 1988); Lorne L. Dawson, *Comprehending Cults* (Oxford, 1998); Meredith McGuire, *Religion: The Social Context* (Wadsworth, 5th edition, 2002); and Kevin Christiano, William Swatos, and Peter Kevisto, eds., *Sociology of Religion: Contemporary Developments* (Alta Mira, 2002).

Second, throughout my career, I have been careful to base my judgements on research methods well-established in the field. These have often involved statistical analyses of sample surveys (see, for example, my first book, *Social Class in American Protestantism*, 1965, and my subsequent articles on "religious dissidence," "religious switching" and American "culture wars"—all listed in the vita that accompanied my earlier report); ethnographic case studies (see my early article on "organizational precariousness and American irreligion" and my forthcoming co-authored work on religious groups in Indianapolis, Indiana, *Sacred Circles and Public Squares*), historical analysis (see the first two chapters in my co-authored book on Springfield entitled *A Bridging of Faiths*), and cross-cultural comparative analysis (see my recent book, *Crossing the Gods* on religion, politics, and the state in some fourteen countries around the globe in addition to the U.S.). Largely because these works involve central methodologies and well-tested conclusions, they have all been very positively refereed before publication and well reviewed afterwards. In fact, the last named above won the 2002 Distinguished Book Award of the Society for the Scientific Study of Religion—the world's largest and most prestigious organization of anthropologists, political scientists, psychologists, and sociologists doing research on religion.

3. *Questions of Law:* First, let me say at the outset that I am perfectly prepared to restrict my testimony to the purely social scientific matters referred to above. Moreover, I do not intend to give an opinion on whether discrimination exists in this case. It is true that I am not a lawyer and make no pretense to a lawyer's expertise. But second, I should add that I have spent a good deal of the past twenty years developing my knowledge in the sociology of law with special reference to the First Amendment clauses concerning religion—a complex area that is now at best an elective rather than required course at most law schools and an area where few lawyers now claim expertise for themselves. I have learned a good deal from lawyers who do specialize on the topic and with whom I have attended conferences and exchanged writings. I am proud of the relationships I have developed with many experts in this small but important corner of the law, including law faculty and legal historians at such institutions as Cardozo, Harvard, Notre Dame,

Princeton, Wisconsin, and Yale. I have also conducted my own research in the sociology of law. For example, this has resulted in my 1984 article on "The Separation of Church and State: Notes on a Mythical Past and an Uncertain Future," which discusses some long-term trends; the aforementioned book, *A Bridging of Faiths*, where a lengthy chapter on "Corner Church and City-State" features a questionnaire survey on the attitudes of Springfield citizens towards religion and the First Amendment, and the also aforementioned work, *Crossing the Gods*, which includes a major chapter on misapprehensions of American church-state law at home and abroad and the sometimes tragic consequences that follow.

4. *Questions of Prejudice:* Here the defense argues that I am "potentially prejudicial" because, instead of providing "testimony helping the trier of fact accurately determine a fact in issue. . . . [my] expert testimony may unduly influence the fact finder's decision." The passage is followed by yet another assertion that "the determination as to whether the Church of Body Modification is a religion . . . is largely a matter of common sense." I have already noted the dangers of relying on common sense alone in these matters. The central issue in this case turns less on a disagreement over facts than on the appropriate frameworks within which to interpret the facts. Here one might think an expert's scholarly judgment would be a boon rather than a bane, especially in the midst of court proceedings that are designed to be adversarial throughout. Frankly, I suspect it is true that if the case is left purely to common sense as the defense would have it, this may be prejudicial to the plaintiff and to the larger and yet more subtle issues at stake. In my forty years of teaching about various marginal groups similar to the Church of Body Modification, I have found a tendency for students to greet the first accounts of such groups with laughter and derision. It is only after the "facts" are placed in legal and social scientific context that balanced and unprejudiced assessments become possible. Those are precisely the sorts of assessments I pride myself in offering as a professional social scientist. My sole interest in this case is to provide an expert's un-common knowledge as a way of insuring that an informed common sense will prevail in achieving a fair decision, whatever that might be.

I hope these remarks are helpful in responding to the motion at hand. I continue to stand by to offer my assistance in any way and on any terms that may please the court.

Signed under the pains and penalty of perjury on this twenty-third day of June, 2003.

———————————

N. J. Demerath III

# Index

# About the Editor and Contributors

## EDITOR

**Phil Zuckerman** is an associate professor of sociology at Pitzer College. He is the author of *Society Without God: What the Least Religious Nations Can Tell Us about Contentment* (2008) and *Invitation to the Sociology of Religion* (2003), and he is currently on the editorial board of the journal *Sociology of Religion*. He lives in Southern California with his wife and three children.

## CONTRIBUTORS

**Benjamin Beit-Hallahmi** is professor of psychology at the University of Haifa and senior research associate at the Institute for the Study of Secularism in Society and Culture, Trinity College, Hartford, Connecticut. He is the author of numerous books, chapters, and articles on the psychology of religion, social identity, and personality development. In 1993 he was the recipient of the William James Award (Division 36 of the American Psychological Association) for his contributions to the psychology of religion.

**Daniel Cady** is assistant professor of history at California State University, Fresno, and director of the Central Valley Institute for Regional and Historical Studies. He has published work on the Ku Klux Klan, the United Daughters of the Confederacy, and W. E. B. Du Bois. He is currently researching southern music and interregional migration.

**Margaret A. Clendenen** is a sociology and religious studies double major at the College of William and Mary in Williamsburg, Virginia.

She is particularly interested in studying feminist and lesbian, gay, bisexual, and transgender social movements, evangelical culture, and the relationship between religions and sexualities. At William and Mary, she has worked as a research assistant for sociologists Thomas Linneman and Kathleen Jenkins.

**Jay Demerath III** is recently retired as the Emile Durkheim Distinguished Professor of Sociology at the University of Massachusetts, Amherst. A past president of the Society for the Scientific Study of Religion and the Association for the Sociology of Religion, the three most recent books among his many publications are *Crossing the Gods: World Religions and Worldly Politics* (2001); *Sacred Circles and Public Squares: The Multicentering of American Religion*, with Arthur Farnsley et al. (2004); and the *Sage Handbook of the Sociology of Religion*, coedited with James Beckford (2007).

**Jack David Eller** is assistant professor of anthropology at the Community College of Denver. He has conducted fieldwork on Australian Aboriginal religion among the Warlpiri people of central Australia and is the author of *Introducing Anthropology of Religion* (2007). He has also published a number of articles on atheism and secularism, as well as two books: *Natural Atheism* and *Atheism Advanced: Further Thoughts of a Freethinker*, both with American Atheist Press.

**Inger Furseth** is professor/research associate at KIFO Centre for Church Research in Oslo and at the Center for Religion and Civic Culture at the University of Southern California. Some of her books include *A Comparative Study of Social and Religious Movements in Norway, 1790s–1905* (2002), *From Quest for Truth to Being Oneself* (2006), and *An Introduction to the Sociology of Religion* (2006, with Pål Repstad). Her research centers on religious diversity, gender issues, social and religious movements, and social theory.

**Thomas J. Linneman** is associate professor and chair of sociology at the College of William and Mary in Williamsburg, Virginia, where he teaches courses on social change, sexualities, and statistics. He is the author of *Weathering Change: Gays and Lesbians, Christian Conservatives, and Everyday Hostilities* (2003). He also has published in the journals *Men and Masculinities, Sociological Perspectives, American Journal of Sociology, Sexuality Research and Social Policy,* and *Contemporary Sociology.*

**Christel Manning** is professor and director of the graduate program in the Department of Philosophy and Religious Studies at Sacred Heart University. She teaches courses and has published books and articles on religion as it relates to issues of gender, sexuality, and family. She is the mother of a young child and lives in Connecticut.

**Frank L. Pasquale** is a cultural anthropologist engaged in research and writing on the worldviews, personal behavior, and organizational life of secularists in the American Northwest and the United States. He is a research associate with the Institute for the Study of Secularism in Society and Culture, Trinity College (Hartford, Connecticut). He has been a research fellow at the East-West Center (Honolulu, Hawaii) and has lived and given cultural education programs in several Pacific Rim countries.

**Gregory S. Paul** is an independent researcher with interests in the evolution of life, human cultures, and technology, including the interaction of religion, science, societal conditions, economics, and politics. Author of *Dinosaurs of the Air*, his academic studies related to religion have appeared in the *Journal of Religion and Society*, *Journal of Medical Ethics*, *Pediatrics*, and *Philosophy and Theology*.